Athlete-centred Coaching

Dedicated to my continued inspiration, my boys Bob, Matthew and Simon

With guest authors David Hadfield and Rod Thorpe

Innovat|ve
PRINT COMMUNICATIONS LTD

First published in 2005
by Innovative Print Communications Ltd
PO Box 6321
Christchurch, New Zealand
Website: www.ipcltd.com
E-mail: info@ipcltd.com

ISBN: 0–476–01445–X

Editor: Tanya Tremewan

Cover design: Hugh Galvan of Ngāti Kahungunu Iwi (tribal affiliation)
The book cover design is based on a traditional Māori (native people of New Zealand) symbol, the 'koru'. The koru signifies "new life" as it resembles a new shoot that grows from the middle of the fern plant and develops into a mature fern frond. The design is comprised of three stages. At the bottom are two dominant koru. These represent coaches as significant in establishing an athlete-centred learning environment. The second stage is the kōiri (one koru turning back to a larger koru). This shape represents turning to the family for support. For athletes, this support comes from being inspired by coaches or other athletes ("the family") when developing skills, confidence and trust. In the third stage, a central stem, the manawa (heart) provides the inspiration for other koru to develop. At this point coaches become less significant and the manawa symbolises the inspiring athlete who enables others to become not only better athletes but better people: a concept central to this book.

Table of Contents

Preface

Athlete-centred Coaching: Developing inspired and inspiring people offers insight on how to enhance athlete learning and development through sport, offered by successful coaches who hold athlete-centred philosophies. Although from a variety of backgrounds, they share similar goals in regard to long-term athlete learning and a quality team environment. All the coaches believe in sharing power with their athletes, enabling athletes to be effective decision makers through focusing on their motivation to participate to the best of their ability. As this book demonstrates, coaches who use such an athlete-centred approach inspire their athletes and, in turn, the athletes inspire each other.

With an athlete-centred approach, athletes take ownership of their learning, thus increasing their opportunities and strengthening their abilities to retain important skills and ideas. This learning also develops athletes' ability to make informed decisions during competitions, an important element in successful performance at any sporting level. It helps athletes to take a leadership role and ownership in enhancing the team culture.

Developing the material for this book involved an exciting project of interviewing and observing the range of coaches who feature in the chapters that follow. I was privileged and honoured to obtain the stories of: Don Tricker, coach of the New Zealand Black Sox (men's softball); Ruth Aitken and Leigh Gibbs, coach and assistant coach, respectively, of the New Zealand Silver Ferns (netball); Ian Rutledge, coach of the New Zealand Black Sticks (women's hockey); Mike McHugh, coach of the Wellington Saints (men's basketball) and assistant coach to the New Zealand Tall Ferns (women's basketball); Team Seagate, world class adventure race team; Lyn Gunson, prior England and New Zealand netball coach; and Wayne Smith, international rugby coach. In addition, it was an exhilarating adventure to research the Riccarton High School Senior Boys' Volleyball team with Mark Norton. All coaches graciously provided insights into their coaching approaches and their philosophies.

Athlete-centred Coaching begins by defining this innovative and successful coaching approach. As well as introducing athlete-centred approaches, the first chapter discusses the benefits of using this term rather than empowerment, which is less valuable due to the nature of the sociological understanding of it. The chapter also compares athlete-centred approaches with their polar opposite—coach-centred approaches—and discusses why coaches should consider using the former. Questioning, Teaching Games for Understanding (TGfU) and team culture are introduced as aspects that are important to enabling athletes to own and take responsibility for their learning. How to develop athlete-centred philosophies and how to relate success (rather than winning) to an athlete-centred approach are discussed as well. The case studies of the coaches have a commonality that all want to develop athletes as people, not just as sport jocks.

In Chapter Two, David Hadfield presents information to show how the athlete-centred approach can be implemented. He discusses how coaches can gain confidence to change what they do now. His major initiative is the query theory approach, whereby coaches question athletes for understanding of technique.

An action research project, involving a case study of the Riccarton High School Senior Boys' volleyball team, is presented in Chapter Three. The coach of this team, Mark Norton, focused on creating a quality team culture for the season in 2003–2004. Acting as a player manager, I followed the team through the season. The chapter represents the story of the season and how focusing on team culture helped the team to meet its goals.

Don Tricker discusses his coaching with the Black Sox and shares his philosophies in Chapter Four. Don is a legend for aiding the Black Sox to become three-peat world champions in men's softball. As an in-depth analyser of people and sport, he offers great insight for coaches to gain an understanding of how to be athlete-centred. His interesting chapter demonstrates how coaches need to be open to change and how the individuals in the team make the team work. Drawing from his business background, Don uses many analogies to demonstrate how people influence an organisation or team.

In Chapter Five, Ruth Aitken and Leigh Gibbs discuss their athlete-centred approach with the Silver Ferns. Their way of coaching enabled the Silver Ferns to become world champions in netball. The secret to their success, like Don's, is the ability to pull a group of individuals together to create an environment where athletes share in the direction and responsibility of the team. Both coaches have come from a teaching background.

The athlete-centred approach of Ian Rutledge, the Black Sticks women's hockey coach, is another athlete-centred coach. Like Don, Ruth and Leigh, Ian believes in creating and maintaining a quality team culture. He believes in taking the physically skilled athletes and binding them together to pursue the same cause and direction. Ian's related analogies and life lessons are an asset to the development of great human beings.

Basketball is Mike McHugh's life passion. He currently coaches the Wellington Saints men's basketball team and is assistant coach to Tom Maher for the New Zealand Tall Ferns. His commitment to the development of his coaching is amazing. His life (as with all the other coaches in this book) has been dedicated to the pursuit of developing fine young people, not just in sport but in life.

Chapter Eight presents Team Seagate, an adventure racing team who believe that focusing on their quality team culture helps them to be successful. All team members recount the story of a team who loves to participate in adventure racing, finding it one of the most challenging journeys in life. Their focus on how they enjoy racing and look for life lessons is commendable.

Chapter Nine is Wayne Smith's chapter, slightly modified from my earlier book *Developing Decision Makers* (Kidman, 2001), and encapsulates his coaching wisdom. Since the chapter was first written, Wayne has been a successful coach at the Northampton Saints from 2001–2003, and is now working again with the All Blacks as an assistant coach along with Steve Hansen, under coach Graham Henry. Wayne rewrote some of the chapter to align it with his current thinking. The athlete-centred approach was a feature of his coaching in Northampton and continues to pervade his approach with the All Blacks.

Lyn Gunson is represented in Chapter Ten. Lyn is an athlete-centred coach who believes that a group within a sports team is a community and develops a team culture based on the notion of community. Lyn has coached both New Zealand and England netball teams, and has a wealth of experience and knowledge to share.

Earlier versions of Chapters Eleven, Twelve and Thirteen have appeared in *Developing Decision Makers*. In Chapter Eleven, Rod Thorpe presents his valuable philosophy on TGfU, adding the current movement through TGfU. Moving away from the use of traditional drills that are irrelevant to the actual sport, the key factor of TGfU is the game. Coaches design their training sessions to make the drills more game-like so that athletes learn about tactics and skills. All coaches in this book use TGfU in various forms, but what unites them is the general model, which is the backbone to understanding the game.

One of the key components to an athlete-centred approach, including the strategy of TGfU, is that coaches ask questions that encourage athletes to be self-aware and learn about tactics and skills. Chapter Twelve gives practical guidelines for planning and asking meaningful questions. The technique of questioning is addressed as well as the art of asking meaningful questions.

As most coaches work with children at least part of the time, Chapter Thirteen concentrates on sport and children, our future athletes. Issues discussed relate to why children participate in sport, the value of and concerns about competition, and strategies to provide child athletes with a positive sporting experience so that they continue to participate in sport. The influence of significant others (such as parents) is also considered.

Lastly, Chapter Fourteen summarises some of the key ideas raised in the book for coaches who are interested in putting an athlete-centred approach into practice. Team culture is further discussed in relation to how coaches can explicitly work on establishing a great team environment. Part of implementation is self-reflective analysis, a tool that coaches can use to monitor their ongoing coaching. The purpose of the chapter, building on the momentum of the chapters before it, is to encourage coaches to start to use an athlete-centred approach, reflect on how they use it and continue to improve.

Your mind is what makes everything else work.
– *Kareem Abdul-Jabbar*

The principle is competing against yourself. It's about self improvement, about being better than you were the day before.
– *Steve Young*

Take the attitude of a student, Never be too big to ask questions, Never know too much to learn something new. – *Og Mandino*

Acknowledgements

There are many people I would like to thank for their various contributions to *Athlete-centred Coaching: Developing inspired and inspiring people*. This book would have been impossible without the constant critical discussion with the students in the Bachelor of Sport Coaching degree at Christchurch College of Education. I thank them for their inquisitive minds and the challenges that enable coaches to be the best they can be.

I would like to express a special thanks to the coaches and athletes who feature in this book—namely Mark Norton, Don Tricker, Ruth Aitken, Leigh Gibbs, Ian Rutledge, Mike McHugh, Kristina Anglem, Nathan Fa'avae, Richard Ussher, Hadyn Keys, Lyn Gunson and Wayne Smith—who selflessly gave up their time to relate stories and share expertise about their coaching, competing and thinking. It is great to have a group of people whose mission is to return athletes to the real values that sport has to offer.

I would also like to thank Rod Thorpe, who inspired me in his workshops and also gives selflessly to the cause of educating sport coaches.

Thank you to David Hadfield, for his neverending belief in the cause to teach coaches about being athlete-centred. He is an inspiration.

To Simon Kidman and Luke Russell, who drew on their experience with school sport. Good luck to these boys for their future endeavours. As coaches, we need to listen to athletes better.

To Dawn Penney who provided a great haven to write the bulk of this book. Thanks for all the motivation. Also thanks to her university, Edith Cowan, who provided some support to help in the writing process.

To Christchurch College of Education for supporting my research leave and providing some valuable monies for travel, which enabled me to observe and interview the coaches and athletes.

I would also like to acknowledge a sponsor for the Outdoor Quest in Borneo. Octagon Media enabled me to follow and interview Team Seagate in a multi sport race. What a fantastic and meaningful opportunity that was. I gained lots of life lessons in that week.

To Anna Mayes, who graciously allowed me to use her Masters thesis interview of Ruth Aitken.

I also want to thank Walter Davis from Kent State University, who believes in empowering athletes and allowed me to contribute to his book, *Understand movement in an expanded context.*

Of course, there is the editor of the book, Tanya Tremewan, who was amazing in her ability to develop the text to make it readable. Thanks Tanya for having such a great talent. You make it seem so easy.

To my husband Bobby, for his, the greatest support of them all.

Chapter One

Being Athlete-centred: the Empowering Coach

Because coaches are responsible for enabling athletes to learn, coaching is a complex process. Like other learners, athletes develop understanding and learn more effectively when they are involved in solving problems for themselves (Butler, 1997). Important tools in the learning process are to develop new ideas, knowledge and the ability to make decisions. If experts merely present knowledge (sometimes quite forcefully) to those who are 'nonexpert' and make decisions for them, the athletes become disempowered. In other words, if athletes' needs do not influence their learning experiences, learning is minimal. The knowledge, understanding, skill and decision-making ability that athletes learn and apply can make the difference between performance success and failure.

When coaches use an empowering style of coaching—or, to use the term preferred in this book, follow an athlete-centred approach—athletes gain and take ownership of knowledge, development and decision making that will help them to maximise their performance. This athlete-centred approach provides athletes with a chance to be part of the decision-making process that is involved in the organisation and performance of sports teams.

Athlete-centred, like the equivalent term *empowerment*, has many meanings. For this chapter, after an outline of the current practice of coaches, an athlete-centred approach is defined and discussed in the sporting context. In contrast to a traditional prescriptive (coach-centred) style of coaching, an athlete-centred approach promotes a sense of belonging, as well as giving athletes a role in decision making and a shared approach to learning. Practices that coaches use as part of their athlete-centred approach are introduced in this chapter, including the three main practices that are highlighted in some form by all coaches in this book: Teaching Games for Understanding (see also Chapter Eleven), questioning (see also Chapter Twelve) and establishing a quality team culture (see also Chapter Fourteen). Then key characteristics of an empowered athlete are identified before the final discussion on how to create an athlete-centred philosophy illustrates one way that an athlete-centred approach can be put into practice.

Current Coaching Practices

To maximise athlete performance, coaches, like leaders of formal organisations, combine the power of their position with a particular leadership style. Although coaching today encompasses a wide variety of approaches, the traditional leadership style has given coaches a licence to 'exploit' their power by taking the choice and control away from the athlete. When a coach takes total control and athletes have basically no say, the approach is called *coach-centred*. This approach tends to be prescriptive. Sometimes it has been identified, mistakenly, as an important element in coaching success.

A coach-centred coach endeavours to control athlete behaviour not only throughout training and competition, but also beyond the sport setting. This kind of coach espouses all knowledge to athletes and actually disempowers the athlete by taking total ownership of the team. A coach-centred coach tends to coach athletes as if they are on a factory assembly line. Athletes of a coach-centred coach are often 'hooked' into a limited form of learning that emphasises memorising rather than understanding or solving problems. This limited approach encourages athletes to be robotic in their actions and thinking. They do not experience themselves as having an active role in contributing to or being a part of their learning.

In the professional era, the performance objectives of many coaches depend on winning. The expectation is that coaches may be held accountable for many uncertainties beyond the coaches' control (e.g. injuries, exceptional play by the opposition, poor officiating, the weather). In reacting to this pressure on them, coaches tend to give athletes extraordinarily gruelling training sessions that demand more than the athletes can give; sometimes they use dehumanising practices to enforce their control (Pratt & Eitzen, 1989). Unfortunately, for coaches like these, the pressure in this professional 'must-win' environment becomes so great that coaches 'take over' in an attempt to ensure their athletes are winning. The directions become coach-centred, rather than mutual between the athletes and the coach.

This disempowering form of coach control actually contradicts why many athletes participate in sport. A coach-centred approach can have detrimental effects on athletes who are controlled. The coach can also suffer when the athletes reject such control. In these controlling situations the benefits of winning can be limited. If a team is winning, the athletes smile, but if a team loses or tires of being bossed around, generally the team environment deteriorates. As all of the coaches in this book suggest, once the team environment deteriorates, it is difficult to win. Winning and success are difficult to achieve without quality team culture.

On the other hand, if athletes truly learn and take ownership of the direction of the team or competition, success is more likely. From the athletes' point of view, *success* is rarely winning; it usually involves achieving their goals. A coach-centred coach makes mistaken assumptions about what athletes need (to win) and seldom determines why athletes participate in sport. Conversely, as part of an athlete-centred approach, one of the coach's first roles is to determine the reasons why each athlete is participating, and to establish a mutual vision and direction for the season that both the athletes and the coach own. (See later in this chapter for more on success versus winning.)

As the above discussion indicates, the opposite of athlete-centred is coach-centred, just as the opposite of empowerment is disempowerment. The traditional coach-centred approach disempowers athletes, yet it is still prevalent in many sport teams. Under this coaching style, reading the game is largely a prescription from the coach (like playing a chess game). Yet this kind of coach-centred coach often fails to realise that the competition itself can be a learning experience that encourages athletes to understand and choose options based on informed decisions. The need for an athlete-centred approach is obvious in many sports throughout the world—specifically, those sports that involve long periods when the coach is not directly involved in making decisions on the field and has limited opportunity to communicate with the athletes. More broadly, in every sport informed decisions by athletes are essential to performance success, as in every sport it is the athlete who competes, not the coach.

When coaching tactics and skills at training sessions, coach-centred coaches traditionally tend to give athletes specific directions on what to 'fix' or the exact moves to perform. In some cases, coaches believe that unless they are seen to be telling athletes what to do and how to do it, they are not doing their job properly. Coach-centred coaches believe that they are expected to win and that successful coaches are (and should be) hard-nosed and discipline-oriented. Others (athlete-centred coaches) view their role as promoting enjoyment and personal development, as being supportive and empowering.

Much of the research suggests that no matter what coaching style is used, athletes respond better to supportive coaches than to punitive coaches (Smoll & Smith, 1989). Ironically, coaches who follow the coach-centred approach often express concerns related to low athlete productivity, poor performance quality and lack of motivation and commitment by athletes (Usher, 1997). In contrast, athletes with supportive coaches show greater intrinsic motivation, enjoy participating and competing in sport, make informed decisions more rapidly in the ever-changing tactical manoeuvres and demonstrate that trust is mutual (player–player, player–coach, coach–player, coach–coach).

Although a coach-centred approach is necessary in some instances, traditional coaches can abuse their influence. Coaches hold the 'power' within a team and this status leads to an unquestioned acceptance of a coach's leadership style among athletes and significant others (parents, administrators, public). In this environment coaches do not and cannot listen to their athletes, as they believe that if they listen they will be perceived as losing their 'power'. Such an environment ensures that coaches do what they want regardless of the personal and collective needs of the athletes. Coach-centred coaches make many assumptions about athletes. For example, they may assume that because athletes are participating, they want to be champions and they will pay the price required to achieve this end. Often teams with this style of coaching have short-term success at the beginning of the season, but start floundering later in the season as they continue to be unable to make decisions.

A very different pattern may be evident with teams coached using athlete-centred principles. Wayne Smith (All Blacks assistant coach) agrees that if teams can keep their cool, react to what they see, talk and guts it out and be relentless, they can get to the top every time. Wayne suggests that teams with an athlete-centred approach tend to be:

> … middling to fair earlier, but as athletes are developing a team culture, developing a way of learning, they are actually going to be more knowledgeable and understand the game better as the season progresses.

In the changing world of sport, the coach-centred approach has been rightly challenged. This book argues that a coach-centred coaching approach takes success away from the athlete and emphasises the coach's total domination of his or her sporting teams (and/or individual athletes). The information here supports and encourages an athlete-centred coaching approach. It is one of the most innovative and effective approaches to coaching, enabling athletes to succeed in and enjoy their sporting participation. Through it, athletes can create something significant and perhaps different from current practices within their sport. Athletes and teams can lead the way by using innovative ideas to make the game or competition more exciting. In the empowering process coaches and athletes work for similar purposes within a motivating environment. An athlete-centred approach helps to motivate athletes and gives them a sense of satisfaction in being part of a common vision so the 'team' can grow in the same direction.

Defining an Athlete-centred (Empowering) Approach

The connotations of the widely used term *empowerment*, especially among sociologists, are problematic. The term is robustly debated among researchers of the social world because of the implied understandings from feminist theory which have wider implications. While this section defines empowerment as it is used in relation to coaching and business leadership styles, it also incorporates the term that I see as an appropriate replacement within coaching: an *athlete-centred approach*. I support the use of this alternative term which seems to be free of the controversy surrounding its predecessor, because an empowerment style is about focusing on the athletes first. To gradually change current coach understandings, however, I will use the terms empowerment and athlete-centred approach interchangeably throughout this book.

At the outset, it is important to understand that the key to the athlete-centred approach is a leadership style that caters to athletes' needs and understandings where athletes are enabled to learn and have control of their participation in sport.

Although both *empowering* and *athlete-centred* may be interpreted in many ways, at a general level both terms describe a process by which people gain control over the decisions affecting their lives. When a coach considers the athletes first and thus gives them choice and control, the athletes are empowered. In other words, through training, empowered athletes and teams gain some choice in and control over what happens in their sporting life as well as in their general lifestyle. They have this choice and control because the 'power' is shared with them (Arai, 1997).

In this notion of power is the suggestion that there are resources that may be utilised to enhance oneself at the expense of others and thus to dominate them. A person with more power can co-opt or appropriate power from others with less power (Eskes, Duncan & Miller, 1998). A coach-centred coach—that is, a person who coaches for himself or herself, uses power to dominate and considers athletes (whether consciously or unconsciously) as only a means to an end—is a disempowering coach. This coach-centred approach is more likely to meet the coach's goals and less likely to meet athletes' goals (Kidman & Davis, in press). In contrast, empowered athletes have the authority and are able to engage actively and fully in shaping and defining their own direction (Freysinger & Bedini, 1994). Their experience demonstrates that people with more power can also act in a manner that enhances rather than appropriates the power of others. In regard to coaching, an important implication of an athlete-centred approach is that athletes take ownership of their own learning and direction.

Some of the main advantages of using an athlete-centred approach to coaching are that athletes are motivated to learn and they have a greater understanding and stronger retention of both tactics and skills (cognitive, psychological, spiritual and physical), which are so important to success in sport. A coach who empowers athletes facilitates their learning but does not control it. This approach is clearly beneficial given that athletes must be self-sufficient in their performance, decision making and option taking while participating in their respective sport. In particular, an athlete-centred approach encourages athletes to become self-aware and self-sufficient, allows them to make informed decisions and emphasises individual growth and change.

Many coaches, who use many different styles, highlight the importance of gaining trust and respect from their athletes in order to enhance performance (Potrac, 2004). In an athlete-centred model of coaching this trust must be mutual, and establishing it is largely dependent upon the coach. Mutual trust and respect between coach and athlete do not mean sameness. Athletes must trust their coaches to make suggestions and decisions and to ensure athlete responsibility in the best interests of the team. Athletes trust coaches to be knowledgeable and prepared, and to provide a safe and supporting environment (Shogan, 1999). Through mutual trust, athletes take responsibility for the learning and performance of themselves and the team, thereby enhancing the team environment. In turn, coaches trust athletes to be serious about their performance goals and the goals of the team. Empowerment (power through enablement) promotes a shared, dynamic power relationship between athlete and coach. Using an athlete-centred approach is a pedagogical strategy that will assist the development of the trust and respect that so many coaches seek (Kidman & Davis, in press).

In the employment world, industrial productivity is related to job satisfaction. A similar link can be applied to sport, in that a team is more productive if they enjoy what they do. Such an overlap between business management and coaching is highlighted by David Hadfield (Chapter Two) and Don Tricker (New Zealand Black Sox coach, Chapter Four). This idea is the basis of an athlete-centred approach, which focuses on the individual and his or her growth in both sport and life. Athlete-centred coaching builds a committed partnership between the athlete or team and the coach. In this partnership, the coach acts as a facilitator or catalyst for athletes' optimal performance. Goals are mutual and teamwork is enhanced, therefore success is achieved. An athlete-centred coach helps athletes learn and enables them to understand how to exceed their current limits. This kind of coach nurtures involvement and autonomy in the athletes' learning (Usher, 1997).

All of the coaches featured in this book base their coaching performance on an athlete-centred approach that encourages athletes to become aware of their own skill execution and tactical play. Their approach is concerned with questioning (see Chapter Twelve) rather than prescription (Hadfield, 1994). When coaches question athletes and encourage the athletes to ask questions themselves, they enable the athletes to take ownership of their learning and athletic environment. The coach who uses an athlete-centred style divests himself or herself of power, however gradually, and shares it with the athletes (Kidman, Hadfield & Chu, 2000).

With the athlete-centred approach it is not suggested that the coach should give full responsibility to athletes. Rather, coaches should exercise their leadership by guiding athletes towards decision making and allowing them to take their own responsibility for sport participation. Clearly in some situations, with some athletes, coaches need to be more prescriptive, but the aim should always be to encourage self-reliance through decision making.

Many people practise coaching without really understanding its process. The coaching process is dependent on the complex dynamics between coaches and athletes, their individual attributes, their desires and ambitions, and the training and competition context. Athlete-centred coaching considers all these complexities, but with an emphasis upon the development of the athlete (Kidman & Davis, in press).

Some Key Components of an Athlete-centred Approach[1]

In all case studies in this book, the coaches highlight three main components of an athlete-centred approach that enhance decision making and form a quality team culture. These primary coaching practices are Teaching Games for Understanding, questioning, and establishing a quality team culture (wairua). In addition, these coaches have highlighted other aspects that they believe contribute significantly to athlete ownership and responsibility, such as the strategies of developing a team full of leaders and rotating athlete roles within the team.

Teaching Games for Understanding

Teaching Games for Understanding (TGfU) (also see Chapter Eleven) is a games approach that has been adapted and modified in various contexts and under various names, including Play Practice and Game Sense. The common feature of these variations is that a purposeful game is used for athletes to learn the skill, technique and tactical understanding of the sport. The ability to use an understanding of the rules, of strategy, of tactics and, most importantly, of oneself to solve problems posed by the game or by one's opponents is the basis of TGfU (Launder, 2001). The TGfU model is understanding in action and providing opportunities to enhance athletes' ability to respond or make decisions, even while new situations are presented. TGfU is about applying game sense—'reading the game'.

With TGfU, athletes can learn about the game and practise skills and techniques within the context of a game rather than separate from it. Learning in context provides a sound understanding of the game and opportunities to apply skill and technique under pressure. When athletes are allowed to play or practice, in a situation uncluttered by coaches

---

[1]Much of this section has been adapted from Kidman, L., & Davis, W. (in press) Empowerment in coaching, In G. D. Broadhead & W. E. Davis (In press) *Ecological Task Analysis: Understanding movement in context,* Champaign, IL: Human Kinetics. Permission has been granted.

telling them what to do and where to go, they are more productive in terms of learning in context, enhancing motivation through challenges, social interactions and decision making (Kidman & Hanrahan, 2004).

TGfU is a physical application of game-like situations to help athletes in their decision making process. Games are used as the learning tool for many aspects of playing the sport. Play Practice (Launder, 2001) uses three rationales to support learning in action within a game context: Shaping Play (manipulating variables, continually changing, teaching through the game); Focusing Play (teaching in the game, pointing out similarities and differences between training games and real games, developing and refining skills); and Enhancing Play (improving performance through meaningful games).

Developing the game to meet learning outcomes is the key to planning and designing games. Some of the ideas around which games could be developed include: freeze replay, shaping applied to invasion games, attacker:defender ratio, altering the size and shape of playing area, nature of the goal, primary and secondary rules, conditions applied to the game, control and development of good players, differential scoring, playing time, tactical time-outs, and user-friendly balls and equipment. Tactical aspects include: deception, risk, shot selection and placement in relation to opponents, time, stage of game, space, decision making, field setting, defensive patterns, minimising angles of attack, attacking patterns, and keeping possession (Australian Sports Commission, 1997).

TGfU fits into an athlete-centred philosophy because it enhances athletes' motivation and thus their intensity of performance through their own problem solving. Athletes increase their effort because of the meaningful challenges offered. These challenges also create opportunities for athletes to respond to the pressure inherent in sport competitions. Achievement is also enhanced as TGfU enables athletes to do something well, to problem solve, and to take ownership for their own learning. Of course, enjoyment is also enhanced because games are fun. Through games, athletes share success and failure; they learn how to trust each other and to know each other's ways of competing and making decisions, which enhances team culture. Chapter Eleven by Rod Thorpe is dedicated to TGfU and its conceptualisation.

Questioning

As all of the coaches in this book have indicated, questioning is the best approach to develop thinking and decision making in athletes. The technique of questioning (which is further explained and discussed in Chapter Two and Twelve) is one way of helping athletes learn to problem solve. It is not simply a matter of asking questions; effective coach questioning requires purposeful questions phrased in a way that encourages the athlete to respond. Stimulating questions are an extremely powerful means of inspiring athletes and enhancing intrinsic motivation (Butler, 1997; Kidman, 2001). Questioning also engages athletes at a conscious level, enhancing their concentration and thus their intensity. This intensity transfers well to games themselves where the pressure is great.

For various reasons, there is a degree of resistance to the technique among some athletes and coach-centred coaches. Because coach questioning is less prevalent than direct coaching, athletes may be reluctant to respond to posed questions at first. However, once they become more accustomed to this practice and see that it gives them ownership of their learning, they will be more accepting of the questions and become more cognitively involved in the sport environment.

Among advocates of a prescriptive coaching approach, there is a perception that coaches who ask questions do not know the answers themselves. Indeed, coaches may find it difficult, and at times daunting, to design questions that generate high-level thinking from the athletes. Yet to create situations where athletes learn best, coaches must listen to their athletes' responses, then redirect, prompt and probe for better or more detailed answers. Succeeding with such a technique demands an in-depth understanding of the game, the athlete, and the context in which a solution is applied.

Athletes will undertake problem solving with enjoyment and ever-increasing effort if given the opportunity. Generating their own solution empowers athletes and gives them more self-awareness; the subsequent enhancement of their performance is well documented (Metzler, 2000; Ravizza, 1998; Schempp, 1982). For example, athletes who take ownership of the content of their learning will remember, understand and apply it more effectively than those who are told what to do, when to do it and how to do it. Solving problems through coach questioning enables athletes to discover, explore, create and generally experiment with a variety of movement forms, skills and tactics or strategies of a specific sport. By enabling athletes to problem solve, a coach enhances their long-term learning (Thorpe, 1990).

Mark Norton (Riccarton High School volleyball coach) reiterates the usefulness of solving problems when he says:

> ... the problem solving stuff was about them [the volleyball team] experiencing the need for certain things, rather than me telling them. Once they experienced them, they started to be able to implement them themselves. They could feel when they needed it rather than wait for me to see when they needed it and me go, yeah right, now you need this. They could feel that they were needing it because they had experienced it in training, then we talked about it, in this situation, this is when they are going to need it. Then, they were able to experience that in a game and implement it when they needed to.

Coaches should test their questioning strategy in each particular situation and adapt it to meet the purpose of the training session and athletes' needs and expectations. Sport and physical activity offer relevant contexts to involve athletes in high-level thinking. Coaches are often surprised and excited by how much athletes really do know and how easily they self-learn.

Team Culture

One key way to encourage self-reliance is to pursue a quality team culture in which athletes gain responsibility for establishing and maintaining a direction for the team. Team culture, a major philosophical underpinning in athlete-centred coaching, is defined as the ability to bring individuals together for the pursuit of a common goal (Yukelson, 1997). In this multi-faceted process, the team's pursuit of a mutual goal informs the quality of its functioning and success. Without quality team culture, success, learning and often winning are difficult. Thus a major challenge for coaches is to bring athletes together for learning and success.

Many athlete-centred coaches have multiple ways of developing the vision (the overriding direction) and the values (ways of acting or of ensuring that the vision is met) of the athletes on their team. Their mix of methods may also differ from those of others with a similar philosophy, as the range of descriptions from coaches in this book demonstrates. One belief that all these coaches share, however, is that either the vision must be mutually created or athletes must buy into an existing vision. In addition, values form the backbone of the team's actions; many coaches and athletes identify such values as commitment and communication. Expectations are often derived from these values. For example, if commitment is a value, then it is expected that athletes, coaches and managers will live by that value. An accompanying action might be to apply that commitment to punctuality of the team members and coach. Whatever values are developed for each team, it is important that the team understands the actual meaning and intent of each value, and that they agree to or buy into that definition. If the athletes themselves develop the vision, values and expectations, they take ownership of them, live by them and take responsibility for monitoring each other.

The notion of team culture is also encompassed in an arguably important Maori word in the New Zealand Health and Physical Education curriculum document (NZHPE)—namely, *wairua*. According to NZHPE, wairua means spirit or the action of spirituality. In a team context, wairua is the spirit of the team, the notion of oneness that all athletes on the team have, a spirit that guides their actions. The team works together as one and develops a sense of spirituality that enhances each individual's well-being. Wairua encompasses all that is positive about team culture: that is, supportive values and attitudes, respect and trust, caring and concern for others. Without wairua, the quality of team culture is diminished and therefore the chance of success is limited.

All of the coaches in this book suggest that wairua is the key to any team's success. Among the prerequisites for ensuring wairua are constructing team standards and having spiritual appreciation. The existence of a quality team culture helps to meet the psychological and social needs of the athletes (Liu, 2001). Further than that, as Liu (2001) puts it, in a team culture all members voluntarily have a 'common faith, valuation view, morality, spirit pillar, ceremony, intelligence factor, and entertainment life' (p. 28). One important outcome is true cohesion, whose foundation, Jerry Lynch (2001) suggests, lies in 'selflessness, willingness to see that the team goal is greater than the goal of any one athlete' (p. 77). Thus the coach who allows for self-responsibility by enabling athletes to make decisions on team direction enhances selflessness, benefits the team vision, goals, values and strategies, and in so doing ensures wairua (Kidman & Davis, in press).

It is important to note that each team is unique. Its individual members have unique attributes as well as some commonality with other athletes. Teams also participate in an ever-changing context. The combination of these components means that a team may develop its own unique culture. As a consequence, what works for one team does not necessarily work for another team. An athlete-centred approach to coaching will take uniqueness into account by focusing on nurturing athletes and enhancing the positive aspects of each environment in which they participate.

It is clear that establishing a mutual direction and goals for a team enhances athlete and team performance (Carron & Dennis, 1998; Kidman, 2001; Liu, 2001; Yukelson, 1997). The purpose of establishing a vision is to formulate season goals so that all athletes strive for the same purpose. In turn, values serve to establish 'rules' for the team and form the basis for setting up strategies to meet team goals. When establishing the vision, values and goals, it is important for the coach to include the athletes in decision making so that they take ownership of them and assume responsibility for monitoring them.

Other Coaching Practices in an Athlete-centred Approach

One of the biggest reasons for using an athlete-centred approach is to encourage athletes to take responsibility for and ownership of their actions and contributions to any team. By providing an empowerment-like atmosphere, using an athlete-centred approach, the coach gives athletes responsibilities not only in relation to problem solving but also in other areas that will aid the team. Thus some coaches create mini-groups, each of which has responsibility for something that benefits the team. For example, Mike McHugh (Wellington Saints basketball coach and New Zealand Tall Ferns assistant coach) supports the concept of a senior group that serves as a mediation tool between the coach and the players. Believing that there is benefit in using players to analyse other teams and their own plays, Wayne Smith has formed several small groups to take responsibility for these various aspects of running the team. Ruth Aitken and Leigh Gibbs (New Zealand Silver Ferns coach and assistant coach, respectively) form mini-groups that have responsibilities for various aspects of day-to-day training, games and sport.

Using mini-groups in such ways promotes a sense of shared leadership—in other words, a team full of leaders. Many of the coaches featured in this book discuss the benefits of giving everyone on the team the experience of being a leader by giving each team member responsibility for an aspect of the team. By this means, everyone takes ownership of the team culture, and each athlete, coach and manager has certain responsibilities to monitor or lead. When training, each athlete should feel like they contribute to the play on and off the field or court. Hadfield (2002) proposes four reasons why teaching athletes to be leaders enhances the team environment. Specifically, shared leadership brings the benefits of: maintaining high standards and motivation; preparing a team that is mentally tough; gaining athlete input to maintain team chemistry; and adhering to team values and expectations.

The issue of captaincy often arises on sports teams. It highlights a difference of approach between those who advocate that teams have a captain as the one who has total leadership responsibility for the team and those—such as several coaches in this book—who prefer a team to have a captain for media representation and name only. Significantly, a decision to single out the captain as the only leader often means that responsibility falls on the captain's shoulders and the ownership from the rest of the team for various aspects of the team environment declines. This lack of assumed responsibility by the majority of the team, where athletes divest their ownership and responsibility to the captain, can be detrimental to team unity. Most teams tend to have a captain because of tradition and because sport competitions require it, not because one is needed. Coaches must take into consideration the roles of a captain and assess what is best for their particular team.

Role Rotation

One of the key features of the process of developing decision makers is the use of role rotation. A major value involved in this practice is trust.

Two key ideas underpin role rotation. First, everyone on the team should be trusted enough to be able to play at any time during any competition. The athletes must believe that others have faith in them to do a given job when called upon to do it. Role rotation can therefore mean that within the team, all athletes play for an equal amount of time and contribute equally to all aspects of the team culture.

The second central aspect of role rotation is that athletes are allowed to play in a variety of positions to establish empathy, understanding, decision making skills and tactical awareness of teammates. For example, in basketball a centre could play a guard role at training to try to understand the skills and tactics needed to play that position. A back in rugby might participate in a line out to determine the roles of the forward in that position. These role experiences increase the cognitive development of others' roles. They give athletes a sense of empathy and knowledge about a particular position which enhances their technical and tactical understanding of the game. Inadvertently, as part of this experience, athletes also learn about coaching as they gain a broader understanding of the sport. It provides self-awareness and team awareness which aids in technical and tactical analysis.

For juniors, no athlete should be 'stuck' in any one position as they are developing and should not specialise until puberty. Athletes change as they develop; a good centre in basketball today might be the best guard in basketball tomorrow.

Empowered Athletes 5

In Chapter Two, David Hadfield provides insight into how coaches can implement an athlete-centred approach. To implement this approach, coaches need to understand the process that athletes go through to become empowered (Jones, 2001). No aspect of this process happens automatically; for every situation, the coach response or interaction depends on the team environment and the impact of the coach's approach on individual athletes. Arai (1997) suggests that in becoming empowered, individuals move through four stages in this order:

1. becoming self-aware;
2. connecting and learning;

3. taking action; and

4. contributing to their own learning.

In the first stage, coaches help to raise athletes' level of awareness (see also Chapter Two). To determine if they are empowered, athletes should assess themselves and begin to increase their self-awareness. To determine their role within the team, they also need to identify whether they feel they belong to the group or whether they feel alienated. It is important for athletes to establish how committed they feel and how important this sport is to their life. Self-aware athletes also understand why they make certain moves and react in certain ways, why they perform the way they do and their own body movement. A coach can help athletes to improve their self-awareness by asking meaningful questions. For example, asking 'Why did you move there?', 'What were you doing when you contacted the ball?' or 'How do you think you can get that pass away quicker?' will help athletes to focus their thoughts on what they are doing.

Stage 2 sees athletes determining their role in learning. To gain an understanding of their own responsibility for learning, athletes must first change their view of what learning is. One of the initial steps is for them to understand that they need to be a part of their own learning. The coach's role is to provide support, to be a mentor and to act as an information source so that athletes can begin to expand on their choices and opportunities.

In stage 3 athletes apply the new information about themselves and learning so that they can take action in the empowering process. They engage in new activities and begin to become decision makers through expressing their own ideas. In this stage, athletes act in empowered ways: they ask questions, they answer coaches' questions; they participate with awareness of their own performance. At this stage they begin to become part of the learning process rather than an observer. The coach's role here is to encourage and support the athletes' ideas and sense of self-expression.

Finally in stage 4 athletes contribute to their own learning by processing their thinking and gaining an understanding that enhances their ability to solve problems and make decisions. They contribute to the vision and goals of the team and of themselves, ask and answer questions and decide on their own fate. Athletes have a sense of belonging and acceptance from the coach and other athletes. The coach's role here is to encourage the growth of this individual and of the team collectively. The role emphasises support and facilitation—and providing these only if needed.

In summary, empowered athletes:

- set their own goals and have an intrinsic desire to reach them;
- enjoy their sport;
- show enthusiasm;
- develop self-efficacy and confidence in their ability and are enabled to control results produced by their skill and effort;
- understand that they contribute to and take responsibility for their learning and direction;
- are accountable for their actions;

- are resourceful and innovative;
- feel that they are important because of the coach's actions in understanding the athletes (e.g. listening, empathy);
- understand that there is mutual trust and respect 'between coach and athletes, and among the team';
- cooperate to enhance mutual goals and directions of the coach, themselves and their team;
- are more coachable because they have freedom and choice;
- are highly committed to achieving levels of excellence; and
- are willing to engage totally in what they believe in (Kidman & Davis, in press).

Creating an Athlete-centred Philosophy

It is useful and important for all coaches to formulate a coaching philosophy or personal statement about the values and beliefs significant to their understanding of sport and life. This philosophy provides the foundation that directs the way they coach (Kidman & Hanrahan, 2004). After thinking about why they are coaching, coaches should write it down and analyse it. Although it can feel quite threatening to put their own philosophy down on paper, the process of thinking through their philosophy is enlightening.

As coaches learn, they tend to change their attitudes and values in accordance with athletes' needs. Because these changes will affect a coaching philosophy, reviewing the philosophy regularly and altering it to fit with each coach's experience are important features of the process of developing a philosophy.

The value systems that underpin a coach's approach are crucial in determining the needs of both coaches and athletes. As the basis of the coach's knowledge, these values will be important to guide any of the coach's actions. In addition, it is the coach's responsibility to communicate this philosophy to athletes so that they are encouraged to achieve their goals. Every sport setting needs a philosophical base so that the team or individual can develop and learn according to a consistent, coherent way of thinking.

Under an athlete-centred philosophy, part of a coach's facilitation role is to define the nature of these guidelines and to follow the athlete-centred philosophy in his or her approach to coaching. As mentioned above, one goal of an athlete-centred approach is to establish mutual visions whereby the coach facilitates the process of setting priorities for the good of the team and/or athletes. By developing an athlete-centred philosophy in which athletes are encouraged to become self-aware and self-reliant in decision making, the coach provides a foundation that contributes to the holistic development of individual athletes. The whole season should be built on the belief system that athletes and coaches have created mutually.

The holistic development of the athlete is central to the success of an athlete-centred coaching approach. The athletes are the main focus of any team and determine the success or failure of the season. The quality of the athletes' experience of a season will depend on the value systems, principles and beliefs of both themselves and the coach. Successful coach Wayne Smith describes the holistic, athlete-centred approach he incorporates in his sound empowering philosophy, in which his role is:

> … to create an environment so that the players feel comfortable in making decisions. In this way, they can cope with responsibilities and they can take ownership of their learning. Players should own the team culture. They should set their own expectations, establish the team protocols, … create the vision and the values. We [as coaches] guide them and facilitate them, but it is their total 'buy in' [collectively] that we are after. It's their programme, their campaign. So my philosophy is to create empowered players and to have … a holistic type approach so that the players are not just sport jocks, not just training for rugby, but have outside interests. I believe coaching is all about trying to develop better people, not just better players and it's important to enjoy the whole experience.

Leigh Gibbs' philosophy is very similar. She sees her role in this way:

> I try to create an environment where the players enjoy and have that passion for the game, but also to create situations where they develop, both as people on the court as well as people off the court. It is satisfying to work with people who are young and inexperienced in that they are still developing and learning. I feel it is my role to help these players expand their horizons holistically by providing lots of learning opportunities for all parts of their life using netball experiences.

Another with a similar outlook is Don Tricker:

> My philosophy on coaching is to take a holistic view as I believe that there is more to life than sport. I like to think that I have not only helped the athlete realise their athletic goals but have helped them become a more rounded person through their experience in sport. Coaching is simply about delivering a service, therefore I need to understand the requirements and expectations of each person that I coach be they five years old or a high-performance athlete. For coaching to be sustainable there must be win–win outcomes throughout the coaching experience—the win for me is that I can sit back and reflect on whatever contribution that I've made in terms of how each particular individual has grown. That's not solely limited to the athlete's athletic ability; it's more a contribution to that athlete as a person.

A philosophy is based on ideas formed from experiences. These experiences stem from influential teachers, coaches or mentors who have had a positive or negative effect on aspects of your life. For example, Ian Rutledge (Black Sticks hockey coach) and Mike McHugh highlight that some of their experiences of playing under and observing coaches have given them insight into how they *don't* want to coach, while other experiences have put them in contact with many positive philosophies on which they can draw in creating their own philosophy.

Specific steps to follow in developing your own personal coaching philosophy are to:

- ask why a particular teacher/coach had such a meaningful impact on you and what happened;
- determine how or whether those experiences may direct personal coaching actions;
- develop opinion(s) based on the knowledge that you have gathered over the years; and
- identify your hopes for the future.

Success vs Winning

To many people, success is measured by how many games or competitions are won or lost. It is a criterion on which the jobs of many coaches depend. Success, however, is not just about winning. More important to the concept is striving to win. Mark Norton highlights that the high school boys he coaches and the nature of their experience are his focus:

> I want to create a positive, enjoyable and meaningful experience for the kids to be involved in. I want the team and the team mission to become a focus in the boys' lives. I also want to create good volleyballers and a team that plays quality volleyball. I suppose. I like to use volleyball and physical activity as a vehicle to teach the kids about themselves, other people and how to effectively interact and function with others. That's how I treat my teaching of physical education also. Volleyball, a game hugely reliant on teamwork and one's team mates, lends itself to do this superbly. At the end of the day, if the kids have developed into better people, then I've been successful.

Certainly winning is a major factor in sports participation but success is more important. An athlete can win without performing well or can lose even though the performance has been outstanding. Success is a measure of how well the athletes are participating, how well they are achieving both personal and team goals. Winning involves comparing yourself to others. Success is self-measured, based on individual performance and contribution. In any competition, it is difficult to win if athletes do not experience success, a quality team culture, an athlete-centred environment, or balance in their lives. The idea of success as athlete learning, enjoyment, performance or growth is often overridden by a 'winning at all costs' attitude, which ignores athletes' needs and sabotages the pursuit of excellence with the result that sport participation degenerates into a means to an end (Boxill, 2003).

Many coaches speak about winning and success as if they are the same. However, winning must be defined within the culture of the team. For example, Wayne Smith's definition of winning is:

> … what you want it to be really. Winning may be (with a poor team), moving them up to a reasonable position on the ladder. It might be walking into the

changing room and seeing smiles on their faces. Winning for me is seeing people enjoying what they're doing, giving it all they have, players to the best of their ability, but playing because they love the game, not just because they are paid to.

There are many success stories about famous coaches but how many coaches have ensured the success of all their athletes? The attitude of 'win at all costs' noted above is prevalent in many societies, including ours, but at what cost? How many athletes have been turned away from sport because of their coach's insistence on winning (as in scoring the most points)? In Australia, it has been suggested that the five most common reasons for dropping out of sport are related to the coach (Robertson, 1992).

We rarely hear news about a successful coach who provided a great training environment and encouraged athletes to do their best. The media rarely portray a successful coach as an educator. Nevertheless, one of the biggest jobs in coaching is to educate athletes, preparing them physically, psychologically and socially. Knowing how your athletes tick and drawing out their athletic capabilities are measures of success. Because coaching is a people-oriented job, coaches must know how to facilitate the coaching environment to bring out the best in their athletes and they need to be committed to the individuals with whom they are working. In addition, given that sport is only part of an athlete's life rather than the whole of it, another measure of success may be whether each athlete continues to participate in sport, either with the same coach or another one.

Athletes have different ideas about their participation in sport, including different reasons for participating, desires, interests, involvement and commitments. Sport offers a setting where athletes can gain a sense of competence, achievement and recognition. Thus taking athletes to the Olympics or coaching an elite professional team is not what makes a coach important. Rather, an important coach is one who introduces individuals to sport and provides them with confidence, success and recognition so that the athletes want to continue in sport. A coach can make the athletic experience positive or negative. If a coach is dedicated to the pursuit of excellence—that is, excellence for the individual athlete—he or she can offer a profound, enjoyable, positive and successful experience for athletes. Our athletes deserve good coaches, dedicated to the athletes' betterment and to the development of confident, motivated, successful and happy people. This dedication is embedded in the values and principles of an empowering philosophy.

Coaches are constantly in a predicament as to whether to do what other people say or to do what they themselves believe. As winning is so important to society and the media, coaches need to be clear about their own philosophy in developing athletes. Is it more important to bow to the media or to keep your own self-esteem? Do the media need to continue to influence humanist approaches by constantly reporting win/loss records? With the power to make or break an athlete, the coach must be able to say that an athlete achieved success by achieving self-reliance and self-awareness. Ultimately, although a coach's job is never complete, by empowering athletes, a coach should make himself or herself all but redundant. To ensure true success, coaches need to strive for the self-sufficiency and self-fulfilment of the athlete.

References

Arai, S. M. (1997). Empowerment: From the theoretical to the personal. *Journal of Leisurability, 24*(1), 3–11.

Australian Sports Commission. (1997). *Games sense: Developing thinking players: A presenter's guide and workbook.* Canberra: Australian Sports Commission.

Boxill, J. (2003). Introduction: The moral significance of sport. In J. Boxill (Ed.) *Sport ethics: An anthology.* Malden, MA: Blackwell.

Butler, J. (1997). How would Socrates teach games? A constructivist approach. *Journal of Physical Education, 68*(8), 42–47.

Carron, A. V., & Dennis, P. W. (1998). The sport team as an effective group. In J.M. Williams (Ed.), *Applied sport psychology: Personal growth to peak performance.* Mountain View, CA: Mayfield.

Eskes, T. B., Duncan, M. C., & Miller, E.M. (1998). The discourse of empowerment: Foucault, Marcuse and the women's fitness texts. *Journal of Sport and Social Issues, 23*(3), 317–344.

Freysinger, V., & Bedini, L. A. (1994). Teaching for empowerment. *Schole: A Journal of Leisure Studies and Recreational Education, 9*, 1–11.

Hadfield, D. C. (2002). Developing team leaders in rugby. *Rugby Football Union Technical Journal.* Retrieved 7 October 2002 from www.rfu.com/pdfs/technical-journal/Developing_leaders_captains.pdf

Hadfield, D. C. (1994). The query theory: a sports coaching model for the 90s. *The New Zealand Coach, 3*(4), 16–20.

Jones, R. (2001). Applying empowerment in coaching: Some considerations. In L. Kidman, *Developing decision makers: An empowerment approach to coaching.* Christchurch: Innovative Print Communications.

Kidman, L. (2001). *Developing decision makers: An empowerment approach to coaching.* Christchurch: Innovative Print Communications.

Kidman, L., & Davis, W. (in press). Empowerment in coaching. In G. D. Broadhead & W. E. Davis (Eds), *Ecological Task Analysis: Understanding movement in context.* Champaign, IL: Human Kinetics.

Kidman, L., Hadfield, D., & Chu, M. (2000). The coach and the sporting experience. In C. Collins (Ed.), *Sport in New Zealand society* (pp. 273–286). Palmerston North: Dunmore.

Kidman, L., & Hanrahan, S. J. (2004). The coaching process: *A practical guide to improving your effectiveness* (2nd ed.). Palmerston North: Dunmore.

Launder, A. G. (2001). *Play practice: The games approach to teaching and coaching sports.* Champaign, IL: Human Kinetics.

Liu, Y. M. (2001). Discussion on team culture. *Journal of Capital College of Physical Education, 13*(1), 28–33, 60.

Lynch, J. (2001). *Creative coaching: New ways to maximize athlete and team potential in all sports.* Champaign, IL: Human Kinetics.

Metzler, M. W. (2000). *Instructional models for physical education.* Boston, MA: Allyn and Bacon.

Potrac, P. (2004). Coaches' power. In R. Jones, K. Armour, & P. Potrac, *Sports coaching cultures: From practice to theory.* London: Routledge.

Pratt, S. R., & Eitzen, D. S. (1989). Contrasting leadership styles and organisational effectiveness: the case of athletic teams. *Social Science Quarterly, 70*(2), 311–322.

Ravizza, K. (1998). Increasing awareness for sport performance. In J. M. Williams, *Applied Sport Psychology: Personal growth to peak performance.* Palo Alto, CA: Mayfield.

Robertson, I. (1992). *Children, Aussie sport and organised sport: Executive summary.* South Australian Study commissioned by the Australian Sports Commission.

Schempp, P. (1982). Enhancing creativity through children making decisions. In M. Pieron & J. Cheffers (Eds), *Studying the teaching in physical education* (pp. 161–166). Leige: International Association for Higher Education.

Shogan, D. (1999). *The making of high-performance athletes: Discipline, diversity and ethics.* Toronto: University of Toronto Press.

Smoll, F. L., & Smith, R. E. (1989). Leadership behaviors in sport: a theoretical model and research paradigm. *Journal of Applied Social Psychology, 19*(18), 1522–1551.

Thorpe, R. D. (1990). New directions in games teaching. In N. Armstrong (Ed.), *New directions in physical education* (pp. 79–100). Champaign, IL: Human Kinetics.

Usher, P. (1997). Empowerment as a powerful coaching tool. *Coaches' Report, 4*(2), 10–11.

Yukelson, D. (1997). Principles of effective team building. *Journal of Applied Sport Psychology, 9*(1), 73–96.

I like thinking of possibilities. At any time, an entirely new possibility is liable to come along and spin you off in an entirely new direction. The trick, I've learned, is to be awake to the moment. – *Doug Hall*

You cannot teach a man anything, you can only help him to find it within himself. – *Galileo*

If I had one wish for my children, it would be that each of them would reach for goals that have meaning for them as individuals. – *Lillian Carter, US nurse, first mother*

People with character will find a way to win, those without character will find a way to lose – *Ashley Jones*

Chapter Two

The Change Challenge: Facilitating self-awareness and improvement in your athletes

Dave Hadfield
Sport Psychology & Coaching Consultant, MindPlus Ltd

I first became involved in empowerment and questioning when I was coaching a group of young cricketers 15 years ago. The slow (and in many cases complete absence of) progress of the players in improving their batting and bowling skills, despite my best efforts in two-hour sessions twice a week, was getting more than a little frustrating. In particular, I recall having a great deal of difficulty in getting four or five of the batsmen to correct one glaring fault. Without going into details, the fault involves moving the back foot towards the leg side (backwards) just before (or at the same time as) a pace bowler releases the ball; this is a real technical problem for a batsman, cutting down scoring options considerably and increasing the chances of dismissal.

In my view at that time, I had been doing a pretty good job with these lads—I had told them what they were doing wrong, why it was wrong and what they needed to do to put it right. Because I also understood that the fear of getting hit was one potential reason why they had been getting it wrong, I took pains to explain that they had less chance of being hit if they kept their back foot still. What more did they need? Yet obviously they did need something more because, despite my coaching, they were still moving their back feet when I arrived for the next coaching session … and the next!

One day, in frustration more than anything else, I picked up a brick that was lying nearby and put it behind the back foot of one of these lads. The bowler delivered the ball, the batsman moved his back foot and the brick went rapidly backwards. Not quite knowing what to do, I put it back again. The scenario was repeated: the bowler delivered the ball, the batsman moved his back foot and the brick went backwards, but not so far this time. I replaced the brick, saying nothing the whole time, and then watched with amazement as this time the batsman kept his back foot still before playing a shot at the ball. I then took the brick away and to my surprise, he continued to keep his foot still for the rest of his batting session. The next step was to try this method with the other boys who had the same problem; it worked with all of them!

It was clear that from this experience I had stumbled upon a key concept for my coaching, but it took me a while to establish exactly what it was. After some thinking I figured out the essential lesson: *true self-awareness is a critical precursor to change.* Despite my telling the boys what was happening and why, it wasn't until they could truly feel it and recognise it for themselves that they were able to change their motor skills in the ways required for improvement. I now believe the learning process starts with *self-awareness*, which leads to the ability to *self-analyse*, which promotes *self-understanding* and *self-improvement*. If athletes are not self-aware, they cannot effectively analyse what they are doing against any kind of template and will find it difficult to develop the level of understanding required to change and improve.

Even after my moment of insight, however, it took time for me to discover that asking questions is a far more useful technique for achieving what the brick had accomplished. Of course, today using video to establish self-awareness is widespread and is an extremely helpful coaching technique; still more powerful, though, is the well-informed use of questions (as reinforced by Chapter Twelve and the coaches who feature in this book). So, instead of telling, I learned to ask. Instead of saying, 'Peter, you were moving your foot back when the bowler released the ball', I started to ask, 'Peter, what was your back foot doing when the bowler released the ball?' With this new approach, as soon as the athlete could reply, 'I was moving my foot backwards', they were able to change—and change quite easily. That is, once they were able to create a clear discriminatory self-awareness between the current (incorrect) way and the new (correct) way, they were able to implement change.

The Query Theory coaching model can account for this connection. It focuses on vividly explaining the correct way to perform a skill or technique; observing the performance, while mentally comparing the performance with a progressive, sequential checklist of key factors (or this checklist may be in written form); identifying strengths and weaknesses; and

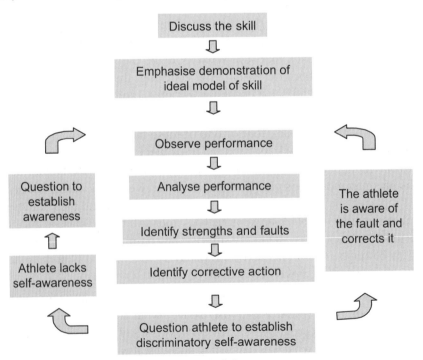

Figure 2.1. The Query Theory Coaching Model

then using questions to guide the athlete to self-awareness, self-analysis and improvement. The Query Theory coaching model is outlined in Figure 2.1.

After successfully using Query Theory to facilitate the changing of motor skills, I discovered that the Query Theory approach worked just as well when coaching the tactical (option-taking, decision-making) side of sport as it did when working with technique and body movement. The traditional approach to working with an athlete who had taken a poor option would tend to be for the coach to explain (using rugby as an example):

> Jack, that was clearly a poor option when you threw that long cut-out pass after the third phase. Their centre rushed up out of the defensive line and smashed Bill ball-and-all and that's what created the turnover and led to their try. You had Rangi running a dummy cut on the inside and you'd have been better served giving it to him. You need to scan more quickly before the halfback gives you the ball and make better decisions.

The Query Theory coach might approach it this way:

Coach: Jack, when they turned the ball over and scored that try, what do you think went on there?

Player: Well, their centre rushed up and smashed Bill and we were too slow getting to him. I shouldn't have thrown the pass.

Coach: Okay, what other options did you have?

Player: Well, I had Rangi running a cut on the inside?

Coach: Any other options?

Player: I suppose a chip might have been the go, especially as they were rushing up and there was possibly space behind?

Coach: Okay, which do you think would have been the best option and why?

Player: Their blind-side winger was sweeping across in defence for the chip, so I reckon the inside ball to Rangi would have been best, especially since he was running at two tight forwards and probably could have stepped them and found space.

Coach: Great. So what do you think you need to do to make a better decision in future?

Player: Well, I knew Rangi was running the cut, so I needed to scan earlier than I did and see their mid-field rushing up.

Coach: When do you need to do that?

Player: I think I need to scan quickly when the half-back is reaching for the ball, and again quickly just before he lets it go before I focus on catching the ball.

Coach: Okay. Let's design a drill that can help to train that …

Having taken a poor option, the player here has been carefully guided by the coach towards understanding what he did, how he did it and why. He is also led towards an insight into what would have been the best option and why.

Certainly the Query Theory approach has its disadvantages. In particular, it takes over twice as long as the traditional 'here's what you did wrong, here's how to fix it' method. Working through the above example would need maybe a minute or so (including some time for thinking) as opposed to 20 to 30 seconds.

What are the advantages? Well, first you are insisting that the athlete tap into his or her self-awareness in order to answer your questions. Assuming that the question is asked effectively (see Chapter Twelve), the athlete has two options: either to say avoid the question with a 'No comment' or 'I'm sorry, I'm not answering that question' (which is rather unlikely) or to answer it somehow. Answering it requires the athlete to analyse the question, tap into long-term memory and retrieve stored information which will then allow an answer according to his or her memory and understanding of what happened. This process will be enhanced if video of the incident is used to augment access to long-term memory and self-awareness.

With the answer that comes from the athlete's delving into memory and retrieving the necessary information, the coach gets valuable information as to the quality of the athlete's understanding and thus can design the next questions effectively. In this way, information and knowledge are constantly being interchanged between the coach and the athlete. Any discrepancies in understanding can be noted and explored. It is a wonderful template for developing self-awareness, self-analysis and self-understanding and for promoting and nurturing self-improvement. Conversely, as mentioned above, if athletes are not aware of what they are doing, they cannot analyse their actions and will therefore struggle to generate the self-understanding required for improvement.

Another advantage of the Query Theory approach is that athletes feel involved in the learning experience. They have a sense of ownership. A couple of observations attributed to the Chinese Taoist teacher and philosopher Lao Tzu (talking about leadership around 600 BC) can be applied to sum up how the Query Theory empowers athletes:

> To lead people, walk beside them ...
>
> As for the best leaders, the people do not notice their existence.
>
> The next best, the people honour and praise.
>
> The next, the people fear;
>
> and the next, the people hate ...
>
> When the best leader's work is done the people say, 'We did it ourselves!'
>
> When the effective leader is finished with his work, the people say it happened naturally.

When asked many years ago to define my own coaching philosophy, I replied, 'A caring guide to athlete self-discovery and self-improvement'. I believe that is in a close parallel with Lao Tzu's aphorisms. In my experience, athletes who have been questioned and guided by a Query Theory coach report feeling that they came up with the answers themselves. This adds to their confidence and sense of involvement in and mastery over the learning and improvement process.

The Query Theory approach has the further advantage of producing a deeper level of understanding than would be achieved if the athlete was merely told what is going on and what to do. Query Theory coaching, allied to the use of Teaching Games for Understanding (as detailed by other coaches and in Chapter Eleven), also creates conditions for implicit learning. Simply stated, *implicit learning* occurs when the learner acquires a skill without being able to describe the rules that govern the performance of that skill. In most definitions, implicit learning is conceived as a natural, simple and conscious learning process whereas explicit learning is described as a process that includes conscious operations such as the making and testing of hypotheses. In a presentation at the University of Bourgogne, Richard Magill (2003) stated:

> Although there are several reasons to promote the use of implicit learning conditions, the primary reason is that people perform implicitly learned skills quite well in conditions and situations that differ from those in which they practiced. That is, implicitly learned skills transfer to novel performance contexts more effectively than skills learned explicitly.

What Magill is suggesting is that implicit learning provides knowledge that is stored more effectively, lasts longer and, because of the way that it is understood and stored, may be used in a variety of situations.

Of course, I am not suggesting that you spend your whole life asking questions. There are many times when you will tell your athletes what to do and what is happening. For example, you may find such an approach is appropriate when:

1. safety is involved (*Move away from that area now!*);
2. you are setting up a session (*Put the cones out in a rectangle, 10 metres by 10*)
3. telling athletes what will happen during the session (*Today we are going to do a speed session before moving into a tactical session using 3 on 3s*);
4. the team clearly needs leadership and you must act to give the team guidance (e.g. at half time in a match, *From up in the stand I can see that their defence is rushing up. We need to try and use the space in behind their defence …*); and
5. you are telling athletes your opinion (*Anne, I can see you're struggling tonight. You're just not your usual self*). Then might come a question (*Is anything bothering you? Is anything wrong?*).

Moreover, asking questions for the sake of it is not useful. To the contrary, aimless, inappropriate or repetitive questions will lead your athletes to get bored or disgruntled, turning them off the questioning approach and thus away from the learning process. Athletes in this situation are likely to say, 'Enough with the questions; just tell me'. To keep the athletes learning, the coach should ask questions with a clear end in mind. That is, the coach needs to know what the athlete needs to understand and change and should be guiding the athlete towards an awareness of this knowledge. Each answer should inform the coach what to ask next in order for the athlete to continue down the road of self-awareness and understanding.

Used appropriately, then, a questioning approach is an effective way of achieving change. Although asking questions might take a bit longer and developing good questioning skills certainly takes time, the Query Theory approach is a key tool in the athlete-centred coach's toolkit. I know through long experience that it will empower both coach and athletes.

Athletes are empowered because the coach recognises and affirms that the real power of learning lies within the athlete and that the coach is merely a guide. This gives athletes a real sense of control over their own learning and of confidence. For their part, coaches are empowered through the discovery that the Query Theory is a powerful tool for facilitating change and growth in their athletes—and in this way achieving the one goal common to all coaches, namely improvement in their athletes. Coaches who are committed to an athlete-centred approach can harness this tool to help athletes immeasurably in the constant search for improvement and optimal performance.

The Nature of Change

The above outcomes of a Query Theory coaching approach lead naturally on to a consideration of the process of change and how empowerment may assist athletes to progress smoothly through it. Change is central to the coach's job. All coaching can be considered as the facilitation of behavioural change. Whether the coach is a teenager teaching a five-year-old to swim or an elite coach fine-tuning the mechanics of an Olympic medallist, the coach's job is to guide the athlete through the learning process. However, there is a difference between teaching athletes a new skill and assisting them to change a skill that is already a habit.

Like all animals, human beings are creatures of habit. Were this not so, we would keep putting our hand in the fire or on hot elements and we would keep walking in front of moving cars. Of course, we do not take any such actions repeatedly. Rather, we learn to do things that work, then we store them in our memory and produce them at the appropriate time. With this knowledge intact, we also resist change. Problems arise when we shift to a new situation or a new level and what we have learned no longer serves our purposes. An example from sport is when an athlete moves from youth to adult grade and finds that his or her existing skills are no longer good enough to be competitive. It could be a tennis player who at age-grade level got away with an average serve which does not cut it at senior level. It could be a cricketer whose inability to play the pull shot is a hindrance when he or she is promoted to first class level.

These kinds of situations are when we have problems changing. For anyone who doubts this, try doing what I have done quite a lot of lately: drive a rental car whose windscreen wiper control and indicator light control are on opposite sides of the steering column from your own car. If you are like me, when you drive the rental car, you will find yourself switching the wipers on (on a fine sunny day!) when you want to turn a corner, and indicating a turn when it starts to rain. Of course, we take these counterproductive actions because we have become habituated to the controls on our own car, which interferes with our ability to learn to operate the controls on the rental car. If you are still unconvinced, then fold your arms as you normally would, then put your hands by your sides and try to fold your arms the other way round from your normal way. If you are like most people it will feel somewhat strange and may even be quite difficult to achieve. Even if we try to learn a new way, we will often revert to the old way under pressure.

This habituation applies not only to motor skills and the development of motor programmes but also to the way we think and the attitudes we form. It applies to your own change and improvement as a coach and it pertains to the athletes to whom you have made a commitment to be the best coach you can and to help them to be the best athlete and person they can. I believe that becoming an *effective agent of change* is at the heart of coaching excellence. If you are teaching athletes a new skill that is different to what they have done before, or you are teaching newcomers a skill that they have never learned, you will not face the issue of habituation. However, if you coach teenagers or elite-level athletes, most of the improvements you wish them to make will involve changing well-formed habits. Certainly changing your own coaching behaviours will require overturning habits!

The other key problem you will face is emotional resistance to change. Imagine that, after you have finished a coaching session with an athlete or team, someone walks up to you and says:

> I am an experienced coach and I couldn't help but notice some of the things you did. I really do feel that you need to make some changes with the way you are coaching your athletes. Your approach needs some radical changes with regards to the way you are talking to them ...

What would your reaction be? Obviously whether you knew (and respected) the person giving the feedback, and whether his or her manner was forthright or empathetic would influence your response considerably. Equally, you may be a person who listens to every piece of critical feedback you get, takes it on board and processes it—indeed, you may welcome it. If you are like many people, however, your first reaction is likely to be resentment ('What do you mean I need to make radical changes? It's worked pretty well so far, thanks'), anger ('Yeah, well you can take a hike, mate!') or disappointment ('Am I really that bad? That stinks').

Usually, a suggestion of change implies that the way things are currently being done is not up to scratch and, to many people, that is a threat. What is threatened is our ego or psyche—our sense that we're okay and that all is well with us. Yet, if we are to change, the first thing that we must accept is that the way we are doing things now is not optimal or perhaps even is ineffective; perhaps it worked well in the past but does not now. It can take courage to admit this and face up to it. For many athletes and coaches, it may be courage that they do not have. So, to protect their psyche, they may push away the knowledgeable person who suggests that change is required, and rubbish the ideas or the person. Now they can feel better because their rejection of the person and/or the feedback justifies them in ignoring the feedback. They may feel that another threat to their self-esteem has been successfully dealt with. However, if they deal with all critical feedback in this way, they will find it very difficult to change and improve unless they are highly and accurately self-aware.

How you deal with this natural resistance to change among some of your athletes will also determine how successful you are as a coach. So, how *do* you best encourage change? Here are some suggestions:

1. Become an athlete-centred coach who understands deeply that the coach's role is to be a change and improvement facilitator.

2. Learn to be a top-class Query Theory coach. Learn to ask questions that lead to self-awareness, self-discovery and change. Especially you should seek to create a clear discriminatory awareness. That is, the athlete (or you if you are seeking to change yourself) should clearly and profoundly understand the difference between the old habit and the new, improved way of doing things.

3. Use a cost-benefit analysis to assist your athlete to see that change is worthwhile. Unless you can get your athlete to accept that the benefits of change outweigh the costs of change, you will struggle to make 'coaching headway'. We are all in sales; you need to be a caring salesperson of the need to change. You achieve this by being empathetic and understanding and by communicating effectively.

4. Ensure that you understand your athlete's learning style. In brief, while many of your athletes can learn multi-modally, perhaps a quarter may have strong leanings towards a kinaesthetic, aural, visual or read–write learning style. In New Zealand elite rugby, it seems many players tend to be dominant in the kinaesthetic sense. Teach using *all* learning modalities wherever possible; be creative. You can find more detail from the raft of resources on learning style; you can also apply simple tests that will indicate an athlete's dominant learning style (e.g. see Fleming 2001).

5. Establish a coaching or team culture in which openness, growth and change are pillars.

Many coaches with whom I have worked find it difficult to become an athlete-centred coach. Why? The prescriptive coach-centred approach is how they were coached and it is how they learned how to coach; now it has become a habit and, like all habits, it is hard to change—especially under coaching pressure. When things are getting tough, prescriptive coaches who are trying to become empowering tend to revert to a 'do this, do that' approach. It is what they know, it is easier, it is quicker and it shows anyone who may be in doubt who is the boss around here and who owns the knowledge. But is it the most effective approach? I would argue that in many cases it is not.

The two main requirements of the athlete seeking to change a habit have already been touched on. The first is self-awareness—awareness that there is an issue and that change is needed. I believe it is the coach's job to guide the athlete to an understanding of this situation. If an issue is not dealt with, it becomes a problem (the athlete will continue to fail) and may then escalate into a crisis (the athlete is dropped from the team or completely loses confidence). In a sense the athlete has to be convinced that the benefits of change outweigh the costs (which are normally time, effort and opportunity costs). The second requirement is that the athlete can clearly discriminate between the current way and the new, improved way of doing things.

If an athlete lacks self-awareness, it is nigh impossible to do any kind of analysis of 'what is'. Without effective self-analysis (either proprioceptive/kinaesthetic or cognitive), athletes cannot develop the self-understanding required to change and improve. One model (used in textbooks for many years, although I am unsure of its origins) sums up this situation well and gives an interesting insight into how athletes actually learn. This model suggests that when learning, people go through four stages (which apply to coaches as much as to the athletes with whom they are working):

1. In the *unconscious incompetence* stage, the athlete is unaware that a given skill area exists or is relevant and that he or she has a particular deficiency in this area. For example, a netball player is unable to pass effectively to her left but is not aware that this is limiting her performance.

2. In the *conscious incompetence* stage, the athlete becomes aware of the skill's existence and relevance and of his or her deficiency in this area. The athlete has a measure of the extent of the deficiency and of what level of skill is required for competence, and is committed to improving. The netballer is now aware that she has a weakness passing to the left, wants to change and understands what she needs to do.

3. In the *conscious competence* stage, the athlete can perform the skill reliably at will, but needs to concentrate and think in order to perform it. The netballer can now pass effectively to her left, but must focus on her skill execution to perform it effectively.

4. When the *unconscious competence* stage is reached, the skill becomes so practised that it enters the unconscious parts of the brain. It becomes second nature; the athlete can perform it effectively without conscious thought. The netballer can now pass equally well to her left as she can to her right under match pressure.

The Query Theory approach, when used in conjunction with modern aids such as video/computer analysis and even with aids as rudimentary as a mirror, is an important tool to help athletes who are seeking to get better. It can be used effectively by the athlete-centred coach across all four stages of change.

Another coaching model that is extremely effective has been developed in Australia by educationalist Harry Lyndon. Summarised very simply, Old Way, New Way (OWNW) is a method designed to create in athletes a discriminatory self-awareness (between the old, troublesome way and the new, improved way) and to enable them to overcome the strong urge to return to the habitual way (*proactive inhibition*) so that they can learn the new skill quickly and retain it. With this method, athletes are guided to distinguish clearly and vividly between the old way and the new way and, as with the Query Theory approach, questioning is a useful tool to achieve this purpose. When the athlete is able to perform in the new way, the coach asks him or her to repeat the old way and to clearly explain the difference. This is repeated several times (OW>NW>OW>NW>OW>NW>OW>

NW>OW>NW) until the athlete has understood the difference and is able to consistently perform the new, effective way of doing it.

Athlete-centred Coaching in Practice: Traps for the tyro

In my experience, many coaches struggle when first attempting to use a questioning approach. For some coaches, one reason for the difficulty is that they do not take the time to explain their new coaching approach to their athletes; instead their athletes are suddenly confronted with a barrage of questions from a coach who had previously been prescriptive. A more productive way to set the scene for a Query Theory approach is to say something like:

> You'll find I may be asking more questions of you than coaches you may have had in the past. It's not because I don't know the answers, or because I am asking questions to trip you up. I've found that asking questions really encourages you to continue to improve your self-awareness and understanding and that it works really well, especially once you really get used to it. I'll be checking in with you regularly to see how you are finding my coaching approach and whether you find it's working for you.

Another reason that coaches may have difficulties in their initial efforts with a questioning approach is that they may find themselves competing with the way that athletes have been coached in the past. Some coaches have said to me that their athletes prefer to be told what to do and why, and struggle with being questioned. My reply is that the preference for prescriptive coaching relates to familiarity—athletes have probably been coached in this way for most of their lives—and I ask those coaches, 'Should you them give them what they want, or what you know they need in order to change and grow?'. I believe that is a question that an athlete-centred coach needs to be able to answer.

A further reason for difficulty with a questioning approach is that effective questioning is a real skill that takes time to develop, and proficiency with it requires additional time and practice. The phenomenon of proactive inhibition will push you to return to the old, 'telling' way especially when under pressure of time, athlete reserve or downright opposition, and your own confusion about what to ask next. You must be aware that you will need to continue to improve your questioning skills—it really is an art that needs to develop over time. Be patient and you will steadily get better at it.

The other two main reasons why many coaches struggle with changing to a Query Theory approach must also be considered by any coach wishing to shift in this direction. First, the coach must decide how far down the empowering (athlete-centred) coaching path—and away from the prescriptive (coach-centred) path—it is right to travel. That is, how much authority should be held by the coach, and how much by the athletes? I will consider this issue shortly. The second issue was discussed earlier: habituation makes it difficult for us (and our athletes) to change. Even if we find that the way we learned to coach no longer works as we would wish and even if we are motivated to change, we still have the human tendency to return to the tried and true whenever we strike any difficulties with the new approach or are under pressure in some way.

To me, being athlete-centred is about taking athletes by the hand and leading them to athletic 'righteousness'. As I mentioned above, in my coaching philosophy a coach is 'a caring guide to athlete self-discovery and self-improvement'. Another aspect to the coach's role is being 'a guide to self-reliance'. Given that we begin working with our athletes when they are at various stages of development, understanding and maturity, it is important to understand that a coaching approach that provides optimal results for a learner with little discipline may need to be altered for mature, self-governing athletes of high skill. The situational (or developmental) model proposed initially by Hersey and Blanchard (1982) illustrates this issue perfectly. In my view, this model offers a meaningful window into the reality of coaching (see Figure 2.2).

The situational coaching model proposes that coaching (or leadership style) needs to change—based on the four approaches (or life-cycle quadrants) indicated in Figure 2.2—according to the situation and the nature of the people being coached (or led). Thus in coaching an athlete (or team) who is a beginner or lacks discipline, you may need to

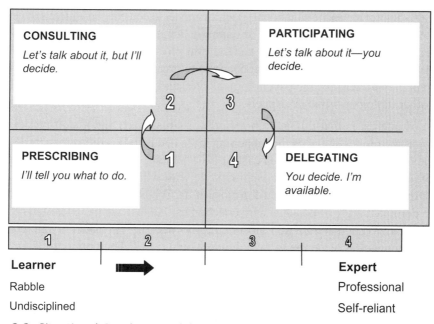

Figure 2.2. Situational Coaching Model adapted from Hersey & Blanchard's (1982) life-cycle model of leadership

be more *prescriptive* and provide considerable resources and support (quadrant 1 in the diagram). As the athlete (or team) becomes more skilful, knowledgeable and self-reliant, then the coaching approach needs to become more *consultative* (quadrant 2) and then *participative* (quadrant 3). When athletes reach quadrants 3 and 4, they are largely the masters of their own development. They know their sport, they understand their own mind and body, and the coach adopts a role focused much more on guiding than prescription. In reality, it is rare to achieve the *delegating* approach in quadrant 4—where an athlete is so self-reliant that the coach becomes an adviser who offers suggestions when called upon to do so. Regardless of which quadrant you are operating in, however, the approach is always athlete-centred, as your coaching is guided by what is in the best interests of the athlete at that time in his or her development.

In my philosophy of coaching, the core objective is to take the athletes (or team) by the hand and lead them, clockwise, round the quadrants. That is, the whole objective of coaching ought to be to guide athletes to become more self-reliant and self-governing, both in and outside of sport. That is the essence of athlete-centred coaching. Of course, the coach must first ascertain which quadrant athletes are in before deciding which coaching approach to employ. What the model rejects is using a quadrant 3 or 4 approach to coach athletes who are in quadrant 1 or 2. For this reason, an athlete-centred approach, where the level of development of the athlete is ascertained and the appropriate coaching approach used, is vastly different from a *laissez-faire* approach (French for 'leave them to do it themselves'), where the coach abandons his or her responsibilities and leaves the athletes to fend for themselves.

It is also helpful to use the situational coaching model to consider an athlete's development stage in various aspects of a sport. For example, an athlete may be well developed and reasonably self-reliant in technical, tactical and physical aspects, but may fold under mental pressure. In this situation, the coach may provide clearer guidance and support (quadrant 2 approach) for the psychological side, and let the athlete drive development in the other three performance aspects.

Also of interest is that this is both a *state* (or situational) and a *trait* model. On the first point, the model suggests that coaching style needs to be adjusted according to the state (level of development in this case) of the athlete. However, it also suggests that each of us as a coach has a trait coaching style with which we are most comfortable. I believe this offers food for thought for most of us. When we learn to coach, we tend to use the dominant style of coaches who coached us—unless we have learned otherwise. Ask yourself, 'What quadrant do I most naturally coach in? If I asked my athletes which quadrant they would place me in, which one would it be?' Then ponder the answer. As Chapter Fourteen discusses, self-reflection is an important task for the coach who wishes to improve. If you lack self-awareness, it will be difficult for you to analyse and understand yourself, and thus difficult for you to change and improve. I am not suggesting that you should be like a chameleon, constantly changing so that the athletes become confused as to what is going on. Certainly you must 'be yourself' when you coach, as athletes will detect a sham or an actor quickly. Rather I am suggesting you should ask yourself, 'Who am I coaching here, what level of development are they at, and how best might I guide them to improvement?' The Query Theory approach will work well with most athletes in all quadrants.

I would repeat here that I am in no way suggesting that a coach ought to forget that he or she is the leader. As coach, your head is on the block when the success of the athlete or team is being assessed; you need to do whatever you think is best, within ethical boundaries, to ensure optimal performance. That means at times you will need to help your athletes understand. When they are struggling and looking to you for leadership, you must provide it. If they are confused about what is going on and what is required, and there is no opportunity for guided self-discovery, you need to clarify the situation for them. Moreover, when athletes are behaving in ways that are below the values and standards set, it is totally appropriate for a coach to point this out in a forthright manner. If athletes do not use the freedom they have been given in their own best interests and the best interests of their team, they need be told so. This kind of 'telling' may be classified as quadrant 1 leadership, but if that is what is required, that is what you do. Of course, it should also be done with respect and empathy.

The Way Ahead

Becoming a master practitioner in athlete-centred coaching takes a commitment from coaches similar to that required from your athletes. You may be using athlete-centred methods to some extent now; if so, that is great. If you believe that you need to change, then you need to ask yourself, 'How am I coaching now? Am I coaching optimally? Am I the best agent of change I can be?' You need to become self-aware, and to analyse yourself using the reflective processes (see Chapter Fourteen). If possible, get someone to video your coaching and study the tape. Get feedback from a knowledgeable peer or coach educator. If you are to change habitual behaviour and move through from unconscious incompetence to unconscious competence as a master of athlete-centred coaching, you will need to be committed to the change process.

To know how to work best with each of your athletes, find out the learning style of each one and decide how far through the life-cycle quadrants each has travelled. Make it your aim to take them by the hand and guide them on their journey of self-discovery. Give your athletes as much responsibility as they can handle—but do not give them more than they can cope with. Become a master of Query Theory. Recognise that it will take time and patience to really get the hang of it.

Good luck on your own journey of self-discovery.

References

Fleming, N. (2001). *VARK: A guide to learning styles*. Retrieved 7 January 2005 from www.vark-learn. com

Hersey, P. & Blanchard, K. H. (1982). *Management of organisational behaviour: Utilising human resources* (4th ed.). Englewood Cliffs, NJ: Prentice-Hall.

Magill, R. A. (2003) Implicit learning of motor skills. Xème Congrès International des Chercheurs en Activités Physiques et Sportives, Toulouse, France, 30 October – 1 November, 2003. Retrieved 6 January 2005 from www.u-bourgogne.fr/ACAPS/congres/Toulouse/Actes%20pdf/pleni%E8res.pdf

Leaders understand the power
of choice. – *Anonymous*

If you want to build a ship, don't herd people together to
collect wood and don't assign them tasks and work, but rather
teach them to long for the endless immensity of the sea.
– *Antoine de Saint-Exupery*

Those who know do not speak Those that speak do not
know. – *Lao-Tzu Tao Te Ching*

Coaches have to watch for what they don't want
to see and listen to what they don't want to hear.
– *John Madden*

When your values are clear
to you, making decisions
becomes easier.
– *Roy Disney, US actor, author*

Mark Norton
Riccarton High School Boys'
Senior Volleyball Team

The coaches featured in this book are using or have used a successful athlete-centred approach. This chapter focuses on the first of them—a development coach, Mark Norton, who for this particular project coached the Boys' Senior Volleyball team at Riccarton High School in Christchurch. For the last five years Mark Norton has coached various volleyball teams at the school, using what he saw as an athlete-centred approach to differing degrees. His interest in participating in this project was sparked by his desire to learn more about this coaching approach. My aims were to observe the evolution of both his approach to coaching and his team from the beginning of the season to the time of the National Championships.

To follow the evolution of Mark's coaching approach, I used an action research model by contributing to and managing this boys' secondary school volleyball team. Before the season started, Mark and I met to discuss the process of working together and my role as a researcher. I acted as a 'player manager', attended training sessions and games for the season and was a manager at the National Championships. The role of dealing with volleyball specifics was entirely Mark's. I noted that throughout the season, he used questioning and Teaching Games for Understanding (TGfU) to work on the boys' decision making skills. One further factor shaping the research was Mark's belief that gaining feedback is important to help him learn more about and improve his coaching and to strengthen his focus on making better players, consistent with his commitment to developing each person as a whole. Therefore my role was to observe and provide advice to Mark on the team culture and psychological aspects of the training and game for the athletes. Mark acted or did not act on my advice according to what he determined was appropriate. It was an extremely enjoyable time and a great research experience.

To collect data for Mark's process of implementing an athlete-centred approach, I interviewed him at length twice and we also chatted informally throughout the season. Two of the athletes, Luke Russell and Simon Kidman, were also interviewed. In addition, I held group interviews with the players during two different barbecues, during which the boys spoke about the team culture and the season in general. Audio recordings of interviews were transcribed verbatim and participant observation field notes were collected throughout the season.

When asked at the end of the season why he had decided to improve his coaching approach, Mark says:

> I have always wanted to have players who were empowered and could run themselves, but through doing this process I think I have learned that there is much more in it than what I was doing previously.

Along with his athlete-centred coaching repertoire of questioning and TGfU, Mark focused on ensuring a quality team culture (wairua). To this end, he mutually (i.e. together with the players) established, reinforced and revisited goals and values throughout the season. Promoting goals and values in these three ways was excellent in helping the boys to take ownership of and responsibility for their learning, decision making and team goals. Mark shared leadership to the extent of establishing a couple of mini groups but did not focus on this strategy extensively in developing his coaching repertoire. The other aspect of athlete-centred coaching practice that I observed Mark using was role rotation. Again he made only limited use of this strategy. It is important to note that, just as an athlete is encouraged to learn one new skill at a time, a coach who is learning new coaching skills should focus on mastering one before moving on to the next one.

In this chapter, Mark's philosophy of coaching, his process of establishing the team culture and a range of his coaching practices are presented. His techniques for empowering athletes are also discussed.

Mark's Philosophy of Coaching

During our interviews, Mark spoke about his philosophy for and his role in the volleyball team. The boys and their type of experience are his central focus, as he highlights:

> I want to create a positive, enjoyable and meaningful experience for the kids to be involved in. I want the team and the team mission to become a focus in the boys' lives. I also want to create good volleyballers and a team that plays quality volleyball. I suppose I like to use volleyball and physical activity as a vehicle to teach the kids about themselves, other people and how to effectively interact and function with others. That's how I treat my teaching of physical education also. Volleyball, a game hugely reliant on teamwork and one's teammates, lends itself to do this superbly. At the end of the day, if the kids have developed into better people, then I've been successful.

For this particular team, Mark decided that long-term development was important. To enable the boys to learn as much as possible from each other, he used a squad system, which meant creating two teams of even ability for the pre-season competitions on Monday nights. Mark believed the squad system would be the most effective way to develop the Riccarton High School volleyball programme. His ultimate goal was 'to have a really high quality top team and a team that would probably develop into a top team the following year'. After himself deciding to put the players into a squad arrangement, Mark gave the boys the responsibility for deciding how to run it and what direction to take. Although he contributed ideas, he regarded what the boys wanted as more important because 'They were the ones who had to do it'.

Once the squad system had been implemented for the pre-season, I asked Mark whether he thought his philosophy of formulating the squad system was working. He believed that the progress achieved to date indicated solid foundations had been laid for the future:

> They are playing some good volleyball, the consistency is not quite there

yet, but they are showing signs of doing some really brilliant things ... we have not even looked at specific team systems or individual roles in terms of developing setters or hitters, we are just really working on all around skills at the moment. I think that everyone's all around skill level is improving ... my setters can hit the ball, can set the ball and everyone can do a bit of everything.

His philosophy of focusing on the boys and ensuring a good team environment was also working, Mark suggested, in that 'We are consistently getting all [team members] attending and the atmosphere they create in their trainings is great'.

Mark's Development as a Coach

Mark holds the position of physical education teacher at Riccarton High School. During his teacher training at the Christchurch College of Education, he was exposed to and influenced by the New Zealand Health and Physical Education curriculum (NZHPE). This curriculum has a philosophy of hauora (holistic well-being), which Mark has transferred into his physical education teaching and coaching philosophy.

Mark has a passion for volleyball and was a New Zealand volleyball squad member until 2003. He says that his coaching before this project was based on a similar coaching philosophy to the one outlined in the previous section but he had never explicitly thought about it or written it down. The very nature of his holistic, athlete-centred approach is in accordance with the notion of empowerment in coaching.

Mark suggests that his playing experience influenced his desire to try the athlete-centred style of coaching: 'I had some pretty clear goals of what I wanted to happen based on my own playing experience'. As his 'serious' volleyball playing days dwindled, he wanted to put more energy into volleyball coaching:

I have always enjoyed coaching, but I have really enjoyed this team. This recent coaching experience is motivating me to put more of my energy into coaching volleyball rather than playing myself.

One of the real coaching skills in using an athlete-centred approach is the ability to 'read' people and situations. In Mark's view, one of his weaknesses lies in his limitations in this ability; for example, he finds it difficult to determine when to change a situation, when to address athletes' needs, when to discuss and when to be quiet. To learn how to 'read' people in the way that he wishes to, Mark suggests:

I probably have to put myself in other people's shoes, and try to think from their perspective more. When listening I need to actually listen. There are all these road blocks to listening ... for example, judging or thinking of a response rather than actually listening to the message they are giving and listen for meaning. That's part of listening too, reading [people].

When asked what he still needs to learn about his coaching, Mark says:

... that's a hard question because you know what you know, you don't know what you don't know. Then there are things that you don't know that you don't know that you don't know them … I suppose it is endless. I experience more and more things and discover more things I need to learn.

The Process of Establishing a Quality Team Culture[1]

Quality team culture can be defined using Yukelson's (1997) components of team culture—namely, unity of purpose, individual and team accountability, teamwork, open and honest communication, positive atmosphere, and mutual trust. These components were trialled, maintained and reinforced with the team through Mark's athlete-centred approach. As noted above, he was already using many practices of an athlete-centred approach, but for this season his aim was to take it further by establishing and maintaining a quality team culture. Although the process of establishing the vision and values was lengthy, it was well worth the exercise. Mark believes that the team's wairua contributed significantly to their success.

As a first step in establishing this quality team culture, Mark decided that the full squad should create the values to live by and the strategies to deliver the vision and values because:

> … I was disappointed with last year with the lack of development the boys achieved. They were a quality junior side but didn't make the required jump into senior volleyball very well. The development of a team culture was out of need. We needed to make more progress with their playing ability but also to re-create the motivation and passion for the game. That had disappeared. I am certain the latter was responsible [for the lack of development] and this was because of my neglect.

To start the process, Mark met with all interested boys who wanted to play volleyball. Eighteen boys, aged 15–18 years, trialled for the team. They formed a squad of two equal teams for the first term. Mark explains the rationale in this way:

> We wanted to have all the boys playing in the top grade because I thought to improve at all, they needed to be playing the top volleyball, even if they were out of their depth a little. So I split up what I thought was the leadership and ability and I tried to make two even teams, so they both would be able to hold their own, not necessarily win, but hold their own.

After the first term with the squad system, 'A' and 'B' teams were chosen in the second half of the season, but Mark indicated that those in the B team could still make the A team up until two weeks before the Canterbury Championships. The boys and Mark decided that the criteria for selection for the A team should be based equally on a player's skills and how they lived the values.

Initially the players were sceptical about the squad system. As Luke says, 'I think

[1]Much of this section has been adapted from: Kidman, L. & Davis, W. (in press). Empowerment in coaching. In G. D. Broadhead & W. E. Davis (Eds), *Ecological Task Analysis: Understanding movement in context,* Champaign, IL: Human Kinetics.

the older guys didn't respect the younger guys that much because we thought that they sort of just mucked around all the time'. Luke changed his mind after he saw how hard everyone on the squad worked. He reflects:

> I think it was really good keeping that huge squad and all training together. I think it brought everyone's level up quite a lot. That made it better when we did split up because we played the Bs and they actually challenged us. If we just split up into As and Bs, then the As would waste the Bs every time we played them and it wouldn't do them or us any good. But having close games made the Bs positive about things because they were beating us. It makes us all step back and see that we had to work a bit harder.

Simon also suggests that being part of a squad made him work harder:

> … it gives you more of [a] chance to get into the top teams …the teams are better so if you want to be challenged then you can train for the A team and get more experience, but if you want just want to play socially; you can just play for the B team.

At the end of the season, Simon still valued the squad system. In his view, 'it makes you work harder because you want to get to the top team and have more fun trying to do that. It makes you attend training.'

As the team was compiled of two teams, a vision and team goals were established with the full squad. First, Mark gave each boy a homework book for writing decisions made during team trainings. To get them thinking about both dream and performance goals, Mark then asked, 'If you were at the end of season dinner and had to make a speech and talk to everyone about the sort of team that we are, what would be the things that you would like to be able to say?'

At first, because of the size of the squad, there was little evidence of interaction. It was obvious that due to comfort and confidence, the seniors had more to say than the junior members, who were hesitant and waited to see what their role in the whole process would be. The squad was curious about the input being asked of them as, even when Mark had been their coach previously, they had never contributed to the direction of a team in this way. Initially they did not understand or know their roles. As this was Mark's first attempt at developing an athlete-centred vision and values, there seemed to be a fair amount of experimenting and 'going with the flow' (which in itself fits an athlete-centred philosophy).

As would be expected of someone new to this process, Mark found it difficult to allow athletes to make their own decisions. However, he was conscious that he had to let the athletes speak and make these decisions if they were going to own the team vision and values. I noted that he made quite a few leading questions and statements but ultimately it was a team decision that the main mission goals were to:

- win six out of 10 Monday night games (with squad system);

- win the Canterbury Championships (once A team was selected, which the boys decided would occur two weeks before the championships);
- be in the top 10 teams at the Nationals;
- achieve a semi-final spot at the Nationals (a dream goal);
- be an exciting team to watch; and
- become known as a team who: never gives up; is the tightest; is mentally tough.

As the next step in this process, Mark explained that the boys needed to establish some values to live by. Providing them with a list of 30 values from Jeff Janssen's *Championship Team Building* (2002), he asked them to pick six values they considered to be important for the team, write down why they were important, and provide a definition of the value so that everyone would understand it in the same way.

At the next training session, Mark divided the 18 boys into groups of three (one senior player and two junior players) and asked each group to collate all of the values identified by the individual athletes and to pick out the six that they felt were the top priority. He then wrote the prioritised values of each small group on a whiteboard and the whole group discussed their meaning. Mark facilitated the discussion and contributed his ideas too. After much discussion and some debate, the team came up with six values for the volleyball team: respect, communication, cohesion, enjoyment, invulnerable and commitment (all worded and defined by the boys).

I thought this process was particularly difficult for Mark as he came to the discussion with his own preferred values for the team. Even though his views were included in the discussion, he seemed to 'bite his tongue' several times to ensure that the values finally chosen were the boys' decision. In this way Mark concentrated on enabling the athletes to contribute to major decisions rather than allowing the coach's power to supersede what the athletes want, as often happens. He also had to be careful not to exploit his social power as physical education teacher for many of the players. Just as the boys had to come to a consensus and go with the majority, so did Mark. He realised that his role was to facilitate the process and follow through with the consensus reached. His intentions are reflected in the views of both athletes interviewed, who identify the goals and values as the players' and regard them as stronger because of that. Luke says:

> We were the ones that made the values. Because they came from us, we respected them a bit more than if they were just given to us and someone says, 'This is how you've got to act'. It wouldn't have been the same.

Simon takes a similar view: 'The coach was in on it, but the kids did most of it. It's better because the coaches just don't make rules and the kids have things to say, so it's better to listen to everyone'.

The next step in establishing a vision and values was to come up with strategies to meet the goals. This time, Mark asked the boys to think about what strategies would ensure the values were practised. The same process was followed; in small groups the boys discussed and prioritised the strategies identified, and then made the final choice of strategies as a whole group. As a result, they committed to the following strategies to achieve their goals and live their values:

- talk constructively at appropriate times;
- take care of things outside volleyball so we can enjoy the game and our season;
- respect each other at all times;
- attend all trainings, physically, mentally and socially (be intense);
- remain positive no matter what;
- always demonstrate positive winning posture; and
- always be there for my teammates.

By about the fifth training session, the team had established the goals, values and strategies for the season. The whole process was enjoyable to watch. I had often wondered how this age group would react to such a process, but the enthusiasm of the boys (once they knew that Mark was going to follow through and monitor their decisions) highlighted to me that these young adults revelled in it. Because they were part of the decisions, they accepted their responsibilities to ensure that each item was followed.

Once the values, goals and strategies were established, the team decided that the they needed one short, precise vision statement to represent it. After much discussion and about two training sessions later, the team came up with 'Binding Together to be Better (B3)'. The boys also decided they needed a symbol of the team's vision, goals and values; to this end they chose a gluestick because it helps to bind things together. Mark bought three-sided gluesticks to match the B3 vision statement. Each boy wrote his name and the team values on the gluestick and carried it everywhere as the symbol of his team's volleyball campaign.

As a result of this process the boys created a tight group (one of their goals) that was well known within their school. To show their commitment (one of the values), they hung the gluesticks around their necks so that they could wear them around school and to volleyball.

The gluesticks became a significant element in the development of the quality team culture. Mark tells the story of the growing importance of this symbol:

> When they developed the values, it was really important for them to say how they were going to show the values, not only at volleyball and our training, but at school as well and in life in general. So, one of the things we ensured they do is not only bring their gluesticks to anything volleyball, but we want them to carry it on at all times in school, so after the first game with their gluesticks, I made sure I had mine in my pocket the whole time and then, I was like a cowboy, I would draw it on them and have them draw it back. If they didn't draw theirs, I would give them a bit of a hard time. They started catching on to that and they were then drawing it on me by the end. They were all trying to catch me out. One of the really cool things was that they

decided that they would take them into their exams. So, they walked into their end-of-year exams, one of the first things they did was to sit down at the desk draw out their gluesticks and they put it on their desk in front of them … the others would look around and they would see each other pulling out their gluesticks and I guess they get that sense of 'we are in this together'. I am sure it stems from it, I don't know, it is spiritual, but …

A more widespread effect was that teachers and other students came to 'idolise' the gluesticks, as Simon explains:

In a way, the year 9s respected us because we were wearing these gluesticks. An example was that last term we were sitting in the hall and a member of the team had a Stage Challenge Practice and they put all their gear down, including the gluestick. The year 9 kid went up and grabbed his gluestick and put it on and was walking around during lunchtime and thought he was cool. The gluestick really helped us. It wasn't just at volleyball, but at school everyone respected [us] and thought we were awesome.

Similarly Luke points to the schoolwide respect that the gluesticks brought them, as well as to their impact on team values:

[The gluestick] was good, that was a way to reinforce the values. It brought all the values together. It was the way for our season and stuff. It reinforced it a bit more. It was really cool to see people wearing them at school. Everyone knew we were a team as well. Everyone knew that we are a pretty good team and that we were pretty close.

As the above accounts indicate, the boys were soon carrying the gluesticks everywhere, including into classes and external exams. The boys then decided that if someone was caught without the gluestick, then that player or coach would get a slit in the eyebrow (i.e. a shaved line through the hair of the eyebrow) as another symbol of the team values. The boys also decided that failing to tell coach if they couldn't make it to training would also earn them a slit. Most boys were happy to take the slit for the team. Some, however, had some cultural issues about it and, after Mark held a team discussion, the boys changed the system. By this time, the coach's monitoring of the system was minimal because the boys owned the values so firmly.

Another part of this process was the creation of a poster that included all of the boys' photos, along with the vision, goals, strategies and values. At an official sign-off ceremony, all members of the team signed the poster as a type of contract that committed them to striving for the team's goals and adhering to its values. This 'contract' proved to be another binding element as, when issues arose, the boys and Mark would always remind individuals of what it committed them to: 'you signed that you agreed to these values'. As a coach, Mark feels that the boys took responsibility for the vision, values and strategies, with the poster.

From a player's perspective, Luke reaches similar conclusions about the role of the poster:

… having the values there in place in writing everywhere, and saying them at trainings and stuff and yelling them out, you couldn't hide away from them. You just had to do them. I think that was different. Other coaches sort of say those things, but [in our team] you've got to do these things …

That the team saw signing the poster as binding in nature became evident after an incident where one of the boys did not live up to the values. This incident was raised in front of the team, which led to a discussion that demonstrated athlete decision making. The team expressed their concern about the boy's well-being because they thought that volleyball was good for his growth and development.

In reflecting on the process of reaching a decision, Mark notes first the team's concern for the boy's well-being:

I thought this was an amazing moment: the boys recognising the work that being a member of the team was towards well-being and saying that they needed to let him stay with the team. On the other side there were the staunch protectors of the value commitment and decided that he had to be let go. This highlighted for me how important the team was to them personally.

Ultimately, however, they decided that by signing the poster he had agreed to the contract but he was not living the values so he must be asked to leave. Mark was given the responsibility of informing the boy of the team's decision, which proved to be another learning experience. In informing the boy, Mark had to remind himself of using the poster as a tool of accountability:

… kind of sealing the deal. The other thing was that they could be held accountable to that if they weren't living up to it. I could say, well hang on, you developed this yourself, plus you just signed it. You signed it and said you were going to do this, what's the problem?

By this time the athletes were managing the direction of the team themselves, with his role largely comprising of instructing and focusing on the values.

For the season, the boys achieved all but their dream goal. They won Canterbury Championships and placed fifth at the Nationals. At the Nationals it was evident not only to the boys and the coach but also to opposing and observing teams that the wairua practised by the boys enhanced their play. The athleticism of the team was considered lower than that of many others yet they managed to beat more athletic teams. The boys, the coach and outsiders put their success down to the wairua they had created, symbolised by the gluestick they carried. Many a player and coach from other organisations wanted to know about the gluesticks. It became a talking point at the Nationals as well as back at school after the Nationals.

The initial squad system helped the team to formulate a mutual trust and practise the values, which were tested throughout the season through different situations. Some situations were simulated, as organised by Mark. Other situations arose spontaneously and Mark used them too to get the athletes to reflect on the values. For the boys to take ownership of the team culture, they had to live the values. Mark notes how the gluestick helped the team to achieve this objective:

> Well, having the gluesticks keeps alive the values for sure. It keeps the values out there the whole time so that we don't forget about them. Part of the coaching also is to make sure that the values are always reinforced. Through reinforcing them, the players took on and lived their values and reinforced their commitment to the values by having the gluesticks on them the whole time, on show. It's almost like the ultimate crime is not to have it because if you can't organise yourself to bring your gluestick, then you are just not fulfilling the values, you are letting the team down. If that is our number one representation of what we are about, and you don't have it with you or you are not respecting it, then that is kind of the ultimate [transgression].

In reflecting on the volleyball season, Mark, Luke and Simon comment that it was one of the most successful sport seasons in which they had participated. They indicate that the success came not from winning (as they did in the Canterbury Championships) but from meeting all their goals except their dream goal and exceeding their expectations. Thus Luke states that success lay in 'bringing the team together, having [everyone] on the team contributing and everyone knowing that they are useful and being positive about it'. Likewise, Simon notes, 'because we knew each other, we knew how we played, we worked out a good game plan and we knocked off bigger teams because we didn't get down and we just played as a team.' They believe that the team achieved the value of cohesiveness, which made the team experience enjoyable (another of the values).

Enabling athletes to make decisions reinforces the natural expectations of any team. Because the athletes chose the direction of the team, they took on the role of self-monitoring which in turn enhanced wairua. With respect to reinforcing the values through the symbol of the gluestick, Mark states, 'I think it gave them complete ownership and I think when they had that sense of ownership, they were prepared to do more, were prepared to work harder and were prepared to sacrifice other things'. This sense of responsibility led the athletes to take ownership of their preparation and performance, a foundation to an athlete-centred approach.

The whole squad was involved with this decision making process of establishing the vision, values and goals, which took about three hours outside of training as a group, plus homework that the boys had to complete in times outside of meetings and training sessions. Simon gives the probable explanation as to why most of the squad seemed quite keen to participate in this kind of decision making:

> …. it's better because the coaches just don't make rules and the kids have things to say, so it's better to listen to everyone. I hated being shouted at in other teams. It makes you want to stop trying.

Although they did not meet their dream goal of achieving a semi-final spot at National Championships, they did come in fifth place. Mark assesses this outcome in this way:

I think you have got to look at success. What is your measure of success? Obviously, one measure could be their results and the level to which they played, which was successful … I think another measure could be, and I suppose is the social benefits they experienced from it. This is the other side to my coaching philosophy. I think just in that alone it was really successful. I thought it taught kids about values and I think it taught them the importance of them and I think they learned a lot socially. They learned how to get on with each other. At the start, there were some rifts. There were some guys who couldn't handle one another, some personality clashes and they learned how to get over those. But for the last game [at the Nationals], it was being tired and having reached your goals and then having this last game to play that was sort of a consolation game.

Simon takes a similar view of the last game at the Nationals, suggesting it was difficult for the team to play because they had already met their goals for the season and it was a consolation game. Yet even in these circumstances the team culture seemed to prevail again and Riccarton won the game. The sets had been tied 1-1, with the last set score at 13-9 in favour of the opposing team. Then John Gibbs blocked a tough spike and Riccarton came back to win the set 16-14. In response to my question as to why the team managed to pull out this win, Simon states, 'We had a belief in ourselves. We just knew we were going to win because we were close as a team'.

When further exploring how the team goals were met for the season, Mark says:

… every other goal, and those little goals like being a tightest team, mentally [tough], exciting team, I think we reached all those. It was those two things [being the tightest team and mentally tough] that enabled the team to beat teams who were more athletic or more skilful. Other teams were more athletic and were more skilful, but not consistently because their mental side of their game didn't allow them to be … All this showed the depth of the team because these guys came in and managed to get us to where we were, and then in the end too, when a couple didn't play so well, still came on full force ready to play. You could count on all of them.

The trust that the coach had in his team, and that all players had in each other, was one of the key characteristics of the quality team culture that developed over the season. Luke notes the motivation that came from:

… the team culture and just being part of the team. That's all I played for at the end. Yes, we were winning but I knew it was because the way the team was working together because we were heaps smaller than and not as athletic as the guys who we played.

Like Luke, Simon believes that:

… because of the team culture and because we knew each other, we knew how we played, we worked out a good game plan and we knocked off bigger teams because we never got down and we just played as a team, we kept together … For an example, we played a team, that through the net, they were telling us that we suck and they were going to smack us, but we kept to our own game. We didn't stoop to their level by doing anything stupid and we ended up beating them three-zip. They were fourth or third ranked team in the tournament ... our team, compared to the rest of the teams in the top seven, we didn't have very much skill. We had one or two good hitters and one or two good passers and a good setter, but the rest of the teams were good at everything. They could probably beat us in skill level any day, but we beat them at volleyball because we stuck together and we communicated well.

Mark's Use of Questioning

As all the coaches featured in this book reinforce, questioning is one of the most important coaching skills to promote athlete decision making and problem solving. Mark used questioning adeptly. He found it to be a fantastic coaching tool for getting the athletes to think for themselves, to solve problems during games, to take ownership of their learning and to understand volleyball better. After putting the team in problem solving situations 'where certain team cohesiveness and tactical strategies were required', Mark would follow up with questioning that:

> ... [the questioning I used] allowed them to discover the strategies that would work in similar future situations. When the same or similar situations arose in the game context, they identified them as problems they had already faced and knew ways of solving them. I don't think I had to call a time out and say, 'You have to do this and this'. Often I would call the time out because they needed a break, but they more often than not did all the talking and problem solving.

One of the highlights of using questioning with his players was:

> I think personally I have challenged the players more. Previously, I didn't have those [team] values set as such, they didn't decide them, and so I had fewer things to challenge them on. I have been able to challenge kids more and more. That's been good for me because ... I think I've become a more assertive coach.

For their part, the players seemed to feel really challenged by questioning. On questioning, Simon says, 'it gets us thinking; instead of just doing things he explains to us why we are doing it, so it helps'. Simon also really liked having to solve problems, and having Mark pose questions rather than tell the boys the answers:

> ... he doesn't just tell us what to do, but then if he asks us questions, we realise what we should do in different situations. It just comes natural, so if we get in a situation in a real game, that we have practised over and over, it becomes automatic. So, he just kept on doing that and by the time the games came up, we were good at the important skills and we read the game way better.

As someone new to some aspects of the athlete-centred approach, in some cases Mark did ask leading questions. Although leading questions are necessary in some circumstances, in Mark's case their main purpose was to communicate his point to the boys in order to get the answer he wanted. Throughout the season, he worked on decreasing his use of leading questions:

> Perhaps I did ask them leading questions … Sometimes I think I am just trying to give them examples, but maybe the examples might lead them a little bit.

By the end of the season, Mark was asking fewer leading questions. He admits that he needs to keep focusing on this skill.

Mark and Teaching Games for Understanding

TGfU (see Chapter Eleven) is a favourite coaching strategy of Mark's. Consistent with his belief in athlete learning, he uses games as a major part of his repertoire to help athletes understand the tactics in volleyball. He says:

> I've always tried to do game-like stuff but I am really using a lot of actual games and scrimmages which the kids are enjoying. I think they enjoy them heaps more. I am just really enjoying the atmosphere in the gym.

When Mark first decided to focus on athlete-centred coaching, he specifically stated that one of his main goals was to use TGfU to help the boys to make decisions. This technique enabled the boys to make informed decisions in the games. It also responded to the boys' choice of enjoyment as one of their most important values. Given the importance that the boys attached to enjoyment, Mark felt he had to have fewer drill-type activities and more game-like activities:

> Traditionally, I have tried to train them through game-like drills but also felt it important to spend some time practising certain skills to hone techniques. But when the kids decided on the enjoyment value, I decided that game-like scrimmages would have to make up the majority of the practice so I was forced to develop some more fun games. These games had to highlight specific tactics and techniques which are required on the volleyball court and then emphasise them by making them the focus. So the game design required they work on certain key things and not the whole game.

Through the focus on game-like activities, Mark himself could develop his coaching further as he designed games to suit specific situations. One of the challenges of using TGfU has always been having confidence to try a different strategy, to find the game most suited to the situation at hand. In relation to this confidence, Mark says his experience with the technique has:

> … been really good for me because now I've got a bigger bank of games. I developed a system in which I go through to design a game. It's much, much easier for me to design them now. At first, trainings took me much longer to

plan as they required much more thinking. So I suppose the time issue was a challenge but, for me, feeling like I am actually putting in a really solid effort and putting in the time makes me feel better about what I am doing.

On deciding when to use games and when to break down techniques and skills specific to volleyball, Mark says:

I think there is a time and a place for the games approach, especially in volleyball, where sometimes I think you do need just some continuous repetitions of things just to nail technique because, in volleyball, technique is so important because often they are completely brand-new skills. So there is very little transfer from other sports into volleyball because you can't just catch the ball. You are just deflecting it and you have to have the angle of your arms just right, which means you have to have your feet in certain places, and it is kind of hard to learn that if there are a lot of other things going on at once. Sometimes it's good just to teach that with some blocked practice or drill training. However, in saying that, you can still make blocked practice into a game! You've got [to] get into your Game Sense [TGfU] and your game-like drills. That's not to say [that during training you are] playing the whole game all the time, but [rather you are] practising situations at training, within your games where you can target certain aspects of the game, where they have to make certain decisions … [We played lots of] King of the Court and the kids loved it. We had good intensity. The key to King of the Court was that we were able to attempt to teach the kids about intensity, but we were also able to create scoring systems where we could reinforce the values they decided at the start of the campaign.

Using TGfU is compatible with many features of skill acquisition theory, as Rod Thorpe suggests in Chapter Eleven. Mark highlights the way that games helped the boys to understand and make decisions of tactical play through game-like situations:

… it was a novel situation and they had to try, from that novel situation, to create a good enough offence to put some pressure on the six who were on the other side. That's something that I don't think a lot of coaches do. I think they train situations that are supposed to happen in volleyball. But, much of the time, things don't work the way they are supposed to work and they are novel … We played the whole game better. Other teams practise getting the perfect situation by closing the environment perhaps by throwing the ball to the setter or by other controlling means. They become good at that situation and it looks impressive, but they haven't had the experience of getting the ball that's not great or dealing with novel situations, which are going to happen most of the time in volleyball.

From the boys' perspective, they really enjoyed playing games. Most athletes who are training love game play, become more intense with it and therefore work hard on specific fitness. The intrinsic motivation they gain from playing purposeful games, as

Rod Thorpe points out, means that they learn more from the different situations. Luke's observations support these ideas:

> There was a lot of game-like drills which was really good. It made it more fun as well. We all played because we wanted to play the game. If we play at games at training, then it is sort of like playing the game at training. If you are having fun, you work a bit harder and the level is higher as well. Other coaches, like at cricket, they throw a thousand balls at you or something and they play this shot over and over and over again. But it is not really helping because if you are in a game then you are not going to get that ball that was thrown.

When asked if he thought that playing the game in training made a difference to how the team played at the Nationals, Luke responds:

> I think it helped us when to play together and be more intense … it taught us to be intense. It didn't necessarily improve our ability a hell of a lot because we had already done that when we were younger. We already had the skills. Doing those game drills taught us how to be intense all the time.

He also considers that using the game situations in practice helped their understanding of volleyball under pressure:

> I think that came from training as well. Like during drills or during game drills, sometimes he [the coach] stops and explains things, explains why we are doing these things. He does that often enough that we know it and can see it by ourselves. I guess other teams don't do that. I think they just say, do this drill and really don't know why they are doing it.

Simon sees both positive and negative sides to using games like King of the Court:

> … the best thing I see that gets us controlled better will probably be pepper [a drill type activity] with two people, you get heaps of reps doing that and you get to control the ball better. King of the Court, you also stand around a lot, one stuff-up and you are off for ages. On a positive, on the sideline you can encourage your teammates and you can also learn from their mistakes.

His concern about the long waiting time for a team once it is eliminated reflects the importance of considering the 'time on task' component when designing any game for a given situation. On the other hand, the prospect of sitting out provided motivation for the players to try harder in this drill. The game also provided a pressured situation for athletes to practise in.

Simon saw some real benefits in using games to practise novel situations that might occur in competitions. The team's practice in novel situations could then be applied to novel situations that they then met in competitions:

> … our defence was good. We picked up the good hitters. Maybe because we did those drills, we could read the offence from the other teams better.

When we were on offence, we knew where to hit the ball or [how to hit] around the blockers. So maybe that did help. It didn't feel like it because we did drills that helped, but now that you look at it, you could probably say, a few things helped us which gave us [practice] in situations.

Simon suggests that Mark allowed the players to take risks. Rather than jumping in when he did not like the risk, the coach left it to the boys to make the choice. They learned through trial and error in games. Simon appreciated the opportunity for athlete decision making, which he compares favourably with more prescriptive coaching styles in the following anecdote:

When I was on duty at the Nationals tournament, I heard a coach say to a player, 'Don't you dare jump serve', because the game was close. The player then served and missed the serve, looked back at the coach with a sour face. The players need to make more decisions for themselves during the games. The coach can say where to serve, but not change how to serve during a game.

Implementing an Athlete-centred Approach

Mark was highly motivated to implement the athlete-centred approach and it was a pleasure to watch his process. His experience as a physical education teacher, I believe, made it easier for him to move to trialling the approach. As he had used questioning in his teaching for many years, he began with an advantage over other coaches who are starting to implement an empowerment style. With Mark's experience, in my view, he began the season at quadrant two of Hersey-Blanchard's Situational Leadership Model (see Chapter Two, figure 2.2).

One of Mark's motivations to take up the athlete-centred approach was his belief that volleyball is a great tool to influence students to do well at school:

I've always had a real mixture and some of the kids who play volleyball tend to be some of the ones who are finding it difficult to achieve in school. I don't know whether because volleyball is an explosive game and hard hitting and it's aggressive and it appeals to that type of student ... But maybe it's the team camaraderie that volleyball can create ... [With previous teams], them getting into trouble at school has gotten in the way a little bit, because we had trainings where they haven't been able to attend because they've had their homework detentions, kids who couldn't travel because they had not been performing in the classroom or behaving well ... I think it is pretty important to do well in the classroom ... using volleyball as a wee bit of leverage to try and convince them to [try hard] in class. [Using an athlete-centred approach] enabled the boys to decide that they had to organise their lives outside of volleyball, so things didn't get in the way of volleyball.

One aspect of Mark's athlete-centred focus was to hand over several areas of responsibility to the athletes, while his own role became to facilitate. As he describes it:

I tried giving the players decisions to make about things like punishments and trainings; pretty much everything. I think it gave them complete ownership and I think when they had that sense of ownership, they were prepared to do more, were prepared to work harder, were prepared to sacrifice other things … It really was their campaign. That was actually one of the things to draw the lines [distinguish the athlete-centred approach]. This isn't mine, this is your campaign, and this is what you [have] decided. I am just the person to help you get there.

He found the process so different from his past involvement in coaching, where 'it has been my goals and my vision and [the players] generally bought into those'. By asking for athletes' input and giving them ownership of the team, Mark feels he helped to make a more cohesive, intense and motivated team. In his previous coaching, he had thought the boys bought into the culture that he created, but he now sees that their sense of ownership was:

… not to the same extent as when they create it themselves … [These days] often other coaches ask me in the staffroom, 'How do you find [various players] not turning up to training?'. We really didn't have any big issues with that. We had the odd one and once that was addressed through the values, we had no problems.

Mark feels he was ready to implement an athlete-centred approach, having used aspects of it for several years already. By formally practising it, he feels that he has improved but still needs to learn more:

… it's more involved, there is more to it. It's the approach I wanted to do but I didn't know enough about it. So, now that I have learned these things, it is the way I want to coach so I'll continue to do it. No doubt I won't get it perfect, there are still lots of things that [have been] pointed out to me that I had to do … There are always going to be things that you don't get, and you don't get it altogether perfect every time. It's like anything. So, if you let those things worry you, then you will never do anything. You have to be confident with what you do know and what you are going to do.

One of the implementation issues that some coaches have raised is the potential difficulty of introducing athletes to the 'different' coaching approach. On the question of how the boys would react to a slight change to his approach, given that he had coached all of them previously, Mark responds:

… they are a good bunch of kids anyway so they were going to be respectful of what we were trying to do to begin with and they were going to go along with it … I still think they needed some proof of its worth before they fully bought into what they were actually creating. I think for a while they were going, 'Yeah, we'll create this because Mr Norton said this is what we are doing and we'll do it.' But once they started to see some benefits of it and …it really snowballed. It got bigger and bigger and bigger.

To find out the boys' views of how Mark implemented this 'new' approach, I asked them to compare his current coaching to previous years. Luke reflects:

> Well, I think the style that he used this year is a lot better than the style he's used in the past. He seems like he was a little bit more organised this year with the things that he did and that helped. It was a lot more enjoyable as well, really enjoyable to coach in that style because we all know what we are working for and stuff. We all worked together to do it. It showed at trainings, it was fun as well.

Simon makes the comparison in this way:

> It's better [this year] because he lets us talk among the group instead of making all the decisions, instead of yelling at us around the court. He lets us choose what we want to do sometimes. We can have fun doing it.

Responding to my request for him to describe what he thinks that Mark did as a coach, what was different or what his style was, Luke says:

> I don't know how to describe it. He put a whole lot of things into one. He is tough when he wants to be but he's not tough all the time. He puts an emphasis on having a good time. I think that makes everyone work harder. He is a unique coach; I have never had a coach as enthusiastic as him before. In his eyes, he was always happy and stuff. He was enthusiastic about the drills and that gets everyone into it as well … you always turn around and he always has a smile on his face, it is really reassuring when you are playing, even though he might not be smiling on the inside.

Luke's comments reiterate that using an athlete-centred style with questioning, TGfU and athlete decision making is fun. This observation is significant alongside research data showing that players drop out when they find that their sport is no longer fun.

A further observation of Mark's approach comes from Simon when he says, 'He still helps us when we need it. He doesn't tell you much; he's just there to help us when we need it'.

What were Mark's perceptions of how the boys reacted to his focus on their learning? I wondered if they realised what approach he was trying to implement. Mark sees it this way:

> My impression is that they will think it was the values that created the success as they were very much in their face! However, the Games for Understanding were [a] huge [factor] in their success also. We never talked about the games as being key to their development, however we did discuss what each game was for and what we should learn from it. I didn't know how crucial this game-centred approach would be either until I saw how well it had come together at the end of the season. That was another thing they talked about in the initial … they do enjoy those games and it is easier to achieve commitment and intensity when you are playing in a game, then it is

in a drill training. I don't know how many Kiwi people are committed enough to pass 200 balls on the left side in a row and then pass 200 balls on your right side in a row, which is what I believe they do in Japan.

One of the unique aspects of Mark's approach, which he had introduced to his coaching the previous year, was that after he calls a time out during a competition he allows the boys to run it themselves. In regard to this system, Simon says:

It's good because if we are down on court, we sort of know what we are doing wrong, so we don't need someone telling us what we are doing wrong. So we sort it out as a team … a few positive suggestions [are good], not what we are doing wrong, but what we can do to improve our situation. Then we try and improve it, then if it is not working, then he will talk to us on the court and say what we need to do. We sometimes need him to get us back up after we are down.

Luke agrees that Mark's unique time out system:

… was good. It was good not having a coach in your ear all the time and just letting us do it. [With coaches who are directive], it always feels like you are being watched. You don't get out of it. With Mr Norton, if you made a mistake, it was really good …you didn't get scared that he was going to yell at you, like you do with some of the coaches, you are too scared to make a mistake or if you do make a mistake it's all doom.

When asked if he would like to be coached in the same way next year, Simon says:

I would've thought that it would be essential. I thought it would be automatic after the way that we went this time. Everyone agreed on it, so why can't we do it again? We can only get better.

The Process of Empowering Players

As part of the process of being an empowered player, Simon says he felt 'valued and important'. Mark makes similar observations from a coach's perspective:

I think the process has helped them understand the importance of the values I used to put into place. But because they have ownership, these values have made it more meaningful for them. Players feel listened to, considered, valued and respected. With their head in a good space, the commitment, passion and dedication were outstanding. Not surprisingly their effort was never in question and their game improved as could be expected. They showed these things at training and games with lots of talk and yahoo which created fun. Then the fun created the good play.

One of the processes that Mark used initially to empower the athletes was to form small groups with the roles of providing leadership and taking ownership and responsibility for aspects of the team environment. As he explains it:

Within the overall squad, we created smaller groups, which were responsible for different aspects that we were trying to do. I empowered each student to have some leadership or have some responsibility. Without responsibility, you can't learn how to use it, learn how to develop it. When we talk about cooperation and teamwork, they are terms that have just been drummed into the kids. You ask them the question about 'What do we need to do now?' ... the kids can always come up with the words *cooperate* and *teamwork*, but they don't actually know what they mean and they don't know how to do them in a lot of cases ... once you have said that you wanted to develop that, then you've got to teach them what they are and then give them the opportunity to practise them.

As mentioned at the outset of this chapter, this aspect of Mark's empowerment approach was not a strong focus this year. Though he talked about using small groups, it was a potential strategy that never really developed. A senior group, which was one of the two groups that Mark formed, met only once. The second group, however, had responsibility for running a parents' meeting and gave some positive indications of what might be achieved with a more general use of small groups. This group designed a great meeting, informing parents of the season, focusing on fundraising and showing the parents what they had learned thus far. The parents were impressed with the evening. The boys showed that, given this responsibility in the quality team culture that had been created, they were motivated to do this extra work for the benefit of the team.

Now that Mark knows the best way to establish a vision and values for the team, perhaps he will form more small groups with responsibilities next season. Other coaches in this book highlight how forming small groups for certain responsibilities helps to create leaders on the team. Many suggest that they want all athletes to be leaders. In a successful team, everyone is responsible for making decisions.

Role rotation is another aspect of an athlete-centred approach that gives athletes great learning experiences. The squad system, which is athlete-centred in nature, is a form of role rotation. To improve their ability to work together smoothly, the boys played in several different positions. Consistent with a squad expectation that all boys played equal time in the games, Mark continued to rotate players equally up to the local championships, which increased trust among the team. He reflects on the result:

I think it came together in the Canterbury Champs, we were still trying to get people on, we were still rotating players on and off trying to get them all playing, even though I'd said and the guys had said, when it comes to Canterbury Champs side, we would play our top six and people playing didn't matter so much, but even then I still tried to get people on.

By this means all boys contributed equally and were trusted to do the job throughout the season until just before the National Championships, where the tournament required an A and a B team. An incident occurred during the tournament where Mark strayed from the wishes of the boys. He made a decision, without letting the boys know of his philosophy of role rotation. Sticking to his plan of role rotation and to demonstrate his trust in the players, he used several players who had had little playing time in a game in which the outcome did not really matter. Luke was upset at this:

> ... that's the game that we had a debrief, I remember him asking what we were annoyed about because he knew we were annoyed. I think he knew what we were annoyed about but he just wanted us to say it. But I didn't want to say anything because it would put a negative spin on things because we had the final in the afternoon. I think he should've left the rotation as it was and put the foot on the floor with all the Canterbury teams, which they were not going to bag us for giving up a game.

Mark also used role rotation well in relation to King of the Court. All three players in this game have to take on every position on the volleyball court, thus they work out the role of each player on their team. In this way they gain empathy for a setter, for example, through experiencing what this player might experience in the full game.

One of the highlights for me as a researcher of adolescents was to observe at the National Championships just how closeknit the A team had become, with resulting benefits for the team. Adolescent boys sang in the warm-up and even danced to their positions in front of the crowds. They did not worry about what they looked like; they were doing it to help the team environment. To me, it was true wairua. To my question about how such shy boys managed to sing 'Row, row, row your boat' in the middle of the Nationals, Luke responds:

> We decided that we shouldn't be taking ourselves too seriously because it made us uptight on the court and we wouldn't talk as much and, so at trainings, we started acting the goat a bit and yelling out our values. It was something we weren't used to doing, but when we started doing it, it was heaps of fun and then we started, we did it in the stadium and we just didn't worry about anyone, it was quite cool. It was cool, I liked it, I didn't care what people think and …I didn't think they laughed at us or anything, they thought it was all right.

Some Challenges of an Athlete-centred Approach

As noted by other coaches in this book, one of the major challenges of an athlete-centred approach is that it takes time to empower players effectively. Yet the focus on long-term learning means that it is worth taking the time to get athletes to problem solve. On the time required to create the team vision and values, Mark says:

> It took way more time than I thought … From the start to the end, it probably took three weeks of maybe half an hour [each training session]. I didn't want to cut too much into their playing time because the boys had come to play and there were some grizzles to start with, so we had a couple of sessions at other times. [Therefore] we didn't feel like we were cutting into their playing time too much.

Luke is positive in regard to the lengthy process of setting up the values specifically:

> Well, I liked deciding the values. I think that was good, even though it was a long time. It was quite painful sitting there for that long and I think it was worth us doing it. I don't think it would have had the same impact if it was put upon us.

Interestingly, Simon perceives the time devoted to make a quality team culture as acceptable: 'Time is fine, it is part of volleyball practice'.

As a coach, too, Mark has found that he must give more of his personal time to the process of implementing his athlete-centred approach:

> … I'll tell you, I have learned some good things, important things, like I can't just rock up to training. I can't just get in my car and drive to training like perhaps I would have done, thinking about the drills I am going to do in my head before I get there on the way. I actually have to do a lot more thinking about the training and how I am going to run it.

In response to my question about other challenges related to an athlete-centred approach, Mark identifies the great depth of the learning and commitment involved:

> I have always wanted to have players who were empowered and could run themselves and, through doing this process, I think what I have learned is that there is much more to it than what I was doing. I always thought I had some pretty good teams going in terms of [empowering players]. I can now see that [my previous teams] were only touching the surface of what is actually possible. By going through this [season's process], I think what the kids are achieving now is huge compared to what I was previously. It is more holistic. So it's been a big learning curve for me for what is possible and how we go about it.

The process of listening to other people and taking on their points of view is an aspect of the athlete-centred approach that he sees as a challenge but also as a definite advantage:

> You've just got to keep checking where you are at personally and keep reminding yourself what you are doing it for and whose campaign it actually is. I think as soon as you start to think that it is yours, then you don't want to give bits away and that is not an empowering approach. So, if you keep reminding yourself why you are doing it and whose campaign it is, then I don't think there are any problems there. I think when I first started out coaching I think the reason why I was doing it was to win for myself. I wanted to have a winning team.

Another challenge that Mark identifies is having trust in the players, as he was giving them power to take ownership of the team. He says:

> I didn't entirely trust all of them; there was one or two of them where I would cringe when they hit the ball, especially serving. Having had the experience that they had in Canterbury Champs and lead-up tournaments, made them less likely to make the error. I think that was important.

A major challenge was the fallout following Mark's choice of the team to play in the Nationals as the A team, based on criteria the squad had identified. Unfortunately, once the A team (of which Mark was the coach) was chosen, the B team's culture faded and was clearly weaker than the A team's culture at the Nationals. Although Mark continued to reinforce the values with the A team, the other coach for the B team was not as strong in reinforcing the values. Without that facilitation factor, the B team, though they had a good time, experienced a decrease in the quality of their culture. Other factors, such as injuries, contributed to this deteriorating quality as well.

The nature of the high school volleyball season added a difficult barrier to the establishment of a team culture. The volleyball season covers two terms, term 4 of one year and term 1 of the following year. At the end of each year (after term 4), the juniors move into senior divisions. Mark's team did not cater well for the inclusion of the 'new' juniors, which added to the numerous learning experiences involved in implementing such an approach. Because the juniors had not been through the process of establishing the team vision and values, when they arrived in the established squad Mark asked them to decide how they wanted to be involved in the squad. The decision the boys made did not work well: they formed their own team, had their own coach and left the squad to its own devices. As Mark says:

> Those guys decided that that was what they wanted to do. They made an error and they recognised that and so they've got that under their belt now.

As the season went on, Mark invited the C team to train with the squad and they started coming along. The biggest problem was that the C team was not party to establishing the vision, values and goals and therefore did not have ownership and struggled to become part of the team. As the boys came in from another team environment, they were basically forced to buy in to the squad systems. I believe that because they did not contribute to formulating the culture that was now firmly established for the A and B teams, they did not have ownership of it.

Plans for the Future

Mark enjoyed gaining advice from an observer in the background. He suggests that in the future he would like to have access to the same kind of advice:

> Getting advice was great. It fast-tracked the learning process. It helped having someone chipping in the odd suggestion. Even just a question like 'Why are you running this drill?' made me think about the benefits of the drill and that there may be a better way of doing it. It also meant there was another set of ideas looking for team dynamics and cohesiveness. So I think that it is certainly beneficial to have someone who is experienced and someone who knows what they are doing to give you suggestions along the way.

Mark admits that his strength is his coaching of actual volleyball specifics. In regard to my question on the ideal way to run a team while maintaining the quality team culture, he responds:

[Ideally] I think you need the eye. If you have got someone watching the volleyball, critiquing and making comments about the volleyball, then I think it is really difficult to look at the other things. Unless you make it episodic and within the trainings, as a coach, you decide to make the focus on watching 10 minutes on their volleyball and 10 minutes on watching their interactions, cohesiveness and how they operate, but then you still might miss something that happens.

As to whether there will be a time when he thinks that he can go solo, he assures me:

Sure there will be a point where a lot of the team building strategies become second nature and I will be able to implement them on the spot when they are required. I feel I am getting a better bank of activities to promote cohesiveness and trust and am learning when to use them.

One area to work on that I identified was Mark's 'reading of people'. When I ask how he will work on that, he reflects on what he has learned from the season:

Sometimes a lot of what happens in the gym, it's hard to pick up on because I know that a lot of the time, when they are playing the game, I am commenting and giving lots of feedback, talking about decisions they are making on the court and I am often focusing on the people who are immediately in the drills or in the game ... I found a number of times a couple of things that are happening out the back were highlighted. Perhaps a rude gesture or a comment that somebody else made that was perhaps not living up to the values and needs to be addressed. That's quite good because [it is] highlight[ed] for me and then we address it at the end or there at the time.

For the next season, I have agreed to act as player manager again to help the team. It was so enjoyable last year that the process has motivated me to continue to be involved. Mark too has been inspired to keep up his coaching because of the success that the boys experienced, the great time that they had and their unanimous decision to come back for more.

Conclusion

Mark continues to work on his athlete-centred approach and says that he will never stop learning about it. Through the way this season developed, he can see that this approach is the way to go forward and enable athletes to reach great heights. Mark is pleased that he allowed so much input from the athletes; during the season he was often heard to say, 'Wow, these boys really have a lot of value to add to our team'.

As other coaches in this book indicate, learning the athlete-centred approach is time consuming but well worth the effort. The rewards for enhancing the athletes as individual people and watching their skill level grow are obvious from the smiles on the faces and from the comments of the athletes reported in this chapter. Given the great success of the athlete-centred approach with these adolescent boys, it is clearly an effective approach that coaches need to use for athletes at all levels.

What a fantastic opportunity this project was for me to be part of a fun, successful volleyball team. The boys were outstanding in a holistic way—cognitively, psychosocially, spiritually (wairua) and physically. I believe that we learned from each other and that, because Mark enabled the athletes to take ownership of their team, the team was successful in all domains.

References

Janssen, J. (2002). *Championship team building*. Cary, NC: Winning the Mental Game.

Yukelson, D. (1997). Principles of effective team building, *Journal of Applied Sport Psychology, 9*(1): 73–96.

The opponent with in one's own head is more daunting than the one on the other side of the net. – *Tim Gallwey*

'Coach', he whispered. His voice shook just a trifle. 'I found it, coach, the thing you wanted me to learn for myself.' – *Schoolboy, 'Split seconds: Tales of the Cinder Track 1927'*, Sports Council 1991

If only the sun-drenched celebrities are being noticed and worshiped, then our children are going to have a tough time seeing the value in the shadows, where the thinkers, probers and scientists are keeping society together. – *Rita Dove, US poet, educator*

Character consists of what you do on the third and fourth tries. – *James A. Michener*

Chapter Four

A wise man makes his own decisions; an ignorant man follows the public opinion.
- *Chinese Proverb*

Don Tricker
New Zealand Black Sox (Men's Softball)
Former Coach

Don recently stepped down as coach of the New Zealand Black Sox, the national men's softball team. The Black Sox are current three-peat world champions, winning two of these titles while Don was at the helm. Although he treasures his time with the national team, Don says he is ready for the next challenge: coaching children's teams. This challenge faces him along with his new role as a team leader in coaching for Sport and Recreation New Zealand (SPARC). The purpose of the SPARC coaching team is to develop a coaching environment that delivers a quality coaching service to whoever is coached. As a volunteer international coach, Don coaches as a hobby while also working in a full-time job and being a father to a young family.

Don draws on his background and experience in business, specifically information technology (IT), to deepen his understanding of human relations. He suggests that the business environment has provided him with the processes that have helped him to become a better coach. Based on his experience as an employee and manager, too, Don believes in using an athlete-centred approach to create a quality team culture, in which all team members work together towards a common goal. This chapter represents a cross-section of his coaching philosophies and approaches thus far. I interviewed Don after returning from the Athens Olympics and just before he decided to step down from coaching the Black Sox.

Don's softball career path started when he was a young lad in Porirua, growing up in a sports-oriented family and a community with plentiful opportunities. It was in Porirua that, as well as competing in rugby, rugby league, athletics, soccer and cricket, he discovered softball. It became his serious sport after injuries sustained in soccer and rugby ruled out those sports. As a softball player, he represented his community several times and played for New Zealand for a number of years. Softball became his passion. Don believes that sport, in particular softball, has played a major role in shaping him as a person. For this reason he feels indebted to sport and will be involved in it for the rest of his life.

Don's Philosophy of Coaching

Don has developed his coaching philosophy from many experiences and says it is constantly changing. As with other coaches in this book, Don's coaching philosophy is athlete-centred. He elaborates:

> My philosophy on coaching is to take a holistic view as I believe that there is more to life than sport. I like to think that I have not only helped the athlete realise their athletic goals but have helped them become a more rounded

person through their experience in sport. Coaching is simply about delivering a service, therefore I need to understand the requirements and expectations of each person that I coach be they five years old or a high-performance athlete. For coaching to be sustainable there must be win–win outcomes throughout the coaching experience—the win for me is that I can sit back and reflect on whatever contribution that I've made in terms of how each particular individual has grown. That's not solely limited to the athlete's athletic ability; it's more a contribution to that athlete as a person.

I have a simple test of character that I call the RSA [Returned and Services' Association] test. The test is based around the athlete walking into any RSA in New Zealand and holding a meaningful conversation with anyone in the RSA that is not about themselves and be genuinely interested in what it is that person has got to say. Again, it is not just about turning out guys in softball who can run fast and pitch the ball hard … It's [about] people who are outstanding New Zealanders. I am delighted to say that the Black Sox are filled with athletes who pass the RSA test.

As the above discussion indicates, the individual athlete is the focus of Don's energies. He says that sport is about developing a team out of individuals who are heading together in the same direction:

… the common denominator in sport is that it is played by individuals, each with different needs and expectations. Therefore, when building teams it all comes down to ensuring that individual expectations are satisfied when developing the core components of the team culture. The components include ownership of a shared vision or common purpose, clearly defined values, standards and role definitions.

Underlining his concern with the individual athlete and his or her needs, Don relates a story about the night before the final of the 2004 World Championships, which were held in New Zealand:

Whenever a group of individuals hear the same address, or watch the same video clip, or read the same passage of text, then there will be different interpretations of what was heard, seen or read. The Black Sox are no different. I only have to look at my address to the team immediately prior to the 2004 World Championship final. To put the environment in context, it was a very emotional time for the team; it was the culmination of four years of effort. We were about to play the World Series final in front of the people who matter most to us—our families and friends, the New Zealand softball community and the New Zealand sporting public. For us, it was a once-in-a-lifetime opportunity as it will be at least another 20 years before the World Softball Championships return to New Zealand.

My final address focused on the environmental factors, how we were going to win the World Championship, and the points of difference that would separate us from the Canadians [the opposing finalists]. The address delivered the desired outcome, with 17 focused athletes who believed that in four hours they were going to be world champions. After the final I have heard a number of the athletes describe the time immediately prior to the final and the final address. What was of interest was that there were many varied interpretations of what the athletes believed the key messages were. The key messages are dependent on what the athlete is looking for. I am only grateful that under pressure I delivered one of the basics of coaching—an address that met each athlete's expectations.

An athlete-centred coach changes and adapts goals and methods based on the particular group he or she is coaching, as Don explains:

… you have different groups each with different requirements and expectations. As an example, the service that I deliver for the kids that I coach is largely about the development of their social skills, it's about being a contributor to that child gaining confidence and having a go at anything. My purpose as coach is to make sure that they have a good time, so that they want to come back week after week after week. Then we can capture them, in whatever sport they choose. This can only take place when we understand the expectations of each child. Typically kids want to be active, have heaps of turns, have some fun and play with their mates … I recruit the parents and get them involved because it is the only way that I can meet the expectations of the kids.

In another example relating to a children's team he is coaching, Don tells of athletes who, as time goes on, seem to be gaining more confidence to get involved with activities outside their comfort zone. His team of softball players became part of a school choir—an unexpected but great outcome for Don and his belief in enabling children to discover themselves:

… that is the biggest part for me. When I went to the school assembly I watched the school choir make their way up to the stage. It was a huge buzz when I realised that all of the kids in my team were part of the choir, including my son, which surprised the heck out of my wife.

As noted above, in addition to gaining an understanding about coaching through his involvement with numerous sports teams, Don acknowledges that some of his thinking about coaching came from his experience in IT work:

… in terms of business, I had many examples of where team culture is driven from the top down. In every instance, it didn't work as the culture was never owned by the staff; it was always someone else's … On reflection I always considered that if I was in the same position I would find a way to obtain ownership through a bottom-up approach. Depending on the size of the organisation. one way would be to pick off the leaders or the pied pipers within the organisation and leverage off their existing relationships with their peer groups to develop and sell the culture at all stages of its development. So, again, it is not just about leveraging off the good examples only, it's about understanding each example and sitting back and reflecting on them and saying, 'If I had a similar opportunity I would do it a little bit differently'.

Don's Development as a Coach

Don had successful experiences as a softball player, which enabled him to take his passion for the game into coaching the sport. Don's coaching was influenced by many along his journey. The first was one of his coaches as a junior player:

> ... we had a coach, a guy called Neil Tuffrey, Mr Tuff we used to call him. He started coaching us as five-year-olds and finished up with us when we were about 15-year-olds. Throughout this time Mr Tuff, in addition to building a team that dominated junior softball in our area, shared many life lessons with us around working as a team: being supportive, respectful and trusting your teammates and always having a plan—do your thinking before the play.

The transition from junior to senior softball marked his next phase of development, when:

> My coach, Haggis, introduced the concept of class—whether in victory or defeat, always demonstrate class. Haggis ensured that we looked beyond every result to ensure that the lessons of each game were recognised and understood. He introduced the concept that losing is part of life—but it is how you handle yourself in defeat and how you leverage off these lessons that is the important part.

Don recognises a wide range of others who have been influential:

> ... through coaches like Mike Walsh who was very inspirational and very strong in terms of motivating ... I am a bit of everyone in the way I wanted to do things, my mum, my dad, my school teachers, all those sorts of people ... where did I pick all this up; it's just over the years and years of listening basically and asking questions.

Drawing from such influences, Don started coaching:

> I coached junior teams, as an athlete ... but not for an extended period. I coached a team for three or four years and that is how I got into it. It all started from there. I believed that I owe a great deal to softball so coaching was a tangible way for me to share the opportunities sport has provided me with other people, in particular children.

This induction into coaching obviously had a big effect on Don, as he then began coaching seniors before moving into the international softball arena:

> Coaching to me has never been about the coach—it is about the athletes and the value the coach can add. For me it all started with the club side that I played for, Poneke Kilbirnie; I was conned into coaching really. I'd say that my ego was stroked. Some of the guys that I played with had a meeting with me and said, 'Look we are looking for a coach next year, we really want you to come and coach us, we've got no one else and you can do this' ... I hadn't even considered coaching at a senior level, so it was, 'Oh yes'.

With my sporting and life experiences I always thought that I could add the value that the team was looking for. We had a very successful time and then the national coaching position became available. The national coaching role was another now-or-never type deal for me. My wife and I had two young children and the timing was right. If I had waited another four to six years, my role as a father would almost certainly have taken priority over any aspirations of coaching the national team.

This coaching job at the national level came up because, in playing for New Zealand, Don had already made a name for himself in softball circles. As a player, he was highly analytical, so taking on a coaching role seemed to be an obvious move. He reflects:

Towards the latter part of my international career, I was a spare-part player. I could hit, so therefore I would always find myself in the line-up, but not necessarily in the same position each game … I would consider myself to be, at the international level, a late developer … it took me a long time to understand how to play the game. Then, once I figured out how to play the game, I was relatively successful internationally, and it was all based around confidence and keeping things simple, which enabled me to make smart decisions under pressure.

Don started coaching seriously in the 1990s when he pooled all his experience in sport and business and applied it to coaching. Don's analytical ability made him a reflective coach, always observing and asking why certain things were done a certain way. Through his own admission, however, he did not learn his coaching trade through the 'traditional' coach education process. Instead, he learned:

… through the ability to observe the coaches … I have picked up little bits and pieces of each of those coaches I thought were quite good and bits and pieces that I didn't think were very good … All the way through my playing career, I was always a deep thinker and listener. I often helped other players to work through and find solutions to the issues they, or we, faced. So I had all sorts of coaching roles, even when I was a player.

Another method of developing as a coach, Don suggests, is to continue to watch and analyse other coaches in his everyday life:

I can't watch sport now without trying to break it down into understanding what happened and more importantly why it happened. Why were poor decisions being made, those sorts of thing … This is in every sport. I go to watch rugby, I go to watch netball, I am not looking in terms of the result, in terms of who won or lost, I am looking at how it happened. I am looking at particular players and attempt[ing] to understand why they chose to execute a particular play that is clearly not part of the role or skill set.

Don highlights his development of coaching the technical aspects of softball. Having technical nous about the sport is essential to athlete learning and decision making and is thus a key component of a coaching repertoire. At the same time, Don says that this component is always the easiest part of the trade for coaches to learn:

> … in softball I had the technical background through my playing it. It was my IT background that has provided me with the processes to package up my technical knowledge into a format that can be understood by each athlete.

Some of the coaches in this book describe how they began as coach-centred coaches then developed an athlete-centred approach after realising it was better for learning. When I ask Don if he fits into this category, he says:

> No, not really … when I said I was having the coaching roles when I was an athlete, it was all still about an awareness of what is happening here and why is it happening, rather than just 'do this' or 'do that'; [it was still about] always asking question[s] in a non-judgemental manner.

In Don's development as a coach, major influences have been mentors with whom he tosses ideas about and whom he listens to and observes extensively. Obviously, any coach uses these opportunities to advance his or her knowledge and pick out ideas that would suit him or her individually. Don describes the process for him personally:

> It is more from my computer background, in terms of how we have shared knowledge … whether it is a lot of transfer or you very quickly establish a relationship with whomever it is that you are working, then very quickly determine, in what part of that person you want to leverage off. It is not necessarily the whole person, or their knowledge; it is a small part that is really going to help me. So you drill down into that particular path … I have had many 'mentors' over the years, where it comes from people who really interested me and they had something of real value that has helped shaped them as a person. So I pick out a bit of each in terms of interest. Typically what happens is that you pick all that out and you find someone else who comes from a slightly different, but related [experience] and suddenly you have a different view of the same subject. That all helped.

The Process of Establishing a Quality Team Culture

A common theme across the athlete-centred coaches in this book is that they are committed to establishing a quality team culture. In this environment, athletes contribute to the direction of the team, taking responsibility for and ownership of setting and maintaining that direction. It is the same for the Black Sox.

Throughout the interview, Don refers to the significant influence from his business environment, where multi-faceted elements must combine to enable a team to function productively. To achieve this outcome, the team must have mutual goals and aim towards common ground. Don transferred this way of working to his coaching. He says that developing a quality team culture is dependent on the individuals and the groups he gets for every campaign. Don discusses the process of building a team culture:

> Part of what we do each year, particularly in our World Championship years, is that we make no assumptions in terms of culture that worked previously. For the Black Sox we could not assume that what was important to the 2000 team would still be valid for the 2004 team. Even though a number of the athletes were part of the World Championship team in 2000, [in 2004] they were four years older with greater life experiences.

> We went through a similar process to 2000 where we had an athlete-facilitated session where three questions were addressed: what do we want, what is important to the team, how are we going to deliver what is important to us? ... [First,] 'What do we want?' ... That is all about our values and standards. Then [we ask] 'How are we going to deliver what is important to us? How are we going to operate on a day-by-day basis to ensure that we deliver what it is that is important to us?' Then the athletes define their roles ... on an individual basis in terms of their individual roles, then by units. To put it in our context, the pitchers would get together and talk about what is the role of the pitcher and then they would draw it up with the pitchers and catchers and say, 'Well, what is the pitcher–catcher role? What is the relationship there? What is their relationship to the infield and outfield?' ... The athletes then defined the role of the coach, the role of the manager, the physiotherapist, everyone in that particular campaign.

As many athlete-centred coaches acknowledge, the management team is part of the whole team. Don includes them in the process of establishing the roles of individuals:

> The role of the management team is to challenge the outcomes reached by the athletes in an effort to make it better. Following this process, the outcomes are agreed, documented and implemented. This process limits the opportunity for mismatched expectations.

Establishing a team culture is initially complex and takes time. However, through forming team values and expectations and identifying the responsibilities of each team member, everyone takes individual ownership of the task of living these values, expectations and responsibilities. The process of communicating and defining meanings together, Don believes, provides individuals with a clear, shared understanding of what is expected of them. Conversely, failing to establish such mutual understanding, Don says:

> ... is a classic downfall in coaching and with any team that you have the coach sitting over here with certain sets of expectations of what he or she believes that the athletes require, but yet hasn't talked to the athletes about it. The athletes may have a set of very different expectations with the result being a huge disconnection. Inherently it's built into us that when things aren't going well, we will apportion blame ...

> In a sporting context, when things aren't going right then typically you don't want to step forward and accept responsibility. Inherently, it's like, 'Who can I

drag down with me?', so you waste a lot of energy before you move forward. Again, with clearly defined role definitions ... should we drop the ball in our World Championship campaign, then it will be very clear to everyone who dropped the ball. The focus is on, 'How can we pick up the ball as a group and move forward without worrying or wasting energy over all the other stuff that goes on?' That worked really well in a couple of instances through our campaign, because clearly things didn't always go right. But the pleasing part was how quickly we got back on track because in sport it's about time. Once you start trying to blame someone else then you lose time. When you lose time, you drift from game plans and then you find yourself in a situation where the game is almost over, rather than retaining your composure and belief in your game plan and just moving forward again.

Being an advocate for an athlete-centred approach, where athletes learn to make decisions for and take ownership of the team and its operation, Don gives the athletes responsibility for helping to develop roles and team expectations. His role is to facilitate this process. He gives an example of how it happens:

... the athletes were the principal architects of our defensive patterns. The Black Sox culture encourages creativity; every idea was respected and cherished. As coaches we would facilitate discussion with the players [about] how we really want to play. The coaches' roles were more about facilitation. It was clear we had a lot of input to provide, but we were leveraging off the knowledge and experience within the side. It wasn't about saying, 'One person has got all the knowledge here, so this is the way we'd better play it'. It was like, 'No, let's respect each other; we have all got something to contribute here and we want to play out every scenario to ensure we have got it right and that we believe in it. Then we will practise it, then we will test it and if it's going to deliver what we are expecting, then we implement it in a real competition.'

As to the process of establishing the values of the team, which Don describes as 'good, classic New Zealand values', Don explains:

It's all about respect, it's about integrity ... We had three questions that we essentially asked: How are we going to deliver this? [What are] the values and how are going to live [them]? The team went through the process which included reviewing what we did in 2000, deciding what's relevant now and what's not. Some [values] survived and some were revised or adjusted. The purpose of our culture was to create an environment that is enjoyable and meets the expectations of the team ...international sport, when you are playing in a world championship final, is incredibly stressful, therefore the environment must be enjoyable. When we built the team we made sure that it was an enjoyable process. We created competitive scenarios that challenged the team. The outcome was a series of shared experiences based on humour. It was these experiences that helped us get through the difficult situations.

Once these values are set up, Don believes that they need to be reinforced. Because the players chose the values, they also take responsibility for reinforcing them:

> … they are policed by the athletes as well because the athletes have built and own them. The values are ours, not mine; they were not imposed on the athletes by me. The athletes ensure that the values are lived. We have a simple expectation that we all must … be prepared to face the consequences of every decision we make. The philosophy that we have is that we will support any poor decision once. But, if the individual chooses to repeat that poor decision, then they need to be prepared to pay the consequence. That may well be non selection. That is the ultimate consequence—an athlete explaining to family and friends that they have not been selected because they could not be trusted.

Like other coaches in this book, Don believes it is important to have meaningful team-building activities to reinforce team values and enhance the team environment. An innovation in his athlete-centred approach was holding a team-building weekend for his first campaign as the Black Sox coach:

> … before we went on a tour to North America in 1998, in our first training camp we spent two days building the team. That was a completely foreign concept from previous national sides that I had been involved in. We needed to build the team so we understood each other and so that when we went on tour, the focus was softball and not building a team. Previously, we tended to focus on softball, softball, softball and then we would get on tour without the team being developed with the result being teams that did not function as a cohesive unit. Then we would try and patch things up while on tour but there would be leaks all over the place. Usually the tour would start really well, but towards the back end of the tour, when the competition was at its most serious, expectations were not satisfied and performance suffered. We leveraged off these previous experiences and ensured that building the team was always the first activity completed.

Black Sox team-building exercises have even involved the army in the Southern Alps. Don tells the story:

> We have used the New Zealand Army to assist us with team-building activities since we started in 1998. The main reason is that the military have been in the business of building teams for generations, [whereas] with us in sport and business we are only starting to understand the process required to build teams. Therefore, we thought it sensible to leverage off the knowledge and experience of the New Zealand Army. In addition the army facilities are conducive to building teams and not filled with anti-social devices, such as Sky TV.

For the Black Sox, practising team values in the pursuit of the team goals and vision is one of the key selection criteria for the team:

When selecting sides, the first thing we are looking for is skill that can be executed under pressure. Then [the next question for selection] is if you've got all the other things ... because we have had the opportunity to build the values, it's not like [the selectors] are coming in and saying, 'This is our core values and these are not negotiable' ... we want to test that each time we bring a team together, so are these still real, are these still valid? If you've got two athletes side by side in terms of skill level and there is not much between them and someone can make another contribution somewhere else for the side, then you go with that person. It still comes down the ability to be successful. You can have all the passion and all the desire and all the belief in the world, but if you haven't got the skills that back it all up, then you are going to be dangerous, but you are not going to be effective ... we want effective athletes on our side—that is athletes who have the skill set, the belief and the commitment.

So what happens if an athlete has the skill but does not live the values or take responsibility for his attitude? Don says:

The athlete will not be part of the Black Sox. If the athlete did not live the agreed values of our culture then [he] would be cast adrift. It is all about respect. Failure to respect the contribution of each individual in the team will result in cliques or divisions within the team. This is generally the first sign of the team breaking down. Loners fall into this category. In teams, you are going to have athletes who don't enjoy socialising with other people, they prefer to be by themselves ... the trick is understanding it. There were times when we first started out where athletes did not quite fit the mould, we tried to just change them so they did fit the mould, rather than actually recognising what is really important to those individuals and then ensuring that the team understands. What is important is that each individual buys into what we are trying to do and they believe that they will be a world champion and are prepared to pay a serious price ... and everyone's price is different.

Achieving such success comes back to quality team culture, as Don reiterates:

... for the athlete to succeed, then he/she needs to believe and own every aspect of our programme.

Don's Use of Questioning

The use of questioning as a coaching tool is demonstrated by Don in various aspects of his coaching, including establishing team culture. Through his verbal questions and physical questions to prompt problem solving, athletes can consider the possibilities, rationalise them and come up with the best solution—and thus become better decision makers.

When Don first started coaching the Black Sox, his use of questioning was a new tactic for many of the players. He reflects on how he has been successful with this method even when players may be hesitant at first:

I have always believed that the solution to any issue we may face is held within the team. One of my roles is that of a facilitator. You know your team, you know your athletes, you know that there are three to four who you know are going to respond in a large group scenario, so when things are getting a little bit quiet, you go to them by asking open questions. 'Mark, what do you think?' You know that he's got an opinion, but he is waiting for someone else to say it, and then out it comes … it becomes infectious. One guy started talking and then some of the other athletes started and then it was like, 'Well what do you think?' The next thing you know, we've got everyone interacting. When I was first appointed as the Black Sox coach I ensured that the athletes understood that I did not have all the answers but, between us, we have a pretty good shot at understanding the issues and crafting the appropriate solution.

The challenge to questioning effectively is to be able to read and understand your athletes and know when to ask the question, to whom and in what situation. Don's philosophy of understanding individuals is highlighted in his method of questioning:

Asking the right questions to the right athlete at the right time is often the most effective way of ensuring that a particular experience has been analysed and the key learnings identified. If any of these parts is missing then the communication will not be effective. Timing will always depend on the athlete and the nature of the experience. If the experience has been a pleasant one then questions may be asked immediately. If the experience has not been so pleasant then the first priority is the well-being of the athlete; questions that reflect on the experience can wait.

Questioning is a great learning tool for athletes at all levels. As well as using questioning and problem solving extensively with the Black Sox, Don achieves excellent results in using the method with children, as he relates:

I ask questions so they think it through and then we practise that and then [I ask], 'Why do you think that happened?' Even these kids at eight and nine years old are starting to capture the purpose of the game. The kids that I coach all want to understand why we are completing a particular drill.

Don and Teaching Games for Understanding

The tool of Teaching Games for Understanding (TGfU) has been shown to enable athletes to become self-aware and solve problems, which in turn develops their ability to make decisions. One of Don's strongest beliefs, on which he bases his coaching, is that:

Sport is not black and white, there is way too much grey. One of my roles is to condition my athletes to make smart decisions under pressure.

Because so much of sport is grey, athletes must be able to understand many tactical situations that arise in the game. It follows that setting up purposeful games helps athletes to read such situations and make informed decisions. Thus when coaching the Black Sox, Don uses purposeful games to create competitive situations in which the players must operate under pressure:

... at the elite level, the [athletes] are there because they are very driven individuals and they are very competitive at anything that they do. Therefore we ensure trainings are set in a competitive environment. All of our drills are designed to ensure that the athlete completes the 'think, recognise and execute' sequence when making a decision. The thinking takes place prior to any action; this process enables the athlete to identify the likely situations before they execute. If the athlete is surprised then typically a poor decision will be the result.

Don disagrees with those coaches who believe that playing games is just about having fun and that the athletes are not learning if the coach is not telling them what to do. As he sees TGfU:

... it's not about always playing with your mates; it's not always about having a good time, because when we train we are at work, with the objective being quality. It's very structured; each training has a purpose. If the purpose is defending the short game (bunts and little slap hits) then, with the athletes, we design how we are going to set up our defensive patterns. We then test our patterns through structured drills that match what we would expect to experience in a game. When we have proven it in training, we then test it in competition. The purpose of the drills is to ensure that everyone in the team recognises the situation and understands what the next action will be. At the Black Sox level, we don't try and overcomplicate things; we only ever focus on one part of a game at a time. We don't try and do a bit of everything.

In coaching both children and adult athletes, Don is always looking for the best way to get them to learn skills through game situations:

... when I taught kids how to throw ... rather than throw backwards and forwards, which can be pretty boring, we went off to practise at the beach, chucking rocks into the sea. [I challenged them], 'Who can make the biggest splash? Who can throw the furthest?' Then we work on the mechanics. We try to go a bit further and then we try to skim a flat rock across the sea and introducing different throwing techniques. Then you transfer that back into the game. There are, in some instances, similarities [between the two situations] and, in some instances, they're not. But at the kids' level, you have to focus on a bit of everything because otherwise they get a bit bored, they want to hit the ball, they don't want to just sit there fielding the ball and throwing the ball and things like that and running around bases, so we just set up lots and lots of games.

When TGfU is part of the coaching repertoire, a coach must be flexible in organising games or situations that need to be practised. Instead of referring to a book for specific games to learn a certain situation, the coach looks to the situation to determine the game that will be played. In keeping with this approach, Don does not necessarily have a game ready when he is coaching children; rather, he reads the situation and determines which game would suit what the children are trying to learn:

... you quickly recognise that they are struggling a little bit, so you introduce them with a game, such as all around ball tag [or] games inside a little wee diamond area, where it is about throwing the ball and tagging someone. It's softball-related skills, but it's all about fun and about physical activity and getting the kids running around. We [might] play a ball tag game inside a diamond with a tennis ball, where the object is that you are trying to throw the ball to try to hit someone. So, again, if you are throwing to someone and they catch it, then they can throw the ball away, so they have to go and get the ball and come back in and it builds the complexity up.

Don believes that the younger the children, the more the focus should be on providing an element of fun in games. As children get older, the games can become more competitive. At any age, however, when games are fun, athletes play intensely and learn because of the natural motivation to play. Equally, each game must be used as a learning tool and be purposeful, rather than just being included in training for the players to have fun. Don underlines this principle with reference to the Black Sox:

Everything we do with the Black Sox has a purpose that can be aligned back to the purpose of the team (winning a world championship). To meet the athletes' competitive expectations we often break the team into smaller groups and set up drills where there is a winner and loser. At the end of each practice the session is always evaluated why teams won or lost. We never lose an opportunity to learn from our experiences. It is our belief that one of the things that separate the effective teams from the rest is their ability to leverage off their experiences whether they are poor or positive.

Implementing an Athlete-centred Approach

Implementing an athlete-centred approach requires some degree of belief in athlete-centred learning. Moreover, as Don highlights, a coach needs to be able to self-analyse and be aware of his or her own coaching:

The process of continuous improvement is no different whether you are a coach or an athlete. Coaching is made up of activities and experiences that must be understood along with the context in which they took place. The coaching environment must be conducive to breaking down the significant points and picking up what are the real key learning points. Every campaign that you have, there would be half a dozen points of difference that have separated you from the rest of the world in terms of the competition, or a half a dozen reasons why the other team won ... so just understand, what are they? Why did that team win vs our team, or did this athlete run faster or this athlete, and try to understand that ... then create your plans to put it right, should you find yourself in a similar position in the future.

Don suggests that a coach has to understand the coaching process before beginning to use an athlete-centred approach. As Don sees it, the process is comprised of five components based on what, who, how, when and why:

The *what* is the technical and tactical part of sport which is the area that is the easiest to learn. It is the area that is the major focus of coach education and can be found in many publications. The *who* is understanding the athletes—what are their expectations, what is important to them, why are they important, what is their background, what is their preferred learning style? The *how* is about packaging up the key messages in a format that matches the learning preference of the athlete, thereby increasing the chance of the message being understood. The *when* is all about timing. I can know what to say, who to say it to, and how to say it but if my timing is not right it will be an ineffective message. The last part is the *why*—that is about, why are we doing this? Why are we doing anything? If the athlete doesn't believe, then the athlete will do what they believe is appropriate …

I have a simple approach—if I can't sell it, then we just don't do it. It is not necessarily about my idea, it is about how I might sell something to the athlete, or encourage the athletes to make improvements to the idea and come back with a better idea. In my experience, failure to execute a game plan can only come down to one of two reasons: the athlete does not understand, which means that it has not been communicated effectively, or the athlete does not believe in it—it has not been sold with the athlete recognising the benefits.

In an example from the business environment, Don vividly illustrates the consequences of imposing an idea on people rather than asking for their input. This particular experience is just one of many that influenced him to become an athlete-centred coach:

… one of the organisations I worked for decided to rebrand themselves … new colours along with the purpose and core values. We knew that something was going on because the senior management team kept sneaking off. Then they launched the new brand to the staff (an organisation of about 300 people) at the same time as they did to the outside world (our major customers) … They said 'This is our new culture'. I [was] sitting there and thinking, 'But aren't the people your culture?' They were talking about all these lovely words and all the things like that, but I had absolutely no connection to it. Given that the culture of an organisation is reflected through its staff, how did they expect it to be lived when the staff had no input into its creation?

One of the highlights of hearing Don discussing his philosophy is his great ability to analyse situations and issues, which includes an apt use of analogies. In one analogy he demonstrates how having ownership is an important aspect to being an athlete-centred coach:

I look at myself at home; I want to build a nice, white picket fence outside my house. I've got two choices. One is that I can pay someone to do it and I might admire a fantastic job but I am not emotionally attached to it. Or I can get out and do it myself. It might not be a flash job but I am emotionally attached to it. The emotional attachment is what lasts.

As with other coaches in this book, shared leadership is an important aspect to Don's coaching. Contrary to what he sees as the traditional stereotype of leaders as older, more mature people who have already paid their dues, he suggests that:

> We don't operate like that. If an athlete has leadership qualities then we leverage off them. Great things happened in this last campaign, where one of our young guys, a 21-year-old, stepped up and took ownership of an issue and its resolution during our World Series in Christchurch. I am not a believer in developing senior player groups as they are typically filled with athletes that have similar backgrounds and experiences. In short, they think alike. I have always considered that these types of groups limit creativity. We operate with an informal leadership team within the Black Sox. We don't believe that we need to formalise it as the leaders are readily identifiable to everyone in the team.

As Don practises the athlete-centred approach, the leadership role is used to enhance understanding and communication among the athletes, Don and the management team. Don describes one of his tools for ensuring two-way communication:

> I prefer to have almost all my messages delivered through the leadership team that we have within the team, not through me. The messages that I delivered needed to basically stop the team, so that we could re-group get back on task and move forward. When you are in a campaign such as our World Series, if I was the delivering all of the messages then it gets a little bit tiresome … what can you possibly say that is different to what you have been saying all along? … During our heavy conditioning phase, if I want to motivate a group of athletes in Auckland, I use a Wellington athlete to deliver my message. It would be in the form of a simple phone call from one athlete to another sharing how hard the Wellington guys are training. The next thing you know, there is a competition going on between the Wellington- and Auckland-based athletes.

Every coach has various strategies for implementing an athlete-centred approach in which the players understand, own and take responsibility for the mutual direction of the team. When a coach understands and shows concern for every individual athlete, trust is obtained. With mutual trust, the team goes forward and becomes the best that they can be, together. The process of gaining athletes' trust and enabling them to learn is specific to the coach's process of empowering players.

The Process of Empowering Athletes

To enable athletes to learn, coaches in this book include them in making informed decisions in all aspects of the team environment. As Don points out, a coach needs to trust in the ability of the athlete to make these decisions:

> It is the athlete that makes the decision in real time; therefore you must trust the athlete to make the smart decisions under pressure. If I don't trust my

athletes to make the smart decision then I would consider that I have failed them. In addition, members of the leadership team take on a mentoring role that results in a transfer of knowledge. We spend a lot of time ensuring that the athlete understands the context in which the decision is made. For example, if a decision was made at club level, we encourage the athletes to consider if the same decision would be appropriate at the international level.

As part of this process, athletes learn and recognise what they should execute to achieve the most informed type of play. Don explains how they do it:

> It's part of their reflective practice. The greater lessons that you learn in life are those where you feel a little bit of pain. If you make some mistakes, then you've got to have that opportunity and the environment where you can go back and reflect on it and say, 'Okay, now that I am wiser and I have got a little bit of hindsight on my side, was that the smart play or why did I make that decision?'

Before athletes can reflect in this way, coaches need to create an environment that allows them to analyse through trial and error. At the elite level of the Black Sox, athletes should come to the team environment with some ability to think and make decisions. Unfortunately, as Don suggests, they have not necessarily had the chance to develop this ability as many athletes at the development levels are never given the opportunity to practise reflecting on decisions made:

> ... when I was coaching the Black Sox, we had some of the best softball players in the world. Yet their knowledge of the game and their ability to make smart decisions under pressure was our greatest weakness. That was simply because, right through their careers, they were always the best kids on the team. Therefore, whether they make a poor decision or a great decision, it didn't really matter, because they could do whatever they liked. They could typically get away with it because their skill set or their athletic ability tended to cover up poor decisions. But the higher you travel in international sport, then that all evens itself out and typically the teams that win are the teams that make the smart decisions under pressure.

In learning how to make decisions under pressure, the Black Sox were allowed to make mistakes so that they could learn and reflect on why the decisions were made. Don describes his method:

> ... we spent two years from '98 to 2000 encouraging our athletes to make mistakes. We spent two years with a small set of signals so that we could enable our athletes on tours of Canada (they were big tours for us) to make decisions where they would actually feel a little bit of pain in terms of making poor choices. We then go through the process to understand whether it was a smart or poor decision. We go all the way through, in terms of process, and we break the play down to understand the critical decision point through asking open questions of the athlete concerned and the rest of the team.

'What happened?' Or, 'Why did it happen?' And, 'Why didn't you think about throwing the ball to first base?' or, 'Why didn't you throw it to third base?' It is an environment where you are not necessarily challenging the athlete, saying that he made a poor choice, it is just understanding the process and improving the awareness of the athlete when making the decision.

In terms of the business model introduced in Chapter Two (see Figure 2.2), the coach must be able to read players' level of ability to cope with taking ownership (especially if they have never been exposed to an athlete-centred approach). With this knowledge, the coach can determine how much to involve athletes in decision making and gradually move through four quadrants towards the ultimate goal of delegating decision making to the athletes. With reference to the Black Sox, Don elaborates on the process he uses to gradually introduce an athlete-centred approach to the players:

When building the culture of the 2000 World Champion team, I was probably a little bit [coach-centred]. This was because of the athletes' maturity level with an athlete-centred approach in developing team culture. In 2000 I met with the athlete leadership team and explained what I was looking for in terms of culture. The athlete leadership team then facilitated a meeting with the rest of the athletes. The outcome of the meeting was a perception that the athletes built the culture of the team, when in reality they delivered pretty much what I sent them away to do. In 2004 the process was very different, with the athletes taking complete ownership of developing the culture of the 2004 team. The captain of the side facilitated a meeting with the athletes; the outcome was the core components of the culture.

There was an advantage to empowering players for the 2004 campaign. Don suggests that one of the reasons for the success in 2004 was the systems that had been set up to empower players:

It depends on the team you've got ... The Black Sox model is built on a solid foundation of stability. The core of the athletes will have had World Championship experience and exposure to our culture. The way we have built the 2004 Black Sox ensures that the next time we go to a World Championship, of the 17 [athletes in the team], there will be about nine or ten who will be back. So the core of the team will be back each time. We just regenerate talent, so coming out the other end is a bunch of young guys who have already been exposed to our culture and coaching style.

Don believes in using an athlete-centred approach for athletes at all levels. So is there a difference in the coaching process between the Black Sox and his son's team? Don considers:

In many ways the process is the same. The kids that I coach are now 10. At the start of this season the kids decided what the main objective is for the year. This was achieved through a series of questions. I asked the kids what they liked most about softball. They all responded that batting was the most fun. I then asked what stops us from batting. After a very little direction by me, the response was fielding—if we can't get the other team out, we never get a chance to bat. Falling out of this conversation was the decision developed by the kids that we wanted to be the best fielding team in the grade. Therefore our main objective for the year is developing our fielding capability so we can get the other team out quickly, which will mean that we will spend more time batting.

As mentioned earlier, part of empowering your athletes is to know who they are. On each Black Sox tour, Don has made a point of getting to know each player—although, as he relates, the process has not been without its challenges:

… for each tour, I spend time getting to know the athletes on a personal level, sitting on the buses with them … just talking sport and life. We have always viewed our bus trips as learning environments. However, this was tested on our first tour when some of the senior players decided that they were going to introduce a ranking system when sitting on the bus. They decided that because of their status they would sit at the back of the bus as they understood the All Blacks did. We let it go for a couple of days, then we sat down with the senior players and talked to them about it. 'Okay, why are we doing this?' 'Oh, because the All Blacks do it.' 'So, we are followers are we, we are just doing this because someone else does it? I thought we wanted to be trendsetters, why are we following everyone else?' We then asked how we could win without the younger members of the team who were sitting at the front of the bus. It was acknowledged that we couldn't. Then I asked why then were they treated differently? How were we going to leverage off each others' knowledge and experience when we did not sit together? The following day the ranking system was removed by the athletes and the bus trips returned to the required learning environment.

Don's insight on how he empowers his players will stimulate others to come up with ideas that might suit their own environment. In coaching, there is no one way that works best; what is central is the athletes. Any campaign is the athletes' campaign. But athletes need some control over their sporting lives. Don gives a personal analogy about how adults need to have faith in their children by allowing them some freedom to be innovative and acknowledging their effort:

I am just thinking of a story of mismatched expectations. One that I always had my dad on about, when I could talk to him about these things, is when I mowed the lawns. I would do what I considered to be an absolutely fantastic job and I could pick up the lawn and take it to Wembley. I had it criss-crossed and everything. My dad wouldn't see that. He would only see that I didn't trim the edges. So that is what he'd focus on and I would get a hell of a letdown …

The key learning from that was how did I feel about that? So I try look at everything in a complete and entirety and how it was done … congratulate the success and if there are some bits around the edges that you want to tidy up, then pick your timing to talk about the edges. So, role reversal, what I was looking for at that stage was my dad to pat me on the back and say 'That was a fantastic job' and then maybe the next day say, 'Hey let's come out and have a crack at these edges together' or whatever, [where] the focus is not on poor performance because I didn't do the edges, the focus is on, 'Hey, that is a fantastic performance' because of the way the lawns looked.

It is so important that we deliver positive messages. Yet we typically feel more comfortable focusing on the negative parts of performance. The childhood saying, 'Sticks and stones will break my bones but names will never hurt me', is complete garbage. Broken bones mend yet emotional scaring caused by what has been said can last a lifetime.

Some Challenges of an Athlete-centred Approach

As for every innovative approach, an athlete-centred approach has its limitations. One of the challenges facing Don when he took over the World Championship team in 1996 was that the athletes had expectations of him, based on their relationship with the previous coach, that did not match his intended approach. He elaborates on the challenges of introducing his athlete-centred approach to his players:

> … the relationship with the athletes was more a player–player relationship because I played with most of them. I started coaching New Zealand when I was 36, so I wasn't that far out from the players. So the first challenge for me was to actually adjust the relationship. My previous relationship with these guys gave me the opportunity to walk through the door with instant credibility. But then the challenge for me was to gain that credibility each day, to where it went without saying … it was because the relationship was completely different to the relationship Mike Walsh had with the team initially. Mine was more like a peer relationship. There were not a lot of things to handle in terms of adjusting the relationship … Because I had that relationship with a lot of those guys, and they experienced me when I was an athlete as someone who would challenge, teach and coach in the same manner as I am doing now, it wasn't a lot different to them. 'Hey, this is Don coaching us, this is not someone else.'

> At this point we talked about my expectations and those of the athletes. The first thing we did was build a team as it hadn't been done in a planned way before. This approach received instant positive feedback from the athletes so straight away we had captured the imagination of the athletes. This approach enabled the athletes to contribute to the planning process that delivered a world championship. From this very first camp we gathered momentum in a structured way, ensuring that we had the right team playing our best softball at the World Championships. They saw that everything was a bit different here.

Don is a 'big picture' coach. He believes in looking to the long-term outcome and direction of his team and then encouraging his athletes to analyse what is needed to reach that outcome:

> It starts with having the desired outcome clearly defined and owned by the athletes. Then it is about leveraging off the knowledge and experience of the athletes and the coaching team to develop the processes that will deliver the desired outcome. The process will include identifying the key milestones where we test our progress. At least annually after our pinnacle event for the year, I facilitate a meeting with the leadership team where we ask a simple question, 'If we continue to implement our plan, will we deliver our desired outcome?' If the answer is yes then the next question is, 'How can we improve the plan?' If the answer is no, then the question asked is, 'What do we need to do to get the programme back on track?'

Don recognises that in their development as coaches, people—in the role of athlete or coach—often experience coach-centred coaches and learn that approach to coaching as the 'correct' approach. This influence is hardly surprising given that, as human beings, we tend to copy what we have seen, based on the reasoning that it has worked in the past so it should continue to work. In this situation, the key is to inspire coaches to question the status quo, as Don says:

> … growing up in terms of my experiences I have had coaches all the way through who were very prescriptive. They tell you what to do, and you do it or you don't do it. But there is no [questioning] what is in it for me. If your style is to challenge and inspire athletes, then the athlete must recognise that there is a real value and benefit to them. If the benefits are recognised then it is easy to adjust the behaviours of an athlete.

So when training coaches it is a challenge to encourage them to take an athlete-centred approach. For the coaches being trained, it is a challenge to be confident enough to try it and believe that it is the athlete who is the most important component in sport. To gain this confidence, Don believes you need experience:

> Coaches must recognise that it is not about us. All we are doing is delivering a service to the athlete. You only have to consider how the media reacts to a win or a loss to realise that the athlete is the most important aspect in sport. On my first tour I noticed that when we won, the media focused on the athletes in terms of interviews. Yet when we lost, they bypassed the athletes and came after me. In terms of confidence in making decisions under pressure—it comes down to experience and having the discipline to reflect after each decision. I store each of these experiences away so that I can use them or a combination of them to craft solutions to issues as they confront me. There is no great mystery to sport and the issues that we are confronted with are not unique—it is only the context in which they differ.

Certainly Don can apply an athlete-centred approach confidently and effectively now. But how did he become confident enough to try it at all? He explains:

I just believed that it was what the athlete wanted. I just believed that it is right for us in terms of our stage of development. I believe it was the right way to go in terms of coaching and hadn't been convinced otherwise through my previous experience. It was these experiences that conditioned me to realise that this is the way forward. Having said that, not all of the athletes were comfortable with this approach, so for them I delivered a coach-centred service.

The first step towards an athlete-centred approach, as coaches indicate throughout this book, is to believe that the athletes themselves will benefit from contributing to the team and making decisions. Because many coaches lack the confidence and/or the experience to implement an athlete-centred approach, I was curious to find out how Don believes we learn how to encourage athlete decision making. He says:

I believe it is just a collection of whole heap of things. Clearly, you want to take the luck out of it, so it all depends on the environmental factors … It's not just about experiences, you can have all the experience in the world, but if you don't have the ability to take a step back and actually understand them in terms of what just happened and why it happened, then you will have to get a collection of experiences that are in no particular order or context, which will make it very difficult for them to be re-used. In short, no learning would have occurred.

Another challenge of using an athlete-centred approach is that it takes time to ask athletes and include them in decision making. Yet the focus needs to be on the outcome: athletes learn and develop more effectively when there is time to work on their learning and development. Don agrees that, if a coach is to form a quality team, it requires some time:

As part of the Black Sox culture we believe that the big prizes in life are hard to win—for if they were easy anyone could do it. Good things typically happen when you have a plan and work incredibly hard to execute it—there are no shortcuts to sustained success. It sometimes takes time for the whole team to recognise the benefit of a particular initiative. The outcome of belief and ownership in the game plan is worth the wait, as it will not break down under pressure. Should I be the initiator of a particular idea, then I look to the team to make it better. It is through this involvement that quality solutions are developed.

Coaches are busy people and are often coaching as volunteers. To be a great coach and great at everything else in your life, it is important to have balance. It is important to not just say the right things, but to practise them. The balance comes if coaches actually live it and learn how to say 'no' in difficult circumstances. For coaches who find it challenging to achieve a balance in their life while coaching, Don offers this advice:

… it's hard to get that balance and it is something that I constantly strive to get right. The most important part as a coach is that you need to have some space for yourself, which is why I've got to have balance. There are four main quadrants to my life that I need to balance: being a father and husband; my employment; my coaching; and my own space where I can recharge and ensure that I remain energised to deliver a quality service to the other three quadrants that they deserve.

I have not necessarily cracked the balance issue; however, what works for me is to use the coaching and family quadrants to provide me with the balance I require. It is these quadrants that I always want in my life. Therefore spending time in them is always rewarding and refreshing. I also use [both] the 30-minute commute to work and the time that I find to exercise as time to unwind and keep life in perspective. The final point about balance is that I have a close group of friends, in particular my wife, who provide advice on the load that I am carrying to ensure that I keep things in perspective

Plans for the Future

In his current employment, one of Don's roles is to develop coaches. Part of his philosophy in educating other coaches is to communicate the potential of our athletes as people. Sport is often discussed as an institution that develops character and good human citizens. However, unless we practise developing character and getting athletes to make decisions, these sport values are difficult to meet. Developing decision makers in life is important to producing a generation who are independent and informed thinkers. Coaches as educators can have a role in producing thoughtful children. Through another analogy, Don highlights the need to allow our children a bit of room to learn from their own experiences:

… it's all the way through life, it's about making decisions. I mean making decisions about when to cross the road and when not to cross the road. I am a parent, and I am having a debate with my wife at the moment …, now it is time for my ten-year-old son to walk to school by himself, with his seven-year-old sister. My wife doesn't believe he is mature enough to do it. Whereas I look at it and say, 'Well we need to have confidence in him and trust him to make smart decisions.' As I see it, our role as parents is to create an environment that encourages our children to make decisions; an environment where the awareness of child is enhanced. If we continue on the current track, we are just going to create a generation of young people who haven't got the ability to make decisions because they have never had to. Sport is like that; even coaching young kids … let the kids find out for themselves which is the best way to do something.

As a contributor to the coaching strategy for New Zealand, Don discusses how coach education can develop athletes who are decision makers as they progress though the system:

The first step is to ensure that coach education is connected to the development requirements of whoever is coached. It then needs to recognise that the constraints for coaches are the environmental factors in which we operate. They are never the same; therefore coaching cannot be scripted. We need to keep the education framework practical and relevant to the stage of development of the child/athlete who is coached. We must leverage off the knowledge and experience of coaches. We have got some fantastic coaches in New Zealand, yet we don't celebrate them. They are off doing their own thing; somehow we need to capture them and then feed them back in ... it's broadly an awareness of the coaching requirement. One of the risks with coach education is that you coach by following the book, you become dependent on an education framework, and you think that there is only one solution. Coach education must move beyond the current what and when, and have a greater focus on the who, how and why.

Training future coaches, Don says, is about:

... recognising that everyone that we coach deserves a quality coaching experience. Therefore we must understand the expectations of each individual. We also need to recognise that not one group has all the answers, but together if we understand each other's roles and skill sets, then we can make a real difference. But it is like anything in sport, it starts with respect. I respect the view of science and I respect the view of the coaching academic, but I have an expectation that they respect my point of view as well. The more we enhance our awareness of the various views, the greater we are positioned to truly understand the issues and craft the required solution.

Contained within Don's insight into present coach education and development is the idea of networking to enhance our application and understanding of a coach's role. There is no one correct method of coaching. It is an extremely dynamic, multi-dimensional role. The coaching method always depends on the situation, and the who, when, what, how and especially why. Don emphasises the extent to which coaches can learn from each other on an ongoing basis:

... within New Zealand if you have coached a successful team, then there is a perception that you must be pretty good at what you are doing, so people tend to want to listen to you. It is as if you have the magic pill. I don't believe that at all. For every opportunity I get to talk to a group of coaches, I get just as much if not more out of the experience than the coaches I talk to. My most valued coaching development experience is talking to other coaches. It's about leveraging off each other's knowledge and experience. You won't necessarily find a perfect fit for each experience as it will always depend on the context in which the experience occurred. But you will find streams and say, 'Yes, I can identify with that.'

Conclusion

Don's refreshing goal of meeting individual needs indicates how a positive environment can be created using an athlete-centred approach. His strong emphasis on planning for long-term outcomes is another highlight in his coaching approach. In combination, these views mean that, rather than catering to outside expectations, coaches should focus first on the needs of their team and athletes and together they will establish the team direction. If the athletes own those outcomes, then the path to success is easier and more rewarding. To achieve those outcomes, certain sacrifices need to be made—like being happy using certain situations to learn, rather than focus on winning. Along the pathway to achieving a team of champions, trial-and-error learning is essential.

Although his knowledge and thinking have developed substantially already, Don believes he still has much to learn about coaching. He is a great advocate for talking with other coaches as an aid to learning, as he believes that 'answers are not found in books—books contain ideas—the answers are held with coaches. [We should] encourage coaches to talk to each other and leverage off each other's knowledge and experience.' Don also believes in constant observation and analysis of other sports and teams to provide insight and challenges as to why certain events happen in a certain way. These insights transfer well into all aspects of coaches' own sport and team.

Given the complex and multi-dimensional nature of coaching, Don favours a close analysis of any given situation in terms of who, what, when, where, how and especially why. The ability to read a situation and the people involved goes a long way to making athletes valued members of the team. As Don says, 'Coaching is not about the coach, it is about the athlete(s) and the value the coach can add.'

Too often we give children answers to remember rather than problems to solve. – *Roger Lewin, US humorist, author*

In every success story, you find someone has made a courageous decision. – *Peter F. Drucker*

To reach a great height a person needs to have great depth. – *Anonymous*

Each day of our lives we make deposits in the memory banks of our children. – *Charles Swindoll*

Chapter Five

If you don't have time to do it right,
when will you have time to do it
over? – *John Wooden*

Ruth Aitken and Leigh Gibbs
New Zealand Silver Ferns (Netball)
Coaches

Special thanks to Anna Mayes (Bath University)
for her contribution to this chapter

Ruth Aitken and Leigh Gibbs share their experiences as coaches, most recently as the head coach and assistant coach, respectively, of the Silver Ferns, the New Zealand netball team. Helping to gather information on their story has been Anna Mayes, who interviewed Ruth while she was on a scouting trip. Based at Bath University in England, Anna is completing a Masters thesis about empowering coaches. Ruth, who is one of the subjects of Anna's thesis, is a busy woman and graciously allowed her interview with Anna to be used for this book. I had the honour of interviewing Leigh while she was at a Silver Ferns camp in Blenheim. At this camp, I also was privileged to observe the Silver Ferns training sessions and practice games with the New Zealand A team, prior to the home series against Australia in 2004.

Interestingly, Ruth and Leigh both have backgrounds in teaching. Leigh has a Diploma of Physical Education from the University of Otago and a Graduate Diploma in Teaching from the Christchurch College of Education. She taught physical education and coached netball teams at Lincoln and Hillmorton High Schools in Christchurch before going back to live in Gisborne. Ruth attended the University of Auckland, then completed her Graduate Diploma in Teaching at the Auckland College of Education before gaining a Masters degree in English from the University of Auckland. After teaching English and coaching netball at Takapuna Grammar in Auckland and then having children, she went to Paeroa to teach English at Paeroa College.

Both women have coached netball, at secondary and representative levels, during and since their days of teacher training. Since they began coaching the Silver Ferns together in January 2002 in preparation for the Commonwealth Games held later that year, they have had some great successes. Most recently the Silver Ferns won the 2003 World Championships in Jamaica.

Ruth's coaching began with the North Harbour netball club and then the Thames Valley netball club. Before coaching the Silver Ferns, she also coached the Counties Manukau Cometz (1998–2000), Waikato (1999–2001), the Magic (2001) and New Zealand A (2000–2001). Leigh coached secondary school sides and Canterbury senior teams and was head coach of the Silver Ferns from 1993–1997, before coaching the Canterbury Flames in 1998, 1999 and 2001.

Coaching philosophies of Ruth and Leigh

Ruth and Leigh make a great coaching team as they both prefer to use an athlete-centred approach. In my observations of the Silver Ferns camp, it was evident that their philosophies—similar, though not identical—are put into practice.

I noted that Ruth and Leigh work extremely hard to set up systems in which the athletes have a major say in the team. They organise training sessions to encourage athletes to make decisions through solving problems for themselves, responding to coach questioning and playing games that the coaches have set up to develop understanding of tactics and skills. It was also refreshing to observe the selflessness of the Silver Ferns: they work to support each other, never operating in isolation. Ruth and Leigh, through their philosophies, have encouraged a quality team environment where the group works together well to achieve team and individual goals.

While acknowledging that her coaching philosophy has evolved over time, Ruth notes that it has not changed dramatically. At the heart of it has always been her interest in using sport as a tool to develop people. In her interview with Anna, Ruth explains:

> I'm very interested in players as people, the whole person. I love the sport, but I also love seeing the players develop both on and off the court. That's the way it's always been, whether I've coached at college [secondary] level or with my representative team.

Likewise, Leigh focuses on developing the whole person:

> I try to create an environment where the players enjoy and have that passion for the game, but also to create situations where they develop, both as people on the court as well as people off the court. It is satisfying to work with people who are young and inexperienced in that they are still developing and learning. I feel it is my role to help these players expand their horizons holistically by providing lots of learning opportunities for all parts of their life using netball experiences.

Given the notable similarity between her athlete-centred philosophy and Ruth's, I ask Leigh if her philosophy has changed since she started working with Ruth:

> Perhaps how I apply my philosophy might have changed. I am in a different role as an assistant coach [after being Silver Ferns coach in the 1990s] but I hope that people leave from the environment [that] I have been working with them in as better players and maybe better people … Seeing how they respond to situations and how they have dealt with challenges in their lives shows that what they gained from the netball experience has been meaningful.

On the topic of successful coaching, Ruth identifies the elements that she sees as part of her own or another's success as a coach:

> I believe with coaching a team, there are so many factors that are involved.

I mean winning's great, there's no doubt about it. But I do think there are many other elements that make me feel successful, such as playing a really good style of netball, and developing where individuals feel valued, but the team is bigger than us all. I also believe what players *leave* in the Silver Ferns is really important; that they leave it in a state better than it was when they came in. What I really like about our players is the experienced ones now feel that it is part of their role to bring on the next level so when they do leave, the Ferns are still going to be strong. So that philosophy of 'you're only borrowing the jersey, or bib', I think is really important.

Leigh relates successful coaching to winning, which she interprets in a broad sense:

Success is winning, but the concept of winning is bigger than the score. Winning is about creating the opportunity for players to be able to perform to their best. In a team environment, the challenge is that all perform optimally at the same time.

As to the potential for media influence on her philosophy, Ruth says:

… it certainly sits there. And for me I have to make a conscious effort to put it in the background because I feel that if I start to change what I do because of the media, I'll really be in trouble.

Although Ruth dislikes the specific term 'empowerment', she is willing to describe her interpretation of empowerment as a coaching approach:

I think of it as involvement of the players and management. It all comes down to communication; an environment of open communication and an environment where players take part in their own development or help direct it. I think it's more of a partnership than anything … it's really important that players feel that they can still question you or debate an issue—without it being used against them at a later time.

Development of Leigh as a Coach

Leigh's development as a coach was largely influenced by her playing and coaching experiences; 'you learn from the trade'. She acknowledges the influence of her own coaches:

When I was a player, I had strong role models—coaches like Lois Muir with the New Zealand team, Kath Brown who had been a Canterbury coach for quite a long time and Kay O'Reilly, another Canterbury coach. While all three were different in their approach to netball, all provided great learning experiences to draw from.

As players, both Ruth and Leigh were coached by Lois Muir, a legend in netball. In commenting on Lois's influence, Leigh says:

In the seventies and eighties, the coach's knowledge was considered very important and Lois's netball knowledge was second to none. Lois's coaching style in her early years as national coach was directive and authoritarian. While I had confidence in it, at times I was intimidated by it too. The more experienced and more confident I became, the less intimidating she was to me. I also think her style changed and she mellowed as a coach.

Georgie Salter, former Otago and New Zealand under 21s coach, was another major influence on Leigh's coaching development and through her she gained a positive experience of working in tandem with another coach:

I coached with Georgie … in a co-coaching role with the New Zealand under 21s. It was a great experience, made even better when we won the World Youth Champs. We worked well together and were both creative. Georgie's style is very vivacious and I am more reserved. We would have the most amazing discussions when planning our sessions. It was the first time that New Zealand netball had appointed co-coaches at national level and it was a successful decision. We split everything totally. During the series, we would toss a coin and whoever won, was the leader for the day … it was a big effort time-wise to split everything down the line, but a great learning experience.

She also says that the Diploma of Physical Education course at Otago contributed to her understanding of how people learn:

My time at PE school exposed me to the holistic approach to learning. Professor Phillip Smithells created an environment for PE students that enabled us to understand a person as a whole.

Leigh acknowledges that her development is a continuous journey. A crucial influence on it was her previous experience with the Silver Ferns as coach. The World Cup in 1995 contributed powerfully to how she reflects on her coaching. She relates the story:

After unexpectedly losing to South Africa in section play, we faced Australia on the fourth day of a 10-day tournament in the game that we expected to be the final. I don't know that we were overconfident but I don't believe [that] as a coach I [had] prepared the team well enough to deal with a very competitive South African team, who had just returned to the world stage after 28 years' absence. They were extremely passionate and played above our expectations. After the game, we were deflated and within a 24-hour period we had to play Australia. In that short timeframe, [we had to] get over our disappointment of losing to South Africa and get ready for the game against Australia. The Australia game was amazing. It was one of those classic New Zealand vs Australia, one goal differences. What I learned from the South African game was how important it was to not take anything for granted.

Part of this process of development was Leigh's realisation that she had to train for quality rather than quantity. In training for the 1995 World Championships, Leigh had still been in the mindset that quantity training is more important:

I believed that the team had to do a lot of training. We had only a small amount of time so quantity was really important to me. I went in as a greenhorn thinking that I've got all these things to do and we only have limited time. What I have learned actually is that less is more. As an international coach with limited time, it's more about quality and being astute in figuring out what the priorities are.

Leigh's journey of learning, as for any coach who is striving to successful, has been complex and full of reflection. This depth is evident in her explanation of how she changed her stance on quantity training:

Another year after the World Champs in 1995 with the Silver Ferns, I thought that I was more laid back … Probably, I was more relaxed. I wasn't so worried about quantity as I wanted players to enjoy themselves … From my first Silver Ferns experience, I learned losing wasn't life threatening and there wasn't going to be anything in the coaching context that could get any worse than that. I had the opportunity … within the next 18 months [I coached the] Star series, which involved working with players who were in the New Zealand high performance programme … I had a group of players, some I had never worked with, and we got through to the final which we lost by one. They played well and we enjoyed ourselves.

In between her two Silver Ferns coaching experiences, and after the Star series, Leigh coached the Canterbury Flames with Nicola Jones. Her confidence boosted, she was ready to try some new methods in her coaching and she changed her philosophy of training from focusing on quantity to quality.

She began to translate her focus on quality into coaching practice in the next stage of her development, while coaching the Canterbury Flames. Then Ruth asked Leigh to be her assistant with the Silver Ferns. Leigh was thrilled and honoured to be considered:

I didn't know Ruth very well even though we had both played for the Silver Ferns in 1979. Mostly we had played in and coached opposing teams … After some consideration and family discussion; I accepted the position of Silver Ferns assistant coach. My confidence had been boosted from the Star series and working with the Flames. I was ready for the challenge.

In working with the current Silver Ferns, Leigh draws on her valuable experiences and reflections. She advocates strongly for coach self-reflection and analysis as a way of stimulating the learning and improving the performance of the coach. Based on self-reflection, she acknowledges that she has needed to dig into her basket of tricks and become more creative in the way she thinks about learning opportunities to help the team to enjoy themselves and be creative, as well as to ensure she trains for quality and remains relaxed despite all the pressure on her in international coaching:

I think I have changed because … you can't promote this when you are overloading them [the team]. It's getting that set time and using it better. I was getting a lot of enjoyment out of being creative and saying, 'Oh we could do that'. But in actual fact, the [players] need to have that time, it's important [for them] to learn to be creative on the court as well.

The purpose behind Ruth's development in coaching has always been to enable the athletes to learn. Ruth tells Anna how the World Championships in 2003 really brought her coaching together and highlighted that what she was doing was right:

… it was great. I felt that in the past, in those 'down to the wire' games, there's been a fear of failure that has come in and then players kind of go within themselves and hesitate. I think that's a quote somewhere, 'If you have the ability to play like nothing's at stake, when everything's at stake, then you've really got is sussed'. And it's being able to still play with that openness and that passion and that freedom, even though there are only a few goals in it … that was what we tried to instil … when the game got tight we still needed to keep attacking.

So is there an end point to development, then—a shelf life for coaches? Ruth responds:

I think that when a new coach comes, it's something fresh and the players enjoy that and that's not being critical of what's been before, it's just something different. My challenge now … as I've been appointed through to the next World Champs in 2007 … is to … constantly be looking at ways of doing things better and bringing in new ideas. That's why I try to get out and talk to different coaches and see what I can apply or modify to the Ferns.

One of the challenges for netball has been that the national coaches were not professional coaches until 1996. When Leigh was first appointed to the Silver Ferns in 1993, she still had to maintain her teaching job and coach the national netball team. She comments on the marked difference that professionalism has made to her coaching approach:

It's only been in the last few years that I am fully coaching and fully employed without the distraction of having to make money outside of netball. Due to this professionalism, I now find I have head space to think about my [netball] job and what we are doing.

Another useful initiative has been the 'carding' system through the Academies of Sport, which helps high performance coaches to pursue their careers in coaching. Both Leigh and Ruth appreciate the support they are getting through this system. Ruth says:

I think the carded programme is a great to support coaches. It acknowledges the benefits to be gained from professional development and provides the support and opportunity for coaches to continue learning and improving.

The Process of Establishing a Quality Team Culture

In many ways, the attention that Ruth and Leigh have given to establishing a quality team culture has helped the Silver Ferns to become world champions. In responding to

Anna's question as to whether she thought that team culture had helped them to win at the 2003 World Championships, Ruth says:

> ... for us the team culture was fantastic in Jamaica ... it was the X factor for us.

Leigh says that establishing team culture by providing a successful environment contributes to a successful team:

> ... the team culture, probably the environment is the most important. If you create the right environment, then you can actually use more time more efficiently.

Leigh herself became interested in creating a quality team culture when she was coaching in Canterbury and was helped in her task by Gilbert Enoka, a fellow teacher at her school. Leigh recalls:

> [As a] Canterbury provincial coach, we did a lot of things on team culture. We were one of the first teams to have a sport psychologist [Gilbert Enoka] to be a part of the team and sit on the team bench who helped us with this. We called him assistant coach in the late eighties because it was a new phenomenon. He participated fully and was fantastic. Gilbert worked with us for five years. We had so much fun and he was great in working on team culture and values.

During my observations, one feature of the Silver Ferns camp that stood out was that every player contributes to the team and supports each other and the team's campaign. During the actual training or game, the manager acts as facilitator while the players fill water bottles, look after bibs, and help each other in different situations. The team's independence and ability to put the value of selflessness into practice help the athletes to take ownership of and responsibility for their team as a unit. This observation is all the more noteworthy in the age of professionalism, when the 'What's in it for me?' attitude often prevails over the 'What can I do to help?' attitude. Thus the Silver Ferns' team culture was a breath of fresh air.

Like other athlete-centred teams, the Silver Ferns have a symbolic representation of their team's vision and have found it to be worthwhile because it is a tangible form of what the team lives. The successful team cultures of Mark Norton's volleyball team (Chapter Three) and Wayne Smith's various rugby teams (Chapter Nine) demonstrate what can be achieved when athletes have substantial input into deciding on the team's symbol and vision. I believe athlete ownership and responsibility are enhanced when both athletes and coaches agree on the team direction through such means.

An important facet of establishing a quality team culture is to ensure that for each season or series the team starts fresh. Each change means new players, new series and new situations. Leigh acknowledges that player evaluations, which the Silver Ferns complete to give feedback on the team environment and performance, encouraged her and Ruth to use a fresh approach for the 2004 team:

... we both felt that it needed a different approach. I think with these players, you can't keep doing the same thing. At times they quite enjoy that organised fun, but most of them (based on a survey prior to the World Champs) said they prefer to let it happen naturally ... This group is probably more experienced, been around; probably a younger group might like to be directed more in that way.

As part of the team environment, Ruth and Leigh work on mutual trust between athlete and coach by ensuring that athletes have input and that both coaches and athletes contribute positively to the team environment. Athletes understand and feel the trust that coaches have in them. One sure way of conveying that trust is to instil in athletes a sense of belonging by providing a caring environment. Ruth gains players' trust:

... once people get to know you and that they know there is a consistency in your selection and that you will give them feedback if there are areas of concern.

Leigh shows how much trust she has in the athletes:

We operate with a team of 12, but on the bench there are five other players that we know could be put on the court and do the job.

Leigh suggests that having this trust in playing your athletes is even more important at junior level:

I hate it when I see young players sitting on the sideline. I think it is a waste of a learning opportunity. You do your learning on the court playing.

Use of Questioning by Ruth and Leigh

Both Ruth and Leigh highlight the importance of using questioning so that athletes can problem solve situations or scenarios in order to enhance their learning. About questioning, Ruth says that athletes learn by coaches:

... asking questions and posing problems rather than always telling them the answers ... I try and put groups together and give them tasks to do—for example, to come up with a play to counteract a particular opposition strategy ... I've always felt in sport that there's lots of different ways to skin a cat, so it's not just my way—it's, 'How else can we do it?'

Like Ruth, Leigh has always focused on her questioning technique in order to develop decision makers but, again like other coaches in this book, she started questioning without really letting the athletes know of her philosophy or intentions. As she recalls it:

I wanted decision makers and I certainly think that caused some [initial] barriers ... I don't believe I explained the intention of what and why I wanted to question. Because of that, these players were thinking, 'Why are we doing this sort of activity on the court? It's not a drill, we have to make decisions, but how does it relate to the game?' ... they were concerned about the value of such an approach to their game … that was my constant frustration. I was trying to create situations where they had to use problem solving to practise making decisions.

Having used questioning with many teams, including the first Silver Ferns team she coached, Leigh still believes in it quite strongly. Her ability to question, however, has evolved from experience and through self-reflection. In reflecting on her past questioning strategies Leigh says:

> Initially, I asked quite closed-ended questions, where the players didn't have to do much thinking to make decisions. Posing a question, whether it is an open question or a closed question, was easy. The difficulty was listening and interpreting the athletes' understanding of the problem and allowing them time to process their thoughts.

Leigh's acknowledgement that it can be difficult to read athletes' responses to and understanding of questions reflects one of the challenges experienced by many coaches. Many athletes are unfamiliar with questioning so want to know why the coach is asking them questions when coaches should have all the answers. Ruth reflects on how different athletes respond to her questioning technique:

> Some athletes like it more than others; some just want you to, 'Let's cut through this and tell me what you really want me to do'. I think there is a fine line. I think it can cause a bit of frustration with some players that if we want them to do a lot of self-evaluation, they would still like to be told what we think, and so there is still that balance and I'm not sure if I get it right all the time or at all.

In her Netball New Zealand coach development role, Leigh has encountered some difficulties in her use of questioning when demonstrating it to coaches:

> … what I have noticed when I am coaching coaches, and using players for the demonstration is that when I question the players, some of them find it quite hard to give answers. I don't know whether it is just the fact that they don't know me, or that they are in front of all their coaches watching, [but] perhaps I need to ask the questions in a different way …

Nevertheless she has gained the confidence to use questioning, which she says developed because:

> I ask the players questions where sometimes I may not know the answers … When I am running coaching sessions for coaches, I may say, 'I don't know all the answers, so why not ask the players? They are doing it, they are out there.'

Another important questioning technique is to avoid giving away the answers and instead getting the athletes to think for themselves. Ruth explains how she stops herself from giving athletes the answers:

I try not to ask many questions to the whole group as often only the same players give the answers. The difficulty is remembering to pause long enough to give them time to answer or else rephrasing the question to be a little more specific. But I think it works better when there are smaller groups, or else if something's happening at a practice, I'll pull a player aside and ask, 'What happened then?' or 'Why did that work well/not work so well?' So it's just a variety and it's really only experimenting.

The questioning process takes up valuable training time. However, the understanding and learning achieved through thought and consideration are far stronger than what could be achieved by rote methods. The athletes need to have this thinking time to process the question, arrive at an informed solution and then apply it to the situation, as Ruth suggests:

[The] hard thing with the questioning is to not make it too long. It's still got to be quite quick as you don't have a lot of time.

When Anna asks if she questions more during less pressured times in training, Ruth replies:

… it does depend upon your stress levels. The more stress, the more you tend to feel that you need to provide the answers.

One of the most interesting coaching situations that I observed at the Silver Ferns camp, and then later in the Australia series, is that Ruth and Leigh's time outs do not necessarily continue with the heavy questioning that characterises trainings. Because the competition games are for putting into play what athletes have learned at training, during time outs and breaks, coaches should use only cues or similar and should not relay new information. In addition, like Mark Norton with his high school volleyball team, Ruth and Leigh tend to let the athletes have extensive input during time outs. For any coach, the difficult part at these breaks in the game is deciding what and how much to say. There is no real answer, except to read the athletes' needs. As Ruth says:

I think that giving players opportunity to talk amongst themselves at a break is really valuable. Sometimes I will simply listen to what they are saying before I add my thoughts.

Reflecting in a similar vein on what should be done at game stoppages, Leigh says:

I am continually learning how much information is going to be of value at the break. How much do they actually take in? How much change can they effect as a result of the input of information ? … Most of the Silver Fern players are experienced and game wise, why do we need to tell them things?

Ruth and Leigh on Teaching Games for Understanding

In my observations of Leigh's coaching, she has become one of netball's promoters of Teaching Games for Understanding (TGfU or Game Sense), helping to develop the use and understanding of it. Through her coach development role with Netball New Zealand, Leigh also promotes TGfU as a great learning tool for enhancing athlete decision making and creating pressure situations.

Leigh has always been a strong advocate for TGfU as a pedagogical approach because of her exposure to it at Otago's School of Physical Education. She says she applies this approach because:

> I like to get them to think … and I want the players to be competitive. Game Sense activities provide the uncertainties that you get in the game.

As to how she sets up trainings to implement TGfU, she explains:

> I enjoy looking at ways to create decision-making opportunities and to develop creativeness in the athletes. I am constantly looking at ways to use Game Sense in my sessions as I think there is huge transference to netball. For example, I try to think of what we are working on in defence, such as two defenders working together to shut down an attacking player who is cutting along the goal line. I think about what attributes the defence will need for this situation and then come up with a game that will challenge the athletes in a similar way as would happen in the game.

At the Silver Ferns camp I observed, most drills were purposeful games where they practised game-like scenarios, which were designed to be played under pressure and to simulate real games. The coaches set up problems for the athletes to solve and often let the athletes play for a period before jumping in to ask a meaningful question. This period of play allows athletes thinking space in which to consider how they might solve the problem, or to learn from their application of the game. Ruth describes how the Silver Ferns have benefited from using TGfU:

> I think we were so much better prepared at World Champs [2003]. We used a lot of scenarios in our build-up practices—90 seconds, we are two goals down … that sort of thing. We tried to give players lots of practice in pressure situations and we felt there was real confidence in the team that when we needed to nail something … we could. It worked really well.

Implementing an Athlete-centred Approach

As noted above, Ruth has believed in the athlete-centred approach since her earliest days of coaching secondary and representative teams. Does she implement the approach in different ways, depending on the level of the players? She reflects:

> I think that I probably coach the Silver Ferns in much the same way that I used to coach College A. Certainly, [with the Silver Ferns] there's a sophistication and higher level understanding that is not there with college players, but I've always felt that if players are involved and understand rather than just being told things, that they will respond better. There is certainly a time when I am quite bossy and that's the balance of knowing when to be directive and when to guide them to an understanding.

Anna suggests that knowing when to implement the athlete-centred process can be a challenge for a coach. Ruth considers:

> It just depends on their [athletes'] past experiences … I think I need to be a little bit more directional to start off with and then put it in gradually.

In implementing an athlete-centred approach in various ways throughout her own coaching career, Leigh has worked hard to avoid being directive. At the same time, like Ruth, she believes that achieving a balance in her approach is useful:

> I do find at times that I have to check myself from being directive, but I think there are still times when it is appropriate. Understanding when it is a good time to be directive and when it is a good time to use questioning is ongoing learning for me.

Within their team environment, Ruth and Leigh include players in team decision making in many different ways. Players have a say in how and why things are run, and in what they are aiming for. As mentioned above, use of player evaluations is one of the processes that they find valuable. Ruth tells Anna:

> … after our tours and camps, we have a detailed debrief from each of the players. They're actually very good now, their evaluations are very useful. We ask for opinions on the trainings, team talks and other aspects of the team environment and performance. We also get feedback during a series or camp from our Senior Player Group, who in turn report back from the player-only meetings that they hold. So, nothing much is held back.

Ruth and Leigh also use 'overload' pressure situations, a training method advocated by Ric Charlesworth. Leigh describes how a presentation by this high performance consultant sparked her thinking:

> After listening to Ric Charlesworth in 1994, one of the things I took from his presentation was that players needed full game understanding and could play in a variety of positions. In netball, apart from shooting, which is the only real specialist skill, players should have an understanding of what is required to play most positions.

This strategy ties in with role rotation which, as mentioned in other chapters, is a practice that underpins an athlete-centred approach. An element of trust is required to demonstrate to your athletes that all of them are worthy of being played, even under pressure. Putting players in a game to give them experience of international competition is crucial to the development of future athletes. With the Silver Ferns, Ruth and Leigh practise this role rotation, including under pressure when it is appropriate, as Leigh confirms:

> … both of us believe that players need to have skills to play in more than one position. Except for the specialist goal shooter and a specialist goal keeper, most of the players are capable of playing more than one position and have been required to do so.

Some Challenges of an Athlete-centred Approach

To gain athlete buy-in to an athlete-centred approach, many coaches have suggested that it is necessary to act as a salesperson for the approach. As David Hadfield points out in Chapter Two, 'selling' the concept to the players is one of the initial challenges of using the approach. Many an athlete has never experienced the opportunity to contribute their valuable ideas in a positive way. To the contrary, coach-centred coaches often ostracise players who attempt to contribute, as Anna Mayes reports from her own experience as a player:

> … that was something I found very difficult, because as soon as I tried to question [the coach about] something I felt that I was actually arguing.

Such experiences prompted Anna to ask Ruth how players respond to an athlete-centred approach. Ruth identifies their response as a potential challenge initially:

> I think to start off players can find it unsettling as they're so grateful to have been selected and don't want to get on the wrong side of you. [They may not feel comfortable with the approach] until they get to know you and start to trust you and understand that their opinion is truly valued—even if it is different to yours …

Like others in this book, Leigh admits that time is a pitfall in using an athlete-centred approach:

> I suppose if you are constrained by time, there are a tendency and a need at times to be directive.

Leigh (again like many other coaches in this book) suggests that one area in which she still has more to learn is 'reading' players and situations. That is, she would like to develop her skills in determining when to sit back and observe and let athletes run things, when to jump in and offer augmented feedback, or when someone needs something that she can help out with:

> Knowing the right time to stop and question or when to let the activity run without interruption. Then with skill development, how many times or repetitions are really going to cause a change, for that group or for that competition that we are leading into? How many will we have to do? Is it enough to just get through it a couple of times and hopefully they have got it.

In its essence, the purpose of coaching is to ensure the athletes' needs are met, as Leigh says:

> I am still learning how much the right amount [of positive and negative feedback] is. In the last couple of years, my philosophy has been to accentuate the positive. The challenge is knowing whereabouts on that continuum I should accentuate the positive and when to be more critical … It changes depending on their confidence levels.

Gaining athlete input is extremely rewarding for a coach. One of the highlights to using an athlete-centred approach is to see that the athletes understand given situations or, better yet, that they teach coaches situations and show initiative in their learning. Leigh agrees:

> I enjoy the interaction and exchange of knowledge that occurs when you are coaching. I do not feel threatened by what the players bring to the sessions in the way of experience and knowledge. They help me to grow and develop as a coach.

Conclusion

Ruth and Leigh have been very successful coaches, not because they won the World Championships (although that was definitely a highlight), but because of their success at following their philosophies in which their aim is to create 'good' human beings. Their attention to establishing a quality team culture has enhanced the team's ability to be successful at international level. They provide us with many life lessons, from their holistic philosophy to their practice of giving athletes responsibility and ownership of their team. They acknowledge how much they still have to learn, and continue in their own professional development by taking up as many opportunities to help their coaching performance as they can. We need more coaches like these two, dedicated to an athlete-centred approach and the development of confident, motivated, selfless, successful and happy people.

As Leigh and Ruth continue into their next international netball adventure, Ruth tells Anna her hopes for the future:

> To continue to love what I do (even though it has some huge challenges) and feel like I am making a difference.

We do not believe in ourselves until someone reveals that deep inside us is valuable, worth listening to, worthy of our trust, sacred to our touch. Once we believe in ourselves we can risk curiosity, wonder, spontaneous delight or any experience that reveals the human spirit."
– *E. E. Cummings*

There is no point in coaching unless the teaching you do helps the student to overtake you. – *Rene Deleplace, mentor of Pierre Villepreux*

If you believe you can, you probably can. If you believe you won't, you most assuredly won't. Belief is the ignition switch that gets you off the launching pad. – *Denis Waitley*

To give yourself the best possible chance of playing to your potential, you must prepare for every eventuality. That means practice. – *Seve Ballesteros*

Chapter Six

Talent wins games, but teamwork
and intelligence win championships.
– *Michael Jordan*

Ian Rutledge
New Zealand Black Sticks (Women's Hockey) Coach

Australian Ian Rutledge was employed by New Zealand Hockey in 2003 to coach the New Zealand women's hockey team, the Black Sticks. The Black Sticks placed sixth in the 2004 Athens Olympics and are ranked sixth in the world. With the team, Ian uses an athlete-centred approach and believes in training players to make informed decisions. Ian has always coached using an athlete-centred approach because of his experience and analysis of coaches during his time as a player, and his choice has been reinforced over his many years as a coach.

Originally from Orange, New South Wales, Ian completed a three-year Bachelor of Sport Science, majoring in sport coaching, at the University of New South Wales. Within his degree, he completed coaching practicums where he often coached with a state hockey coach. After obtaining his degree, he went on to gain a graduate diploma in teaching and then a Master of Sport Science, which emphasised skill acquisition, focusing on talent identification. In his role as a national coach, Ian uses his Masters interest informally to give advice about the high performance structure including talent identification.

Ian has been coaching since he was 16 years old. His first team was an under 13 representative side. As he recalls it:

> I got involved coaching rep teams. I come from a small, country town and begrudged a little bit the lack of opportunity that was given to me. So, as a coach, I wanted to make sure that I provided a better opportunity for the people who came after me. I got into coaching early so I could provide opportunities for people to go further than I was going.

Within the Orange Hockey Association, Ian was involved in a mentor system (as a player), where two young players would learn from a young coach. Although unfortunately the system lasted only a year, Ian has high praise for it and believes that it really benefited his coaching. He comments on the innovative approach:

> It was a pretty forward-thinking environment. I was involved in the mentor system early and I just picked up coaching while I played and through my education … Then I went to uni and worked part time for the New South Wales hockey as a development coach, where I went around schools and coached.

Professional coaching was not yet a viable long-term option. After completing his graduate diploma in teaching, Ian worked as a teacher and then a development officer for Sport and Recreation in New South Wales. Thereafter he did coach in Scotland for a year but then became a lecturer in pedagogy, skill acquisition and biomechanics at the Canberra Institute of Technology for five years. Throughout this period, though, coaching continued to be part of his life as he coached several representative hockey teams in a voluntary capacity.

Ian's coaching journey continued with the national under 18 and under 21 men's hockey teams, then as an assistant coach for a men's national league team. Next he worked with the ACT Academy of Sport hockey team, first as assistant coach and then, after the 2000 Sydney Olympics, as head coach. After working with Australian elite players for two years, he applied for and obtained the Black Sticks coaching job in New Zealand. In response to my question as to whether he had ever coached women before this job, he explains:

> … when I was in Sydney, I coached a women's club team. I was involved in a very successful club team where my wife (well my girlfriend then, my wife now) was playing. I came out to watch her play hockey, they didn't have a coach and didn't have a coach in line … but I hadn't coached elite women's hockey before I got the job [in New Zealand]. But I don't coach males and I don't coach females, I coach athletes.

Ian elaborates on this last comment by pointing out that coaches can fall into the trap of coaching based on their expectations instead of treating their athletes as individuals:

> All athletes appreciate good coaching and respect, so I think the biggest mistake I have seen with men coaching women is that they don't treat them as athletes. They see them as a different type of citizen … I was asked that question in my interview, 'What do you see [as] the difference between men and women?' I said, 'Well I am coaching athletes, I am coaching hockey players. There [are] obviously different things that need to be considered, but not a lot.'

Does Ian have an impression of any differences between men and women in terms of their response to an athlete-centred coaching approach? He observes:

> I think men are more prepared to pressure each other in terms of coaching. I am speaking very generally, but I know with men you've got to actually reel them back for what you are trying to achieve and I think with women you have got to encourage them to get there. Women can also be a little too prescriptive. If you say, 'Go and do A', they'll go and do A; they are very dedicated and committed … It is environmental … that they have been conditioned in a certain way … I think if they are prepared to make decisions and understand that situations are not black and white, but grey, they will function well.

Ian's Philosophy of Coaching

Ian's athlete-centred coaching approach is based on a *situational management* philosophy. This philosophy focuses on analysing each situation for its merits and making decisions based on the needs of that situation. He believes in approaching each situation with fairness to ensure each individual's needs are met. Pervasive to his coaching philosophy is his use of novel situations for learning in order to develop decision makers. He is concerned with enabling athletes to learn based on what he suggests is his own unique approach rather than an approach that comes from a textbook. About his coaching philosophy, he says:

> It's funny, because every book you read always has a coaching philosophy and every course that you go to and that you deliver has a coaching philosophy. I have a number of them; I have a philosophy on life. I see hockey as an extension of life, but I don't have a catchy philosophy saying. I think that my personal aim is to make sure that any team that I have ever been involved in, will be better off when I am gone than when I arrived. That is what drives me. I think my sole motivation is to provide athletes the opportunities to achieve their dream and goals … but also to do it in a way that makes them better human beings [rather] than just hockey players. If my players become better human beings for my involvement with them as hockey players, I am successful. The organisation is probably more concerned about winning and losing but, to me, hockey is just an extension of life. I am in a position where I can actually learn from people and make them better holistically for their involvement in sport.

Throughout the interview, Ian came up with a multitude of great principles and concepts related to how he thinks as a coach. Ian really focuses on learning as an outcome of athletes' development in any team:

> … it's like standing on the shoulders of giants, so whoever stands on my shoulder, will see further than I see, so if I can provide these players with the right kind of grounding … then I will be [successful] … All of this groundwork is foundation building to really accelerate New Zealand Hockey as one of the world powers of our game. I explain things to the players in a way that will allow them to be a better coach than I will be. It is a learning process … The thing that motivates me the most in coaching is that I want to be able to explain to my players in a way that they can understand the concepts and strategies that we are using and go off and explain and teach it to somebody else … it sounds so simple, but it shows true learning. The first thing I say to any group that I present to, coach or teach is that 'If I explain something that you don't understand, that is not your fault, it is my fault. My job is to teach and therefore, if I haven't given you the right information or opportunity to learn, then I haven't done my job' … But teaching someone very theoretical [concepts] and not understanding what it means, and then explaining to confuse other people, that is not teaching. They have not learned from my method.

As Ian sees it, providing athletes with opportunities to learn more than coaches know is a major achievement. It is a view found among many coaches who employ an athlete-centred approach; Wayne Smith quotes Rene Deleplace, 'There is no point in coaching unless the teaching you do helps the student to overtake you.' Ian has similar firmly held views:

... the ultimate goal is that I can actually walk away from that team and know that they don't need me and they can say, 'We did it' ... It's funny because when the players are performing at their best or at their peak for major events, I don't coach. At the qualifying tournaments, the players just played and performed. Anything that needed to be corrected was corrected after the game, between that match and the next match. You've got to trust your preparation. A lot of coaches don't trust their preparation, that's why they give their athletes a thousand instructions before they go out on the field. If it is so important, why didn't you actually do that in training? Why didn't you actually spend time practising, rather than just talking about it when it was too late for learning to occur?

Winning has always been a goal within Ian's philosophy, but he places more emphasis on a winning *mindset* since his experience at the 2004 Athens Olympics. Winning should be the main goal for elite athletes; it may involve changing their attitude from just competing to wanting to win. As Ian suggests, the process of pursuing winning is what enables athletes to win:

To go to the Olympics, we need to go to win. What I found is that we aimed to be competitors, but it is a different mindset than aiming to be a winner. An example is an athlete who just aims to make the team. They play to the level to make the team; once they are in the team, they compete for different positions. It is an unconscious laziness to just be satisfied to be selected. A team with that mentality has difficulty seeking higher ideals. After the Olympics, I believe that we need to change the paradigm of the player mindset from competitive thinking to elite or excellence thinking and being the best they can be. We had a benchmark and when we got to the Olympics, the benchmark was a lot higher than we expected. That is awesome for our hockey future because we will be able to set higher ideals of excellence, elite or whatever you want to call it ...

Elaborating on the importance of the winning mindset, Ian says:

Our goal is to be the best team in the world, and you do that by winning a gold medal. To get that gold medal, you have to win the final, before that the semi-final, etc. To do that, we need to have the mindset of winning that takes place under the process of performance, so it is a higher ideal. Rather than having a process-oriented mindset, we need to develop the attitude to be winners ... We don't need to change the environment, we need to change the mindset.

Ian believes that the process must be in place before a team can win but what is pivotal is to shift the mindset to being excellent and pursuing winning. Ian explains what this philosophy means for his future teams:

There is a process for performance and there is also a parallel process for winning. What this means for me is that I am not going to change too much, other than putting a different pressure on the players. The priority needs to be the team and the individual in changing the mindset from training to compete, to training to win.

In this process of pursuing winning, many coaches believe that they need a group of people (e.g. sport psychologists, physiotherapists) whose 'expertise' helps the team. Ian's team does draw on the help of 'experts' but Ian believes in being selective about who to involve: those who are recruited must understand and value the team environment, and gain the trust of the team. He gives the reasoning behind this approach:

> ... we don't want to bring somebody in to invent a job for them just because everyone else has one. That is the biggest problem in sport ... this team has one person, this team has another person and therefore we should all have those positions. Why are there some organisations with different terminologies? Why does every sport have a high performance manager? Why don't we think outside the square?

As both a player and a coach, Ian has experienced many a coach at the coach-centred part of the continuum. In his view, it is inaccurate to call them directive coaches—after all, every coach needs to give direction; rather, he argues, these coaches should be labelled dictators. One clear disadvantage that he sees with this approach relates to knowledge. A dictator coach has a finite amount of knowledge, which he or she espouses to athletes. Often observers interpret this behaviour as a sign of an intelligent coach. Yet an athlete-centred coach must have an abundance of knowledge because each athlete thinks differently. When questioned, athletes often come up with the unknown (to the coach) and with great ideas. An athlete-centred coach must be able to analyse such answers, draw out the athlete's knowledge to elaborate, and draw on a multitude of information (some of which might be new to him or her) to help athletes take risks and make innovative decisions. Ian contrasts athlete-centred coaches with dictator coaches in this way:

> [With athlete-centred coaches,] maybe it is as simple as somebody being led to say that they don't know and that they are not afraid of not knowing. Whereas the dictator coaches, in my experience, are people who are afraid of people thinking they don't know. So therefore, they humiliate people. That is deflection technique ... I remember where I was [sitting at] the back of a course ... This person in front of me asked a really good question. It was a challenging question, and was a good point. Instead of saying, 'There is a thousand ways to skin a cat, and my preferred way would be to say, run with that, that's a good idea', the teacher annihilated the person asking the question ... he demonstrated his lack of knowledge by getting personal with the guy who asked the question. I thought, 'You are just making up for a lack of knowledge and you are fearful of people finding out that you don't know what you are talking about'.

Many of Ian's experiences on his journey contributed to his philosophy as a coach. Understanding athletes' needs is a key to how he coaches.

Ian's Development as a Coach

Ian has had an interesting journey to get to his present coaching stage. Responding to my question of why he wanted to be a coach, he says:

> I have always wanted to coach; I always wanted to be a player first … But your playing days don't [last]. I wish I knew then what I know now. I probably was a bit of a frustrated player and wanted to stay involved with sport to give back to the sport that I love and continue to develop the sport, so … when playing fell over, I just thought 'coaching'.

Moreover, as Ian's goal was to be a professional coach, he focused on training to be one. Everything he worked for was to get the ultimate prize of being paid to be a full-time coach:

> I trained myself to be a professional coach. My education and my previous experience, every job and every course I have done, has allowed me to train to be a coach. Some people train to be accountants … I trained to be a coach … I first started to get paid full time in 2001, when Hockey Australia employed me. The funny thing was that I ended up getting paid for hours that I had already done for free for the past few years.

Ian progressed quite quickly through the system: he was only 31 when I interviewed him. He explains his rapid rise in this way:

> … the biggest restraint placed on ourselves is ourselves. I often listen to people I know who believe in a 'pecking order' and in 'hierarchy' and my attitude has always been that I want to accelerate myself through the process by doing as much as I could to improve and find out where I am strong and where I am weak and try to build up [and maintain] some of my strengths and develop my weaknesses. But most people sit back and think they are going to get there through longevity by staying in one position long enough and thinking that by doing that and saying the right things, you get somewhere.

It follows that Ian believes in being proactive in pursuing one's goals:

> My thoughts have always been if you coach and do the best job possible, learn as much as possible, as you come through sport, you actually work with some fantastic coaches. I've always seen myself as grabbing those opportunities. Rather than working with a colleague, I have been a student of him/her and tried to learn as much as possible, as often as possible. It is just something that I love. I think that is why I have accelerated my own development, through education and enjoyment and not believing in any hierarchy …

Some of the coaches in this book are 'carded', meaning that the New Zealand Academy of Sport has identified them as high-performance coaches who need support, which may be financial assistance, professional development or support within the sport. Ian is one of those coaches. About his carding, he says:

I am supported by the Academy, so I use it as one vehicle for my professional and physical development. I use massage and podiatry to keep myself physically fit. When you are coaching, the thing that you neglect most is yourself ... it is so easy to spend time with other people. You are often away from your family and when you get back to the family, you hide from your own deficiencies. So, from a physical point of view, I keep physically fit.

I wondered if Ian has a coach consultant through this 'carded' system, to advise him or help him reflect on his coaching. He replies:

I talk with coaches purely about coaching, philosophies and my performances. You need to respect somebody a lot and understand and appreciate the advice ... Ideally, I would have a 'critical friend', one who I trusted, but realistically, this is difficult due to time. I know, however, that I cannot let time be a distraction and use it as an excuse, I must find this person. There are so many egos in coaching that often you have resistance, so you need to trust people that you work with. At this stage, my focus, in reality, has purely been on my team and not on myself. I am confident with how I operate.

The way that he checks that he is being successful is to:

... look at my key performance indicators every time we come together, or every series or every training session. ... [What these key performance indicators are] depends on the series. One example is for the last series we [Black Sticks] were together, we were working on defensive circles, to focus on our defence and also the effectiveness of our attacking circles. That is just one example [of] training for that period of time. That has usually dropped out of something previously, so we work on that with the players.

At a general level, as a way of assessing the training and measuring whether athletes are learning and moving in the direction set, Ian uses the performance indicators. At a more specific level:

What I do after each training session is to go through a self-reflective process where you ask a whole series of questions, such as 'Could I have done it better? What areas didn't I cover, was I you happy with it? Did the finish reflect the planning?' From there, it gives me the direction for the next game or training. You need to be reflective in your learning. There is never a point when I don't go home and say, 'Oh I could do better'. I walked out of this meeting with you thinking that there is a process that I could have done better.

Coaches working with national teams may have many opportunities for professional development but often are unable to take them up due to the nature of their work. Although Ian finds himself in this situation, he also looks beyond conventional boundaries to identify professional development (PD) in a range of past and present experiences:

PD happens before you become a coach in my mind. In theory, you would like to do a lot more professional development than you are allowed time for. I find it really hard to find the opportunity for PD. For me, coaching development is about watching hockey. I'll watch hockey live, watch it however I can watch it … The last job I had allowed me to go and watch coaches and the two questions I ask, 'Is there something that I can take out of those situations that are positive?', or 'Is there something that I wouldn't do?'. Even when I was a player, I asked myself, 'If I become a coach, would I do that?' or thought, 'When I become a coach, I am not going to do that'. I think coaching is a very unique job because … you are pretty much in operational [mode] for the entire time. When you are a younger coach, before becoming a head coach or full-time coach that is when you have to get your PD done … when you are a young coach and you are learning your trade, (you are always learning) … and are motivated and keen to be a full-time coach … I am not saying it is the best practice, but it is just the reality of the time available to do the right things.

One opportunity for learning that Ian seizes is reading about issues directly or indirectly related to coaching. Although he does not read fiction, he says:

… I am [a] religious reader of books and the more you read, the harder it is to find something that actually isn't verbatim [from other coaches]. I find that [reading books] often reinforces the path you take.

Ian believes that the holistic development of athletes is important and that one of his responsibilities is to teach and speak with development coaches about what this means:

… if you believe in the holistic development of the sport you are involved in and want to make the environment better, you have to make it part of your job. At every possible opportunity, I spend time with development coaches … When we go somewhere; I make myself available to the local organisation and to their coaches. Every coaching course I speak at, I have to get the word out.

Ian has a great ability to find meaningful examples and analogies in relation to coaching development. In discussing the development of junior innovative coaches, for example, he provides this analogy:

It is like driving around the Canterbury Plains and seeing those wind breaks. To me it is just amazing the amount of forethought that went into building wind breaks. The person who put in the original wind breaks is not going to be around long enough to see the effect. It is no different with junior coaching. I won't be around to benefit from developing juniors. That is why I reckon a lot of coaches don't take time to develop juniors. Elite coaches don't have enough time to develop junior sport because it is about surviving the next hurdle, so therefore you look after the people in front of you now. That is not what coaching is all about. That is sad. Ideally you are coming in with a philosophy that you want to make the sport better and all you really need to do is look after the people in front of you. You don't have time to break it all down to reform it because if you do that, you take away from your core job which is to coach the elite people in front of you. But ideally, you could do some special things and look forward if you had the security to do it.

It is evident from Ian's statement and from the comments of other high-performance coaches that, in regard to national sporting achievement, junior coaching is the way forward. Enhancing the holistic development of junior athletes will give future national teams innovative, well-rounded individuals with good decision-making skills as their New Zealand representatives.

Given all of Ian's great advice and insightful contributions on educating coaches, is there anything else he needs to learn about his coaching? He says:

Everything. It's such a dynamic sort of environment that you are constantly changing your coaching. You always read about coaches ... especially the older coaches who have been around for a long time. They look back on their younger experiences and laugh about how they used to do things. So young coaches have got a lot to learn. I think society changes and if you don't change with it [and] change the experience of the athletes, you [will] be left behind, so I have everything to learn about my coaching.

The Process of Establishing a Quality Team Culture

Ian has such refreshing ideas about developing values and attitudes with his athletes. He leads the way in analysing how to set up team culture and ensuring he meets his philosophy of developing athletes who are well-balanced individuals. Ian also believes that having a quality team culture is essential to success. In explaining how his team culture is organised and monitored, Ian focuses first on goals:

I think the most common thing a coach and players share is generally where they want to get to. Both parties want to be the most successful they can be. As for us, we want to be the best team in the world ... That is my goal for the team. The players have the ability to do it, so now it is just a matter of them buying into it and once they have bought into the team goal, they bring their goals into it and we work out what is realistic and what is not realistic. [I ask them] is my goal too over the top for them? Can they handle the pressure I am putting on them by having such an extreme goal?

The players' general answer to such questions, Ian says, is that:

... they enjoy somebody having that much belief in them. They want to be the best team in the world and who doesn't want to be the best team in the world! You can easily sell that. So once we've got that down pat, we just need to make sure that the direction that we take is decided upon. I think coaches should always provide the direction. Where empowerment doesn't work is when trying to build a foundation from scratch; you might get there eventually, but you actually need to accelerate the process, you actually need direction.

Once the direction is agreed upon, Ian asks the players to determine how they will get there. To help this decision-making process, Ian breaks the team into subgroups:

> … like forwards and backs, oldies and youngies … we do it in different ways, just to break up the group thinking a little bit. It is better to have small groups so you actually get people thinking. In big groups, the dominant people function, so we have nothing over a group of five. We just run over situations, from the plays to what values they want to instil. It's more about how they want to be perceived and then we make a check on reality by living up to the values that we put on ourselves.

To introduce the process of designing the values and practices that will enable the Black Sticks to be the best in the world, Ian asks some pertinent questions:

> … how do we want to be perceived? If you are on the sideline watching the Black Sticks training or playing, what do you want observers to see? If you read a newspaper article, how do you want to be perceived or described as?

The subgroup meetings are the first step. The information is then collated and they write up a draft paper for the team and Ian sends the players away to think about what has been written because:

> … I have been involved with teams in the past who have had goals and values and they look great, they take the playbook home, fantastic, and they are all happy with it. Then we put them into the back of our locker and we never see them again. We wanted the values to be something special, something that you could live and breathe and actually demonstrate. So we actually pick terms that could be demonstrated and [made] visible, something we can measure, not necessarily statistically measure, but something we could physically observe and measure … they chose the direction they wanted to take, I just made sure we took the path towards the goal that we decided upon.

The process of establishing these values for the Black Sticks' Olympic campaign took eight months. The team addressed them every time they came together, which was every four weeks during the national season. Because they are a national team, time together outside of games is limited to a few weeks together at camps at different times of the year. To establish the values they took full advantage of such times, as Ian says:

> We had this camp in Christchurch for five weeks. We sat down and dedicated a whole week to it. We did team building and team activities as well. We wanted it to be [part of] the selection criteria.

The values for the Black Sticks for the Olympic campaign were:

> Kaizan, a Japanese word for continual improvement; winning attitude; mental toughness; bravery; courageous communication; the ability to perform and respect ourselves and our vision.

Once established, the Black Sticks put their values and vision on a laminated card. The players carried it around with them to remind them of their campaign. In response to my question about whether the team has a contract or something similar, Ian explains:

> Sometimes you want people to sign a contract, but it is of more value to reinforce it by using it. For example, we want to be one of the most physically fit teams in the world. If people shirk away from that responsibility, they've broken a team value. So we want to make the contract a usable document … Every year, you want to get the players together and create a new set of values as it changes with each different group, players and competition.

To create a quality team culture, Ian believes that athletes must drive the values. This ownership enhances the mental toughness needed in sport as they take ownership to practise the values:

> … it is driven by the players, it really is. I am just there to provide facilitation … the values I buy into as well. Some of the values that they have, I don't agree with, or I might not agree with. I agree with them at the moment, but if you want your players to make decisions and truly believe in empowerment, like [in] any organisation you have to walk out of the room and with compromises. There is no point in walking in and saying, 'I will buy into six of … [those seven values], but the seventh one I am going to do my own thing.'

Ian cannot understand why New Zealanders as a whole are not mentally tough. Believing that New Zealand has a great history of toughness in its ancestry, he is mystified by the lack of a strong desire to be competitive:

> We are not tough in New Zealand. Our ancestors and grandparents were Maori warriors and ANZACs … why would toughness be an issue with New Zealanders? We want the athletes to be mentally tuned, practically smart and be physically ready. We don't want them to be gritty; gritty assumes that you are going lose so you want to be tough losing.

To become mentally tougher, players must live the values and take ownership of and responsibility for contributing to the direction of the established team vision. To ensure the mutually decided values are practised, Ian reinforces them in training:

> We talk about being committed and being brave … I remember one time where we were training and a defensive player had her nose broken in a tackle … [The defender] was so committed in training that she made a tackle and that's how physical our environment gets. We had a meeting after that training session and the team awarded her a box of chocolates in front of the group for being brave, one of the values that the group decided upon …

As to whether the selection criteria for picking players are based on ability or values and attitudes, Ian says:

> … the ideal athlete is someone with a fantastic attitude and … awesome

ability. You can't win without ability … When it comes down to it, my selection criteria for athletes would be in the order of attitude, attendance, application and then ability. Ability at this level is a given, it's assumed. I want good people with good character, that's what I am after. The attitude is important, the attitude to be part of a team and to give something of yourself to the team. Attendance at training is important, you can't improve unless you attend training. The way you apply yourself at training is important. There is no point in just turning up and going through the motions. You need to turn up and want to improve. That is the responsibility of the athlete. We want to provide an environment where learning is paramount, but you also want to provide them with the responsibility to turn up and learn. They have to turn up with the right attitude. Then it comes down to ability. If you've got ability and you haven't got the three above, you are going no place. But without ability, it is pretty hard to go places. Ability is a given, but in my own criteria, it is not the most important.

It is a combination of the less tangible factors of the desire to win and attitude, Ian argues, that makes a great team environment:

I think it is a sign of a successful team environment [when] the players can see where they can go. I think for some of our senior players, if there was no hope of them training hard to be the best team in the world, regardless of how much fun they are having, they wouldn't stick around. They want to be the best team in the world; that is part of it … I'd rather have a winning environment that was fun or exciting to be around, and making progress. To my mind, I don't think you can have long-term sustainable progress without a good environment. The athletes have to be careful when a coach is in it for a short period, they realise that you are only using them.

A promising sign of a good team environment, Ian suggests, is 'if somebody really struggles to tear herself away or doesn't know what to do because they know they are leaving something special'. On the other hand, a problem is signalled where players can easily part from a team temporarily or permanently.

One factor that can contribute to a detrimental team environment is the failure to put good values into practice, as happens in some professional sports, much to Ian's distaste. Ian gives the example of team bonding sessions, which sports like rugby league and rugby union claim to be important to them as a form of team building. In reality, however, such sessions are excuses for those athletes to perpetuate their reputations along with their actual approach to sport and life as selfish athletes who do not make good decisions; they may even be associated with extreme behaviour such as a nasty situation with an Australian rugby league team that had been in the media just before Ian's interview. In describing his 'anti-philosophy' in this regard, Ian points to the wider and long-term ramifications of the 'pack mentality', of which the team bonding session is an example:

… you tell me how those people are good human beings? Where have they learned that? The sport has taught them. Athletes only survive in an environment created for them … then you sit back and listen to sport washing their hands of different people …

This observation leads Ian to identify sport, and specifically the coach, as being at the heart of an athlete's narrow and selfish attitude:

> … the sport has actually created that problem. It is the attitude that people will overlook any discretion because of sporting ability. That is not developing well-rounded human beings … it just develops a use and abuse relationship, and that person who is very good at sport and doesn't care what else they do … [has] a very selfish approach to sport and to life. It is one person using another person to get something. For a coach to use a player to better their own coaching record and the success of the team, they are coaching at the expense of personal integrity.

In contrast, the Black Sticks as a team are bound by their personal integrity. Because they have ownership of their team and their actions reflect the team values, Ian explains:

> We don't have curfews, we don't have late fines, or anything like that. We just expect people to understand human decency.

Ian's Use of Questioning

As emphasised throughout this book, questioning is an important strategy for athlete-centred learning. A particular kind of questioning that Ian uses to develop the decision making of the Black Sticks and to enhance their cognitive processing is *problem solving*. His reasoning is that:

> As these athletes bring so much knowledge and experience to the team, I need to ask questions to gain the ability for the players to make informed decisions within various sporting situations … so by questioning they will be able to learn how to make these decisions.

He gives this example of a typical problem that he sets up for the team:

> In this situation we need to achieve A, so what are the options available to you so you can do A? What are the options available if you don't do it?

In my observations of a couple of Black Sticks training sessions, it was obvious that one of the greatest tools Ian uses to develop decision making is asking questions and applying Teaching Games for Understanding (TGfU; see below) by setting problems for the athletes to answer. He discusses the process that he thought was his initial learning about questioning, during which he realised that he has been using the strategy all along:

> … I read something about questioning and I thought … 'I don't question enough. I need to question, but I don't know the logistics of how to question.' For example, I didn't know what an open-ended question was. I didn't know what a leading question was … but [I came to realise that] I have been questioning, it's an area that I am really interested in but I have not been

conscious of, which is hard because most of what I do I am quite conscious of. I know I ask questions … but only just recently I started questioning my questioning technique … I was surprised with all the definitions and examples that were laid down in [a] book, but I follow most of the techniques to questioning and discovered that I could do certain things more, but on the whole I am pleased with my questioning.

As well as using questioning, he can articulate clearly his reasons for doing so:

… I want to check understanding, that assumption thing. I do it a few ways too; you don't just do it verbally. You can do a 'show me' activity where the players demonstrate the answers. I give players feedback books where they write down any questions that they have raised. That's an opportunity for them to put their hand up … If there are players asking questions or challenging the coach, sometimes their ego gets in the way and they don't want to show that they don't know it … I think for me to see whether I am on the mark and also to test the knowledge of the players and to make them think about their decisions. Sometimes they can't answer it, they have to go away and think about it, [e.g. to answer my question,] 'Why do you think we do this?'

One of the many important techniques in questioning is for the coach to refrain from answering for the athletes. The coach must give the athletes time to digest and understand the question, then time to think about the answer. Ian says although the length of silence required can be difficult for coaches:

… you have to feel comfortable during those uncomfortable times of silences. I reckon it is a true bit of advice because I think that when I ask questions, the thinking takes time and as a coach, you want thinking activity … As a naive coach, I used to feel uncomfortable by those silences and I would give the answers. Now, I just sit tight and allow players valuable thinking time and then get the players to answer.

Ian also advises coaches to plan their questions. It is important to have a purpose to the series of questions, an answer that needs to be resolved:

… If you have got purpose to a subject, you have to have a plan for questions. I think if you have no plan for questioning, you won't know what the problem is. You have a coaching plan, a training plan; you have to have a questioning plan. I think having an awareness of the coaching points [is important]. I still [see other coaches] who don't use training plans … Even if you are working with a mentor coach, you need to have training plans. I ask my students, 'Out of this drill, what are the coaching points that you are trying to achieve?' You need to plan that. Somebody had a simple drill set up the other day and asked the mentor coach to give them an example of each of the coaching points. He couldn't answer what they were … you have to understand coaching points to ask the right questions.

Ian and Teaching Games for Understanding

I observed Ian using TGfU (or Game Sense) in several different ways. The purpose of all the games he used in training was to work on a particular strategy in hockey. Sometimes he stopped the game and asked a few questions; sometimes he let the athletes play the game several times and then had them discuss the situation. In explaining the fundamental reason why he uses TGfU, he pinpoints the complexity of hockey:

> Our sport has such a dynamic environment. We can move in three dimensions. We've got 22 people on the field, all doing different things. There are plenty of skills involved, but it is such a [complex] game that as soon as you start to assume it is simple, it puts pressure on the players because you don't understand the pressure they are under. So for us the biggest thing about hockey is decision making ...

Recognising the implications of this complexity for training, reinforced by his dissatisfaction with the training environment he had experienced as a player, Ian shaped his own coaching accordingly:

> To me as a player, the training environment never actually replicated the complicated [nature] and sophisticatedness of the game. So, when I became I coach, I wanted my athletes to experience the complicatedness of the game, giv[ing] them options to be able to make decisions ... I have a set of options that I prefer the athlete to take and we actually train those options, to give them coping mechanisms ... The only way to do it is to provide them with multi-stimulated training drills or training exercises. So one of the things in hockey is that under pressure you can freeze, and in turn become indecisive. So how you train decisiveness or how you set up decision-making drills is how I got into Game Sense or decision making ...

Ian believes that TGfU has learning value for training children's sport but that the fundamentals are equally important:

> I reckon that in a lot of junior coaching, they spend too much time on the technical and we get technically very good players, but not good decision makers. The opposite also happens; we are giving them so much time making decisions that they can't hold a stick properly. Unfortunately, our game is very technical, so it is a balance between the technical and the tactical. Ideally when people have got all the information, you can do pure Game Sense.

The problem he identifies is a lack of balance to training as directed by the many coaches who design boring drills to work on the hockey fundamentals:

> ... you need to spend more time allowing the kids to learn the skill. Children think that repetitive skill learning is boring. That is because the delivery is boring. You need to make a purpose to the drill and make a challenge ... our players will practise the basic skills for a lot longer than most other people

do … If you live by the old credo that the basics are important, you shouldn't get bored by doing it. All we do is make it a challenge for the players … we actually see that they are getting bored with this drill, so then it is time to switch and work with a partner and put the pressure on …

As Ian sees it, achieving the right balance when coaching children means that:

… we actually need to spend good quality time teaching them the technical part of the game, but we also need to spend time for kids to give them the applied part … I want the players to be very good technically, but I don't judge them in isolated technical environment. I actually assess them in the heat of the battle, whether they can apply the skill.

Ian reinforces that using TGfU or similar tactical strategies actually shows that coaches understand their sport. He suggests:

New Zealand is very big on technical and physical development of their athletes which is extremely important. Unfortunately, that is the level of knowledge that coaches have. Therefore, they are afraid to work with the athlete in areas that they are not strong on, which is the tactical and mental development of our game.

The Black Sticks respond well to TGfU, but Ian highlights that it is not sufficient to introduce games to training; instead, the coach must develop games that specifically allow for athlete learning:

[The Black Sticks] like playing, that is what they train for, to play in the game. I always say if you come and watch our team training, most of the time it looks like they are playing … the bad part of Game Sense is that people just play games, they just play and there is no actual development or learning. There has to be a purpose to the game … We want to reinforce the things we are trying to achieve out of TGfU. You want to accelerate the time that you have together … Every training activity has to be purposeful and have meaning. Players get frustrated with no purpose. I think if athletes can't see a purpose to a drill or game, they want to know why we are doing it. But if they see the purpose in it, they'll walk on hot coals to do it.

In other words, Ian's thoughtful approach to TGfU underpins the Black Sticks' responsiveness to it.

Implementing an Athlete-centred Approach

Ian has a sound background in sport coaching from his study at university. As he remembers it, however, player empowerment did not feature in his university course work. Instead:

… when I was going through university it was more about abusive substances, arousal theory, team dynamics and team culture. It wasn't necessarily about team ownership. I think empowerment is probably more of a mid nineties onwards thing … I have definitely been aware of player empowerment, but it is not something that I read once or twice and said, 'This is how I want to operate' …

Even without a strong theoretical background in empowerment, though, Ian supports an athlete-centred approach with the Black Sticks because:

… the players are adults, our team is taking responsibility for their own actions, so they are responsible for the decisions they make. With an athlete-centred approach they get the opportunity to make decisions that they will be held accountable for.

So where did his belief in athlete-centred coaching spring from? Did it have anything to do with his own experience of coaches who were dictatorial? Ian reflects:

I know people say to me, 'How do you motivate your team, do you yell at them?' When this question is asked, that person must have a real primitive understanding of coaching if he/she thinks that is how a coach operates … I have had those [dictator] coaches all along … what I learned from all of them is what *not* to do. I remember as a player thinking, 'When I become a coach … I am not going to do that. I am not going to treat my players that way. I am not going to run my training that way. I am not going to do my debriefs that way' … I know how my teammates felt and how I felt about that approach. I reckon coaching should be about accelerating the development of your players. That has been my goal … how I can accelerate the development of my team? … the fact that the players have done really well in an exceptional amount of time, it's great. Their development has been accelerated.

When I then start to explore where Ian has gained the confidence to use the athlete-centred approach, he identifies a range of sources from his childhood to his accumulated coaching experience:

… I always ask myself this question, where do I get the tenacity to be brave? … If you are going to do the job and be successful, you have to do it your way. If you are going to fail, you might as well fail doing it your way … If you are going to be successful, you do it your way and you take great confidence out of each time you step up to the challenge. My attitude is always live by the sword, die by the sword and that is why if I am going to go down, I am going to go down my way, then I can take confidence out of that … I suppose it was the fact that my mum told me she had confidence and believed in what I was doing as a kid, that is probably where I get the confidence … you take confidence out of knowing that you can work with other people. Then you still have to have the conviction to do it yourself.

Perhaps having such confidence is part of what being a coach is. After all, as Ian points out, coaching is a role that demands fearlessness in many fundamental respects:

When you think about the philosophy of coaching, it's uncharted territory and I don't think you can show fear of looking back. If you've got people following you, it's like a new frontier ... the philosophy of New Zealand hockey, winning the gold medal would be lovely for us. It might never be done, but we are going for it.

Finally, in reflecting on some of the interview questions, Ian observes that a variety of people and ideas have contributed to his journey in which he has developed his own version of an athlete-centred approach:

... To improve in certain areas, you operate consciously and then you get to the state of operating unconsciously ... It's rare that any ideas you use are exactly your own ... You do a lot of reading and observation and you have to take the good and bad of everybody and put your own personality on it. Every person who you come into contact with moulds you with how you operate. It's subconscious.

The Process of Empowering Players

Before Ian introduced an athlete-centred approach to the women's hockey team, they hadn't really been coached by someone who asked them what they think. As Ian describes it:

... When I first came on board, the players were still very much in the stage of cognitive development as a team. You could just see the big wheels grinding every time. They'd go out and I think they were so keen to impress; for example, I'd ask them to transfer the ball and they would spend the entire game transferring the ball, not realising that ... they needed to pick out the optimum [situation] where we are doing this because it creates this, or we are doing A to create B. They did A because the coach wanted them to do A.

The process of changing the mindset of the players—developing them and encouraging them to solve problems and understand situations so that they could make decisions—Ian sees as a positive:

... I didn't see it as a negative that they were very restrictive but, with development, I knew that we were going to get to the automatic stages of performing, that we needed to go through a very cognitive stage initially and that would mean decision making and performance errors ... In the last 12 months, we have seen this rusty, grinding team become more fluent. We are pretty much at the stage now where we are very fluent.

To athletes who have never been enabled to make decisions, the process can be unnerving. Yet Ian has total confidence in the players, which is an important element to empowering them:

I am really impressed by how quickly the players have learned and picked things up ... They've been conditioned for such a long time not to make decisions and to just follow set options. Now I have to teach them by providing them the environment that allows them to make their own decisions and not the decisions preferred by the coach … at the elite level most coaches have to spend a lot of times re-coaching people, because what has happened in the development stages hasn't been appropriate.

When implementing empowerment it is important to have the athletes understand that the coach intends to use an athlete-centred approach and what the implications are: that the coach will ask questions, will care about the answers and will include athletes in the decision-making process. Ian expressed his satisfaction with what he considers to be successful implementation of his coaching approach:

I take great satisfaction out of … the pride in knowing that you have the ability to get people to do a certain thing … Then they take that pride into doing it as well. As long as they can see the benefit, I think our athletes will buy into being empowered. If they don't understand the benefits, they don't know why they are doing it, they will do it but they do it because the coach wants them to do it. If you explain the purpose behind asking questions, what you are trying to achieve from using such an approach and how it is going to make them a better team, by [encouraging] the individual to achieve a goal, then that is when the athlete buys into it. Until you actually get to that stage, they don't really buy into the approach … or dedicate themselves to the task. But when they understand that this way will make us a better team, allow us to win and allow [the athlete] to achieve [her] dreams, that is when she buys in … she has to see how this is going to make her achieve her dream and justify the sacrifices she has made.

In implementing an athlete-centred approach with the Black Sticks, Ian believed his team had a good chance of winning an Olympic gold medal. For such a major competition, athletes do not go to develop their skills and expand their experience; they go to try to win. The campaign for the Athens Olympics presented a good challenge to the Black Sticks. Certainly they were in something of development period but, as Ian reiterates, 'I think the present team is the best team available to win Olympic gold medal'. However, development constituted a successful outcome even if it is not the purpose. Moreover, he saw the team's success—whatever form it took—as inevitable:

There is no bad outcome for us. If we win, that's great. We need to make semi-finals to be in with a medal chance, but if we come dead last, we will still be a young team that we can take through to 2008. Part of trainability is making sure that you can sustain some part of your player numbers. The Australian team that won three consecutive gold medals were together for probably 10 years of their lives. The Argentinean side, who are current world champions, have been together for eight years. In 1996, they came eighth in the Olympics. It is pretty much the same team … that is why I am really happy with our team, because we have enough talent to be successful now, but we have also got enough youth to be successful in the future. We have people that are going to be around. That is the important part of sport, so the expectations are always high, I know that the motivation behind the team will make it successful wherever we come.

Part of the team's motivation is likely to come from Ian's consistent practice of including the athletes in making decisions on what they want to do or whether they are on the right track: I always ask the athletes what they require. If you want to see whether the picture you have in your mind is what the team is developed, much of that is what the players want. Every probably seven weeks, I ask the players, 'Over the next two weeks or next week or when you leave the camp, what do you want to be able to achieve?' The biggest thing that players suffer is … [when] their performance is due to a lack of preparation. So, if you ask the athletes where they need to improve on or what areas you want to spend the next eight sessions on, they'll tell you.

So does Ian think his players know more than he does? He responds to my question in this way:

> I hope so. I don't assume they don't know anything. It's something I have never thought about, to be honest. I don't think that I am superior, or I am perfect or I am the world leader in what I do. I hope that the players bring something as well. They all have different experiences. We want to cut into the experience that they have had.

Pivotal to an assessment of an athlete-centred coaching approach is the athletes' response to it. Ian's reflection in regard to the Black Sticks is that:

> I think they respond well. I have seen them defending well, I see them getting on, I see them quite happy … I did a presentation in Dunedin to coaches and they came and watched the warm-up and a training session. I was pretty much down one end and the players were warming up on the other end. The players were just having a fantastic time. This was training before meeting India the next day. I remember looking down at the players and hearing them laughing and really enjoying and working really hard in their warm-up and I thought that that was great … When you are dealing with elite athletes, they have already made sacrifices in their life, just because of who they are. You have to keep the fun; it has to be part of sport.

In his presentation of this training session, one point that Ian noticed was that the observing coaches did not pick up on the team culture, even after prompting from him:

> I asked [the observing coaches] afterwards, 'What did you notice about them having their warm-up?' They told me, 'The drills they did'. And I said, 'Well what about the environment?' They couldn't answer the question, but I said, 'Did you not hear the players laughing? Did you not hear them having a good time? Did you not hear them about their excitement?'

Another important concept in the process of empowering athletes is enabling them to have flair. Flair is what makes a good athlete, great. Ian describes it in this way:

> I think we have to define what flair is within the team because being selfish is not flair … Flair is a person making a brave decision which is outside the normal of what is expected of them, but not making a decision which is

self-serving. We often spend time talking about flair and what it is. You don't want to coach flair out of players, but you want to coach selfishness out of players. Sometimes people make decisions in frustration, which is being selfish. I think probably, there are certain things from your own experiences that you find successful, so you actually coach towards those things. But the players are always opening their eyes; the borders are movable.

A dictatorial coaching approach is less likely to encourage flair as athletes are often expected to behave robotically and are not allowed to take risks. It is well known amongst educators that learning occurs through taking risks and making mistakes. Certainly some options have been discovered as best practice, but other solutions or practices have not been discovered or used yet (novel situations). In an athlete-centred approach, coaches believe in practising these novel situations (the intention of TGfU), which gives athletes the opportunity to make errors in order to learn. In applying the approach to hockey, where every situation in a game is novel, Ian underpins athlete decision making with a strong sense of accountability:

> … you have options for making decisions. There are some preferred ways, there are the black and white ways, but you turn them grey. What we say to the players is that you can make any decision that you like in regards to what we are working towards, in lines with these options but, if you go outside the options, it has to be successful and, if it is not successful, you have to be accountable for it …

There is room within this approach for working on poor skills but, for Ian, the way that the coaching focus is prioritised is important:

> You coach habits before you redirect bad habits. If something poor happens once, fine, I won't talk about it. If it happens twice, we think about it and talk about it, but if it is three or four times, then you coach it out of them. We use Sports Code [a computer game analysis programme] and give every single play a description in this code … The players don't see the information, only I see it. I never give the players their completion rates, because they would play to the statistics rather than to the real dynamic nature of the game. If I sit down and watch it and see five incompletes for a defensive player and out of those incompletes, for four they were indiscrepancies of the game, that's okay. The things that interest me are the things that are habitual … all our team tactics have been derived to try to expose the opposition's bad habits, or to diminish our own bad habits … We will look at the bad habits and fix them and turn them into good habits or redirect the decision making into something more desirable.

One practice of athlete-centred coaches is to share leadership within their team. It is a practice that Ian says he promotes:

> We split our teams up into groups and ask them to do a SWOT [strengths, weaknesses, opportunities and threats] analysis of our team, our positions

and our processes. Where can we be better? We want the players to have ownership over their environment. We split up into groups that are workable … we actually want people to be heard. We talk about people being leaders for their position, so we have 11 leadership positions.

So, if he believes in shared leadership, why do the Black Sticks have a captain and a vice captain? Ian explains:

We named a captain and vice captain … we have 16 leaders in our team … [but] in my mind a captain is somebody who is an extension of what the team stands for—the summary sheet, … the abstract. If we had to describe a typical Black Sticks player, [we would say that] she lives and breathes the team values. She is somebody who is well respected by all the players. Given that we have a regional profile within the community, it's important that the community has someone to identify with. To me our current captain is that person … I think the reason why I wanted her to be captain was because she reflects the team values and she operates in the best practice in pretty much everything she does. That's really putting her on a pedestal and saying to all the younger athletes, 'We want you to operate like her.'

Ian admits that all these expectations can put pressure on the captain in various ways, but there are also strategies in place for dealing with those pressures:

… when it diminishes her performance, that's when she is focusing on everybody else … There was an experience … in a game, where she was concerned about the team's preparation so much that she played terrible in the first half. The team played quite well around her, but she was probably the worst for us. She is learning. It does put pressure on her … If it puts pressure on her from a media point of view, I talk to her. We need to make sure there is nothing destructive and then she honestly must say what she can't handle. We pretty much share that role around. We have other players on board who they want to talk to. We ask [the media] to respect our own performance environment, so no phone calls unless they know the cut-off period. There is a time when they can ring. So there is definitely pressure on her, but we just need to make sure that we are communicating with each other to make sure that we can alleviate the pressure that she is under.

Ian aims to develop the responsibility of every player in the Black Sticks. In many teams with one named captain, other players are known to shirk their responsibility, deferring instead to the captain. However, Ian is not deterred by this potential. He reasons that leadership is clearly distinct from captaincy, pointing to research that shows shared leadership rather than shared captaincy increases group productivity. Under the approach to leadership that he has implemented, any shirking is soon evident:

There is opportunity for people to shirk, there is no doubt, but it shows up in their performance. For our team, the reason why we play the way we do is that everyone is required to perform a certain role. If we have a role-playing team when we do great play, somebody has executed their role or a combination of people have executed their roles in a desirable fashion to get the desired outcome. If we play the set play, or we get a goal scored against us, it's because somebody hasn't achieved their role, or a superior play has occurred ... For us, that is leadership. We will actually go back and assess who didn't execute their role in a particular play and then it becomes an educational situation. It provides a direction of learning, it is just a habit. She has to justify, 'Oh look I just got out of position because I didn't know what I was supposed to do there'. If somebody doesn't stand up and take ownership of her role, then it is obvious by the way we play ... the person furthest away from the ball could be the shirker then everything else falls down. It is beautiful. If we do everything well, we have to play as a team, we can't hide individual weak decision makers. We can't hide a lack of leadership. Leadership is a good one.

Our interview also covered a more comparative discussion of coaching approaches in relation to the age and developmental level of a team. Ian's view is that:

In under 15s, well you change, but you adapt, but they definitely learn. I think being self-reflective is important. My general philosophy, whether I am coaching under 15 boys' hockey or whether I am coaching the New Zealand women's hockey team, the approaches are the same ... you change the language you use; the processes don't change ... what you do differently is that you are working with a different audience. So therefore you have to know your audience and what they require ... with children ... you want to make it exciting for them.

Expanding on the theme of children in sport, Ian discusses the problematic nature of adult influence:

I believe that the biggest problem in kids' sport is adults. You go down to the park and watch kids play; the thing that interferes with the sport is adults. The kids have been playing there for half an hour and then the adults come along and they want to complicate the situation, for example they say, 'There are not enough rules, there are not enough bibs ...'

One obvious implication for coaches is that they need to be highly aware of their influence and to have strategies for channelling it effectively. Ian suggests that the best coaches should be coaching children because quality coaching is important to children's development:

... the best coaches should be coaching kids. That would be ideal. I know that in the current model of New Zealand hockey, they are trying to get that thinking to the national coaches ... that the children understand the terminologies of how we operate, so when they become elite athletes, they will already be developed.

Some Challenges of an Athlete-centred Approach

One of the major challenges for a coach using an athlete-centred approach is to ensure that athletes are well prepared, developed and have holistically learned to play hockey. In every sport, the public and media put pressure on coaches, but the biggest pressure comes from the coach himself or herself. As Ian says:

> I know it does have to come from the athletes but at the qualifying tournament, I was a bit concerned that if I didn't live up to my job, I would let the athletes down, athletes who have worked so hard to achieve their dream … It is a big responsibility … that was the biggest pressure on me. I was fearful that all the athletes might not be able to achieve their dreams because of something down to my decision making or how we went as a team. That scared me the most; it motivated me though to make sure that I do the best job possible for the sake of the athletes.

Ian also elaborates on the emotional cost involved in using an athlete-centred approach when he must deliver bad news to a player:

> … the way I operate is … [to be] very personable and unfortunately in elite sport you've got to make some decisions that impact on people's lives. It's actually tough to give messages to people you like. It's something you have to live with. You spend so much time and energy developing individuals to make them the best they can be. There are so many times a year where you actually have to tell that person that they are not up to it, or remind them that they are not up to it for whatever reason. That's the hardest part … if you want your athletes to work well in that environment; you have to give something of yourself to them … you have to become connected with the athletes on a personal point of view, you get to know them, and they get to know you.

So when he must deliver bad news to a player, is he honest? Ian says:

> Definitely. Not brutally honest, I am honest. You have to justify your decisions. You get paid to justify your decisions, so why wouldn't you be honest about it? If the athlete doesn't like what they hear, then that is unfortunate, at least you are all on the same page then. I think at the time, they don't want to hear it, but if you have coached them right and been up front with them throughout the process then you have been true to the player. If you haven't been true to her, you've actually been a coward and hidden behind your position. My athletes know this from day one. As soon as I know who's been picked, I know their strengths, I know their weaknesses. If an athlete is on the border line of being in or out, they definitely know what they have to do to maintain that position … They might not like what they hear, but in the end they'll respect you for being open with them …

The toughest situation, for Ian, is where he must tell a player that she has not made the team, even though she is good enough, because 'selection just comes down to numbers'.

As Ian sees it, the greatest pitfall for an athlete-centred coach is to be indecisive:

> I think the biggest trip-up is not making decisions, asking people what they think all the time, freezing as you do. At different stages you have to say, 'I think this is what we are going to do'. But then, you explain the rationale behind it the thing that you are about to do. I think people might not agree with you all the time, but if they understand why you are making a decision, that helps them to become part of it. I give the players information about everything ...

It follows too that a coach can fall into the trap of assuming that people have skills in decision making that they don't have:

> I am not saying that people can't, but we assume that people have the skill set to be able to go through it ... I am a big advocate for showing belief in people and therefore giving people the opportunity to do their job as best they can ... one of the pitfalls is that you can actually make more work for yourself if you assume they can do it and you don't give them enough direction or lead ... to do their job ... that's why the sporting environment can become a breeding ground for a dictatorship because if they haven't done the job properly, you do it yourself.

The potential for dictatorship relates to a final pitfall for an athlete-centred coach that Ian identifies—namely, the risk of a lack of balance:

> If we do too much coaching and [give] too much direction and you become a dictator, or if you get too relaxed and the athletes get too much empowerment [and] then there is a lack of direction, that lack of balance is a pitfall ...

Conclusion

Ian has provided some wonderful insights into how he coaches and, specifically, the type of athlete-centred approach he uses with the Black Sticks. It is great to see his emphasis on continuing his own learning through self-reflection on his coaching. This self-reflection was obvious when he acknowledged his change of mindset after the Olympics. This is a sign of a learned coach.

Ian's central focus is on his athletes—on making them the best they can be, both on and off the field. His attention to values and attitudes of players and personal integrity will benefit his athletes and enable him to win with grace. He advocates a balanced lifestyle, in which the coach teaches athletes holistically and encourages them to be more than just hockey players.

I really enjoyed the analogies Ian came up with in our interviews. He has a deep understanding of how life experiences and life lessons influence the capabilities of his team and players. Due to his prolific reading, he always seeks innovative tools and methods to enable his athletes to learn. He continues to seek an understanding of sport and its role in society and, to his credit, he practises what he preaches.

For success, attitude is
equally as important as
ability. – *Harry F. Banks*

Chapter Seven

Mike McHugh
Basketball Coach

Mike McHugh currently coaches the Wellington Saints, a New Zealand National Basketball League team, and is assistant coach to the Tall Ferns, the New Zealand women's basketball team. He also works for Sport and Recreation New Zealand (SPARC) as the national coaching consultant. I first observed and interviewed Mike at a Junior Tall Ferns camp held in Auckland. Later in the year, I also observed Mike working with the Wellington Saints.

This chapter represents Mike's thinking and practice as a long-serving coach. He describes how it started:

> Unlike a lot of people who go into coaching, it was purely by accident … I was only about 19 years old at the time and I was playing in a regional tournament in Australia for my hometown team [Griffith, New South Wales] in the men's competition, and the women's team didn't have a coach. Someone asked [me], 'Can you help coach?' So, just to help out the team, I coached through this tournament. We won the tournament and I was asked to coach the regional team (all-star team) at the NSW Championships … We went to the NSW state divisional championships and made the final against Bankstown, who had two or three former national players. They beat us, but not by much, but anyway, I kind of got the urge from there.

While running his signwriting business, Mike continued to coach, including several state representative teams. Then in the mid 1980s, 'the opportunity came along to work with a NSW representative boys' team at the national championships'.

As Mike gained a passion for coaching, he realised that he would have to change his life direction, as he was a businessman who needed to earn a living, coaching was his hobby and he was a volunteer. Mike discusses his willingness to make sacrifices for the love of coaching:

> … then came a point in my life where it was, 'Are you going to be a coach who works or are you going to be a businesvsman who coaches as a hobby?' … By this time, coaching had just become totally a passion for me. I was working to support coaching, rather than the other way around. I lived in a small country town; our training sessions for NSW state representative teams were in Sydney. In those days, it was an eight-hour drive to practice, an eight-hour drive home. Later on, I tended to fly because it was just too demanding. You would do that for three months at a time, every weekend … and I had a business to run, but I was often away. I estimate in those days, it used to cost me about $5000 a year to coach, along with the time. I had a young family, two young sons who were both brilliantly raised by my wife.

The change of direction came just two weeks after he took up the position of development officer in Lithgow, New South Wales. He was offered another job as head coach as one of Basketball Australia's Intensive Training Program (the first one) in Bendigo, Victoria: it was the opportunity for Mike to live his dream of coaching as a paid job. Though he missed his family who chose to stay in Lithgow after the big move there, he met with great success as a basketball coach in Victoria Country. As Mike recalls it:

> … within a year, [Victoria Country] went from having no structured development programmes to having a very effective player and coach development programme. Country Victoria had a history of having great talent but no structured development systems. I stayed in that programme for five years and by the end of that programme Victoria Country kids made up almost half of the scholarships to the AIS [Australian Institute of Sport]. On the national women's team who won the world championship in 1993, there were four Victoria Country girls. I also coached the under 16 boys one year; the Vic Country boys finished runners up. And I coached the under 18 girls in another year and we won the national championship title.

Despite the phenomenal success, however, Mike sees his role in it as being the coach in the right place at the right time:

> I was extremely proud of what we had achieved in a short time, but would point out that there was a conveyer belt of talent there just waiting for someone to come along. I happened to be the fortunate person.

After coaching coaches and his stint with Victoria Country, Mike was asked by national women's coach Tom Maher to apply for a coaching position at the Australian Institute of Sport and was subsequently offered the position. He moved his family to Canberra to take up this new challenge:

> The next five years, I worked solely with elite athletes in an elite environment. We travelled two or three times a year internationally, we played in the women's national league. Each day, you would work with some of the best players and some of the best coaches in the country, the best sport scientists in the world, the whole programme. It was a tremendous period of growth, both personally and professionally for me.

Next Mike coached the Canberra Capitals, a women's national basketball team. Mike felt his role was to build up the team:

> They were a team who had limited resources at that time … some good young players and some good local players, but they had never done particularly well, usually a good middle-of-the-road team, apart from 1992, when they made the finals. I realised it was a long-term building project.

True to his intention, he was responsible for recruiting some strong players and built up the base of the team. Since then the Canberra Capitals have been successful, as Mike says:

We built a good core of players and then recruited an iconic player in Australian women's basketball, Shelley Sandie. Her recruitment then enabled the club to get players like Lauren Jackson and Kristen Veal, at that time the two brightest prospects in the country.

At that stage, the club brought another coach into the programme (Carrie Graf), which Mike sees as creating new opportunities for himself:

… to go to the ACT Academy of Sport … I went back to coaching developing athletes … I had two squads, an ITCP [Intensive Training Centre Program] squad (14- to 17-year-olds) and an 18- to 24-year-old squad, both males and females through that period. Also I was on the coaching staff with the Opals … working with Tom Maher and Carrie Graf, Jenny Cheesman, Phil Brown and Jan Sterling, all great coaches. This experience allowed me see what happened at the international level and I could transfer that back to the athletes I was working with.

Mike's next adventure began when he accepted a job with SPARC in New Zealand:

… in one week, my whole life changed. I was contacted by an employment agency advising of the position, flew over here for an interview on the Thursday; by the following Monday, I was contacted and informed that I was the preferred candidate, which meant another lifestyle decision that we had to make as a family. We enthusiastically chose to come to New Zealand and I now have a great job with SPARC, developing and implementing a coaching strategy for New Zealand, and I believe we are going to make a difference for coaching in this country. I am working daily with great people, like Don Tricker, Paul Ackerley and Waimarama Taumaunu and coaches and sports throughout New Zealand.

In addition to this job, Mike kept busy with his coaching career. At the stage of our interview Mike had been coaching the Wellington Saints for two years, had begun to develop juniors through the Junior Tall Ferns, and had been appointed as an assistant coach to the Tall Ferns. Interestingly, although his move to New Zealand was motivated by his desire to develop coaches, his passion for coaching continued and he got drawn back to work at the coal face. He explains how each of his coaching roles gradually built up again:

I didn't come over here to coach. I came over here to develop a parallel career path. Anyway, I was asked if I'd be interested in coaching the Saints when their coach suddenly resigned. I had no intention of taking on a bad coaching experience, so I went and watched [the Wellington Saints] practice sessions for a week. What impressed me was that the players were a hard-working group that just seemed to lack a bit of direction and support, so I agreed to do it for a year. From being 2 [wins]–4 [loses], we strung together an eight-game winning streak and ended up winning the national championship.

I was always going to help out with the Junior Tall Ferns, just because I believe very much that if you don't have effective development streams in the junior area, how are we going to have good senior players? So I wanted to help with that. That programme was going to be my little hobby coaching experience and then the Tall Ferns opportunity came along.

Since my time with Mike at the Junior Tall Ferns camp, he had to leave the Junior Tall Ferns because he was overcommitted and needed to devote more time to the Tall Ferns in their Olympic year. The Tall Ferns performed well at the Athens Olympics, playing above their own expectations.

Mike has had many great coaching experiences. When I ask him which he considers his favourite, he reflects:

I think you continually draw on your experiences, good and bad. As I said, sometimes, they weren't all great coaching experiences, but I learned a lot from [them]. Coaching the Canberra Capitals in the WNBL [Women's National Basketball League] at a time when we had a young team that got beaten almost every game, was personally very difficult but, looking back, a great learning environment. Each week you could see incremental improvement and you knew that down the track, if you could stick it out, ... they'd get over the hump. That was hard, because you would see those kids lose a lot and you were trying to keep their spirits up, help them learn to play the game, and to experience play at that level ... I learned so much, not only professionally, but personally, a maturity that comes with hard lessons. Obviously the Saints' NBL championship and the Athens experience [with the Tall Ferns] were highlights.

Mike believes strongly that experience helps create better coaches. He certainly has had some great experiences from which he has learned.

Mike's Philosophy of Coaching

Mike believes that winning is important. He uses his coaching repertoire to enhance athletes' learning so that they can achieve that outcome of winning. Everything he throws into coaching and athlete learning is for the purpose of achieving that outcome. Winning is one of the two reasons why he says he coaches:

What drives me is that I want to teach people to play the sport technically well, I want them to be able to perform effectively, at a high level, but I also have a very competitive streak that drives me to coach to win too. I believe winning develops high self-esteem, and provides performance and life goals to achieve; winning gives you reasons to celebrate the things you do in your life and in a team environment, share those achievements. There is a whole bunch of good reasons to win rather than lose; underachievement is not something that I personally subscribe to. It also is relative to the environment you are working in; at the professional level, evaluations of success are entirely based on performance outcomes and do not acknowledge limitations. You are a prisoner of your win–loss record.

The second reason behind Mike's coaching has a broader focus:

> However, when you are working with developing athletes, your philosophy and commitment also has to include the development of the person along with sporting performance. You are coaching within a recognised range of constraints such as age, time, place and organisational situation

Mike coaches according to the need of the team with which he is involved. For professional teams and junior teams, it is all about the process used to develop athletes – an athlete-centred approach:

> I have thought about what coaching is for the best part of my working life. I think now I understand the elements essential to doing it well. By far the best way is keeping it simple. I guess this means I have been around long enough to know how to identify character differences and how that impacts on your interpersonal skills. [For example,] the Tall Ferns are going to the Olympics, how do you define achievable goals and compete proficiently in the best tournament in the world? Given our status in world basketball, you can't focus on winning a medal; in reality that mountain is too high. Your objectives have to focus on the athlete and on process, to achieve the highest placing we can by concentrating on the process rather than the outcome. It is also about representing your country in a manner that reflects the sports psyche of your country. This is where you become athlete focused, for them to learn to be able to perform effectively at the international level is certainly a goal for the coaches ... So I think that you've got to be able to focus the coaching performance on the particular situation, you focus on winning in some situations, and you always focus on the development of the athlete.

Mike believes that creating a coaching philosophy is important in itself:

> Coaching is a means of self-expression. Determining and formalising your philosophy is therefore a principal undertaking; a coach must decide before anything else what it is he or she wants to say about him/herself through the sport.

When asked to elaborate on his philosophy of coaching, Mike begins by identifying the centrality of coaching fundamental skills:

> I think firstly you have to have a good understanding of and the ability to teach the fundamental skills of the sport, for a lot of good reasons. Firstly, if you can develop good basic skills in your athletes, then they will be successful in the game, at whatever level they play, which leads to two things. One, they will enjoy the sport experience and also they will have some longevity in the sport ... The other value of this philosophy is that when you get to the champion athlete, and they are well developed fundamentally, they can survive at any level of competition. The first thing that is exposed under pressure is a lack of fundamental skills. They are punished very quickly at the highest levels. So, every player that I come in contact with, I want to teach them to have

good fundamentals because I know I am doing the best thing for them for all those reasons ... players can survive and enjoy and flourish in the game if they have good fundamental skills, whatever sport it is.

Though fundamental physical skills are extremely important to Mike's way of coaching, he suggests that cognitive learning is also important:

... it is not what I know; it is what [the athletes] know that is important. So I have to build an extensive knowledge base in order to impart that information to them; they have to be able to use that knowledge on the court. I have to develop the skills to impart that information in a way that is easily accessed by my athletes. That's where teaching them to be decision makers, teaching them to understand the appropriateness of the play in every situation and every environment is essential.

Physical conditioning is a third important component of Mike's beliefs about what athletes need to learn in basketball or any other sport:

... you have to be in a very, very heightened state of physical conditioning if you want to be successful, so achieving the level of physical conditioning required for the level of competition is extremely important ... the thing about being in great physical shape, you can minimise injury, you can always be on the practice floor, therefore you can always improve [and] you can always grow your skill package.

In addition to the three components discussed above (physical skills, cognitive development and physical attributes), Mike—like other coaches who feature in this book—believes that athletes should develop psychosocially and that coach role modelling contributes significantly to this outcome:

... you are trying to teach them to be the best basketball players they can be, but hopefully you are also teaching them to be the best person they can be. Some of that will be apparent by the way you behave and act, so that they'll replicate some of your behaviours and, if you are standing on the sideline abusing referees, well then the likelihood is that your players are going to end up doing that too. Being an appropriate role model assists in the development of life skills for your players and even more importantly they will not make mental errors at big moments because their focus is somewhere else. I think the mark of all champions is high focus; they play the moment, not what has happened or what might happen.

Correspondent with David Hadfield's message in Chapter Two, Mike believes that a coach's philosophy should recognise the need for self-awareness. Coaches should understand how they work and, most importantly, how they affect their athletes. He suggests:

Effective coaching begins with self-scrutiny, so there is a self-awareness element in there as well. To develop the coaching process into a confident, effective state, you have to be able to objectively self-evaluate, to be aware of your skill set and how to use it, aware of your behaviours and how they affect other people; that is a communication skill. The ability to challenge and be challenged … if you are not receptive to challenge then you can't improve. If you can't improve then you can't be an effective coach or a manager, you can't be any of those things; your ability to be a good decision maker will be hindered.

Mike acknowledges that a coach's job is all about preparing the athletes. Once the game starts, the coach is there only for support:

For me it is all about preparation. I believe the coach's job should be done before the ball gets tipped off. I believe that my work is done on the practice floor. I work very hard to have my players 'ready to play' independently of me. I believe in the adage, 'Practice time is coach's time—game time is players' time'. However, in my sport there is a component of game management, I just try to prepare the players to have a greater role in that aspect. If our preparation can allow my players greater 'think time', then we have an advantage over our opponents. If we have greater think time, understand the decision-making process and accept responsibility for our performances, then I believe we are putting ourselves in a better position to win.

Of course, Mike says, he prepares himself for every game and is there 'trying to assist my players with every tactic or direction at my disposal'. But there are major advantages in developing athletes who are effective decision makers:

… it works better when they have that same mental approach and that they can make those same decisions or adjustments on the court in the heat of the battle. Think of the advantage that you have when decisions can be made and executed with no reliance on the coach or without having to go through the coach for approval. Think also of the well-rounded and informed athlete you have developed.

However, Mike agrees that competitions provide great learning experiences, including opportunities for learning by trial and error:

Competition, for me, whilst trying to achieve your goals and objectives, is a fertile ground for trial-and-error learning. The coach that ignores this opportunity for developing his [or her] athletes, particularly in the area of decision making, is just making life harder for himself [or herself]. This is where the players actually learn, not from coaches, but from the environment. This is also a valuable learning arena for coaches.

Mike's Development as a Coach

As indicated at the start of this chapter, Mike developed as a coach through experience, making mistakes and doing things well. A significant part of this development was his move from being a coach-centred coach for a substantial part of his early career to being an athlete-centred coach. What influenced the change? He says:

I can't pinpoint a specific period or time, it has just evolved over time and to a point where from being totally autocratic to, with the Saints in 2003, almost total empowerment. But you have to understand with the Saints I had no other option, I came into the team when they had already played six games in that season, I had no familiarity with the players either technically or as people and certainly no preparation time. This was a situation where the best method for successfully completing the season was to make no radical changes but to allow the team to move forward by gently providing direction and support.

In taking an athlete-centred approach with the Wellington Saints, he says that:

The biggest change I made was to instil the concept of collective responsibility. The media used to give me all the credit for turning the Saints programme around. I had to continually tell the players not to believe what they read in the papers. I did not want them to have a reliance on their coach; I wanted them to take some responsibility for their own development and the development of the team. I am a huge believer that team development is about collective responsibility. I might provide some direction and some ideas, but I want the players to take some part in deciding what is good for the team and themselves individually and to learn how you go about it, how to get the job done. I coach for players to be independent of me because I am not always going to be their coach. Those Saints players now could run a practice session without me ... they could work on the skills they know are important and at the tempo that you'd know I'd want. But it is more about making the right decision at the right time appropriate to the situation and those involved. It is about taking ownership for their performance.

In explaining how his coaching knowledge and practice developed, Mike pays tribute to a wide range of influences. First, his mentors include coaches from his playing days. He recalls learning so much from them about how to do things and how not to do things:

While as a player I wasn't blessed with talent, what I was blessed with was that I always had good coaches and I know some players can go through their whole life and not have any. Every coach I had was a good coach. They didn't turn me into an elite athlete, but they gave me many other valuable lessons, although they and I did not know it at the time. Also throughout my coaching career I have been very fortunate to have had fantastic mentors.

Mike suggests that his experience of and learning about coaching came mostly from role models or previous coaches:

Simply imitating the style of another coach is not the same thing as determining your own coaching development. However, learning from experienced effective coaches and adapting this learning to your own personality is a delicate skill. These skills arrive with experience and maturity. I tried to keep things pretty simple, which even today I still do. I was able to rely on coaching instincts that had been learned over a period of time ... When I first started playing, there was a coach from the Police Boys' Club in my home town who was a basketball coach of pretty high stature, so from my earliest playing days, I had good coaching and then in school, I had a fantastic school teacher who was a good coach. When I came out of school playing club basketball, my club coach was an American who had come out to teach school in Australia and had a good background in the game. So from an early age I had a taste of what good coaches do.

At the same time, Mike believes in coach education and gaining more knowledge whenever possible. He was one of the first to complete Level 1 coaching in the new coach education structure implemented in Australia. In addition, he completed a referee's course because:

I am a great believer that a coach should have a very specific knowledge of the rules of their sport. The rules are designed so that the players have parameters within which to play. If you don't know the rules of your sport precisely as a coach, then you are not going to provide your players with an appropriate learning environment. This is especially important in the heat of battle when you have to quickly make adjustments to the officiating style or interpretations.

Mike admits that as well as learning from his own coaches, he has gained invaluable learning through observing and working with other coaches, finding what he likes and dislikes about their coaching. One such experience was being initiated into coaching as a process beyond just learning about the game—as assistant to another influential coach, Warwick Cann, with an under 18 representative team in New South Wales for two years (before Mike himself took over as coach). During his two years with Warwick Cann, Mike says:

I learned a lot about the game ... [but also] that was my induction into the socialisation of how coaches behave and the ethics and etiquette involved when coaching on the sideline: the way they communicate with their players, the way they interact with the officials in the game, the way they behave ... while as a player I had good coaches who taught me about the game, I had never had anyone previously who could teach me about being a coach ... Warwick was able to do that, his background was in school teaching. He knew a lot about individual learning styles, and he taught me a lot about stages of learning, very valuable for someone like me, who didn't have an academic background.

One of his main coaching influences is Tom Maher, with whom he has worked for a number of years and who has directly and indirectly been his mentor. Mike reflects:

That was a special time, being involved with the Opals and Tom Maher was a wonderful experience that provided not only sport-specific learning but also the maturing of the coaching process for me. Getting the opportunity to reunite with Tom with the Tall Ferns and the Olympics in Athens was also very special. I am an unabashed admirer of Tom's values and his approach to coaching.

Another major influence on Mike's coaching development has been Bob Turner, a coach who came to Australia from the United States:

> Bob was a guy who had a passion for coaching. Bob was a very, very good player who came to Australia in the years just prior to the birth of the NBL. We were playing a tournament in Shoalhaven, NSW and someone said, 'Look you should go and talk to this guy, and he might be able to help you with coaching.' At that stage, I had got the bug and I was eager to learn. I subscribe to the wise saying that in coaching 'learning is a daily pursuit and a lifetime mission'. I now felt like it was something I'd like to do, I now realised that it could be a career path. I went and met with Bob Turner and he gave me direction, he advised the pathways and development I needed to undertake. So in a short period of time, I accelerated my learning around coaching, through completing coaching courses, meeting other coaches and talking to coaches at a higher level, basically bugging anyone I thought could help me.

Among those from whom he has had a chance to observe and learn are coaches with an international reputation:

> Fortunately, coaching has taken me all over the world. I have spent a lot of time internationally professionally developing myself. I have visited lots of international coaches and learned a lot of things, but the sport was able to provide that for me. I would never have been able to do these things if it wasn't for basketball. I have been to sports schools in Russia and Olympic training centres in St Petersburg. I have travelled to China, Spain, France and the US looking at how they do things. I have been to able to observe a lot of good college coaches in the US, and spent some time observing two NBA programmes—the Detroit Pistons when they were the world champions and San Antonio Spurs the year before they won the NBA.

As well as providing the opportunity to work alongside some highly regarded coaches, international experience gave Mike some development time, as he now appreciates:

> … you look back now and realise that you pick up certain number of things from the environment you participate in. Being involved at an international level taught me about transfer, how to take the lessons from that environment and convey these to developing athletes, which ultimately is another stage of my development that has rounded out my coaching background.

However, among all these development opportunities, the best coaching experience is gained from working with the athletes themselves. Mike believes that athletes are our biggest and best teachers:

> … we have talked about coach education, we have talked about coaching

experiences and you put them all together and you end up with a rounded profile of a coach. But working with great players is the best way to accelerate your coaching development provided you are willing to learn off of them. Particularly in the area of skills and technique, you observe how they execute and perform skills; this can provide you with the ability to coach these skills from a more relevant platform of knowledge.

Working with players and experiencing the highs and lows of coaching are invaluable to coach development. As Mike says:

My time at the Australian Institute of Sport was just a fantastic time in terms of my development. I learned so much, not only professionally but personally—how to conduct myself better as a person, how to have a more balanced view around athlete development and specifically how specialist support personnel could aid the coaching performance. It is difficult to imagine in today's sporting climate that a sophisticated coaching process can be devised and delivered without a team of support personnel. In any team approach a system of communication is essential; a good deal of energy needs to be expended between the coach and the specialists on enhanced communication. But keep it simple.

His learning through practice has been reinforced by his experience from his playing days. He comments how important observing the game has been to his learning:

… because I wasn't a great player, I was often sitting on the bench, so I was observing. I do think that my greatest skill is observational learning. I sat beside the coach, hoping that he might put me into the game, so I was observing what they did anyway. So I think that was a great learning experience for me; it certainly helped me develop some instincts for the game.

In his job in Victoria, Mike learned about coaching through educating coaches. Through this experience, he says, he developed communication skills and 'learned about the elements involved in the coaching process'.

Mike is rightly grateful for the opportunities to develop professionally and personally. He feels quite privileged that he has been a part of basketball for a number of years:

I would never have been able to do that if it wasn't for basketball. I owe the sport much more than it owes me. If I worked every day for the next 100 years, I would never be able to repay the sport for what it has given me, in terms of the life-long friends I have made, the life experiences, and especially the interpersonal relationships I have had with players and coaches. The support of my family that allowed me to do it, that makes it special as well. So, for me it has been a fantastic journey, hopefully not yet over.

Now that Mike is involved in coach education, he has used some of his experiences of developing as a coach to suggest what other coaches need to do to develop:

There is a difference in learning to coach, and learning to be a coach ... this requires an induction into the coaching process.

Somehow I don't believe that Mike's coaching journey is over. We continue to focus on this journey as we now turn to discuss how Mike has developed into a great, athlete-centred coach.

The Process of Establishing a Quality Team Culture

Mike believes that establishing a team culture is one of the most important elements to a successful team. It is a principle he learned from Tom Maher:

> ... I observed and learned how he achieved this with the Opals, who had a tremendously robust team culture ... but with all teams I have coached over the years, I would have tried to develop some form of culture. From Tom, I learned how to formalise it. This is what we are, this is what we hang our hat on, and this is how we want to be seen. Developing this type of culture is a lot about identifying shared goals, about collective responsibility, about living the ideals of the team. Mostly it is about self-sacrifice.

Tom establishes the vision and values for his team culture. He develops values and goals in terms of what the team should do and how athletes should act as an Opal. I ask Mike about this process: how can the athletes take ownership of the values if they have not been involved in developing them, and what happens if the athletes disagree with Tom's ideas? Mike responds:

> Tom was emphatic about the formalising of the themes he felt would take the Opals to where they desired to be. At the time of my involvement this was to be in contention for gold medals at pinnacle events. Tom felt that if the players were able to embrace and 'live' the Opals' themes, then as players came into the programme they could progress very quickly. Mainly Tom felt that this was an excellent way to evaluate and provide precise feedback. I think that coaches who are able to establish effective cultures in their programmes don't impose it, they direct it. If something is right, it is because it has always been and will always be right. However, you still have to get buy-in from the players. In the Opals' situation, all senior players had bought into Tom's formalisation of the themes, and they had the ability to project these themes both on and off the court.

Mike reiterates the importance of establishing a team culture with visions and values in a basketball team:

> The team culture is what helps them become the right people for your programme. It is about formalising your values around honesty and integrity and loyalty and collective responsibility so that when players embrace and project these values, you have an environment where all team members can grow.

To develop this invaluable culture, Mike says, he begins with guidelines to encourage athletes to take ownership of the process:

> … you have to have some guidelines. I learned not to use rules because that inferred external compulsion. I want our players to self-impose specific behaviours and, by projecting these behaviours, they adopt that as their ethos. So … anyone who comes into the programme from outside of it has to adapt or they won't develop as part of the group … those values have to be determined by the individuals within the group …

The coach's role in this process is:

> … to sit down with them and discuss those particular traits and how within the group they might make that work. Now, that might be through senior leadership helping the younger players to understand the importance of these values to the group. A coach develops ideas, communicates them to his players, and through them tries to realise his conception of how the sport ought to be played and the team project itself … I always like to communicate my ideas, through our practice sessions and team meetings. We have to exhibit those things that are important to the team and the growth of the group as part of our everyday lives. So, when we come into camp, we display mutual respect, we exhibit unselfishness and we show regard for our teammates … Team sports are fertile grounds for development of this philosophy.

Mike suggests that reinforcing values and visions throughout the season establishes the quality within a team culture. His teams revisit values and goals:

> … usually in team meetings away from practice. When we come to practice, we focus on the sport-specific. Once we determine our guidelines, we remind players through evaluation and I document this in our playbooks, they all get a copy. Then they will be tested on their knowledge of those guidelines, mostly through the evaluation process but also in briefings.

Mike also uses appropriate situations during training to reinforce the values that the team has determined. For example:

> Sometimes we might be getting tired and we are not focusing, so I'll say, 'Look, one of our values is about a team who can handle adversity. Here is adversity, here is fatigue.' So you point it out in those sorts of ways too. Every principle can be used to evaluate. This affords an effective communication process.

As our location is the Junior Tall Ferns camp, I ask Mike to explain the process of establishing a team culture with the Junior Tall Ferns specifically. He says:

> That is part of the induction process. They might come into the first camp and not understand at all, but again … my expectation is that, you don't come in and get told all these things. Sometimes it is just an assimilation

process rather than an induction process, but it is long sort of induction process. But they get a playbook, they get to read my values and understand my approach.

One of the principles for the Junior Tall Ferns is the notion of 'we', as Mike explains:

… if you can't communicate with your teammates or your coaches, then you are not part of the 'we' team. It's about self-sacrifice. It is also about learning to be assertive; if you can't communicate you will not be assertive. It is about being unselfish; selfish people choose not to communicate or communicate in a poor way. Selfish people find others to blame. There is no place in a team for selfish people; an effective team will also have an effective system of communication, it will be a group that will share goals and responsibilities.

Part of developing a team culture, Mike believes, is to create the best learning environment in which players can develop:

For me a learning environment consists of two elements: you have to have discipline around your team, discipline assists learning, and this comes back to your established culture. This is the way we behave so having a strong discipline around the team and around the club actually helps the learning process. The other thing is that you have to encourage them to be eager to learn. They have to understand that learning is something that will help them be better players and better people. If you can achieve that, I don't think some form of empowerment is a difficult thing at all.

Mike's Use of Questioning

Questioning features as part of an athlete-centred environment as it gives athletes thinking space to solve problems. Mike continually works on players' decision making through problem solving and asking questions:

… at the end, we review, 'How did you do this? Did you run the right play?' 'You scored three and you were down by four, then when you went back and went into the zone and they got a three and you were back down by four. Do you think that was the right defence at that time?'

Mike asks questions relevant to the athletes' learning level as he perceives it. With the Junior Tall Ferns, he did not ask many questions as he thought that they needed more information during that stage of learning. For the Saints, however, he uses questioning extensively through the session. Through verbal questioning he gets athletes to reflect; he also sets drills and games as problems to solve. With both strategies his main intention is to get athletes to think and make decisions. Mike gives some examples of his questions with the Saints:

'Is that the most effective to defend that screen? Is that good shot selection?

What is the consequence of a bad shot? Why did we as a group of people make that play, when this might have been more effective?' They have to come up with the relevant answers. They have to answer it with some validity.

The technique can run into trouble, he says, when athletes cannot come up with valid answers. As Mike sees it, this undesirable situation is a sign that 'you as a coach are not communicating in the most precise way'.

Another challenge is determining when to be directive, when to let athletes carry on because they are learning, and when to stop activities to ask questions. Mike suggests the following as a response to that challenge:

There are times that you have to be firm, there are times that you have to be challenging, there are times that you have to be demanding, but if you do that within the parameters of your philosophy and you evaluate within the parameters of your culture, then you are going to be effective. The players now know that when I am critical of something that they do, that it is not personal attack. Once the players understand they need to be critiqued, demanded of and challenged because it is going to help them be better, they can accept the fact that the coach can communicate certain things to them. You've got to be careful how you couch phrases and address things in a particular way because mutual respect is also an essential ingredient to effective coaching.

Mike and Teaching Games for Understanding

Teaching Games for Understanding (TGfU) forms a large part of Mike's coaching repertoire, especially at the level of the Wellington Saints. His games and drills are purposeful, designed to meet athletes' needs, and adapted to fit with his focus on developing fundamentals (see his philosophy above). Because Mike feels that specific fundamental techniques cannot be learned correctly through playing games, he includes a fair amount of repetition in initial stages of athlete development, as I observed at the Junior Tall Ferns camp. He explains:

… the first thing they have to do is learn the techniques. I will work on the basis [that] to acquire the skill you learn the correct technique. So I have got to be able to teach and demonstrate the particular technique I am looking for. So then the process is: you learn the skill, you refine the skill, you rehearse the skill and then you perform the skill in competition. That is the learning structure that I use. And then it is repetition, repetition, repetition. With shooting mechanics, you've got to learn correct technique because shooting is about muscle memory. If you learn bad technique to shoot the ball and you shoot a thousand shots a day, you are practising bad technique. But if you shoot a thousand shots a day with good technique, muscle memory will now remember how to shoot the ball correctly. So, whatever stage of the game [you are at, when] … you shoot the ball, you shoot with correct technique and that is the result of repetition which is an important facet of skill acquisition.

An important concept in TGfU is providing games and activities whereby athletes learn through trial and error. The game itself sets up the situation that enables athletes to make errors and then learn how to do the task better next time. Mike agrees:

> I am a great believer … that people who learn from their errors, progress quicker than people who don't, so if you don't put them in the trial-and-error environment, and give them the skills to recognise the lessons, their learning is accelerated and enhanced.

Although clearly committed to developing fundamental physical skills and techniques, Mike is particularly supportive of TGfU (or Game Sense) at the level of children's sport. Children need to understand the context in which they apply the necessary physical skills and techniques, so running a training session in which young athletes apply the fundamentals in purposeful games creates a learning environment in which they come to understand game play as well. As Mike observes:

> Game Sense is important, but I think the real impact is at the junior level with athletes in their formative stages. This allows kids to sample sports; this provides for longevity, understanding and enjoying sport and ultimately having success in the sport they choose. To me the biggest benefit of Game Sense is the positive experience and enjoyment associated with the activity.

While observing the Saints, I noted that the entire training session included TGfU activities. It was interesting that after setting the game (based on what the team needed to work on), Mike would totally back off, just standing and observing. Left alone in this way, the players were very good at pulling up the game and reflecting on choices they made. Mike's role, where he did get involved, appeared to be to occasionally jump in with a question to clarify something or to get athletes to think about the decisions they made. He was interested in getting the athletes to make informed decisions through playing purposeful games.

During the session I observed, Mike planned to train for two hours but ultimately only trained for 1.5 hours. The session finished early because the games the Saints played during that session were intense and the session was of high quality. The players were intense because the games were meaningful and the effort was great, therefore their intrinsic motivation was high. It is with high intrinsic motivation that athletes learn more, as Rod Thorpe suggests (see Chapter Eleven). Mike believes trainings should be run for quality rather than quantity. For this session, he felt the quality was of such a high standard, the athletes did not have to carry on until the scheduled finishing time. It was an exciting session to observe.

Implementing an Athlete-centred Approach

Mike has developed his athlete-centred approach with input from many different sources. Through his experience, he has learned about providing quality opportunities. He adapts, modifies and implements these challenges according to the levels and abilities (cognitive, psychosocial and physical) of the athletes. With reference to an occasion involving advice from Tom Maher, he discusses one of the platforms on which he built an athlete-centred approach:

> I remember the Opals were playing Cuba and the Cubans were reasonably close, closer than expected, and it was going into the last minutes of the game. One of the assistant coaches asked Tom if he thought a time out was appropriate. He turned around and said, '[Michelle] Timms knows what she is doing; I don't need a time out'. He was right. What he was saying was [that] the players on the court knew exactly what they had to do because of his preparation with them at practice and the experience of the players would allow for the correct decisions. By stopping the game, you were allowing the opposing coach to have a time out, a chance to talk to his players. So all you were doing was helping their team … that one situation alerted me to the fact that it was the people on the floor that were imperative. It's not what I knew, it's what they knew that was important.

This incident seemed to be a turning point for Mike as he became convinced that enabling the athletes to learn was most important:

> So from that time on, in every practice and in everything I did, I tried to ensure that the players had some ownership of it. This was not divorcing my responsibility as a coach but allowing the players a greater role in the decision-making process, having them accept a greater responsibility for the team's effectiveness.

Mike values the knowledge that the players bring to trainings and games. Unlike many coaches in basketball, he does not call time outs just for the purpose of having time outs, or to draw plays and give the athletes directions on how to play the game. He explains:

> With the Saints, because we have experienced athletes that have been around the programme for some time, I don't overuse the time out process. They know exactly what they need to do. If I were to have a time out, it would be more for a tactical reason than to discuss what they are doing on the court. They know the plays, and they know when plays are appropriate to the situation. I want them to feel like they have ownership, with my role as an adviser rather than a director, but we also have collective responsibility; we win together and we lose together. This is not to say that there aren't times when my role is to provide specific direction, I have to be alert to when this is appropriate. They also know that when I call a time out to question their intensity or focus, … it must be really significant.

Mike suggests that the Saints have total ownership during the game. When they are on the court, they call the plays. The decision making is up to the players as well as the coach providing the support. So who designs the actual plays—the players or Mike? He says:

> I would say, 'Look, I think this is a good idea to do it this way, what do you think?' If they come up with a good idea, I say 'Great, let's do that, that's a

better idea than the one I had'. I am not afraid to say that to them at all …
Then we'll set up a specific situation—there are two minutes on the clock,
we are seven points down, it's your ball out of bounds on the sideline, you
have a time out. So now they've got to understand specifically the scenario:
that they are in a catch-up phase, they've got to run a play where they get
a quick shot, they have to come up with the defensive plays that will get
them back in the game, so they have to talk about what defensive pattern
they're in. At this point I don't interfere, I let them workshop the scenario. I
let the players practise decision making. Of course, if they are not able to
come up with the correct decision, then my job is to provide them with the
relevant information and direction.

As other coaches in this book observe, the coach has to prepare the athletes for an
athlete-centred approach. The coach is the facilitator and the person who maintains the
integrity of the players and coaching staff by following through with athlete-centred
beliefs. It is a view with which Mike wholeheartedly concurs:

From a coaching perspective, the coach has got to be a bit of a salesman as
well. You can't just walk in and say, 'I am going to be about empowerment'
and then say, 'Don't do that'. You have got to let them make some mistakes as
well. Your intervention then has to point out those errors and the appropriate
responses. They have to learn, they have to … perform their own trial and
error. And sometimes you have to be patient when it is extremely difficult
to be.

Whatever the challenges, Mike continues develop and expand an athlete-centred
approach:

… because I do get a good response from the athletes. I do get a response
that helps me be able to coach the skill aspect better because I can build the
relationship through this approach. It also allows for an enjoyable coaching
experience. You are building a team relationship, but you are building a lot
of individual relationships as well and they all see you in a different way,
but because of the collective, because of the ownership the team has. With
your individual relationships … you can identify the particular methods your
athletes utilise to learn and develop. Not everyone gets it the same way. I
find that some people learn [by] hearing, some people learn [by] watching,
but most people learn through doing things. The very great may be able to
learn in all ways but in my experience, most people cannot.

Mike advocates experience as the key to gaining the confidence to use an athlete-centred
approach in coaching. He believes a coach really has to know the players well in order
to determine what is best for the individual and the team:

I think the longer you've been coaching, you find ways to do things because
it connects that experience that you can relate back to. People are different,
but people change as well, so you've also got to monitor for change. I think
a delicate coaching skill is being able to recognise those traits, not only

recognising them, but know[ing] what approaches coaches should use with different types of people. Some people are driven and can find their own direction. Some people you have to give direction, they are not self-motivated enough to direct themselves. Self-motivated people you can give some ownership [to] and let them go on their way. Other people need you to be enthusiastic and supportive; some feel neglected if the coach is not giving them attention. I have seen players who actually mess up so that they get that attention. Experience is the key to accurate identification of the correct approach.

The Process of Empowering Players

Mike feels that each platform the coach is dealing with has different implications for the process of empowering players. In particular, the level of experience and knowledge of the athletes determines how much power they have. For Mike, the Saints' level means they are suited to the Situational Coaching Model's quadrant 4, which represents the most empowering, delegating coaching approach (see Figure 2.2, Chapter Two). With the Junior Tall Ferns, Mike's approach seemed to be more consultative, in line with quadrant 2, and to focus on developing the athletes to gradually take on more responsibility. Mike confirms that initially he needs to be more directive with athletes who have lesser cognitive and physical skills:

> The first three days I had with these girls [Junior Tall Ferns], we just did fundamental skills because there was no platform to work with. They just didn't have good fundamentals; we had to get a lot of fundamental development completed. For this camp, now that we have a fundamental platform, we can actually show them some plays, now they have a fundamental base to refer to they can learn to sequence and execute the plays. In this situation you will hear me saying a lot, 'Are you happy with this?' Which means, it is my way of saying, 'Are you comfortable with this? If you are not, tell me.' They are so young that they aren't going to say to a coach what they think; they are not going to say that. I know that, but I am going to continue on that theme with, 'Are you happy with this? Are you comfortable with this? Tell me if we need more practice. Tell me if you need further explanation.' This allows for attention to detail, both by me and them. We will break it down into little pieces, then connect the pieces. I will teach whole–part–whole. I teach the whole thing first, in its broad brush sense, come back and then do all the detail stuff and then go back and put the whole thing together again.

To give athletes ownership of the team, Mike creates a small leadership group that is given or takes on the responsibility of helping others with team needs or goals:

> We'll identify a senior leadership group. Empowerment doesn't just mean empowering everyone. There are degrees of empowerment. What you are doing is authorising or sanctioning ownership, but demanding responsibility in return. You know sometimes you are empowering people to empower others … the concept that we are establishing is not about running my system, it is

about playing the game … I am trying to teach them how to play basketball, not just how to run plays. I think if you can play the sport well, in this case basketball, then you can run any plays you are asked to.

Mike believes that athletes need to learn how to be leaders, as part of the athlete-centred approach. He encourages this leadership:

… one of the things I try and do is teach them all to be leaders … even the ones who are quiet and shy, after a while, they will feel confident enough to say, 'Oh I think it is this', or 'This is how we do this'. So it is a bit of a trick to allow that to happen. Obviously, they don't assert themselves right away. But I want everyone to be leaders. I don't subscribe to the team captain theory at all. I subscribe to the collective responsibility concept. That's taking ownership; it's about everyone being leaders—at the same time, everyone being helpers as well. I want leaders and I want them all to be leaders in their own way … I think, if you are going to play sport at a high level, you have to be an assertive person. Assertiveness is one of our guidelines and, while being assertive, you are being a leader.

As noted by some other coaches in this book, when athletes are empowered because they have ownership of the team, they are highly motivated, which also brings intensity. Mike suggests that this intensity can sometimes cause problems as the athletes are training so hard that, at times, disagreements among them have to be solved:

They'll say to the player who is not working hard, 'Look why should everyone be training hard and you are not', but that is leadership too. With the Saints players, it can get that competitive at practice that they are almost having fistfights. There have been times when I thought I would nearly have to step in and stop this because you don't want to go over that line, but you want them to be as competitive as can be. They have never, ever gone over the line, but boy it has been close a couple of times. But you know, at the end of every practice, everyone shakes hands. At the professional level, or semi-professional level, you can just deal [players] out. At the [junior level], you can't just deal them out, you have to try to help them become better.

Mike refers to a directive, coach-centred approach in basketball as a 'systems' approach. A coach with a systems approach basically creates his or her own system, which athletes have to buy in to in order to be successful. From Mike's experience of observing and working with other coaches throughout the world, he judges the systems approach to be detrimental to athletes' learning about their sport and their general lives. While acknowledging that it also contains holistic coaches, he identifies the US college system as a good example of how the systems approach is fundamentally flawed:

They recruit players who can exist in their system and for four years you learn that system. When you come out, that's it, you are an expert in that system, and you haven't learned anything else. So, if you go into any place in the world that runs that system, you'll be okay. If you go to another team that doesn't, you won't.

In his own approach, Mike aims for a directly converse outcome:

I take the view, as a coach, my job is: if a player leaves the Saints, he can go to any other coach in this league or in any other country and be able to play basketball and fit into that particular programme. So I teach them about the game, not about the play … I want players to learn to play the game … you are teaching them about decision making as well and you are teaching them about how to learn to read the defender … For me that is what coaching is about. The play we run is incidental. I tell them all the time, 'If we are running this play and you have an opportunity to drive or shoot, you drive or shoot.' The play is to give some organisation and some direction but is secondary to the game. The players' correct response to any situation is the key aspect. To teach players to be proactive, they have to respond not to what has just happened but to what is going to happen. This allows them to have the initiative. To understand this you have to understand the game and be able to execute the correct skill. To teach the players these things is my responsibility.

One of the most exciting outcomes of empowering athletes is that they are able to be innovative and show flair when performing. When athletes are allowed to make decisions, they are allowed to take risks. In a systems approach, by contrast, athletes are not allowed to take those risks. Taking risks increases the number of learning opportunities and makes the competition more exciting. Mike agrees:

… they are allowed to use flair, they are allowed to be innovative, and they are allowed to [learn by] trial and error. Making a mistake is not all that important as what you learn from it and how you respond to it. You learn not to repeat it too often. I want players who have initiative, who have a work ethic, who have to desire to set and achieve goals. I am going to adapt my coaching performance to their skill set, but I am also going to determine the style of game we play by what they can do. You have to have confidence in their ability to do that too and your ability to recognise the correct approach.

Some Challenges of an Athlete-centred Approach

In comparing the training of New Zealand and Australian junior basketball teams, Mike observes that:

… the big difference is that kids in New Zealand don't have that individual development mentality because they haven't been conditioned to it. Kids in Australia who come through ITC and AIS programmes and other development streams are conditioned to it. So, when they are 13, 14, 15, they know they have to go and shoot, they know they have to go and run, they know they have to get into the gym and lift weights because the ITC programmes have conditioned them to do that. Here, the kids don't know how to do that …

I think the stamp of the New Zealand athlete is that they work hard, they try unbelievably hard, they are determined, persistent players with a lot of athletic talent but they have not been conditioned through development programmes to know what techniques to work on, the tempo you need to work at and how much time you have to spend going about it and, most importantly, how to have some balance in managing their sporting and other commitments.

Perhaps the way that children are trained in Australia allows them to understand the benefits of doing the individual fundamentals. On the other hand, when they experience coach-centred coaching, children don't take ownership of the need to learn or perfect the skills. A challenge for New Zealand coaches then, which Mike highlights, is to establish mutual responsibility and ownership in sport. He underlines his argument with the observation that coaches work hard, so athletes should work hard:

I can say to these kids, 'I can't help you if you haven't been doing the work. This is about self-improvement; you have got to help me help you.' It is also about knowing what and how to do and when to do it.

A challenge to Mike's own coaching is that most of the players he coaches have not been trained to make decisions. Like many elite athlete-centred coaches, he often has to start from scratch with his elite athletes because junior athletes come through a sporting system where coaches generally do not develop thinking people. Mike says that most athletes coming from this system:

… have never been given the experience of being a decisive element. Some coaches will tell you that players do not want to make decisions, they need to be driven and that they want to be told how to go about it. This may be true, they just want a prescription. What I am saying is, I don't want those types of players who will rely on someone else to drive them; I want players who will drive themselves, who wish to take responsibility for the decisions that are required during competition. What I want to do is to prescribe the techniques and teach them how and when to use them in a game situation. This sequencing requires decision making at that moment in time.

It is decision making to a depth that some athletes are reluctant to adopt. Here Mike identifies one of the pitfalls of an athlete-centred approach:

Sometimes it takes a long time to have your players fully accept that this is the way it is. As I said before, some players do not want responsibility, they want to have direction, but want the coach to take responsibility. I want the players to take responsibility and I am prepared to extend ownership and decision making if they are prepared to take responsibility.

As Mike says, 'It may take a long time for players to want to accept responsibility.' Here he acknowledges, like other coaches in this book, that time is another challenge when empowering athletes and pursuing long-term learning. Yet equally he emphasises that the time invested brings major benefits:

I also think, if you take a long time, you have a longer time at the other end. I think the Black Sox are a great example. For three world championships, 12 years, they have developed their culture. This culture changes from team to team as new players and staff become involved. However the platform is always there. You know that if Don Tricker walked away now, that culture is still there ...

In regard to his own coaching, Mike reiterates:

It does take time, but I always feel that anything that is good takes time anyway. With the Saints, I am not just coaching to win the title this year; I want to bring a winning basketball dynasty to Wellington. That does not mean we will win the championship every year; what it means is we will try and put ourselves in a position to win the championship every year. The championship is a reward for excellence. I am about trying to achieve excellence every time we play or train; in this way, championships will take care of themselves. That's about building a culture, that's about building layers of development for your programme, so you have good succession planning. It's about making playing for the club more important than playing for themselves. That's about having administration and the other peripherals in the club, the management, the sport science area, the managers—you all have to be thinking the same thing, going in the same direction. My goal for the Saints club is that they develop a strong connection to their community, they don't take shortcuts and they make sure that everything that is done, is done for the right reasons ... Then when times get hard, you survive because of that community support that you built. I want to build a succession plan that the players and coaches of future Saints teams will always be able to compete in this type of environment.

The need for a quality team culture relates to another potential pitfall that Mike identifies:

... bringing together the personalities involved in the programme is always difficult, for anything to be successful I believe that everyone has to work together whatever the style of the coach, there has to be a shared vision and goals, everyone has to embrace hard work and give more than they receive and there can be no room for selfishness.

Given that it can require considerable confidence to implement an athlete-centred approach, I ask Mike how a coach might develop that confidence. He replies:

The fundamentals of success are communication, trust, collective responsibility, caring and pride. I think you have to instil these principles and then demonstrate belief in the players. You've got to let them know that you believe in them, you care about them and you trust them. Once they are convinced of that, once they are confident that you have belief, trust and care, they will respond in the same way. Sometimes that is ... not an easy lesson.

In making his own transition from coach-centred to athlete-centred coaching, Mike says he was able to hand over decision making to the athletes because:

> ... it comes back to your values, your beliefs that this is what is going to work best for you. I am not saying that coaches who empower or give ownership to their players are better than coaches who adopt any other method. I'm not saying it is right for everyone, what I'm saying is that it is right for me ...

Mike says that flawed communication can be a pitfall for an athlete-centred coach:

> ... one of the lessons I took from working with Tom Maher was his communication. He always used to say, 'Listen to my words, don't read anything into them, I am saying this exactly how it should be, don't put your slant on it.'

As Mike sees it, however, it is possible to overcome this pitfall by providing 'precise communication'. He explains that athletes must have an understanding of what a coach is trying to do:

> ... a heightened state of communication is essential. I try to develop my teams around the concept of offence, the concept of defence and a system of communication. It is not only what you communicate, but how you communicate. The players can never be mistaken about what you are doing and reasons you are doing it for ... You are using all the individuals in the team to help you grow the leadership and build the concept of collective responsibility.

Another pitfall is to fail to communicate with honesty, which Mike believes to be one of the main attributes of an athlete-centred approach:

> If you say one thing to this player and another thing to that player that will not build the culture you want ... Honesty builds trust; once you've got trust you can achieve many things, particularly on the court.

Coaches also must find the approach and methods that work best for them. As Mike points out, another pitfall is to imitate another coach without developing your own coaching philosophy and style:

> You cannot just imitate another coach; what you can do is study the things that make them effective and adapt these elements to your philosophy. I have said previously that coaching is a means of self-expression. Determining a coaching philosophy is a primary task. If I imitate Tom Maher, David Parkin or Tab Baldwin, it is not Mike McHugh; it is an imitation of those coaches. You have to identify successful approaches and effective processes and adapt them to your own philosophy and personality and deliver it in a way that reflects this. I find myself sometimes using Tom Maher's terminology, that is natural—you just pick these things up when you are around people like that. I am talking about the context of your message and how you deliver it.

Plans for the Future

Coaching is about the athletes. We coaches are there for them, and our goal should be to provide them with the best opportunity to better themselves. Mike agrees that the athletes are the most important part of coaching:

> You have to be athlete focused. It is about them, and they are the clients. They are the people who are going to suffer [when things go wrong]. It is how you respond to their needs that will determine whether their sports experience is positive or negative. But, if your players are saying that the coach cares about us, believes in us, trusts us, a lot of people want to play for those types of coaches. The people that will embrace that culture will want to play for those types of coaches.

As Mike is now a coach educator by profession, I ask him what he thinks about the big picture and whether we should be educating all coaches on how to use an athlete-centred approach. He reflects:

> I think the best way for coaches to see [possible coaching approaches] is that at this extreme you can have total empowerment and on this extreme you can have total dictatorship. In between, there are all degrees of those two things and somewhere along that continuum; you will find your space. You will also move back and forth along that continuum depending on the type of athletes you have at that point. You have got to understand yourself. Effective coaching relies on efficient self-analysis. You must be driven by the desire to improve. You must be able to honestly and objectively appraise yourself and your performance. You have to continually evaluate and correct your behaviours. If you aren't aware of your strengths and weaknesses and the way you communicate, the way you behave, how can you provide for self-development and continuous improvement in the coaching process?

In regard to our role as coach educators, Mike says:

> … effective coaches possess extensive specialised knowledge … To gain knowledge you need information. The role of educators is to ensure that the coaches who go through the educational process learn to develop a sound base of knowledge, acquire the skill to impart that knowledge in an effective manner and understand the importance of relationship building and management.

Learning is one of the keys to enhancing anyone's coaching. Once coaches stop learning, the athletes suffer. Mike offers these words of wisdom to all coaches:

> The moment you stop and wait, someone is going to go past you. That's not just about technique development; it's about your array of coaching skills and behaviours. As you become more confident in your performance and your development, it becomes automatic. Coaching skills become instinctive. You will see that your coaching philosophy is a constantly evolving phenomenon as well … If you don't have that thirst for more knowledge and

more information and more ways to do things better, then you won't evolve as a person or as a coach.

Conclusion

Mike's vast experience provides coaches with a story of a journey that is never ending. Through this journey, Mike continues to enhance the way he thinks about coaching. Mike has found that giving the athletes power to make decisions enhances their learning and performance. This power should be given gradually and be dependent on the level of the athletes.

Mike acknowledges that coaches should become highly self-aware, just as they encourage their athletes to do. This self-awareness keeps coaches fresh and looking for innovative initiatives that enable athletes to learn more and to learn more effectively. Keeping up to date with current coaching philosophies is part of this self-awareness. Coaches must use self-analysis—and look beyond game analysis alone —to identify what they need to enable their athletes to perform better. The art of coaching, especially communication, is a key to athlete success.

Mike also strongly espouses collective responsibility. By encouraging athletes to be decision makers and take on leadership roles, a coach creates an environment in which this collective responsibility flourishes. Athletes taking ownership of their direction and having responsibility for their learning is a key to an athlete-centred approach. Gaining experience in enabling athletes to grow through the process of coaching and learning should be considered by coaches pursuing their journey to success.

It is not only by the questions we have answered that progress may be measured, but also by those we are still asking. – *Freda Adler, US educator, criminal justice specialist*

I can do something else besides stuff a ball through a hoop. My biggest resource is my mind. – *Kareem Abdul-Jabbar*

It's really impossible for athletes to grow up. On the one hand, you're a child, still playing a game. But on the other hand, you're a superhuman hero that everyone dreams of being. No wonder we have such a hard time understanding who we are. – *Billie Jean King*

Everybody wants to be somebody. The thing you have to do is give them confidence they can. You have to give a kid a dream. – *George Foreman*

Chapter Eight

Team Seagate

Team Seagate are a New Zealand adventure race and multi sport team whose philosophies are similar to athlete-centred coaches. In the time that I observed and interviewed them, Team Seagate demonstrated their focus on establishing a quality team culture in a condensed time span (one year). I believe that this focus and, more generally, the team's athlete-centred approach have contributed to their status as one of the most successful adventure racing teams in the world. From when they first came together, the team's mutually agreed direction was to address individual and team expectations that demonstrate a strong and quality team culture. Interestingly, one of the main reflections they use within the context of adventure racing is the ability to discuss and identify life lessons learned through each of the races.

The four team members are Kristina Anglem, Richard Ussher, Hadyn Key and the captain, Nathan Fa'avae. Although it seems logical for an adventure racing team to adopt an athlete-centred approach, it is not common practice. Therefore this chapter highlights how Team Seagate builds team dynamics through a purposeful process. It also covers how the team and individual athletes have evolved to their present stage, their learning experiences and life lessons, which these athletes relate as an important aspect to adventure racing, some pitfalls of their journey in building such great team dynamics and the team's plans for the future.

At this stage, defining both adventure racing and multi sport will help to put their process in context. *Adventure racing* can be described as an expedition, a journey that requires multiple outdoor sports skills, endurance fitness, mental and physical energy, and the ability to work well as a team. In an expedition race, athletes race through the elements of nature for hundreds of kilometres, demonstrating skills in sea and river kayaking, mountain and road biking, running/tramping, navigating, inline skating, mountaineering plus many mini adventures, like rope work and caving (just to name a couple). *Multi sport*, also known as *stage racing*, is where athletes compete in stages, returning each evening for a break, then completing another stage the next day. Multi sport racing is usually a five- to eight-hour race per day and typically goes for one to six days, but occasionally up to 30 days.

So what drives the athletes who take on such a physical and mental challenge? Richard Ussher describes why he races:

> You are alive when you do a race. You can be walking along a ridge as the sun sets or rises out amongst nature, you get to see those things that people never see.

Kristina Anglem says that when she adventure races:

> … I get into these meditative states and the clarity of thought that comes

out is what I think that people who meditate seek and strive for … [that is] the confidence and sense of well-being and drive to attain a higher level of excellence. Going to races gives me the opportunity to experience adventure and then apply what I learned to life. Adventure racing is not just an amplification of life but also a fast forward of life. What you learn and then immediately apply makes the experience so intense; the learning curve is huge …

Kristina also enjoys the challenges that adventure racing brings:

For me, racing is an extension of the outdoor sports I do; a competitive situation challenges me mentally and physically. The appeal is to race efficiently to do this … I need to learn to deal with challenge and process a solution quickly.

Keeping fit and healthy is one of the motivations to which Nathan Fa'avae alludes:

I love what it's all about. It supports one of my deep-down goals of being fit and healthy … I am addicted to spending time outside for a wilderness experience and occasionally the kind of spiritual experiences I have. I can't imagine a life without adventure and the experiences it creates.

In contrast to multi sport, where athletes race from point A to point B in the shortest time with only check points to go through, an adventure race or expedition is 6 to 10 days long, with no scheduled sleep time. Hadyn Key describes adventure racing:

Adventure racing is more of an adventure, much more of an expedition. It's longer, there are more tactics that come into play, different strategies, positioning in the field, maximising your strengths [and] minimising your weaknesses. They are a lot slower, relatively … There is a chance to recover from minor mistakes, whereas you don't really have that luxury in the multi [sport] side of things. Navigation itself provides a huge challenge in adventure racing.

To obtain information about Team Seagate and its practices, I interviewed Kristina at different times during the year. All four team members also gave their individual perspectives in interviews and I observed the full team in action when I was privileged to accompany them to the Borneo Outdoor Quest, a multi sport adventure race, at the end of October 2004. That, for me, was an adventure in itself, a week of discovery and my own expedition to determine what this sport and this team are all about. I would like to thank Octagon Media for its sponsorship and support in my quest for further understanding to write this chapter.

Development of the Athletes

As with their journey to adventure racing, each of the athletes has had a unique journey to becoming a member of Team Seagate. Common to all, however, were an athletic childhood and a continued love of the challenges that sport brings to their lives.

Hadyn was a surf lifesaver, representing New Zealand, and an assistant coach for the New Zealand development squad. At university, a friend introduced him to the mountains, which became his first encounter with adventure. He moved to Wanaka in 1992 as he loved skiing and has made the Southern Lakes area his home ever since. His first adventure race was the Kepler Challenge and, after he thoroughly enjoyed it, continued to compete in other races. He entered the Southern Traverse in 1995, when someone pulled out of a team, six weeks before the race. His next challenge was the Coast to Coast race, where he competed in the one-day individual race and had a great learning experience; he placed fifth the following year. As well as continuing with the Southern Traverse and the Coast to Coast for a number of years, Hadyn competed in other races such as his favourite, the Gold Rush, which he appreciated for the countryside, the people and the relaxed atmosphere. In 1997 he competed in the EcoChallenge, where his team finished eighth.

After being asked to be a reserve for Team Seagate a few years back, Hadyn was invited officially to join Team Seagate in 2003. He jumped at the opportunity. His first race with Team Seagate was in 2003, competing in the last race of the Balance Bar series. In 2004 he was a full-time athlete with Team Seagate. Hadyn self-coaches through reading books and research and by watching and talking with others.

Kristina started sport as a gymnast, continuing with it until she was 11 years old. Like Hadyn she also coached at an early age. Her brothers introduced her to mountaineering when she was 16. At this time she climbed many of the peaks around Mt Cook and fell in love with the sport. Her last year in high school (at age 17) was spent in Bolivia, where she expanded her climbing horizons, climbing 6500-metre mountains. She finally summitted Mt Cook at 20 years of age.

On entering university, Kristina began to discover other outdoor sports. While her first year was spent mountaineering, her second was spent kayaking, and she continued adventuring while she was at university until 1996, when she completed a physical education degree. Also in 1996 she entered her first multi sport race in Tuatapere, then moved on to the Coast to Coast. At the end of the Coast to Coast race, a team asked her to join them for the Canadian EcoChallenge because of her mountaineering background. She competed in another EcoChallenge, two Southern Traverses and another Coast to Coast before doing a year's cycle tour from Singapore to Belgium in 1997–1998. Upon returning from the cycle tour, she continued on with adventure racing as an individual and won the length of New Zealand race by a large margin in 2001.

After she had raced individually for a year, she was approached by Team Seagate in 2002. She is coached by John Hellemans and is the only one on the team to receive advice from a sport psychologist about mental strategies for racing.

Richard's background includes competing in several sports when he was growing up in Wellington. After leaving school at 17, he moved to Wanaka. There he joined a ski programme, following his coach's advice that he had to learn how to ski all over again. He skied for four years, which included up to eight months of each year in the northern hemisphere. He represented New Zealand in the Winter Olympics in Nagano, Japan in 1998. After the Olympics, he took a year off, and then went back to Wellington for two years. He began to take an interest in multi sport and completed his first race in 1999 at the age of 22 (he is the youngest member of Team Seagate). Since moving back to Queenstown in 2000, he has focused on multi sport while working various jobs.

Richard was asked to join Team Seagate in 2003 just before the Outdoor Quest in Borneo. To train, he writes his own programmes and gains advice from Mark Elliot about ideas to improve his physical training.

Nathan began playing sports like rugby and soccer from the age of five. At 16, he went to an outdoor adventure programme for 'at risk' students and discovered his future career path. On this programme he met his goal of being an outdoor instructor and developed many of his initial outdoor skills in sports such as kayaking, windsurfing, caving and mountain biking. During this time, he also decided that it was time he started looking after his body and began running regularly to change his life and become fit and healthy. Running his first marathon at 17, he completed it in less than three hours. From this experience he learned that he had the ability to push himself hard physically and tried it out in a local endurance triathlon.

Nathan completed the two-day race of the Coast to Coast in 1990, when he was just 18. Although his goal was to finish, he was leading on the first day after the run and came in 11th or 12th at the end of the two days. After being dissatisfied with his result in the following year's Coast to Coast, he turned to mountain biking competition for the next seven years. He qualified for the Atlanta Olympics but in the event did not go as the Olympic Committee decided not to send any male mountain bikers.

After that fiasco, having continued his career in outdoor education and adventure tourism during his mountain biking years, Nathan tossed in mountain bike racing and went back to do the Coast to Coast where he surprised himself by qualifying third. For the next year, the Coast to Coast was his focus in training. He then signed a three-year contract with Outward Bound and, after eight months, decided to do the Southern Traverse in his home town of Nelson. He took a month off work to train then compete with a group of friends and won the 1999 race. The next year he competed in the Southern Traverse again, which by then had become an international race, and qualified for the World Championships in Switzerland.

Nathan was then asked to do several races with Team Seagate. With one thing leading to another, he has effectively been a full-time athlete with Team Seagate for three years. Although he mainly self-coaches, he has had three coaches for ideas to help his adventure racing.

Nathan is the captain for Team Seagate and has been proactive in pulling the current team together. Team Seagate won seven out of ten international races in 2004; for the other three, they placed second or third. They are definitely a team with mana (a Maori word for respect). They are well regarded throughout the adventure racing fraternity, not just because of their success, but also as a team that practises values and standards, and focuses on lessons that are learned from such a sport.

At the end of 2003 and through 2004, Richard, Hadyn, Kristina and Nathan competed as a team. An advantage of their team environment was its stability, with all members planning to be together for more than a year. Many adventure race teams swap team members fairly regularly. It is obvious that because Team Seagate has been proactive in ensuring a quality team, they have created advantages in many of the races.

Philosophies

Team Seagate are a professional team in that all members are full-time adventure racing athletes. The money they win, however, is a bonus in their eyes; it is the journey and experience that is of utmost importance to them. Part of the journey, they acknowledge, is making personal physical and mental sacrifices to compete, as well as needing their families to make sacrifices when they train or are away from home, and their sponsors to put energy into such a team. Each team member also suggests that through their racing they have learned many life lessons (see the next section for more detail).

In discussing the team philosophy for adventure racing in general, Kristina describes it as 'working for team unity, learning for life, giving it our best and having a laugh at it'. To Richard, it is '… not to want to take anything for granted'. Hadyn focuses on one important feature of the team philosophy:

> I think that one of the overriding philosophies is just to get everyone travelling as quickly as they can as a team. When you are doing that, you are not thinking about yourself personally, you are thinking about the team. You are thinking about the slowest member at that time and that can be any team member … I guess we all enjoy racing and by enjoying it, I think we do so much better.

Nathan sees Team Seagate's philosophy as still evolving:

> We are still working on what it is. To me … my ultimate goal is for us to have a safe experience; and secondly to have a good time. I know when flying back to [New Zealand], no matter what happens in the race, if we have had fun and we are safe, than that is okay. We have achieved our primary goals. That is the most important thing. The next thing would be that we have obviously done well.

Based on my impressions, the overall philosophy of Team Seagate involves: processing experiences and extracting learning; constantly developing each athlete so that each one can learn from his or her experiences; celebrating as a team for every part that they accomplish; practising life values; and making the team go faster through a quality team environment, which includes caring, empathy, humour, honesty and trust.

For every athlete in the team, fun and enjoyment are also essential to competing with Team Seagate. When I ask Nathan how he knows, as the captain, if the team are having fun, he explains:

> It's obvious when people are having fun; they sing, laugh and smile. There are certain times in the race when people may not be outwardly having fun,

but I can sense by talking with them or watching them that they are doing okay. If we can't laugh at what we are doing, then that tells me people are really hurting, and maybe not enjoying the moment. We suffer out on the race course. Our sport often puts us in discomfort and pain. Usually you have forgotten the pain when you cross the finish line.

Life Lessons

A belief held by every athlete on this team is that adventure racing provides many opportunities to learn life lessons. The challenges that they face in adventure racing provide great learning opportunities that have the potential to influence everyday life.

Nathan explains one of his life lessons: that he is lucky to be an adventure racer. Races are often held in third world countries and in the most beautiful places on earth. He tells the story of passing through these countries, seeing people lying on the ground with guns pointing to their heads. The stress of not winning the race plays largely on his mind, until he sees the reality of others' stress. It shows him that if he does not win the race, then the world is not going to stop spinning. He therefore constantly feels privileged to be able to compete in adventure racing.

In athlete evaluations at the end of each race, one typical question is: 'Name a life lesson that you can take away from the race'. Team Seagate are always conscious of these lessons—lessons that all sports should acknowledge—and it is great to see a team that explicitly uses them.

Nathan identifies why he sees life lessons as important:

> … a lot of how I want the team to race and how to be is part of a big picture. I want people to be able to take what we learn in sport and transfer that learning into everyday life. We have had many examples of learning we have taken from racing and applied that to our home life. One of my big things is accepting things and moving on, solution-based thinking, real positive thinking. I think it's a great bonus to take learning away from sport and use it again in other areas and I enjoy seeing that happen.

A challenge to which Nathan alludes is the team's focus on solution-based thinking. That thinking is about getting over a mistake quickly and moving forward to think positively about what the solution is. In everyday life, this is good practice: rather than dwelling on mistakes, look forward to solving the problem and moving on.

Hadyn relates a story about getting stuck in a river at the Primal Quest (PQ), where the team had to practise solution-based thinking:

> That was a bit of an effort because we were stuck in the river for quite a period of time, with Nathan going over first as he is taller and stronger than the rest of us. He got through the river okay and then the rest of us fought our way across one at a time with our bikes. Once we were halfway across and looking to the other side, we realised there was no way we were going to get across the rest of the river. It was extremely difficult to get back to

the same side we had come from as we had to go upstream against the current to get to an eddy pool. It was a lot easier to get to halfway than it was to get back. Nathan did a mammoth job of getting back with his bike and then shuffling the rest of us across. Without Nathan's efforts we would probably still be there and the situation may have resulted in very serious consequences.

In relating the same story, Kristina focuses on being safe and discusses her life lesson in regard to solution-based thinking:

We were in a life-threatening situation [trying] to get back on the right shore of the river. When we reached the shore, it was so relieving that the frustration of the situation was dimmed by the fact that we were all alive. What followed was a quiet time while we retraced our tracks to get back on the main road. Once we hit the main road, Nathan broke into song and from then on we just started singing. It helped us get into solution-based thinking instead of stewing over what [we] had done and how much time we had lost [and] the fact that we were now in tenth place. There were many factors which could have entered our minds, like who was to blame. Rather, we thought of what we needed to do from here, which was essentially catch up and stay on the right track … breaking into the song and spending the next couple of hours singing whatever came to mind, songs from movies, etc., gave us something else to think about. It totally changed the mood and certainly helped with the solution-based thinking strategy. Once we had made progress and we were on the next section, which was a walk, we were powering up the road. Time had moved on and we had moved on from the event.

Another life lesson that came from this Primal Quest experience, as Kristina describes it, relates to the acceleration and intensity of thinking and feeling:

One of the things about adventure racing that I learned in this PQ race is that while people describe adventure racing as a condensed version of life, it is also a fast forward of life … what I thought of [before PQ] was that you had really heightened emotions, so you feel things more strongly and you experience and you express things more strongly than you normally would. [Now] I think all that is true, but I think also that you process things much quicker, so it is not just an application of life; it's a fast forwarded life. The time that it took us to sing our group of songs and get onto the walking leg, was the time it took us to process that information, focus on that mistake … While racing, you are essentially processing information in your own time. If you want to discuss things with your teammates, you can because they are right there. You can say a couple of words to them, or a sentence, and then leave it for another hour and just think about their response or think about what you could have said, but chose not to say. It is really clear thinking time for even the most severe challenge; it actually doesn't take long to focus. I think you can process things so much quicker because you don't have the media throwing things at you and you are not looking or hearing the emotions of the other people. You are just back in your own thoughts and you can let thoughts come as you want them to come. It's an incredibly free feeling.

Two other incidents during the Primal Quest race that produced life lessons were mentioned by the athletes in our interviews. First, tragically, the athletes lost an adventure racing friend and colleague. Nigel Aylott died when a boulder loosened from a mountain and hit him while he was descending. The race was halted while the race organisers decided what to do. Nigel's team AROC was in the lead at the time of the accident.

The leading 10 teams were called to a meeting to discuss what should be done. They were 50 hours into a 130-hour race. For about 45 minutes, most teams suggested that the race should stop, that the teams in the lead should receive the prize money. This agreement among the top 10 teams seemed to prevail.

However, Nathan, representing his team (having spoken with the team first), suggested that the race should continue. He said that, although the accident was very unfortunate and tragic, 56 teams had come to race, made sacrifices, put in much time for training and organising, and paid lots of money to get to the race, as well as having sponsors to please. He even presented the parallel example that in a 10-kilometre race, if someone falls off at 5 kilometres you do not stop the race. Of course, the full PQ adventure race was not even halfway through at the time of the tragic accident.

In the end the PQ advisory board met with all the teams to determine what each team wanted to do. The vast majority wanted to continue; apparently only two teams voted against it. Thus the first life lesson to come from this experience was that the elite are not the only ones to be consulted and considered. Secondly, individuals must stand up for themselves, communicate honestly, and look at the big picture rather than make decisions based on emotion.

The other incident that brought important life lessons was Team Seagate's decision to share the win with Nike. Because of the shortened race and the concern for safety, on the second day of the restart there was a forced dark zone at the white water paddle section of the river. The lead team, Nike, arrived at the river too late to continue and had to stop for the night. Team Seagate arrived two hours later and were now, according to the new rules, considered equal with Nike and also had to stop for the night. Several other teams also arrived to the dark zone and all were considered in equal position with the lead teams when departing the next morning. The Nike racers were weaker paddlers than Team Seagate and they knew it, so in a sense they were worried about losing the lead that they had built up until then. A protest made was rejected because of the changed nature of the race course.

Next morning, Nike set out 10 minutes before Team Seagate who, sure enough, caught up with them in no time. Yet, as Nike drew into sight ahead of them, Nathan began to wonder about the fairness of just overtaking them and going on to win, especially considering everything that had happened to reach this point. He obviously had some empathy with Nike, who were forced into this situation. Nathan asked Kristina what she thought about proposing that Nike draw with them for the PQ. Kristina said she had been thinking about the situation as well and wholeheartedly approved of Nathan's idea. They then pulled up alongside Hadyn and Richard, who were up ahead, and asked them their opinion. After a bit of discussion Hadyn and Richard agreed. The consequence of this action would be that they would have to share the first and second prize pool if the two teams arrived at the finish line together before all the other teams.

So Nathan and Kristina paddled up to Nike and put the proposal to them: would they like to draw the race? Nathan says that the Nike's first reaction was total shock at the gesture. But it was a gesture they appreciated and they decided to go with it. Nathan suggested that Nike and Team Seagate would have to cross the line together. However, because he was worried about competition from other teams, he also specified that, if they saw other teams were catching up, Team Seagate would race for first to the finish—the deal would be off. Nike again agreed.

This agreement caused some logistical problems in that Team Seagate now had to give Nike a bit of help to stay in front, while also being aware of the potential for some teams to catch up to them. So instead of working as a team of four, they were working as a team of eight. During the river leg, Team Seagate helped tow Nike and encouraged Nike to use drafting techniques to keep up the lead. Team Seagate helped Nike down the river for about four or five hours.

At the end of the river leg, the teams had to portage their boats for about 19 kilometres from the river to the sea before sea kayaking in the next leg of the race. The teams arrived at the portage together. Nike had skates for the portage, which would make their trip shorter than Team Seagate's, so Nike decided to go ahead and start paddling in the sea where they knew that Team Seagate would catch up with them. Working as in effect a team of eight, everyone had total trust that the others would keep up their end of the bargain.

Once hitting the sea, Team Seagate did indeed catch up with Nike fairly quickly. The two teams paddled together for several hours. Then at the last checkpoint, in a culmination of the sporting gesture, the teams swapped paddlers, so each kayak held a Team Seagate member and a Nike member to paddle to the finish. They finished the last leg in unity and crossed the finish line together—the ultimate gesture of sportsmanship.

What life lessons we can learn from this occasion? For Kristina, the central lesson was that 'unity and sportsmanship hold more at heart than straight-out winning'. Nathan talks about the mana that Team Seagate seem to hold now, with other teams respecting them in a different kind of way. He sees the gesture as the ultimate action that perfectly matched a race full of tragedy. In a captain's report after the PQ race, Nathan observes:

> It is often said that sport is a metaphor for life and that an adventure race is a condensed version of life where you pack a year's worth of thoughts, feelings, experiences and emotions into one week …

It is reassuring that Team Seagate actually focus on the many life lessons that they have the opportunity to learn and that can be applied to life more widely.

The Process of Establishing a Quality Team Culture

When I began to research Team Seagate, they had just recruited two new members (Hadyn and Richard). As in any team with new members, the team went through a process of accommodating and understanding each other's needs. They started off on a high because they won the first race they had together, the Borneo Outdoor Quest in December 2003. This was a stage race, so the expedition races had yet to be tested. As in all teams, too, they experienced some teething problems. All were getting to know each other. This familiarisation included learning others' mannerisms and expectations, which was the team purpose for the 2003 Borneo event—winning the event was a bonus. From that race onwards Team Seagate continued to work on their team culture explicitly.

Then in mid 2004, in an interview with me after a race in Sweden, Kristina reflects on the development of the team culture to date:

> I think that some of the foundations are there, but some are missing. As an example, it still feels like the new boys have an urge to prove themselves on the team. The team feels really progressive ... but it is still fragile, not yet an open forum with everyone surefooted and keen to create; rather there are still 'human', ego fragilities, etc. there ...

As expected, the process of establishing the team culture was taking time. But as the year progressed, so did the quality of Team Seagate's team culture.

Honesty and Trust

To expedite the building of the team culture, it was important at first to focus on honesty and trust, two values essential to enhancing performance. Interestingly, these two values had not been acknowledged as important by the range of other teams to which Team Seagate members had belonged previously. The difference for Team Seagate was that they needed to consolidate as they planned to be together for several years. Moreover, unlike other teams in the adventure race circuit, who have been together for 10 years and have learned through experience, Team Seagate aimed to establish a quality team environment in a short time. They believed the condensed timeframe was necessary to enhance their racing capabilities, as Kristina acknowledges:

> ... the team just feels like it can go so far... we are trying to create the team by shortcutting time. Normally what we are trying to create would take three or four years. But we want to cram this 'team' development into a year. I think that is fully possible because everyone is so keen and eager. This year is really the year that we are going to develop ourselves into a team and next year will be the year that we actually gain the benefits of that.

In their period of adjustment, all the athletes admitted that the one factor that would help them was experience. So experience is what they got by competing in 10 races in 2004. Some of that experience involved sleep deprivation in the expedition races, making decisions (or not) when exhausted, navigating well when times were rough, enjoying sensations and good times together, working out support for each other (perhaps through towing people), working out when someone was struggling and needed help, being honest about needing help, and trusting each other to ask for help when needed. After the Swedish race, Kristina demonstrates the team's initial concern with pursuing honesty:

> I wonder if that honesty will come, in which you can really say what you feel needs to be expressed for the betterment of the team. I think there needs to be a balance between recognising when honesty towards someone is your opinion and recognising how self-assured that person is to receive such honesty/opinion. I believe I put across honesty in how I feel if I am down, need help or I feel like I can be completely honest with that. I don't feel that I can be honest about how I think someone else is feeling, I can't express that yet because I don't feel everyone on the team is in a position to receive it.

The reality of any given race can change the dynamics of any team. So one part of gaining honesty and trust has been to experience many different racing scenarios and focus the team on solution-based thinking. Like Ruth Aitken and Leigh Gibbs with the Silver Ferns, Team Seagate's tactics in this area include *what if* scenarios, which they practise in debriefs outside of races and which they use to enhance the team's solution-based thinking, one of their directions this year. Kristina explains the rationale behind what if scenarios:

> As yet, we haven't covered all the scenarios or at least covered enough of the core ones to be able to mix and match responses [in races] ... I think ultimately we will have addressed so many different ways, such a variety of scenarios that new things won't come as a shock to us any more ...

The team use what if scenarios to develop their honest communication about the support they need or do not need from each other, as Kristina points out:

> ... in training, quite honestly, there was just a magnificent feeling of understanding and support between us all. At the end of those three weeks [in Colorado, after the race in Sweden], [we had] the scenario of someone needing help totally down pat. I was completely comfortable with it, the boys were completely comfortable with it. We knew what to say to each other, when to ask for help and when to give help without explicitly yelling things out.

Becoming honest has been an ongoing process for Team Seagate. In an interview before the 2004 Borneo race, Nathan says that honesty continues to improve:

> I would say that only recently Kristina ... has been honest with me about what could happen. It is also to try to make them feel that their position is not threatened or whatever. I think for the other guys, that is still there.

In regard to his own development in accepting honest communication and becoming more honest himself, Richard reflects that:

... doing a race, or a training mission, ... is a chance for you to say, 'Are you okay?' If you have had a real crap day, and you are feeling bad, as soon as you go to evaluate, you want to hear how everyone else is feeling ... Like, is there a chance to tow someone who is feeling bad or to get some help if I'm feeling bad? We are getting to the stage now where we think we are really enabled to ask. The ideal is not just for people to offer help, but is also for people to feel able to ask for help. It can be quite hard the first few times. It also takes time to learn how to evaluate how everyone else is feeling. For the first races I was just learning, it is a fine line between whether you are suffering [to an extent] which is normal in a race or whether you or someone else needs help. If someone else is suffering, you need to share the load. That is the probably the hardest thing to do, ... ask for help.

Hadyn offers the following perspective on the team's process of being honest before the 2004 Borneo race:

I think we have all become more honest and we have all realised that honesty is the best approach. We also trust that everybody is being honest. It didn't happen initially, but ... there was probably an awareness that total honesty was going to be important. And then through discussions, training weeks and races we worked on and developed our communications. Getting to know each other better also helped.

To help develop honesty quicker, the team decided there should be team debriefs (which began in the race after Sweden) about their races, and meetings to discuss strategies. Before and after each race the team have regular meetings and some structured feedback sessions. Because they are not together regularly outside of race events, they often email feedback to each other and follow up with a phone call. Through this process they learned that everyone had different needs, so the focus then changed to what each person needs to be successful. They also obviously continue to discover strengths and weaknesses in each other.

Certainly many of the individual needs identified can lead to differences of opinion and struggles to understand. Nonetheless Team Seagate are still pursuing open communication and honesty because their main focus is to function well as a team. Kristina underlines this point:

... in this team it's just great. Sweden was the first big race for us, even though we raced [in two other major races]. There was really opportunity after Sweden to give individual feedback, so you weren't just brushing issues under the carpet and not worrying about them again, you were confronting them. That is the bigger picture stuff. We were confronting them and saying, 'I am going to race with you for the next two years. This doesn't work for me, so we need a way of working it out so we are both comfortable with the situation, or with this personality clash, or with this trait, or whatever.' So there are not [unresolved] issues, we sort it out.

Trust, the other underpinning value needed to progress the team culture, existed on a basic level with Team Seagate initially. Subsequently, however, the team still believe they need to work on trust to build a good team environment. They have set out to feel comfortable with each other so that they can work on the team values. As Richard describes the process:

> That is something that has evolved. I have always trusted them and I think they have pretty much trusted me, but it was a process … especially with the amount of racing and the racing to that level.

As the process continues, Richard feels that trust is rapidly gaining momentum:

> … it feels as though there is much more of a confidence. All four of us have our own opinions and with the trust we can suggest ideas freely. In the end, [whoever's] idea we go with, we all trust that it will work the best for the team in that situation. To me that process hadn't really been completed until PQ. There are lots of things like that which come down to trust.

Kristina agrees with Richard:

> I think we have a huge potential to be a really fantastic team, but the [Sweden] race showed that you just need time as well. Something that came out was trust. You can want to trust someone but actually, until you have done the time with them, it's really hard just to give that trust, regardless. I needed to build my trust with them and they needed to trust me.

Earning trust over time is a theme in Hadyn's reflections too:

> … we haven't known each other for that long, but we do trust in each other a lot now and trust that the other person is being honest as well. If you're asking a teammate how they feel and they say 'great' when they feel like shit, then they aren't giving an honest answer. If you feel like shit, you have to tell people you feel like shit.

At the Borneo Outdoor Quest 2004 I observed that Team Seagate's honesty and trust had become much more evident. Their constant emphasis on creating a quality team culture enhanced their honesty, open communication and trust. It is a process that continues. As Hadyn notes:

> … there was a period where we were all getting to know each other … we still are. The team dynamic changes with the people you race with. When there are different combinations of team members, each team member takes on different roles.

In Hadyn's view, the ongoing process of getting to know each other is tied up with the challenge of creating good team dynamics through honesty and trust:

> What we are trying to do is to focus on how we could use our collective knowledge to help us travel better as a team. Getting to know each other is ongoing but we are at a very comfortable level now. We are trusting each

other and being completely honest … if there is a start of any frustration, it comes out then and there. Nothing is withheld.

With trust and confidence in a quality team environment, Richard says, 'there is more belief and you start to live it'. He believes the accelerated process of creating a quality team culture is working:

When you come into a new [team], there are a lot of things you can't really control; it just takes time to get in on it. It takes time to know the history and … Until you have the complete picture, it is really hard to feel ownership of something. You feel like, maybe in a year. That is really where by really pushing the teamwork and the team building and doing all the exercises that really formulate us, is going to bring that on a lot quicker. Whereas the likes of Nike, they have been together for several years. I think we have managed to re-create that in only a year. We already have a really, really close team.

Richard sees a number of reasons as contributing to the team's ability to work so well together. In part it is because of:

… everyone's commitment to making people go faster. There is no one thing … there is a professionalism, so differences don't become issues—especially on the race course. I think we generally get along well which is a huge help and I think everyone genuinely wants to see the others have the best race they can.

The Feedback Process

One of the tools Nathan introduced since joining Team Seagate is feedback sheets. Although initially unsure about the worth of the new tool, as they continue to use the sheets the other team members acknowledge the benefits of having debriefs and giving and accepting feedback.

As the year progresses, Nathan acknowledges that they have been using the feedback sheets to focus explicitly on 'a bit of team building or team planning'—that is, building team culture:

There is probably a lot more emphasis on that, as opposed to just getting out there and letting the experience sort itself out. We are doing a lot more processes and things like that … I was aware that Kristina had some ideas or links or direction that she wanted the team to go in. But I didn't think it would've worked with the last team, but I definitely feel that it will work with this team. I have supported her on that kind of stuff.

Kristina speaks of a questionnaire that Nathan designed as a method of giving everyone feedback to enhance individual and team performance. This approach to team debriefing began after the race in Sweden:

What is new in this team is that we talk about the race. After the race we spend some time filling in a questionnaire that Nathan drew up, which has team things to improve upon and things we did well. Also, [we identify] our own individual things to improve upon and things we did well, and then look at each of the team members from our perspective, what each of them did well and what each of them could improve upon. We go around in a circle and first discuss the team stuff, our own individual did well/improvements and then take turns focusing on one person and everyone gives feedback to that one person.

From Hadyn's perspective, the feedback discussions are a positive influence on the process of establishing team culture:

I think things continually fall into place. There was one trip where (at the time I didn't realise it) we had a great time. It drew us closer together as a team. These times are very important. We have had a lot of discussions and I believe we have accelerated the process of getting to know each other through discussions, team meetings, emails, self-analysis and honest communications … teammates give their opinion as to how you can perform better, or where you are performing badly, what your strengths and weaknesses are. Each person does that for each other person. You've got to be honest.

Nathan has designed several different questionnaires which vary in their questions but are all concerned with identifying what the team did that worked well. They seem to function as one of the key elements in establishing a quality team environment. The following are sample questions from the questionnaire after the Sweden race:

- Name three things the team could improve on.
- Name three things the team do well.
- How can the team help you or the team at Primal Quest?
- What are some concerns you may have about the person (things that worry you)?
- What comforts do you have about the person (things that reassure you)?

Following the same general themes, these questions were used before each stage of the Borneo Outdoor Quest 2004:

- What are any anxieties/concerns/fears?
- What are you looking forward to in this race?
- What do you want to work on in the race?
- What can the team do to help you?
- How do you feel?
- List one word that describes the race for you.
- How do you want to feel when you cross the finish line?

Another part of the pre-race team brief for this multi sport race in Borneo was for Kristina, who was organising logistics for the race, to go through each transition and report what equipment needs were for that day.

Then at the end of each stage, the team reflected on the day's racing with these questions:

- How did you feel today?
- What were high points and low points?
- What did you learn today?
- What did we do well?
- What do we need to work on?

Finally, at the end of the entire race, team members filled in an official feedback sheet about the full race:

- What is the one word that describes this race for me?
- What went well for me in this race?
- What went well for the team?
- What can I improve on?
- What can the team improve on?
- For each athlete, give feedback on things he/she could improve on and on what he/she did well. [They save the positives for last.]
- What can I take away from this race and how can I action this?
- What am I going to leave behind from this race?

After the team had experienced this feedback process for almost half a year (from its mid year beginnings in Sweden to Borneo in late 2004), Kristina acknowledges its strengths:

> The team feels so professional now. We know we have weaknesses in areas and stuff, but to be able and talk about them and then be able to go away and work on them is a completely new professional approach.

Kristina suggests that what comes out of these evaluations is:

> ... things that we have to work on. We do not begrudge those because they were going to come out at some stage as we are not a perfect team, we accept that.

The feedback initiative has allowed the team to take ownership of the team direction and to buy into ideas to work on. Richard admits he struggled to become accustomed to a process that was so new to him but over time he began to see its benefits:

> I guess the biggest challenge has been just accepting, just learning how to deal with things within teams and how to be a bigger part of that team. That is just experience ... taking as much of the opportunities, rather than just going on. Just allowing yourself to go out on a limb and say things. The first time you do it, you feel a bit silly, then it gets better ... It can be quite a good thing, sometimes it would be easier to go and do your own thing and then forget about it. Sometimes the hardest points can be when one person is

keen and the others aren't so sure, you notice some of the cultures in other teams and I think the difference is how open our team is to trying things and always looking for the edge to improve. I think that dealing with people and getting the confidence to voice your own opinion is quite important. As an individual we are doing similar evaluations, goal setting and planning, but I find that it is quite different in a team situation doing it, I haven't been involved in it like this [before]. It's quite hard to start with, but it has formed the culture and it has been getting easier as we go … The easier it gets, the more powerful it gets.

Moreover, he now appreciates the reason for doing it:

We started to get to the point where there could've been issues, or there were issues that people brought out and we aired. I think the whole culture evolved quite rapidly, so everything we have worked through has helped develop the culture very quickly and … at a much higher level because everyone has helped to solve the issues. It has really made the team as good as we can be.

The notion of team evaluation was also quite new to Hadyn. He speaks of the context in which the feedback process was introduced:

The last few months have been relatively new for me. I am not sure whether the others have previously done this process or not. I think what has happened is that prior to Richard and myself joining Seagate, this process would never happen. I believe that this is something that Kristina has been striving for, for a long time and now that there is the opportunity to do it we have gone essentially quite deep into the psychology and teamwork development processes.

Like Richard, Hadyn now enjoys the process:

It's fine … I think there are things that we all want feedback on. It's your teammates' perception of you, and you can take away from it what you want and can leave the rest of it behind … if I bring up a point and it doesn't get picked up on, so what of it? It doesn't matter, but if it helps a teammate that's great. Everybody throws their ideas into the hat and you take what ideas you want out of it … I believe we have become better as we have gotten to know each other. I don't know whether I would've offered my opinion a year ago. I was the new guy and I would sit back and watch and learn, and when I was ready I would apply it. We are now all taking more ownership in team decisions. We all jointly own the decisions made. If you don't input into the decision-making process then it is assumed that you agree with the decisions made.

For Nathan, this feedback process in particular has allowed him to learn a lot from the other Team Seagate members:

I prefer the team as it stands now. One of the reasons [is] … I think that I have been able to explore potential … of where I want it to go. Each of them have some great ideas, we couldn't have done [this] with the last team, partly because of resistance, partly because they wouldn't have approved it. I think this team, from a competitive point of view, as a unit … I think I find our skills will be stronger, a stronger team.

Nathan sees this process as the really important focus when creating a team that works well together. Given that most competitors are fantastic athletes in adventure racing, Team Seagate must certainly maintain their physical prowess. However, attending to the physical side of racing alone does not create a good team environment. Nathan puts it this way:

… in adventure sport and multi sport, there is often a lot better athletes at the races. But for the athletes to perform as a team, the team has to work well. Same at this [Borneo] race: there are probably 10 or 15 guys in this field, if you went on physical [prowess] and they are strong and fitter than me, but their teams are not winning teams. I think we effectively have a great horsepower team, but it really needed to be channelled rather than focused on raw ability alone. I don't think we would have had the success that we've had. Particularly since it has only been a year since we have been together.

In his captain's report after each race, Nathan summarises the race, relates stories and identifies great aspects as well as areas that need to be improved. He always uses a sense of humour to communicate his message, which the team seem to appreciate.

For most of the team, the training week in Nelson before PQ was a turning point that led them to feel closer and really work on team culture. As Richard describes it:

It has all built up over the year. We went up to Nelson for a team camp; it was a long way to go but as the week progressed we started to really explore some of the issues and extend the team culture. By the end of the week I think everyone was really quite drained, but once I had had time to process everything and had some recovery time, then I felt great. On reflection, I think the combination [of the Nelson trip and working on team culture] worked quite well …

Hadyn has striking memories of the Nelson experience:

One of the nicest times we had was in Nelson when we were sea kayaking D'Urville Island; Nathan had organised a number of trips that week. We camped on the beach, had a campfire, sat around. It was wonderful, it was really, really nice.

Establishing Team Values

The Nelson training week was also noteworthy for its impact on team values. Kristina feels that, prior to that week, the boys were still focused on building skills and physical fitness more than on developing as a team:

… it seemed that when we have that time away, they're not being recognised as actual team development times; rather the focus was still on training and fitness and stuff. At first, I think the new boys saw the week in Nelson as more fitness-orientated, or hard-skill-orientated, but not really as team time.

Contrary to their assumptions, however, the time in Nelson proved to be an opportunity for team development. Kristina enjoyed introducing a process to establish team values for Team Seagate. She explains how everyone came up with a saying linked to team values that would help establish their team culture:

The saying that we have come up with is 'swells up'. We spent a bit of a time thinking of a saying that would have meaning for all of us. In general, ['swells up'] means the pressure is rising so just chill out, though to different people it means different things … H[adyn, for example,] is a real sea boy; he grew up with surf lifesaving, so he can immediately go to a nice happy place.

Kristina then relates an anecdote that gave the saying particular meaning for her:

When we were sea kayaking in Nelson during that training week, Nathan and I were on the outside of a sea cave, a particularly ugly, gnarly one, deciding whether we should go into it or not. There was quite a swell. We had to come down on the swell to go into the cave and then the rising swell would lead up to the arch. So timing was really important. We had it all sorted, went to go in, looked back and there was this massive wave coming at us. We backpaddled madly to get out of the cave. It had been the seventh wave and was huge. If we had been in the cave, it would've been all over. There would have been smashed bits everywhere. Fortunately, we hadn't been pushed in, but we still had to decide whether we would go into it or not. Now that the seventh wave had gone, and we were back to the normal with intrepid excitement, we went in and came out the other side safely … The term 'swells up' reminds me of this moment, of the excitement, challenge and relief giggling … 'swells up' or sea swell brought in the idea that Seagate was behind us and helped us remember that Seagate related to how much we were sacrificing to be here.

While Kristina respects the values they established and continues to use the sea swell imagery, the boys claim that they have less need for the words. Nathan says he does not use the term because it does not fit with his style rather than because he does not support the concept:

I don't *not* want to [use it]. Part of it for me is because it is not how I operate. I have gone with that because I felt that it has been good for the team. It is better for some people than others, but I supported it because it is important in some ways to the team, then I am happy to go with it … I just find that often I am navigating as well and often with navigation and [focusing] … how we are getting along as a team and general race strategy, I feel like I am [exhausted].

Richard similarly supports the team's key words as generally helpful to the team culture without feeling the need to make them integral to his own practice:

> I am really happy to participate to help Kristina and at some stage the key words might come up … when you use them and need them, but not if you don't have to … that was one of the things where it showed to me that we had matured a lot, was that everyone had ownership of that even though it didn't necessarily fit exactly what they were going to use. With the whole team participating and helping to formulating them, for Kristina it gave her what she needed … When we got to PQ and we were formulating our race strategy, that was probably where the key words became quite relevant, e.g. controlling the race and consolidating it with sleep. So that helped though it wasn't part of my coping strategy. It was part of the overseeing and it helped build the strategy around the race.

While also regarding Kristina as the central figure in the process, Hadyn feels that the sea swell terminology has helped him:

> There was another thing that came out of that from our Nelson trip. We had discussed ways of trying to help us through certain situations during a race, when we were feeling down, when we were feeling up and ways of dealing with frustrations and negative situations. The phrase 'sea swell sac' was one of them that came up. Kristina was the instigator, she was the one who facilitated the word play, it was important to her and we felt we could all learn from it. She was searching for something that she could take with her into a race that would calm her or lift her when needed … in the process we went through a number of words that we thought would match a situation, or that we could all relate to. So we developed the phrases and these have worked well for me.

For the Primal Quest, they continued with same theme but used different values, still based on Seagate. Hadyn shares his idea about Seagate and what it means:

> 'C-gate' was a phrase that arose at the PQ. The 'C', in this situation, stood for Confidence, Control and Consolidate. 'Sea Sac Swell' was also there from our Nelson trip. We respect other teams and this leads to a number of situations. If we felt that a team passing us didn't respect us, then it is much more of a chance that we are going to get our backs up and we would go a lot harder. [That is where we need control.] I guess it's better to be beaten by a team that you respect rather than a team that you don't respect.

As Kristina recalls it:

> The Seagate and sea swell stuff was ours from Nelson, but coming up with the four C's, I think it was [Hadyn] coming up with those at one of our team meetings, putting forward four words and all relating to Sea. … it sparked a little acronym thing and then we were all coming up with 'C' words.

As with the sea swell word play, Richard was less enthusiastic about the wording developed at PQ than about the values and goals it represented:

The values were really good, but it was … more the words and phrases [that] didn't work for me. As far as the goals, they were good, what we wanted to achieve out of the race, the C's: we wanted to control the race, be confident we could do that and then we looked at scenarios whereby if we end up getting ahead, what are we going to do, and that was consolidation, so we would take a sleep rather than trying to [continue], we had to consciously do that.

So did the values help him to race better? Richard believes:

They did because there were a few times when we said, 'We'll just take the opportunity to sleep now and consolidate our position.' At times in the race, we said 'How are you going?'; the lead teams hadn't slept at all and ultimately, if the race had continued, we were still in with a shot because we consolidated. While we were racing it was quite easy to look at the words. We were just out here conserving ourselves—that was the other C, conserve—for the 40 hours and we were just going to treat it like a couple of 24-hour races.

But one of the most powerful team-building events arose entirely unexpectedly through music. That event involved their adoption of a song based on mutual experiences. Though it seemed like a coincidence, I believe the link to the song was forged because of the team's focus on sea swell and Seagate values. This song proved to be crucial to their emotional stability at the PQ race. Kristina tells the story of how the team tuned in to the power of this song:

Actually, the song was decided after the training week. We were driving back from Nelson and it played on Nathan's car stereo; the song is 'As Good As It Gets'. Then, by coincidence, we raced back to Nelson, finished the week off, went to Hanmer and were watching the Olympic triathlon double medal and it was the song they used when they were showing the highlights … I've got this absolutely delightful memory that will stick forever, and it is a wonderful memory of our team at PQ. We were just about to go down to race registration and we had been sorting gear and having a team meeting … We were back at the campervan, collecting everyone and Brayden, Nathan's brother, was there with his guitar. He had written the words [to the song] on a big piece of card. Before going to registration, we went to the camper[van] and sang the song a couple of times until we really knew it. It was powerful … there we were singing this powerful song about giving it our all and accepting this is as good as it gets; this opportunity we have, we are living it, it doesn't get any better than this. Then we walked down together to the registration singing … the atmosphere of the team was brilliant.

Nathan identifies with 'As Good As It Gets' in this way:

… we represented that stuff … humming that song, singing words to that song during that race was my connection with that session about the words.

Richard relates how the song influenced him:

> It was just a Feelers song, I just found it was a really good distraction ... we had some times in PQ, where we were dragging our bikes through the bush and things couldn't really have got any worse, and the song was a really good thing. It was knowing the words, the song would just make you feel good. So that for me was really powerful.

Hadyn also enjoyed the song:

> ... we all ended up singing together for awhile. I hate singing with others around and I am crap at it, but it was one of the first times that I felt comfortable actually singing. It was good to know that everyone was into it as it really gave you a mental lift. PQ was a big race and we did a lot of things that we thought would help us and they did. There would be times when you were feeling low, you'd just start humming or singing the song to yourself. The effect that it had on you was quite cool. Sometimes you kept it to yourself and sometimes you would hear someone else singing and join in.

'As Good As It Gets' will remain a powerful memory forever because of the experience the team shared at PQ. It will remind each person of what Team Seagate means to him or her. It enhanced the great team culture that they were already forming.

As an aside, I was curious to compare the sport of adventure racing to popular team sports. Why does the process of establishing team culture take longer for an adventure race team than, say, a volleyball team, who only meets two or three times a week for a limited period? Kristina addresses the question this way:

> My guess would be because ... the experiences you have in adventure races are so much more raw and intense [compared] to normal sport settings. If I was to sum up adventure racing, it is a year in a week. Everything is so much more intense. The physical and emotional extremes you go through, the level of tiredness which brings out all sorts of demons, you can't hold anything back when you get that tired. My guess would be, because adventure racing is such an intense sport, the process just takes that much longer because you get that much deeper into a personality. In volleyball, there are some practices in the week, and you have the game within [a two-hour] timeframe ... then the people step back from each other, vent out frustrations that they may have before then they meet up again. That same space doesn't happen in adventure racing. You are with the same people for the whole week. You can't go away and vent off frustrations. You have to be within 100 metres of them ... You have to have all the venting sorted, and the working together sorted beforehand.

Team Goals

In the process of team building over the year, team goals became a stronger feature. Kristina indicates how they began to become more important:

> I said [after Sweden] that I felt like I needed to have a team goal established so [that] when things were really tough I could think back to the team goal, because having a goal worked for me in my other races. The boys became open to the idea … I put it across that I need a team goal and it would be good if it was created by the team because it would make it a real team goal.

Now, team goals are established before each race throughout the season. Nathan points out the advantages of setting goals in both the short and longer term:

> It is all good and well to sit down at the start of the year and say, 'This is what we want to do', but you really have to check in at the start of each race and actually see where things are at and make a plan for that race. The only goal that I have been really keen to have is that we have a goal to race together and that at the start of this year, it was for two years at a time. I think we probably need to readdress that at the end of the season. I think that is incredibly important, that commitment thing, so we all know that we are in for the long haul.

Richard provides a perspective of creating team goals for a multi sport event in particular:

> For a race like this [the Borneo Outdoor Quest] it is a little bit different because there's probably less strategy involved. You don't have sleep to manage, you don't have equipment to manage and if you lose a lot of time then it is going to be harder to catch it up. You pretty much have to race in front of the race. So tactics are a lot more obvious. If you race to the front and get a chance to get ahead, you take it … you never get to the point that you can give the lead, you are always trying to extend it. It's quite different tactically from adventure racing. For any team, the goals are always to help put on the best performance you can. For us the goals also include to be true to whatever the values are and not to win by cheating, and [to aim to win] by racing in a good spirit of sportsmanship.

Roles

One of the best methods of enhancing team culture, as athlete-centred coaches in this book suggest, is for athletes to understand each team member's responsibilities and roles. A role for both Nathan and Kristina, for example, seems to be to monitor the team environment and look for opportunities for feedback. Nathan explains that leadership and other roles of individual team members vary according to the conditions of the individual race:

> I think in the teams for adventure racing … it is not like a rugby team, where you've got forwards and backs and wingers. Really all we have are navigators. It is a huge role, but often Hadyn and I share that navigation role. The roles are slightly different … we've all got different areas of expertise, so often whoever's area of expertise it is, they'll effectively slip into that leader role. Kristina has the most mountaineering background, so when we are in the mountains, we look to her for leadership, or she makes the calls, so to

speak. When we are near water, especially rivers, I take that [leadership role]; I don't ask questions, I basically dictate this is going to happen. The team trusts that. Richard has come from Olympic skiing, so he is really familiar with ski or snow conditions, he knows lots of stuff about things like that. Hadyn has come from surf lifesaving, so the ocean and swells and things like that, he knows a lot about. I think the roles go around for a lot of different things. The race is so long …

Hadyn describes his role:

Well, I have [navigated] the bikes in the last few races and navigating can be tricky. You expend a lot of [mental] energy, (well I personally do,) when you are navigating. It's nice to be able to pass the maps over and not have to think about navigating for a while when you are into a trekking section or a paddling section. One of the reasons I enjoy the multi sport, or the shorter style of racing is that often there is not the navigation involved … it's pretty much the gun goes and you know where you are going. You follow the tape and you can just focus all your energy on performing the task of getting there or assisting your team as opposed to having to be pawing over the maps and expending mental energy on that.

As to whether there are roles on the team more generally, Hadyn says:

Yes, we realise the strengths of certain people. A lot of the stuff if we each individually did it, we would waste energy. Nathan is the captain and the leader and he performs certain roles; he is also the lead navigator. Kristina's great with logistics as well as the discussion and communication side of things. Physically we all have to be relatively strong, but Richard would be the strongest overall.

With a view similar to Nathan's, Kristina suggests that the nature of the race, rather than assigned roles, shapes the leadership role that each team member takes on:

In the past, Nathan has always been the leader, though essentially we have all put in our opinion and rather a consensus been made. If there was any wonder, we would back down to Nathan. A team of us three as happens in the 24-hour races without Nathan is different. We are feeling our way. At the moment, I think the boys are looking up to me for my experience, and again offering their opinions, like with Nathan, but backing down to mine, whatever that is. Though we all have our roles. H[adyn] for example is navigator, so he leads any decisions on that matter … I would say, we all very much contribute, and the percentage [of each contribution] depends on not only the situation, but also how we are feeling. That is important in this type of racing, we aren't always in a position to lead, even if this is our strongest discipline or situation normally.

These reflections lead Kristina to conclude that the team's flexibility in regard to roles may be linked to its success:

Maybe that's a key to a successful team: one which has roles assigned but enough skill within the team to allow those roles to change depending on how people are feeling at the time. I would say roles are by no means clean cut; rather they 'flow'.

Leadership in Team Seagate

As the captain of Team Seagate, Nathan is the identified leader. He also works hard to implement shared leadership, as is evident from the discussion of roles above. Nathan's leadership characteristics confirm the observation of Lao Tzu (a Chinese Taoist: see Chapter Two) that 'when the effective leader is finished with his work, the people say it happened naturally'. He is a leader who ensures that athletes take ownership of and responsibility for the team and its performance. He can be classified as practising an athlete-centred approach because in making decisions he considers the best interests of the athletes in the pursuit of the perfect performance.

As with some coaches in this book, Nathan started off in the first, prescriptive quadrant of Hersey and Blanchard's Situational Coaching Model (see Figure 2.2, Chapter Two) because there were two new members on the team. Very rapidly he moved into quadrant 2—consultation—as though the team members were responsible for their individual training, for races he needed to facilitate establishing mutual team goals. I observed that Nathan operated in the more participative quadrant 3 in Borneo: although he facilitated the athletes, he divested the power more. He feels that, although Team Seagate is not strictly the first team he has captained, it has been his first experience of particularly active and more confident captaincy:

> … I have been team captain a lot but really until this year, team captain has just been on paper really. There haven't actually been different roles or responsibilities … Just the way we race … I definitely think that in this team, I have seen the benefit of having a little bit of leadership, at certain times. It is only natural for me to be in that role … because of my position with our sponsor and I am the person who liaises with the races. I usually have a bit more knowledge than the other teammates do. I know what is going on. So definitely the team captaincy role has been more active this year than it has in the past … I think the captaincy role for me I have grown into and have had time to put energy into. I thought it would be a good thing. I thought the team would benefit from having that leadership. I guess part of that is acknowledging the value of leadership. I have also realised that my extensive experience in the outdoors and racing holds a lot of influence that can be used positively to make decisions. I haven't actually been aware of that in the past.

As to where he learned about leadership, Nathan says:

> I have had coaches who have been inspirational and then there were things I noted in a lot of the theme[s] of my coaches. I have earmarked coaches who have been life coaches as much as sport coaches. Often [in] sports

training [there have] been little lessons there about life … It keeps it all in perspective, I think, in a lot of ways.

To enhance that all-important athlete input, Nathan continually seeks information from his teammates. He believes in asking questions to get athletes to think about issues and solutions:

> I ask questions about things, more so to Kristina. I keep a little bit of control on that … I have had the most experience in racing competitively in this sport. Since I have been through this evolving team, I have come up with a lot of themes that are better to help us achieve more. One of those themes was to surround myself with incredible athletes who were also open to my ideas and were kind of running with them a bit. That's where I have felt that with this team there has been a lot of trust … I do [ask questions], but it actually takes quite a long time for people to answer. So you can question and question and question, but it takes people a while before they are actually comfortable with putting their ideas forward.

One of Nathan's assets as a leader is his ability to 'read' people and empathise with them. He admits that leading people, and especially reading people, takes a lot of experience. There is an art to getting the timing right to approach a person to question or discuss issues, although Nathan feels it comes naturally to him:

> It is just my style. I guess it is looking at the appropriate time to say things or looking for opportunities to say, I think I am quite good at timing and then when I feel something may need to be said about something that relates to that stuff, then I say it.

Shared leadership has been important to the creation and development of this extraordinary team environment. Nathan agrees:

> I guess on top of that, with those shared leadership [roles, in] my role as captain, I see myself as the main facilitator; I am the person who is looking at an overview, looking at the whole picture. I have to do that as much as I can.

An example of his leadership that clearly represents his principles came at the Borneo Outdoor Quest 2004. He and other Team Seagate members are opposed to a rule that each team of four must include at least one woman or else at least one man who is 45 years old or more. At the awards ceremony of the race, Nathan spoke out against the inclusion of the provision for a man aged 45+ years in races like the multi sport stage races. He explained that by keeping the men's teams, it is possible to omit the female competitors completely. In his eloquent presentation, he sent a powerful message that without women, racing would not be worthwhile. In conclusion, again demonstrating Team Seagate's values and class, he declared that if the rule stayed, Team Seagate would boycott next year's Outdoor Quest.

Nathan admits that the leadership role is much more enjoyable when others take on different aspects of it. He believes strongly in delegating and, for their part, the other team members are happy to have ownership as it makes them feel part of the team. One of the factors contributing to the success of Team Seagate is the athlete-centred leadership style Nathan has adopted.

Plans for the Future

The morning before we left Borneo, the team had another meeting to decide their plans for 2005. On a sheet they had been given to complete, they wrote the races they wanted to do for the year, including a wishlist for 2005. Having enjoyed their 2004 training weeks, Richard and Hadyn wanted to have another in Queenstown where they could organise it. They also talked about their wishes for gear and getting sponsorships—wanting to keep Seagate as a sponsor, but perhaps looking at increasing the base salary. Nathan took notes and will begin to organise what will happen in 2005. Each team member suggested that they would like to set aside a minimum time for being at home to spend time with family. As they all live a long way away from each other, they wanted to enhance the communication both home and overseas.

Team Seagate reviewed 2004 by asking how each athlete feels about racing in 2005. All team members are committed; all are inspired by their potential for achievement next year. They are excited to see how far they have come as a team in just one year, how much they have come together and striven together to improve. Their one concern is the potentially limited number of races on offer in 2005. There is talk that several major races will not take place for various reasons—including lack of sponsors and organiser concern over risk taking. Therefore they want to maximise every opportunity they can take. They love the sport, they love the team and its direction, and they want to continue on together.

Conclusion

Team Seagate (along with the coaches in this book) have shown that the public and the media need to understand the true educational value of sport. It seems to have been lost in translation. Some would argue that professionalism has brought a need to do well in order to earn money and look after 'number one', rather than creating athletes who are human beings, not just sport jocks. As a professional team, however, Team Seagate has demonstrated that that the 'me' culture that pervades professional sport is not a given. To this team of four, what is most important is learning and applying life lessons through sport. The money is a bonus.

By continuing to praise winners (that is, the people who come first, at no matter what cost), the public loses the true value of sport. Sport can build moral character but it does not happen through osmosis. To the contrary, it is very difficult to develop morally when we are constantly receiving messages that cheating helps us win, that violence is more entertaining, and that sport is an *I* institution, where *I* receive more money if *I* wear certain clothes. Typically, the first question from an athlete today is, 'What is in it for me?' Coaches, administrators, educators and media have a responsibility to build moral character through sport by educating the public about the true value of sport.

We are inundated with 'Bring Back the Biff'—replaying episodes of people falling, being knocked out or fighting in the sports arena. One of the most-reported features of the Athens Olympics concerned supposedly world-class athletes who use drugs as a way to win. We also get replays of violence or injuries to sensationalise the stories. Come on now: winning is important, but the *process* of winning is the true way to build character through sport. Certainly winning remains the aim of any sporting campaign, but it is the process leading to the win that serves as a learning opportunity. You need to lose to learn how to win too.

The Team Seagate Adventure Race team are one of the most recent examples of a team full of moral character, striving to win and to be the best in the world. They treat sport as a privilege and exude life values. Adventure racing is about testing the human body and mind to the extreme. It is about learning life lessons that enhance our character and enable us to be better human beings. This chapter has presented some fantastic stories that highlight the life lessons that we should be taking from sport. Here's to Team Seagate for putting sport back into the perspective it should be.

And the trouble is, if you don't
risk anything, you risk even more.
– *Erica Jong*

Truthfulness is the main element of
character. – *Brian Tracy*

When you make a mistake, don't look back at it long. Take the reason
of the thing into your mind and then look forward. Mistakes are lessons
of wisdom. The past cannot be changed. The future is yet in your power.
– *Hugh White*

To be able to look back upon one's past life with
satisfaction is to live twice. – *John Dalberg Actor,
English historian*

Chapter Nine

Wayne Smith
International Rugby Coach

This chapter discusses the coaching approach developed and used by Wayne Smith, one of the two current assistant coaches of the All Blacks (the New Zealand national men's rugby team). A prime proponent for the athlete-centred philosophy, Wayne Smith is noted for his ability to formulate a team culture that is more successful than that produced by traditional rugby approaches in the modern era.

An athlete-centred approach, as suggested in Chapter One, is ideal for sports teams as it gives athletes control and choice, it enables them to make decisions while competing, and it brings back the 'fun' of participating in sport because athletes have greater internal motivation. As well as using an athlete-centred approach with elite rugby squads, Wayne has used it when coaching children. His philosophy, vision and values can make rugby, in his case, a sport of the 21st century.

Wayne was interviewed at length while he was still coaching the Canterbury Crusaders, a New Zealand regional men's rugby team that plays in the Super 12 international rugby competition, which he coached from 1997–1999. Then, after he became assistant All Blacks coach in 2004, Wayne edited and added to many of his quotes from the original interview; therefore some of his experiences since 2000 are integrated here. Since the interview and editing, Wayne has coached Northampton Saints in England before returning to New Zealand to be an All Blacks assistant coach. The interview remains an honest reflection of his views, as what has changed in the interim is not his thinking about coaching but his experience. His wisdom remains widely valued.

The chapter begins by focusing on how Wayne has developed his athlete-centred philosophy. Wayne then discusses his own development as a coach and reasons for adopting Teaching Games for Understanding (TGfU), the advantages and implementation of such an approach, and the process of empowering players. He also covers some of the challenges he faces in continuing to use an athlete-centred approach and how he will use it with the All Blacks.

Wayne's Philosophy of Coaching

To give some background to the development of his philosophy, Wayne discusses the contribution of the players to the team. He prefers people on his team to show real *character*, which he suggests is:

> … the ability to persist, be relentless and not give up when the chips are down … the ability, when away from home, when faced with adversity, when conditions are against them and they haven't got their star player, to still perform with character, with persistence. People with character don't look

for the easy way out or for excuses when up against it, they achieve the unexpected. They leave a little bit of themselves on the field every time they play and they take responsibility for their own performance.

Likewise, the coach has to be resilient and consistently optimistic under pressure. After five games in the 1998 Super 12, we [Canterbury Crusaders] were last and coming in for a lot of criticism. One of my sons (Joshua) was in hospital for some major surgery and my contract was up at the end of the season. In this situation, you have to lead the way—the players deserve your best effort every day. It takes huge reserves of energy to dig deep and keep fighting, but once you give up, the players will give up. Your job is to keep hope alive for yourself and your players.

Building character among a group of players, so that they take responsibility for their preparation and performance, is part of the foundation of an athlete-centred approach. Wayne suggests that every member of his team (whether he is a wing or loose forward) should have the ability to be a leader who can communicate what he is seeing on the field, where to go, what space he is in and what the opposition is doing. All players should have the ability to 'see it, understand it, call it and react to it'.

Wayne believes in traditional values and works hard with players to identify and develop those that are meaningful to the players and that are bone deep—that is, with them for a lifetime. Wayne's philosophy also relates to the importance of developing the whole person, not just the rugby player. He suggests that a focus on career goals is a key to developing thinking people who are able to empower themselves. He supports this focus by encouraging players to study, work or help in the community. He also encourages players to think and creates an environment in which players are not scared to have a go. All these elements in his philosophy are reflected in his description of himself as a coach:

I am a coach that likes to learn and believes that learning faster than the others is critical. I communicate that attitude to the players, making sure that they also are open to new ideas. Players generally like innovation, but it's important they treat everything on merit. You've got to be prepared to make mistakes and allow your players to make them. The team that makes the most mistakes wins the game because only 'do-ers' make them. Your job as coach is to ensure they're not making the same mistakes over and over.

Another key area in Wayne's coaching approach is his belief that the principle of honesty with players is extremely important. He believes that it is essential to act on this principle, not just talk about it:

Being honest with the players is crucial. We establish a protocol where we expect people to 'stab in the belly', not the back. Telling players why they are not playing on the weekend is fundamental to achieving an honest, up-front team environment. I like to back my selectorial opinion with statistical and video evidence, making suggestions on what the player should work on to get a starting spot in the team. The players get an opportunity one on one to discuss these issues. A player [at the regional level] once suggested I was using different standards to measure him than I was using to assess the other player in his position. He was right. There was a flaw in the data we were using. We named him to start the following game, and he was outstanding. He is now an All Black.

To be successful, you need players with a hungry attitude to accept the challenges you set them, and to improve their strengths as well as their weaknesses. When you give them an opportunity, they know what the team needs from them and have a greater chance of performing well. Establish your expectations and stick to them. If [the players] don't come up to scratch, you need to help them improve until they do. Worthwhile people seldom let you down if you are up-front and honest with them.

In the three seasons that Wayne was coaching the Canterbury Crusaders, the team won two Super 12 championships. His athlete-centred approach with the Crusaders was innovative. Many of the players had never been coached in this way. Wayne became a leader in rugby coaching by learning how to empower players. His example has provided encouragement for many coaches of rugby (and other sports), who are now beginning to learn about and use an athlete-centred approach.

One of the first steps in initiating such an approach is to set up a team of people to help empower the players. Wayne sees the merit of finding the right people for the job:

You should spend the time to get the right people around you. You need the right players, obviously, and the best support staff you can get. Getting great people going in the right direction is important. You need a really strong vision that everyone is part of formulating. Ensure the best systems and processes are set up, commit to excellence and consistent work habits, develop a hard mental attitude and smother it all in good, old-fashion values. If you adhere to that model, you'll (at the very least) get satisfaction as an outcome.

Getting the right people for the Crusaders was fundamental to our success. I've been fortunate in having people like Peter Sloane and Steve Hansen as my coaching partners. I've also got other people around me who are able to teach and learn. We work well together. We enjoy what we are doing. Often you neglect the journey in your eagerness or anxiety about reaching a goal. John Wooden (ex-UCLA basketball coach) said, 'A successful journey becomes your destination'. Try and make your journey better than the inn.

Wayne indicates that having a great bunch of people to learn from is a major part of developing a successful team (as well as contributing to his own development as a coach—the subject of the next section):

Gilbert Enoka (sports psychologist) is really helpful as an educator. When I was playing, we got him along to talk to the Canterbury team the night before a Ranfurly Shield match. He spoke to us about the mental side of rugby … I become convinced … a psychological skills training [PST] programme was important. I went on to develop my own PST programme as a player with Gilbert's guidance. Once I became coach, I reintroduced him to the team. Now, he is an integral part of the Crusaders and All Black set-ups, not just in PST, but just as importantly in time management and game review systems.

It seems obvious that Wayne has been successful in attracting the right people to develop the Crusaders and the All Blacks. The staff that work along side him are teachers and keen learners. His players have become learners of the game and of life by being enabled to take ownership of their direction and reasons for playing rugby. By giving the players a measure of control over their campaign, Wayne believes burnout can be avoided and a deep love for the game enhanced. He believes passionately that better people make better rugby players.

As part of the athlete-centred process and giving players ownership of the game, Wayne also believes in the rotation system of play whereby all players have an equal opportunity to be selected for particular games:

You've got people on the team who you selected, so you've got to give them the opportunity. You have to trust that they can do it. At some stage you are going to need them. Also, the players who are starting players, so to speak, need that competitive guy behind them. They need to know that people are keeping them honest. You need to receive the message that someone is ready to step into your spot if your performance drops.

Wayne's Development as a Coach

Wayne has a passion for rugby. After finishing his playing career with the All Blacks (1980–1985), he saw it as an obvious progression to coach the game he loved. In 1986 he went to Italy to play for a club. He learned Italian and was thrown in the deep end when he began to coach an Italian team:

When I went to Italy, I'd already been an All Black and a captain of the New Zealand Sevens team for which I took almost a player/coaching type role along with a very open coach, Bryce Rope ... We were the first New Zealand team to win the Hong Kong Sevens (in 1986) despite the fact that most of our team [had] never really played the game. Fifteen-aside rugby is much more important in New Zealand. I took responsibility for researching the game. I read books about sevens ... I made sure I understood the fundamentals of the game ... The experience gave me the knowledge that I could research and apply skills and tactics that I was unfamiliar with. I was open to learning, wasn't threatened by the fact that I knew little about the game. I was quite prepared to do my homework to ensure I was giving it the best shot I could.

Wayne has continued to use research as a major form of developing his coaching. He believes a coach can never stop learning. He also realises that the way he played and was coached is not necessarily the best way for the modern game:

When I first went to Italy I couldn't speak the language and I was coaching players who had grown up in a different system to mine. Putting them through the sort of trainings that I had been used to wasn't going to motivate them, wasn't going to work. I wanted to get the most out of the opportunity. So I had to adjust pretty quickly to what I call a global coaching methodology, which in its pure sense is playing the game, rather than analytically developing individual techniques. The French coaching influence in Italy had developed a style of coaching based on opposed situations designed to develop intuitive (or recognitional) decision-making skills in players.

Wayne clarifies the idea of a *global methodology* to coaching:

If you look at a range of coaching methodologies, 'analytical' would be on one end of the spectrum and 'global' on the other. Using an analytical methodology you'd instruct a player, 'Put your foot there, put your hand there, drop your shoulder and finish up in this position'. A global coaching instruction would be more along the lines of, 'This player has the ball, stop him from scoring a try', … It's about doing it, the coach observing and letting the players sort out the most effective way themselves. I think effective coaching moves up and down this spectrum.

Wishing to develop his coaching further, Wayne began to think about the athlete-centred type of approach from his experiences of coaching in Italy. The factors motivating his learning were:

… experience and a realisation that to survive I had to change. I had to adapt to what they'd [Italians] been used to. It was sink or swim, but I went into it with an openness to adapt rather than change them from what they had been used to. I then gradually brought in some of my analytical [tools] … to try and make a technical difference.

A large part of Wayne's initial coaching development was observing the Italian coaches:

I went and watched coaches who literally threw the ball in the air and two teams played, tackling each other as they would in a game. It was very unstructured but I thought that I could adapt and improve this style. I developed activities that had one area of a field strongly defended, then threw the ball to the attacking team to see if they could figure out the space and make some ground. That's a situation in the game that's real. I modified the approach to develop my own style. I was still (at this stage of my learning as a coach) telling them what to do and where to go, but at least I had started developing this raw Game Sense type approach.

This approach reflects elements of TGfU as discussed by Rod Thorpe in Chapter Eleven. Rod developed the use of game-like situations in which players learn about technique and tactics of the actual game. TGfU allows the development of greater intrinsic motivation among players and more movement appropriate to the actual game for which players are being trained.

In his coaching development Wayne observed and spoke with a French coach, André Buonomo in Benetton (about 15 minutes from where he was based in Italy). Admiring and seeing some real worth in André's athlete-centred approach to coaching, Wayne decided, 'This is for me, this is the way to mix the analytical side with a game simulation side'. As he continued to learn from André's model, he began to use a similar approach in his own coaching. Questioning was a big part of André's approach and Wayne too began learning how to question. Wayne returned to coach in Italy from 1992 to 1994. It was at this time that he started using athlete-centred approach at a more elite level, and continued to learn about it thereafter.

After returning from Italy, Wayne was the chief executive of Hawkes Bay Rugby from 1994 to 1997. This job enabled him to think further about and develop an athlete-centred approach in a different context. When taking up this job, he accepted a new challenge and a new area of learning was involved:

> It was at a time when Hawkes Bay were reconstituting the union and they wanted to set up a board structure. I had no skills in that area at all, so it was a huge learning curve for me. I had to manage change, set up systems and facilitate board meetings.

> I learned the necessary skills from some exceptional business people on the Hawkes Bay board. They educated me. They taught me to apply myself to become a little better every day. They helped me develop a systematic approach to running a project, a team or a business. The job taught me about the processes a team [organisation] needs to put in place, like how to set goals and review them. The role really fitted in closely with what we do as coaches, so it was a great learning experience for me. I read a lot of corporate-type coaching and business management books. Complementing our traditional values, rugby's heritage, with a vision-driven process and systems-based model has stood me in good stead. I like to learn from the past, but not live in the past.

Wayne talked further about the many books he read, which combined with his professional experience in helping him to think about and set up his athlete-centred approach:

> I read books like *The Tao of Coaching* [Landsberg, 1996] and *The Flight of the Buffalo* [Belasco & Stayer, 1993], about empowering people, giving them ownership of their responsibilities to perform. This is an ongoing education process really and by the time I was ready to apply for the Crusaders job, I felt I was ready to combine the coaching methodology I had developed with the skills I learned running a business.

When asked for his advice for coaches who are interested in learning about an athlete-centred approach, Wayne suggests:

> The key thing I think is the openness to learning. I think coaches need to look at things on merit and understand that just because they've played the game, they don't know everything about it. This is particularly so in sports

like rugby where laws are changing all the time. Having a passion to improve is important. Knowing that you are part of the problem means you can also be part of the solution.

As part of the journey to discover solutions and search for best practices, Wayne created the 'crow's nest', an innovative way to look into the future:

Every season we put groups in an imaginary 'crow's nest' where they can view the horizon. Their task is to look into the future and determine how new laws will affect the game … They report back on how they think teams will play and what new styles will develop. This allows you to adapt and meet changes before they happen. Whilst it is critical that you have core game plan that you perform better than anyone else in the world, you also need enough flexibility to innovate and incorporate changes to your game that will make a positive difference.

An issue that Wayne reiterates extensively in the interview is that he is still learning about coaching and about how to use an athlete-centred approach. Coaches always need to be developing, learning and asking plenty of questions. On his own learning, Wayne says:

I am always trying to do things better. Progress for me is not going back to my natural or learned instincts from years of being coached in a certain way. The tendency for me under pressure is to bark out orders and say, 'Do it this way'. Sometimes, I'll come home and think, 'I know that wasn't the way to handle that' or 'I had a poor night tonight'. It is good practice to film your training runs so you can review your coaching performance. The next day I make a conscious effort to make improvements.

A questioning approach encourages the self-awareness that players need to get better at what they're doing. This doesn't mean you abdicate your responsibilities as a leader. You set your standards and expectations. Your job as coach is to then ensure the players come up to them.

Much of his thinking and development came from people who coached Wayne when he was a player:

My coach for Canterbury, Alex Wylie, had technical nous, hardness and knowledge of 'bush' psychology (he seemed to know inherently what to do). His coaching offsider, Doug Bruce, was calm, thoughtful and knew the game inside out.

My last All Blacks coach, Brian Lochore, had all these qualities. [He] had extraordinary mana as a person and the wisdom to 'know' his players. He had (still has) real credibility as one of the great All Black captains. He technically knows what he is on about, is calm, composed and steeped in the values that make the All Blacks great. You could talk about anything with Brian in a social situation (not just rugby). You'd talk politics, farming or whatever. He is well rounded. He is the only All Blacks coach to win a World Cup, but it never changed him as a coach or man … His record speaks for itself and, more importantly, he has influenced his players as people.

In his modern coaching, Wayne uses others' knowledge, including the styles and methods of other coaches, to help develop his coaching and continue his learning. He seeks the advice and information he needs, often by email. He sets up relationships with coaches and experts who can help him, such as those who use an athlete-centred approach, and asks many questions. Elaborating on his past and present approaches to learning, Wayne says:

> When I first committed to using empowerment in my coaching, there was no one else really using it, so I needed to look at other sports to keep learning. I still like to see what other coaches do and whether I am on the right track or not. I know the way I want to go … to continue empowering my players and to get better at questioning (rather than instruction). I also want to be my own person and develop my own style. I work hard not at copying, but at understanding and adapting what I learn.

> I have to work on my ability to discriminate between the need to ask questions about the skill and the need to ask about the tactics, i.e. understand whether it's a skill issue that let the player down or a game understanding one. Did he fail to pass because he couldn't technically execute it quickly enough, or did he pass because he didn't see what was [going] on? You can get the answer quickly … by asking, 'What did you do?', 'What did you see?' and 'What did you want to do?' You can soon find out whether he wanted to pass and couldn't or whether he ran with it because he didn't see that the pass was on.

> The skill is in understanding how to use the questions and doing it quickly and selectively so that you're observing more than talking. Let the players have a go, then if you see the activity being done correctly you don't need to step in. My biggest fault is overquestioning.

As evident from Wayne's statement, asking meaningful questions and 'reading the play' is important. (For further information on how to ask meaningful questions, see Chapter Twelve.)

A key component of a coach's development and enhanced performance is *self-analysis* (see Chapter Fourteen). It is used by many coaches to gather feedback and reflect on what is working and what can be improved in their coaching. Wayne also believes strongly in obtaining feedback on his coaching to help him self-analyse:

> I've participated in lots of coach evaluations. I've always tended to evaluate myself through videoing practice sessions, or by getting feedback from the players. Gilbert Enoka and Peter Thorburn are my coaching mentors. They make comments after training which help me assess how the session went in general and, more specifically, how I performed as a coach. They can often see things more objectively than I can. It's important, though, not to let negative feedback get you down. Just stack the learnings up as building

blocks that will make you better as a coach.

Steve [Hansen] and I evaluated each other's coaching performance constantly. We sought each other's views and listened to them.

As part of a coach's development, it is important to get feedback from the players about the approach:

The players will give you feedback if you have the right culture. We have a simple rating system at training. I am convinced that players love learning about the game and genuinely want to improve something at every session. However, you need to ensure they are not just saying what they think you want to hear. That's all about trust and respect, which you shouldn't just expect as of right—it is hard earned.

Wayne and Teaching Games for Understanding

TGfU (see Chapter Eleven) is an approach that has become popular in New Zealand and Australia. It can be a useful tool in an athlete-centred approach because it encourages athletes to understand and appreciate the game. In addition, it enables them to make informed decisions, take ownership of their learning, and exercise choice and control over how they play the game.

On TGfU (or Game Sense) as a part of an athlete-centred approach, Wayne says:

We never trained like that in my playing days [using Game Sense]. The closest we came to it was pick-up games as kids. All my life we'd always trained without opposition, not really simulating game situations or pressures. [There was] no thought of where the tackle line was or what you were looking for to make the pass or run through the gap. Game Sense is a logical way to create tactical understanding and awareness, getting players making the right decisions in various situations.

The use of TGfU enabled Wayne to begin to develop a non-traditional approach to help athletes learn. TGfU had a great influence on his thinking and the development of his empowerment approach. Wayne admits that, before he started using TGfU, he was a coach-centred or prescriptive coach:

I was still very much an instructional person who told them what to do, how to do it and when to do it. It wasn't really until I came back and got involved with kids at KiwiSport level in my job that I started to understand about learning. You can tell people how to do something until you are blue in the face, but unless they understand it or believe in it themselves, they aren't going to take it on board. So, I started to ask some questions.

Then while doing some personal development ... I came across David Hadfield who had written a paper called Query Theory on a questioning approach and how it created self-awareness. It was exactly the sort of support and evidence that I was looking for to validate the approach. Coaching is all about raising self awareness and generating responsibility. Effective questioning achieves this, whereas giving people the answers stops them from being either responsible or aware.

I try to use this coaching approach] all the time, a mixture of positive reinforcement, Game Sense and a questioning approach. I don't always succeed. I still fall back into old habits at times. I can also be a bit reactive, especially when things aren't going well. Patience and composure are two virtues I am still trying to master.

The games in TGfU are a key to designing training sessions. Instead of using the traditional practice drills, which have no real relevance to the actual game, Wayne tries to design games that match the purpose of a particular drill:

I have used the Game Sense-type approach for training since 1986 when I started playing and coaching in Italy and saw the French influence. I was putting players in match-like situations and changing the rules or the situation to develop adaptation. Game Sense ensures players practise having to make decisions all the time.

If there is no purpose, a coach tends to use questioning for the sake of using questioning, which is a common occurrence when coaches are learning about TGfU. In TGfU, the questions should come from and be geared towards achieving an objective the coach and team have identified. Wayne observes that questioning without a clear objective can be counterproductive:

Not knowing what to achieve or not having an objective is a common fault. Questioning, for the sake of it, was a big problem I saw when reviewing a video of one of my sessions. The players participated in very little activity because I kept asking questions. Observation is a big part of a Game Sense approach. Look before you question so that you can be more incisive and meaningful with your queries.

When Wayne designs his training sessions, he is still learning and developing TGfU ideas. To coaches, he suggests:

Take a drill, then try to think about how you can change the rules, the size of the field, the time limit, the scoring systems, etc., to get what you want to get out of it. I try to give [the players] a framework so that they can design their own drills. I don't have a book of drills because every time I go out there, I do something new. Drills develop from the last training and reflect what we are trying to achieve next week.

Wayne is aware that his coaching style is different and that his knowledge of rugby is extensive. From this perspective, in regard to planning for using games at training, he suggests:

You don't have to do what other people do. Think of how *you* can do it e.g. if you want to work on your forwards picking the ball up and going through the middle of the defence, you create ways to spread the defence at training. They are not even drills; they're mini-games.

In identifying the biggest advantage to using TGfU within an athlete-centred approach, Wayne also gives a practical example of how he uses questioning as a major coaching technique to ensure athletes are learning from the various games:

> The biggest advantage to a Game Sense approach (opposed activities/ games) is that it develops tactical awareness. You put [the players] in real game situations with similar pressures and you require them to choose the right options. It ensures that they have the skills to make the right tactical decision. You ideally want all the players to see things the same way so that they make the same (right) decisions and you get a measure of synergy in your game.
>
> For example, when you create three attackers against two defenders, the obvious thing would be for the second attacker to draw the last defender and pass to the outside guy because he is the one in space. If you can see that the player understands that, but cannot execute the skill, you need to ask some questions. For example:
>
> Wayne: 'What did you do?'
>
> Player: 'I held on to it.'
>
> Wayne: 'Where was the space?'
>
> Player: 'It was outside.'
>
> Wayne: 'What was the reason for you deciding to hold on to the ball?
>
> Player: 'I couldn't get the pass away.'
>
> Then you know it is a technical issue. You could then ask:
>
> Wayne: 'Why couldn't you get the pass away?'
>
> Player: 'He was on me too quick.'
>
> Wayne: 'How could you give yourself a bit of time?'
>
> Player: 'I would slow down.'
>
> Wayne: 'What would you need to do to slow down?'
>
> Player: 'Take short steps.' Or maybe it's a hand speed issue and: 'I had enough time, but I couldn't get the ball ready, it was going to be a bad pass.'
>
> Wayne: 'What was the reason you didn't have time to get your pass away?'
>
> Player: 'I took the ball into my chest.'
>
> Wayne: 'Where were your hands when you caught it?'
>
> Player: 'They were out in front.'
>
> Wayne: 'Where do you think your hands should have been?'

Player: 'Towards the passer. If I met the ball earlier, I could have passed it.'

So you can get them through to the answer and they come up with it … They will learn from it better than having been told the solution.

I like the approach. It is logical. Players are working on understanding the game, not just the skills required. You can work on all the skills you like, but if you can't use them in the game, you are not going to get much satisfaction. If you have detected that a behaviour has become a bad habit, it may take more than just this process to change it. Old Way, New Way [see Chapter Two] is an effective method of turning bad habits into good ones. I'd suggest you [coaches] do some reading on this in order to trial the approach.

It is also worth remembering that there are times when athletes do need to be told what to do—the trick is to identify that moment. This is part of the art of coaching, as Wayne suggests:

There are times when you need to say, 'You had more power in the tackle that time, what did you differently with your foot?'

They might say, 'I am not sure.'

Wayne: 'What did you do that time with your leading foot?'

Player: 'I put it closer to him.'

Wayne: 'So what did that do?'

Player: 'It generated more power from my front leg …'

Wayne suggests that players learn from the approach because:

… they understand it … I could tell them 10 times, 'You've got to meet the ball early', but if they have self-awareness that meeting the ball early allows them to get the pass away faster, then they are probably going to try it a lot more quickly. The thing about questioning is that, whilst coaches should have some knowledge, good observation skills are really important. You have to be able to see the three-vs-two or the two-against-one situations.

… most times I use a technique where I carry a second ball and I'll look and see if there are two attackers against only one defender. I will blow the whistle and throw the ball to the two attackers. I want to see how they react and how the play develops. It is not just the skill of questioning, but it is the understanding of the game that is important. There are a lot of skills associated with a questioning approach, but it can be quickly learned if you are motivated to do so. It's not coaching by abdication. You also need to ensure your players understand why you are using it.

One of the benefits indicated in research about TGfU is the ability to increase intrinsic motivation of players. Wayne agrees:

People are more motivated if you've got activities that are meaningful and fun ... I think most of my players would say that our trainings are interesting because I put them into game situations all the time. If it is fun and they can see the purpose behind it, it is motivating to them. If they enjoy doing it, they will do it well.

If you make [the questioning] logical and you start steering them towards learning and playing the game better then they are going to get motivated by that. If it is illogical or poorly done, it can be frustrating. Just asking questions for the sake of it is meaningless. I've had the odd player say to me, 'Let's just get on with it'. This normally indicates I am asking too many questions. Those are all skills that you learn as you go along.

Learning TGfU as part of an athlete-centred approach is like learning any other skill. Coaches need to be prepared to trial it and search for ways to continue to develop it:

You have to understand that if you are going to use the approach, you're not going to be perfect at it: you have to keep practising it, keep learning it. It helps you expand your armoury, drills and ways of doing things. It helps you improve your own understanding of the game, as well as your players'!

Implementing an Athlete-centred Approach

Before his recent coaching successes, Wayne lectured about empowerment in a practicum course at Massey University. He said that at that stage, 'there was a lot of scepticism because I hadn't been coaching in New Zealand' and he lacked credibility. Nevertheless, he suggested to the students that he would use an athlete-centred approach with the Crusaders: 'I am going to empower my players. I am going to use a questioning and a Game Sense sort of approach.'

Yet he also admits, 'There would be times where I fall back into the way I was coached.' As part of the process of learning about this approach, coaches will tend to revert to the coaching style that they experienced as players. Wayne reflects on why people, including himself, tend to fall back to old habits:

Sometimes it is because of frustration or time pressures, or things not going right ... we film our trainings to look at the drills we are doing and make sure they are valid, see whether the players are doing them really well and to check our way of communicating. Quite often I go home and think, 'Gee that wasn't the right way to handle that player tonight'. I've had to learn strategies to cope with people making mistakes. I have very competitive instincts and like to see everything done well. It has been an ongoing learning experience allowing the players to make errors along the way, which is now an important part of our team environment.

One of the concerns Wayne raised, from his perspective in a very public position, is that people tend to criticise something new until it has been proven (usually by winning). An athlete-centred approach draws away from a traditional coach-centred approach (which has been considered successful), where coaches claim control and ownership of their athletes. Wayne suggests that initially the public was not convinced of his approach:

> One of the problems that I faced early on in my career was that people thought that I was a tree hugger, too soft. There was a public perception that I wasn't tough enough ... If you ask the players [now], they'd say that in my own way I am a hard coach. I preach attention to detail, expect my players to work hard and am not afraid to front [up to] them over form and selection issues. I don't want my players to be better than their opponents—I want them to be the very best they can be.

As Wayne proceeds in using his athlete-centred approach, he learns more and continues to improve, and he gains more credibility. His approach has now become something of a goal for many coaches, but other coaches still have not been convinced. To Wayne the success of an athlete-centred approach does not just lie in the results. He also points to the team culture it produces:

> ... we have people coming here [to Canterbury] to play from the draft who invariably put pressure on us to keep them here. They want to stay and play their rugby in Canterbury. There are other players around the country who speak highly of our organisation and they'd like to become Crusaders. I think these are the real indicators of the sort of environment that we've got.

When asked about how to lessen the emphasis on winning a game, coming first or becoming a world champion, Wayne suggests that perhaps the media and sporting bodies need to:

> ... be aware that enjoyment is going to be a critical factor in professional rugby because if players are playing only because they are getting paid, then we are already losing. Well-balanced athletes are more motivated at training. They perform better on the field and cope better with losing.
>
> Ultimately, I suggest that the best balanced teams are the ones that win anyway ... you can't guarantee winning, but what you can guarantee, if you create the right environment, is that they will roll their sleeves up and do the best they can. If you prepare well, play with passion and enjoy what you are doing, then you'll do justice to the jersey you are playing in.

When convincing various bodies within the rugby union about an athlete-centred approach, Wayne ran into some obstacles. The traditional thinking had to be challenged and Wayne offered a different approach. The Canterbury Rugby Union was happy for Wayne to 'do his thing'. Wayne has found that, 'It's only since we forged the boundaries that we have been successful'.

As coaches develop an athlete-centred approach, one of their most important goals will be to organise a good team environment and culture. With both the Crusaders and the All Blacks, the team culture has been a major focus for Wayne. The success that came from giving it priority has been proven in many ways. One of the many techniques used to establish a team vision and attitude was a videotape based on *Henry V* which Wayne, Crusaders co-coach Peter Sloane and Gilbert Enoka created. This video contributed significantly to the spirit within the team but at the beginning there was uncertainty, as Wayne recalls:

> The first time we showed the team a video we had put together was groundbreaking. The idea of the video was to set the scene prior to us facilitating our team vision, values and attitudes. To see the response at the end gave me so much confidence. It's something we'd never done before that turned out to be really powerful. The players got into the whole thing. They ended up buying into something bigger than themselves.

Wayne spoke about other ideas implemented after this first video that were similarly designed to develop a successful team culture among the Crusaders and to empower players:

> Since then we've tried all sorts of different initiatives, we've pushed the boundaries—e.g. we've used a team song, trained in different ways, used different methodologies and encouraged our players to look to the future and adapt before the changes occur. We've also done team-building type activities in association with our vision and values.

> In 1999 we did something that at the time, again, I was nervous about. We undertook a wilderness experience at Mt Kosciosko in Australia. We had to climb the mountain, which could only be done with the help of your mates. We reached our peak, but we did it by working together. We contrasted this with how we had achieved success in 1998 when we had stuttered along as individuals, not really gelling as a team until it was almost too late.

> We designed the adventure to show the importance of team unity. To win Super 12 again, we'd have to pay a higher price, go in the same direction and help each other more. We fed these ideas throughout the season, creating a really powerful and selfless team ethic.

The Process of Empowering Players

So Wayne put all these systems in place, using an innovative type of thinking, but what really happened? How did the players react to this approach?

> I think the reaction initially by some of the players was a bit of scepticism, things like, 'This guy doesn't really know what he is going on about'. I know I had a bit of credibility problem with a couple of them initially because they wanted me to come and say, 'This is what we are going to do and this is how we are going to do it'.

> They responded this way because they are used to people coming and telling them what to do and they can tell from what a coach tells them whether he knows the game or not. It took a while to establish the fact that I did know the game, that I wasn't asking questions because I didn't know the answers. I was asking for a reason.

It also took them out of their comfort zone a lot because I was trying to get players doing things they traditionally didn't do. Rather than just carry the ball into contact and set it up, I wanted forwards to be able to pass and get the ball into space. I did that by asking questions like, 'Where was the defence?', 'Where was the space?', 'How could you have got the ball there?'. Initially, the players really struggled with it. Forwards didn't see it as their job. Their role in the team traditionally was to set up rucks and mauls. It took a while for them to start understanding the concept of team attack. By them knowing what we were trying to achieve and playing like the backs in certain situations, we were going to be more effective. The vice versa is true as well, i.e. backs have to know how to perform the forwards tasks at the breakdown.

There were some personalities on the team who felt that while I was questioning, I was criticising or bringing up negatives in their play. Often, the question I asked should have had a positive response from the player because it was about a good thing that they'd done. However, because I'd asked it in the wrong manner, it created defensiveness in the player. For example:

Wayne: 'Why did you do that?'

Player: 'I did the right thing.'

Wayne: 'Yes exactly, but tell me what you did.'

Player: 'I passed the ball.'

Wayne: 'Why?'

Player: 'Because that #### defender came in on me, so I passed to the guy that was clear on the outside of me!'

Wayne: 'Great.'

That showed me that the player understood the situation, but I should have avoided using 'why' as a question—it can cause players to feel like their ability is being question[ed] and often results in them seeking justification for what they did.

There are still two or three players that tend to react negatively to questioning. I think, in general, all players initially had some problems with [being questioned]. The activities I used were also new and different for them. They were used to doing the traditional ruck and run type practices for rugby rather than being put in game-like activities. I'd throw a ball to the attack and if they couldn't get through, I threw the ball to the defence. They had to switch roles quickly. It took a great deal of trust on the players' behalf to forgo what they had been used to (and felt comfortable with) and commit wholeheartedly to my methods. Now those same players, when they go back into a more traditional coaching environment, quite often become frustrated with the lack of learning.

Wayne also encourages input from the players:

> The players will quite often come up with extensions to activities, progressions if you like. They will quite often come and say, 'Why don't we do this?', 'Why don't we put this player here and create this?' or 'Why don't we make the field bigger?' or whatever.

The players' input encourages creative thinking. The players have to play the game, so their ideas and ways of reading the game are highly relevant to training for it.

When Wayne began coaching the Crusaders, he spoke about how the players were empowered. Here he provides an account of the procedures he followed to enable players to take ownership of their learning and playing:

> Pre-season, the players and coaches agree on what qualities they most need to be the best player they can (in each of physical, tactical, psychological and attitudinal areas). Then for the first month I sit down with players weekly and go through their game on video. We discuss some of the issues, we look at the statistics, then we agree where they're at and what they have to do to improve. We do check-points every month to ensure they are getting ongoing improvements and are also working on making their strengths stronger. Their own week-by-week reviews (using videos of the games) tend to be both skill- and situational-specific and throw up areas that they need to work on at both individual and team training sessions.
>
> … This review system, together with individuals identifying their mindset and skill/tactical needs in preparation for each game, is very effective, but it shouldn't always be coach-directed. Ideally, the players would review the game on their own and meet with the coach on a need-to basis. We are trying to make them responsible for self-analysis, but early in the season I find I need to lead it more, so they can learn the process.

To empower players, it is important that they gain the skills of self-awareness (see Chapter Two). Athletes need to understand how and why they are performing, including in their tactics and skill development. Wayne had initial difficulties in trying to get players to become self-aware:

> In the first year [of coaching the Crusaders], they were so lacking in self-awareness that I would ask 'What did you do?' and players would have trouble remembering what they did. They played like robots. They did what they were told to do and didn't really *feel* their performance.

Empowering through questioning has other advantages along with increasing self-awareness among players. Questioning also focuses athletes in their thinking and thus their concentration remains consistently higher in trainings, which transfers well to the game. Wayne agrees that questioning 'really makes them aware the whole time. But also you know that your trainings can't be quite so long. It's … hard to concentrate for long periods of time.'

Wayne suggests that sometimes players can take an athlete-centred approach for granted and not be genuinely empowered. One of the real arts to any coaching is to be able to read the players all the time:

> You need to recognise when the players are just going through the motions. Recognising that is an art. That is where an inexperienced person using a Query Theory and empowerment type approach might fall in a hole.

As a development officer with the Canterbury Rugby Union from 1989 to 1992, Wayne was responsible for teaching various courses to coaches and teachers. He worked with and coached children at many different primary schools, which gave him a valuable learning experience in his coaching development.

Wayne advocates the use of an athlete-centred approach and TGfU with children (see Chapter Eleven), so that they can understand what they are doing and why. Children who become self-aware learn about the game and themselves as players. On the sideline, we always hear parents and coaches directing the children as to where to go and what to do. We take the decision making away from them. On the other hand, as Wayne observes, if we used an athlete-centred approach with children they:

> … will make better decisions and enjoy the experience more. If you can give kids lots of game-specific activities, let them have fun, use a questioning approach so that you develop self-awareness, and empower them to be responsible for what they are doing in the game, you'll get a good response from them. They may not win, but they'll enjoy it and make gradual improvements.

A key feature of Wayne's approach is his idea that players need to enjoy themselves. Wayne has worked with Bruce Pinel, a PhD student from the University of Otago, to introduce enjoyment to players' quality profiles (profiles which are made in collaboration with each player). He describes this venture as 'a really good initiative … it's an obvious challenge to professional sport'. Wayne feels that enjoyment is a major factor in coaching because if players do not enjoy the sport, they will give it less effort. Recognising that this enjoyment is a key to young children's participation as well, he says:

> The first thing to do is find out what they enjoy about their sport and make sure you are catering for those things. Do enjoyment profiles. Find out what they expect from you as a coach. Do they expect you to be a ranter and raver, or do they want you to give them fun activities? You need to know what they want … You have that one hour a week [to coach them]. You don't want to waste that hour so how you structure the training sessions will determine how much you all enjoy it.

On the development of rugby players in New Zealand and the importance of coaches learning to empower them, Wayne suggests:

> I'd like all rugby coaches in New Zealand to encourage greater player ownership of and responsibility for performance. Our players need to

understand the game better. They need to be able to question their coaches and in turn be questioned. We need to influence young players more positively, instil values at a young age and encourage all-round skill development. Developing intelligence in players and ensuring they are more self-directed will bear huge rewards for New Zealand rugby in the future.

Some Challenges of an Athlete-centred Approach

Although, as Wayne's experience indicates, an athlete-centred approach offers many advantages, it also brings challenges to coaches who wish to make use of it. This section draws attention to some of those challenges (many of which are also identified by other coaches in this book), along with Wayne's response to them.

A challenge indicated in both research and practice is that using an athlete-centred approach is very time-consuming. It takes time for athletes to become accustomed to being coached in a different way. It also takes time to develop athletes into thinking athletes. Yet the long-term advantages ultimately override this challenge, as athletes begin to make informed decisions, have fun and increase their self-esteem. In line with this idea, Wayne notes:

> It is going to take a while … and that's what people don't understand. If the quality outcome you are after is satisfaction, then we got that straight away. My first year with the Crusaders [of building the team culture, without actually winning the Super 12s] was exciting. Since then, we have won the tournament twice, but to me it's not the winning that counts—it's doing your best to win. Having fun and learning together is a rewarding experience. We've had hard times, but generally the smile on their faces is the biggest indicator to success. Seeing a group of talented individuals selflessly giving to each other and enjoying the experience makes coaching worthwhile.

Another possible time constraint that Wayne identifies is:

> … one player who is struggling, the rest of team is going well and they want to keep the momentum up. Particularly if it is a Thursday night training, the last training before the game, you want flow, you want continuity, you want a bit of feeling being built up. If you step in and stop that through questioning one player or trying to get instructional, it is quite often negative. The hardest part about the art of coaching is understanding when they are on a roll, and when to step out.

> Observation is a big part of empowerment as is getting the questions right. It is quite hard … One thing I found difficult earlier on was sitting back and observing for three or four minutes before coming in. When you are trying to establish yourself, you'll find a lot of young coaches feel like they've got to get in there to espouse their knowledge. They have got to show that they know what is right and what is wrong. Even when [the coach is] using a questioning approach, they feel they have to show that they are involved.

Another concern for the development of athlete-centred coaches is the perception that a coach has to reel off all his or her knowledge to the players, when really coaching is about enabling them to learn.

Wayne reflects on differences in success between a prescriptive (coach-centred) coach and an athlete-centred coach:

> It depends whether you want long-term success or short-term success. A team that you hear in the changing room yelling and screaming as the coach gets them hyped up, are often beaten because they will only have short-term success against you (they are going to be really tough in the first 20 minutes). If you just ride it out and keep your cool, react to what you see, talk, guts it out and be relentless, you'll get on top of them every time. It is the same in a seasonal sense. The teams who are autocratically run have short-term success, do really well earlier on. Teams like ours tend to take a while for everything to come together.
>
> I know one of my faults is that early in the season I tend [to] work on too many things. The players can sometimes get too cluttered, but I believe it's important to show improvements throughout the season. Whereas autocratic teams are really good earlier on, they tend to peter out a wee bit. In contrast, empowerment ensures a dynamic, living, learning environment. You've got new players coming in, new ideas, new intellectual capital, [and] new leaderships. It is ever changing and for that reason, long-term success is often sustainable.

As he explains above, Wayne is still learning about how to use an athlete-centred approach. Here, he describes some of the interesting learning processes that he went through when he introduced empowerment to the Canterbury Crusaders:

> When I first came to the job (my first year working for the Crusaders was 1997), we didn't make the players follow our systems and processes rigidly. For example, with regard to individual game review systems, I said, 'Look this is what we'd like you do, but if you don't feel comfortable doing it, don't do it'. It is no longer the case. [The player has to] be able to sit down with me and go through the game. Effectively, players have to be able to identify what needs to be improved and how they are going to do it. Players have to schedule individual sessions in a weekly planner to ensure they fit in with team commitments. I want to see players organising other guys to help them get improvements. We like the players to go out and actually simulate the situation or skill they are trying to improve, and to coach each other.
>
> One of the mistakes I made when first using empowerment was to not explain what I was doing. This created unnecessary conflict at training. Instead of just giving an answer, players often tried to justify their actions. In my second year, I explained that we were using a questioning approach to develop self-awareness and tactical understanding, which was bought into by the players.

Wayne tells the story about when some players decided that they needed traditional coaching. Their concern drew Wayne's attention to the need for flexibility in coaching:

> In 1998 we worked hard to make the players proud of the ownership they had about the way the team operated. We met often to ensure things were operating effectively. We established the game plans together, and the players were responsible for their own game reviews and debriefs. The players owned and understood every area of the game. The coaches facilitated these processes, provided guidance but became directive only when necessary. We laid the foundations; the players won the football games.
>
> In 1999 we started the season the same way and it was going pretty well before we hit a trough. At one stage when we were playing the Stormers in Cape Town, we lost the game and dropped to eighth in the competition. Things weren't happening. We weren't playing the way we wanted to, we weren't effecting what we'd been doing in training.
>
> Two senior players came to Steve and me that night and said, 'You have to lead us out of this. You are going to have to take control and show us the way'. It was an interesting response. They felt that things were being taken for granted by some of the players. They were getting a little bit sloppy and needed direction. It taught me that a coach must be flexible enough to provide what is required at the time. Sometimes all the players need is to be told what to do.
>
> I didn't know at the time [of this challenge] because we'd been so successful in 1998. I just assumed that [athlete-centred] was the only model we should follow. It really showed that you have to be on your toes. Being a leader means you have to adapt to the team's needs at the time, and not let winning be your enemy by making you complacent. If there is incohesiveness in your team, you have a responsibility to sort it out. If you notice morale dropping, you must take decisive action before the situation becomes chronic.

Wayne describes his reaction to the players' concern and how ultimately the players too saw the advantage of an athlete-centred approach:

> We didn't change the methodology ... really. I think their point was, 'You make some of the hard calls that need to be made. Be definite about the way we are going to go forward in training and what our game requires ...'. For a while, we became more instructional at trainings and more directive about how the game was to be played.
>
> Another turning point for the team in 1999 was also in sending signals that no one is beyond being replaced in the team. Even though the next game (Northern Bulls) was the most crucial game of the season, we played Aaron Flynn at halfback and Leon MacDonald at first five. Regular stars Justin Marshall and Andrew Mehrtens were on the bench. It demonstrated to the team that we trusted everyone in the squad and expected every player to be up to the mark. We won the game and we went on to win the championship.

One further challenge in using an empowerment approach, Wayne indicates, may arise if the right team culture is not in place:

> I can't see too many disadvantages to the approach, unless you haven't got the culture and you can't trust the players to be genuine about it. You need to have an honest team to get improvements.

Adapting the Approach to the All Blacks—Wayne's Plans

After he had been appointed All Blacks coach for what turned out to be his first stint with the national team, Wayne talked about his plans for implementing an athlete-centred approach with the All Blacks. At that stage, he identified time constraints as a major concern, but he was prepared to take on the challenge:

> It is always a concern in that we don't have a long lead-in period to our first game. However, this is the approach I am going to be using. I'll modify it, ensuring that I am being really clinical in the way I use questioning. We have plenty of time prior to assembly for our planning to be excellent, so there shouldn't be too many hiccups.
>
> Simplicity will be a key, culling out the peripheral stuff, so we can get quickly to the core of what needs to be done.
>
> I think the players will respond really well. There is so much intellectual capital in the All Blacks. They know the game. You can't be dumb in the All Black world, so I think we'll all enjoy it.

Conclusion

Although Wayne does not have all the answers and does not claim to be an expert, he provides coaches with some insight into how to implement an athlete-centred approach. He has suggested that the players are intrinsically motivated and learn well when coaches use questioning and TGfU to enhance decision making.

Learning an athlete-centred approach is not an easy task, but the benefits to the team and individual athletes are immense. The learning process is easier when coaches begin by considering *how* such an approach might be suitable for them and remembering that the process of implementation requires time. Coaches will make progress by trying new ideas and continuing to self-reflect on how the approach is working within the team. There are also techniques, such as questioning and understanding TGfU, that need to be practised. The more coaches practise, the better they will be at ensuring athletes have ownership of their learning and direction of their sporting and life experiences.

References

Belasco, J.A., & Stayer, R.C. (1993). *Flight of the Buffalo: Soaring to Excellence, Learning to Let Employees Lead.* New York: Warner.

Landsberg, M. (1996). *The Tao of Coaching: Boost Your Effectiveness at Work by Inspiring and Developing Those Around You.* London: Harper Collins.

Chapter Ten

Lyn Gunson
International Netball Coach

Lyn Gunson's coaching experiences are many and varied. Having coached both New Zealand and England national netball teams, she is now the Director of Coaching for the South and Southwest England Netball Performance Unit. I was able to observe Lyn's training sessions while on a visit to England in 2002. Watching Lyn's teams train demonstrated to me her emphasis on athlete-centred coaching so, when she visited New Zealand in January 2005, I jumped at the opportunity to interview her to find out what being athlete-centred means to her.

Sport has always been a part of Lyn's life. She grew up in a rural community in Waikiekie in Northland where her parents introduced her to sport as a means of establishing social networks. Lyn suggests that the influence on her coaching philosophy came from her farm and country upbringing. Her experience of sport had similarities to being part of a community, in that team membership was stable for a long-term campaign and teamwork occurred in response to an external need and with an identified and defined purpose, thus creating a mutual direction. This focus enabled a committed effort when striving for a goal for a given period.

Professionally Lyn has a background in teaching. She undertook a Diploma in Physical Education at the University of Otago, while beginning to play netball in the national team. She also played provincially at various times for Otago, Auckland, Northland and Waikato. Upon completing her diploma, Lyn attended Auckland College of Education and became a physical education teacher, as well as holding a careers and counselling role, at Melville High School in Hamilton for 11 years. While teaching full time, she coached the New Zealand netball team from 1990 to 1993. During this coaching period, Lyn aided New Zealand's win at the World Games for non-Olympic sports. The team then lost the World Championships to Australia by one point and Lyn was not reappointed.

Ready for a change, Lyn moved on to work as a physical education adviser for a short time before accepting a position at the Waikato Institute of Sport where she helped her organisation introduce a leisure studies degree at the University of Waikato. She then lectured in the management stream within the leisure studies degree. At the same time she completed a Masters of Business Administration (MBA), which she highlights as an experience of wonderful learning through her interaction with people outside of the sporting industry. It provided some intriguing background information that enhanced her understanding about different trends and how others outside of sport view the world.

Since 1999 Lyn has been living in England. In the first instance she was there to work at the University of Bath in an attempt to do her doctorate but she became involved in setting up a project to develop elite players and coaches in netball. During her time there, too, fellow New Zealand netballer Waimarama Taumaunu (England Netball Performance Director) involved her in coaching the English netball team, starting six weeks before the 2002 Commonwealth Games. Thereafter Lyn coached the team through the 2003 World Championships in Jamaica, in which England came fourth.

Lyn started her coaching in high school where she helped out with junior teams. She also spent much of her playing life in roles that enhanced her coaching—as a player-coach and captain. Within both these roles, especially the difficult position of player-coach, Lyn could not be autocratic in the style she observed in her coaches. So she developed much of her athlete-centred philosophy in coaching from having to work with fellow players.

Lyn's Philosophy of Coaching

Lyn's coaching philosophy is athlete-centred in her belief that 'each individual needs to have their own space and be who they want to and can be'. She also believes that 'people who are truly elite, often get there themselves despite everything else around them. It is the others just underneath that need more construction. Coaches can often limit these athletes.' External influences from coaches and others are insignificant compared to an athlete's internal desire. The coach's role is to encourage this internal desire by providing the right environment for athletes to express themselves in a manner that leads them to reach their capacity. Coaches are nurturers of internally motivated athletes rather than builders of motivated athletes. On tapping into this motivation through an athlete-centred coaching approach, Lyn says:

> … ask the athlete, 'Do you really want to do this or not? You decide.' If they really do decide then they will have the passion and desire; it has to come from inside them. It is not just about motivation, it's about whether they can see that they can … One of the things I have asked the players is, 'What is your capacity?' If an athlete can get to the point where [he/she] knows what that might be and have belief in that, then go on to look for more, you begin to have an international athlete. They may never discover it if somebody else is always telling them what to do, think and believe.

Lyn believes that coaches can create the environment to support athlete learning and performing but their role is 'one step removed' in that, when the athlete is ready to move on, he or she 'will come in and you can tell from a particular comment that something is happening and you know straight away, [the athlete is] identifying [his/her] need'. Sometimes athletes gain an idea or suggestion from an external source, or a realisation from some experience, but as a coach, 'the influence you have is to point them in the direction where they will find what they need. That is athlete-centred'.

It is always tempting to identify the answer for athletes and deliver that solution from outside. In a coaching role, when the pressure is on for a short-term performance, there are times when it is simplest and easiest to simply tell the athletes what to do. Yet although imposing that external solution may suit the short-term situation, it is not the answer to long-term needs as the athletes do not own it.

By learning in, through and about sport, Lyn has become very good at analysing and contextualising it. As noted above, doing the MBA helped consolidate some of her ideas on how outside views and trends might affect sport: 'I did it so that I challenged myself to see another world view and so that I could think about sport and its context and the way in which it was going to be affected'. Sport has notoriously focused on the short term, giving priority to an immediate result. This short-term fixation perpetuates the practice of coach-centred coaching and thus of creating dependent athletes. However, working in opposition to this current construction of sport is that many sport situations require independent thinkers and decision makers. In this regard, Lyn's analytical thinking extends beyond coaching to evaluate sport as a socially constructed industry:

> Sport is quite an exclusive society and it takes little if any responsibility for [creating these dependent people], but if you can actually have the athlete willingly participate in [taking responsibility] and making genuine choices, then it's much better than if they fall off the treadmill at the other end. Of course the question arises, is sport responsible, and therefore are coaches [and others] responsible for the athlete's holistic growth as a person? I think that sport [constructs] children. We tell children what to wear, we tell them when to turn up, how to behave, who to be involved with. Fine, it teaches them some good things. But what is missing [within this] constructed environment? Many sportspeople do not recognise how constructed the sports environment is. They then demand thinking players ... not easy from an [coach-centred] environment.

In addition to her education, two other major influences in her life have shaped Lyn's philosophy. Both have been mentioned already: first, the rural community in which she grew up and the sport experiences in her junior years; and, second, her extensive player-coach and captain experiences. Lyn's present focus on community stems from her experience of locals pitching in to help out when needed. She gives an example relating to her community analogy that demonstrates what this collective effort means:

> ... where there is a good community, there are some underlying principles. One of them is that you help your neighbours ... the village and wider district coexists quite happily until the school committee decides they need a fundraising exercise or there is a fire somewhere and someone's house is burning. All of a sudden, a group of people come together who have previously been co existing and because of other and past experiences they become a very tight team. They put the fire out, they organise themselves ... leaders emerge and people fall into specialist roles according to their skills. Somebody leads [the task of] putting the fire out and somebody else takes up the role of coordinating the relief and aid effort, food and clothing and whatever else is needed. All of a sudden, you've got this team operating. When the main bulk of that effort is finished, it just slides back into coexisting again. Over long campaigns, teams operate more as communities; I think the best ones do. That allows the freedom for the way in which it can develop and grow. There are of course some important aspects that make this work,

like a sense of value and cohesiveness and finally a common purpose that clearly identifies the direction and action.

The philosophical base established through Lyn's community involvement as a child also supports the notion of getting involved. Lyn played any sport she could because small schools needed athletes in a variety of sports in inter-school country tournaments. Lyn would play a hockey game, then run and play half a game of rugby, then soccer, then netball, plus help out with her other community teams, all in one day. She says about this experience, 'it was all about this participating in the way that you put your shoulder to the wheel, the collective wheel because the school needed you to do this, so that's what you did'. The collective school points system meant everyone contributed even if it was only a few points.

Lyn believes that the best coaches are those who 'read' people. She is unsure whether this skill is instinctive or if people gain it through experience. She believes her skill in imaging situations, replaying them in her head and knowing what somebody is going to do before they do it comes from her farming background:

> … I have often been asked about how I instinctively know if someone is going to do something. Now, where does that come from? … Certainly what helped me develop it is part of the farm situation. I remember having these experiences with animals. If a dog was going to bite you or a bull charge you, you had to know about it. They weren't going to tell you, it wasn't a person you were dealing with, so there were lots of other signals that you started picking up on, including the electrical energy and atmospheric situation around the animals you were dealing with. I started to really read the signs, and if I hadn't I would be dead now.

This need to read athletes is mentioned in different ways as part of their philosophy by coaches throughout this book. 'Reading people' seems to be an essential skill to coaching. Coaches need to understand athletes and their behaviours, as well as to have empathy for their individual situations and needs. As Lyn says:

> Anticipating situations is huge in coaching and it's how you get the information so that you do start to anticipate things … I think that it is quite strongly in you and that you either develop what is there or it just stays dormant … I think part of it is that there is the physically obvious, which is often to do with biomechanics and seeing through the external body extremity. Then there is a whole lot of other material around the energy and the non-observable. Some people seem to almost be able to see them. Others just feel them and others are just completely not aware that they exist … some image by seeing pictures, but I feel energy and myself doing the activity as well … this is a completely different level of imaging. It's much more complicated, but people can use all their senses quite instinctively depending on all manner of experiences. Coaching a variety of cultures has taught me a great deal about the differences in how people view the world. The English [netball] team has been interesting from this aspect. Many live in large cities and their view

of the world is quite different depending on which part of the country, which culture they are from and how they have grown with their environment.

The instinct or art of reading people and situations is just the beginning. Once you have anticipated the situation, the next important step in successful coaching is timing. As Lyn explains it, the coach must be able to make the challenging judgement of what to offer the athletes and when they are ready for learning:

> It is such an intertwining of observing what's happening, looking at the contextual relationships and then deciding is this the time and is this the way forward? Does this intervention need this type of information, process, experience, support … not just what to do but when to do it. That timing is incredibly difficult to teach. I experienced this when lecturing teachers in training. I have seen people [who'll] react to [a situation] or they'll get a piece of information and they'll react to it. Two days before or two days later they might react completely different to the same piece of information or activity, so it's matching up when that person is ready to take on that experience or information; in other words, are they ready to learn?

Reading people and empathy are dominant characteristics of Lyn's coaching. She describes how she uses them with Bath athletes and coaches:

> What we have done at Bath is try to make it completely athlete-centred and we are trying to read all the time …when different things are needed and when those players are ready. What I find is that if [I] can match up [their readiness], the learning is extremely fast… [the learning] entrenches itself very quickly and they work with it straight away. They use the feeling, emotion, information or behaviour and start to work off of it themselves … They lock in one piece of something and take off with it in an integrated form … the ripple and domino effects cascade to many other actions. To find that timing means you've got to listen to them a lot and hear what is happening behind the words and actions, see their reactions and see what's going on … all of a sudden when you do this, that information that they might be receiving back and analysis makes them able to go away and apply much more themselves. There are some good international tennis players at present who can do this.

Lyn also believes that the capacity to analyse situations and then 'translate them into something practical' is a key to athlete learning. She uses analogies in her coaching to convey particular points to her players. The analogies are real situations or experiences, sometimes unrelated to the sport, that athletes can relate to in their own lives so that the information is translated into their own cognitive understanding. The athletes remember the ideas better through hearing them as stories or analogies, as Lyn suggests:

> You are not telling them what to do, but you are drawing or focusing their attention on something that they are already doing and engage in themselves and then, all of a sudden, they make a connection because their awareness has been raised.

Lyn follows these coaching beliefs in developing and teaching athletes. However, for national teams, coaching by this method becomes more complex as coaches do not have the athletes all the time and the general demand is for instant results. To deal with these problems, coaches tend to revert to a coach-centred style. Lyn observes:

> Often when people take a national team … it feels easier and quicker to take on a directive approach as it suits the 'measurement by winning' required by public and administrators. Athletes are often controlled both on and off the court … The athletes are almost emotionally blackmailed as coaches want to know every little piece about them so that they can be manipulated. While it is helpful to know some of what happens, players need their own space as well or they are limited by their coach and do not grow as much as they can.

Against the general trend, Lyn practises her philosophy of athlete-centred coaching even for national teams. She finds that people's perception of her coaching is problematic because they have different expectations often brought about by their previous experiences of coach-centred coaches. Nevertheless she adheres to her beliefs:

> … people want instant results next week for a one-off test series regardless of its place in a long-term plan. The modern-day event series in netball does not allow for the lead-up games where less experienced players are able to be conditioned. Consequently some teams are developmental at the national level in stages of a four-year cycle depending on the prior experiences of the athletes. If the context domestically is highly competitive, the prior conditioning into this level makes it easier to step straight into the national arena. So, to [be athlete-centred] is extremely difficult as it seems slower. It can be seen as more analytical depending on how it is achieved. But I have always tried to do it because I believe it is the most permanent way to get change of behaviour and produce long-term success.

Long-term goals can leave a coach and team open to criticism when competing in the international arena. Because of public and societal expectations that have been constructed in the past, sport tends to focus on creating robots rather than human beings. As Lyn sees it:

> Good international performance should also push the boundaries of performance. In the national, high-pressure situation, most sports now have events that they want to sell as commodities in the commercial arena and each year there is a big event. [In netball] it might be the World Youth Champs followed by Commonwealth Games followed by the World Champs … Each year there is a big event and so if [we] want thinking players who own their performance and own their own development and are supported by the coaching staff, that's completely different. It's much easier and much faster to be autocratic. Or so it seems. That's the problem. It depends on your philosophy, which one you are going to activate or which combination of effects you want at any given time. It can be fast if you are skilled enough

once you have got past the barriers. Many players like autocratic as they then have someone to blame when things do not go right. The athlete-centred way demands they take responsibility for their performance and learning.

Though athlete-centred coaching is more difficult, its advantages of developing better performers and thinking athletes represent a key to long-term success.

Lyn's Development as a Coach

Lyn's coaching development began in high school when, in her rural community, she was needed to coach the younger ones. There were many participants and not enough adult coaches, so everyone just pitched in. Lyn also recognises the huge influence of her parents on her coaching. As a youngster she used to tag along to all her mother's netball coaching sessions, learning so much about people and coaching from watching and being there. Being involved in many different sports also assisted by widening her range of experiences.

Although she believes her physical education lecturers gave her some ideas, Lyn feels most of her coaching evolved through time and personal experiences. Another major influence on her coaching was her teaching experience at Melville High School. Again, the philosophy of a collective community was pervasive in that school, where the rate of sports participation was high. As Lyn says, it was not 'winning' that made this school excel:

> It wasn't known as a sports school but, when I became Head of Department there later, I did an analysis of it … We had over two-thirds of the school participating in sport, but not one of the teams were the top teams in the area. You wouldn't say that that was the best school for sport because we weren't winning a lot of competitions, but the students were actually involved and many as individuals were achieving national honours both in sport and academic studies, which did not make sense. It was a good school because it had a huge heart … it had a lot of different divisions in the school and the staff there were fantastic. I felt quite privileged teaching there because the people had that collective focus. People pitched in and really helped each other. It is such a precious thing and it allowed the flexibility to let the students feel as though they could achieve whatever they really wanted to. The school often turned around difficult children because of the approach of the staff and I began to realise the way in which excellence and excelling was really being achieved. We often had students achieve well outside their recognised capabilities and I felt [the collective focus] was the cause. I began to evaluate properly how narrow sport coaching was.

Lyn's player-coach experiences in netball ranged from actually being a player-coach for several teams to taking on the role of coaching the team as part of her role as captain, which was her position on several teams. The first of these experiences was in Otago, where players, especially Lyn, were required to help out. She gained quite strong coaching experiences through these roles. Taking on the role as leader within each of her netball teams was a necessity. Lyn says she:

> ... coached using examples or just sharing ideas. It was more of a leadership role because I was playing as well ... you certainly can't be an autocratic coach when you are a player ... If you try and [be coach-centred], it simply does not work, it is more a collective effort, but it was extremely difficult not to [coach autocratically] because of the nature of what was happening [within the team]. I suppose in lots of ways, I always tried to help other people to believe in their own ability and act as an agent for that. [I guess] you call that coaching ...

Lyn notes that it was difficult for a captain to take on a player-coach role as well. All the same, the experience obviously developed her as a coach. She recalls:

> There are a lot of things which have shown me what *not* to do, not *what* to do ... I spent a lot of my time hatching up ideas that I thought were missing. In actual fact, it made it extremely difficult to be the captain because I was doing more than I should've been doing as the captain. It was a completely different way of captaining when you are responding to your environment ... One year we had been away and won a tournament and I didn't play, but I coached ... I just felt that at that particular year, they needed all my energy off the court, as opposed to on it.

Lyn's player-coach and captaincy roles gave her some real insight into coaching based on situations and needs, which contributed to her development:

> I think any captain that is any good is going to respond to their environment. If they were 10 years later and they were in a different environment, there would probably be a different captain. Responsiveness is a basic leadership skill; it depends is how you lead in that particular time.

Most coaching Lyn experienced as a player was autocratic. Again, it was her wider life experiences that had the greater influence on her coaching development. She reflects:

> The main bulk from me, came from a wide variety of experiences I had, not only in netball, but in other life experiences, but I think that a lot of things for me came from my rural community upbringing and the fact that you lived so far away from others, you had to do it yourself anyway.

The Process of Establishing a Quality Team Culture

Lyn's emphasis on community pervades her thinking about how to form a quality team culture. Like other coaches in this book, Lyn believes that team culture is the glue that holds a group together and that, without it, athletes aim in different directions. Lyn believes that teams should have a direction that is purposeful to the team. She also believes that to bring a group together, a coach must enable them to accommodate all the different cultures in the team. Lyn explicitly works on developing this community by instilling meaningful principles.

On any team, there is a variety of athletes, and therefore the team comprises a community. Lyn describes how it operates:

> Of all the teams I have taken, there are sometimes five different cultures in the team. Netball seems to be a game where there are socioeconomic differences, intellect differences, age differences and life experience differences. I actually believe more in the concept of community. You've got a community of people on your hands for a period of time … depending on how long you've got these people. It may be that you are part of a four-year cycle programme and that you have to think about how you want to be at the end of that. When are the big events? When do we have to put the best performance out that this team is capable of producing? Also you need to leave a door open … for competitive pressure outside [and] for those people who will grow and develop within the group … who come from other aspects, like another country. It would be highly unlikely that you could pick a team at the beginning of a four-year cycle and have the best group and it remain the same for all that time. The culture rises out of the group you've got. However, I strongly do believe in having some basic principles which establish a connecting forum from which to go [forward] and pulls them together.

To pull this community together, coaches need to think about how to start with a new group. Initially, Lyn believes that a coach needs to analyse, reflect and observe the cultural elements of the new team and where each member has come from:

> For each team I have taken, the first thing I have done is look at the team and say, 'What have I got in here? Have I got older players, younger players, less mature players? Have I got people who are used to being in charge? Have I got people who need information?' and have a complete assessment [of] who this team is in its current form. I don't ask them, I just see them operating …

The culture of the New Zealand national netball team was of interest. When Lyn started coaching the team, the senior players had just been part of winning the World Championships. Lyn explains how she began looking at that team culture:

> Many members of the World Championship team were about to or had retired. The team had [been together] for a long time … many wanted to finish at the World Champs, which was understandable because they had been to a couple of World Champs anyway. Some of them had hung on, partly because I think someone talked them into it, it wasn't me, but this produced its own challenges for me. The first thing I did was actually recognise that the coach is often the new person in a functioning group and there is plenty of residual culture left over from prior experience. I needed to pay attention to the obvious subgroups within the team. I called a meeting of the senior players to discuss their contribution in support of the captaincy. We discussed their roles and the expectation that they could lead by action in a variety of ways and in support.

Lyn's major theme in creating a quality team culture is to instil and practise life principles. Her four major principles with the English team were having direct communication, taking responsibility for your own and the group's performance, being honest and celebrating difference. She elaborates:

> Those basic principles that I think are important in any group of people operating anywhere, are, [first,] direct communication—[for example,] there is no point in me discussing [something] with you if the person it affects is sitting on the other side of the fence. My view of that is that women's groups gossip a lot and they get a lot of negativity into a group by not really getting directly to the issue and sorting it out and it continues to develop and fester rather than killing it and moving on. My view with players is that if they don't want to sort that out, then they shouldn't be talking about it because that's how we undermine group behaviour.

> The second one is take responsibility for your own performance but also for the group performance. The third is [honesty, which] we can operate on [through direct communication]. I discussed with the players, 'This is how I think we should approach this, from these principles. If we can manage these … then we are going to do okay as a group …' and the most important for me is to celebrate difference … When you have got people of the variety that you have in some of these groups, trying to make them be the same is not only impossible but also undesirable. It is much better to approach it in the community sense and get them at least adhering to similar principles that can then make their differences co exist rather than saying, 'You have to like each other'.

Lyn discusses activities that she has used to instil the principle of celebrating difference:

> I think there are important exercises you can undertake. One is to change the discourse of the group to reflect the principles. Enlist the senior players to take leadership actions. There are functional ways to achieve [a celebration of difference] as well—e.g. group meetings, individual interviews, use of outside activities in order to create situations where people understand how each other perform and think … I try to create situations where people can either get to know one another … and understand how each other think about something, or can demonstrate the behaviours they might display in situations of stress. Therefore, if you can get them accepting the difference and then working with that, that's much better than getting into conflict …

The importance of establishing principles and values is recognised by all the coaches in this book. However, one key concept in developing principles is that the athletes should have a say in developing them so they can own them and thus take responsibility for living them. To create these principles with the English team, Lyn says:

> Normally … I would try and draw those out of a group [my]self … it depends on what the situation is; you would want all of the group to come to the same types of principles that they had all bought into. That is the classic team setting, the environment. In the case of the English team, we didn't

have a lot of time, six weeks before the Commonwealth Games. What we did was more directed to begin with; we said, 'Here are some things that might help this group right now' … I put them up and asked for additions and deletions. It was quite fascinating to watch that process because they virtually just took them on … I am quite a strong believer in discourse as a way of changing social behaviour. So we gradually start to eliminate some of the words and phrases that people were using, by introducing new phrases and words and ideas that would get them to start to understand what was around them differently. The players needed knowledge and to be involved mentally in what they were doing. They then had a chance of taking ownership. However, one of the real issues is whether the support staff also behave in this way.

With the English team, due to a lack of time, Lyn had to be proactive in promoting her own principles:

I did some other things like establish some continuums of behaviour where they physically stood where they thought they were on these continuums. It was a public acknowledgement to their group of their own thoughts about their contribution. It was trying to get an openness and honesty that wasn't there before. One of the things that we talked about was that if you are not honest about what you are doing, the opposition are going to be more than honest about what you are doing and [their words] are not going to be very nice … We gave them some examples of what some other team might say about their team … What I was trying to do for that particular situation was say, 'Here's how you have been operating and you can all see that is not successful'.

After considering the context of a given team on its own merits, Lyn decides how to establish the team principles for that particular team:

In other situations, I'll get [the athletes] to formulate the principles. I often want to see what the natural behaviour is first because the natural behaviour will develop according to who is in the group … You only have to take one person out of a group and put one person in and it can change a lot. So, each time, it is better to just let them go for a while, see what's going on and gradually just draw an activity together. It might be really important with that group to have [the principles] written down.

How does Lyn gain athlete ownership? She says:

Mostly by asking questions, to focus and refocus players by highlighting various instances or behaviours—sometimes in a general way; other times very much one-on-one, and at other times casual.

The key to these principles in the end is to practise them and try to live them. Lyn suggests that, in many cases where you are bringing together a group of very different backgrounds and cultures, the group would normally not mix well. It may go all right for a while, but with one glitch the whole community can be broken apart. So Lyn uses these principles to pull them together. Each situation that arises, there is a lesson to be learned, so to revisit the principles and ask the athletes if they are adhering to the set team principles is an ongoing process of learning, as Lyn explains:

> In netball, it's timing and it's a very quick game which requires a lot of trust and a lot of cohesiveness in a very short space of time. These people are going to have to try to share ... In some games, you can go and score, but in netball, one half of the court can't do that. So it's equal ball, and very much a team game. You can't get mad at the other person for not doing their job because you can't go and do it for them. You've got to actually somehow contribute even more with what you can control ... People get really angry if they are contributing a lot and they can see another person not contributing as much. So that's why teams need some form of common ground ... I have seen teams scrapping inside themselves within their team, but they bind like concrete when they have an external threat ... where a group is not cohesively going very well, we've said, 'Let's stop focusing internally and let's focus on something external ... establishing the purpose. The real threat is what that opposition is going to do to you. Let's focus on that and stop the internal focus' ... we have magnified issues that are external to the group to make them bind as a group.

The external influence is one factor that can bind a team to a common goal. Lyn makes this point with reference to a wonderful example of a tour that she was on:

> David and I saw [the team bond] on a bus trip once. For three weeks no one had a cross word to say and didn't get on anybody's nerves at all. There were 58 people. The reason was that they all hated the tour director. That was the external source. They respected his knowledge, but they didn't like him as a person. So the entire group coexisted quite happily because of the focus on this external influence.

Lyn has never been a proponent of team-building activities that centre on external motivation:

> The [English] team did a lot of external team building and, while it gave the administration of the team an idea of what was happening, the transferability of the activities was quite limited.

By contrast, the types of team-building activities that enhance the team environment have a mutual meaning to the team, enabling them to go in the same direction. Lyn relays an example relating to the English team:

> Team culture to me is best established when there is common purpose and that common purpose is meaningful to the group and highly transferable. There is quite a bit of research about team building in external situations that shows low transferability. Some of the team-building activities that I have seen that work best [have] been when it is related to what you are trying to do ...

For example, we found there were some financial constraints going into the English development campaign. So we got the players in and said, 'We've got some issues here about how the finances are and what the priorities need to be. What do you guys think you can do to help this problem?' They were fantastic. They got together as a group, one or two of them took the lead automatically. They started doing things differently and they produced a significant cut in their spending behaviour. That was a project that had meaning for them. So if I was to engage in a team-building type of activity, it's more about what has meaning for the group.

When another opportunity arose for Lyn to put a problem to the athletes and thereby enhance the team culture, she grabbed it. This is the sort of purposeful team-building activity that Lyn uses:

... the English group was ... taking two-and-a-half to three hours to get taped before games because the one physio was doing it all ... That is not a good amount of time to have the tape on. I asked for the group to do as much of their taping as possible in a half-hour period. There were moans and groans about that at first but, because we identified why and that it was a constraint, they could see what the purpose was. The interesting thing in observing that was that after a while, it became a team-building activity: players coexisted doing something that had meaning and it gave some a sense of control over themselves [which] they needed before playing. The time was cut to 27 mins. Obviously, people [who] were injured were taped by the physio, but there were others who were preventive taping and quite capable of taping themselves. I favour those types of team activities which have meaning for the whole group and in effect build team. In our efforts to support international players, we sometimes take away their sense of responsibility and ownership.

So this example again demonstrates the practical application of Lyn's philosophy of community and athlete responsibility, which perpetuates her belief in creating a quality team culture. She also favours establishing principles for the team, preferably with the athletes. Of interest is her view that it is valuable to find an external threat to bind the team. Lyn also advocates that team-building activities are only useful when they serve a team purpose and are meaningful and transferable to that situation, at that particular time, with that particular team.

Lyn's Use of Questioning

Coach educators are highlighting the need for athletes to become more skilled in decision making along with increasing their awareness and knowledge of the sport. Lyn believes that questioning is an important method of enhancing the learning of a particular experience, which is achieved not just through applying the correct technical process of asking the question, but also through the art of timing the question, formulating it and choosing it appropriately. In England, she says, coach educators:

... have been encouraging the coaches to start questioning. What I find interesting is that they are taking the pieces of activity in isolation without that integrated approach. It doesn't work. People are saying they want more athlete decision making and taking responsibility, [therefore] we have to use more questioning. I have been asked to take sessions about this a lot. Some of the coaches have really attempted this approach and I have seen them struggling with it.

Lyn relates how her experiences in her careers and counselling role at high school focused her attention on questioning as a technique:

What I noticed in guidance groupings, was that although people said things about what to do and what you should do with interviewing people, the one thing that they didn't talk about very much was how did you genuinely feel? Many went into a mode of behaviour that was quite false, I felt. This goes back to what I feel about understanding how the emotions and the energy fields are because if you translate that, even though you are saying the right thing, if [the person's] feelings are different or you think a particular way, you will actually communicate it ... So, if you genuinely can't like the people who you are trying to help, then it makes no difference how trained you are. I saw it time and time again where people tried to help other people, but they didn't genuinely like doing it so it didn't work or it had very short-term effects.

Lyn has been asking questions for years because athletes need to learn to be better players of the game and to make better decisions. She can ask one good open-ended question, which appropriate to that person in that situation at that time, and get the athlete to think in depth. Lyn believes in asking the question relative to the need, personality and desire of the player involved. To ask a good question, coaches must consider 'the timing and the mood' and the question must be 'totally open-ended and leave ownership with the athlete'.

In saying this, being time efficient has a great effect on the ability to think in depth. Any training session involves a variety of experiences, creating a context that coaches must be able to analyse so that they can coach according to the atmosphere at the time. Lyn suggests that the major consideration in formulating the question is what outcome is required:

What is the question that is going to open up the outcome possibilities? It's being conscious of the situations all the time. We constrain [players] by our inability [to ask questions] and focus their attention ... How do you know that person you are dealing with doesn't have the next revolutionary idea about sport? [For example,] who started two-handed backhands? Who starts wearing their cap on back-to-front and sets the trend? Where is the one who has the confidence to do that? So are you going to be a follower or somebody who keeps ahead of the game? Coaches have to allow [innovation] to happen, otherwise the game doesn't develop and champions do not emerge.

As Lyn implies, using well-formulated questions is a key strategy for an athlete-centred approach. She understands why coaches take the coach-centred approach: it is certainly easier. A truly athlete-centred coach faces the challenge of catering to the learning of the athlete and his or her individual needs. Any coach who pursues 'athlete thinking' must be:

> … very brave in this current world of sport. For me, I don't have any question as to what I am going to do, but I can understand the constraints of a lot of coaches who aren't given the time by administrators to actually get to that point where [developing thinking athletes] is having an effect because it may appear to take longer and look softer … People who have come through sport might have come through another method, so they are looking at this [athlete-centred] person thinking, 'What is this? This isn't coaching.' They are already judging [the athlete-centred approach] because of their own experience. My experience is, it is more demanding on the athlete.

Lyn advocates the use of questioning because she is committed to enabling athletes to learn and develop. The athlete-centred approach is different to the dominant public perception of coaching. To take this approach, coaches must strongly believe that the athletes' needs are most important, despite the pressure from outside groups. Even though it is difficult to shake of the influence of our predecessors and the media, coaches must ask themselves, 'Who am I really here for?'

Lyn and Teaching Games for Understanding

In observing Lyn's coaching, it was evident that she uses Teaching Games for Understanding (TGfU or Game Sense) to teach athletes about the game. To develop international players, Lyn believes that teaching the athletes game sense is crucial. Many players she coaches come from other clubs or associations who have not taken the time to get athletes to think about the game. 'Many of their backgrounds and experiences are limited', says Lyn. She believes in 'getting athletes to experience those feelings about spatial concepts'.

Lyn began using TGfU in New Zealand, making up different situations and games to satisfy a need for athletes to become game aware. By focusing on game understanding, Lyn stresses her belief in developing international sportspeople, rather than just athletes who play for their country:

> I think they are two different things because quite often the player who plays for his/her country is aiming to do things just well enough to get on the national team … so if they are just going for the national team, it is all right if it is the top individual side in the world, but then everyone is chasing you so you have to be better than that … there is a difference in actually understanding what the context internationally is and what you have to do for it. It is important to continually get better and make sure that you can answer whatever anybody else will put to you. If you can't do that, then you are not an international sportsperson. You are only a national player. To be an international sportsperson, there is decision making, there is a whole

contextual difference, there is a difference in the variety of physical skills and the way in which you use them and in what you have to understand socially. All the social implications [some external] of being in international sport can crush the person who may be physically talented before they even get off the ground.

These international players are developed according to how they are oriented. As Lyn says, 'If they are only oriented in the motivational sense, in being excited by the challenge of getting better, then that is how they will approach the international scene'. What she is aiming for with her athletes is for them to be able to sit on the sideline or go to a training session and be able to analyse the opposition in a totally unemotional and rational way. Once players get this international feel, their training goes up another notch. Lyn explains:

It's whether you want to be the best as measured by somebody else, or whether you want to be the best your capacity can manage. If you take the second attitude that most people use, then in the first one you are just edging out the opposition all the time. You see it quite often in athletics, where somebody has a world record and they run against the clock really well, but when they get into an actual event it all changes for them. Some people will win to beat other people, but they won't crack a world record. Other people will crack a world record, but never win a race … In team games, it expresses itself by teams that get ahead and they can't pull away, they are just winning all the time. The New Zealand team is like this.

To develop players' ability to analyse and strive for that extra notch, and in this way to nurture an international sense, Lyn's training sessions are full of problem-solving situations to enhance their game sense:

The best example is that we have a bunch of players who came into the team who did not have good spatial awareness and game sense awareness, just in a general sense. So we said, 'How can we combine training, make it fun and do some other things as well?' We started making up these games in the morning and they would have whatever the fitness element was (speed, endurance) then we created invasion games that had spatial concepts which were teaching them about some of the spatial context that they need in netball and some of the game sense that they were missing. We added other elements that tested their attitudes to rules and other team players by changing rules and making up red herrings. We simply pressured them mentally. What we were doing was just constantly trying to create a game environment situation. I don't go and find the games, I just make them up from the elements that they need and that they need to learn.

Lyn suggests that when the players begin training with her, they often have great knowledge and ability to train and play in discrete units but do not understand how to integrate these units into a full game context. Lyn has really noted a difference in the English team using TGfU, she can see a big change in her players' application and understanding for the game of netball.

To enhance the international game of netball, Lyn uses TGfU to teach for pressure situations that may arise on the court:

> We use [games] all the time to make decisions and add pressure, like risk taking, pressures. We want people to take risks ... There is a time to skill and drill, hone something up technique-wise, but the rest of the time, once they have got that technique right, they need to apply it. They can have the best techniques in the world, but if they can't apply them, then it is a waste of time. We quickly get to the application which has risk taking, decision making and pressure ... The other thing is recognising that they are in a ball game and they should be using the ball as much as they possibly can.

Through TGfU, Lyn creates a learning environment that enhances the desire for athletes to get competitive. What kind of environment that should be depends on the national culture in which you are coaching. She says that coaches need to be aware that:

> There is a real art in a strongly competitive nation where there are a huge number of people participating; you can have a harshly competitive environment. But if you've got a quasi amateur situation with a small population, then you have to handle that differently.

When I ask Lyn if she learned the TGfU approach through any particular training, she responds:

> I probably picked up on it from teaching, actually ... When I first started teaching, I was teaching a lot of home room and disadvantaged groups ... they taught me a lot about human behaviours. They didn't do what you expected, they never did. They never responded to language as you expected either. So it taught me a lot about what I was effectively doing and how people will respond to different pressures. These groups were bluntly honest about everything.

Lyn has been using TGfU throughout her coaching life without putting a label on it. Her intentions in training have always been to create situations in which athletes develop an informed understanding of the game or situation in a holistic sense and with integrated training. She has also seen it as essential to develop this understanding by creating pressure situations through using games to train the players.

Implementing an Athlete-centred Approach

One of the major challenges Lyn has faced in her athlete-centred coaching is that many athletes have experienced only coach-centred approaches before starting with her. She says it is important to help the athletes through this process of change:

> ... the players, when they first experience how you are doing this, they think you are soft and confusing. It is a whole change of behaviour for them. At times, they don't cope with that very well. Sometimes you have to be autocratic, e.g. 'Stop doing that and do this', and then they feel comfortable.

> If you are really, genuinely trying to help them get into this whole scene, you do have to assist them through that process of change.

The challenge continues for her athletes as, when they go back to coach-centred coaches, they must adjust again. However, Lyn feels that these athletes, having been enabled to think and learn about the game, have an advantage as they begin to use their knowledge and experience to enhance their performance under each different leadership style. Going back to a coach-centred coach, these athletes may also begin to challenge the coach's ideas, which many coach-centred coaches cannot cope with. In Lyn's view, it is important to give athletes some guidance about how to return to such a situation:

> It is interesting watching [the high performance players] who've come out of a highly autocratic system and into this completely different way of doing things and there isn't one of them that does not now like it. They are having great difficulty at the moment going back to … very autocratic coaching and teaching situations. Of course what you've got are athletes who challenge, who ask questions, people who think about things and say, 'Excuse me but you are not making sense to me'. So it is a much more challenging to the coaches who are autocratic now and we've had to counsel the players who have gone from that programme back into autocratic coaching, to teach them how to cope with that. It is quite specifically different. What is interesting for me about that is when I first went there, I didn't realise I was that different [in my coaching approach]. I have now realised that it is extremely different.

Players who will be the best international athletes will have a special passion. That passion exudes through training if you can offer them an opportunity to enjoy what they are doing and know why they need to understand certain situations. Using an athlete-centred approach, a coach can enable athletes to gain that passion. Lyn relates two other analogies to illustrate what can be achieved with passion:

> It happened last year when Temepara [Clark] came back on the court in the final of the World Championships. Australia would have won that game, but Temepara came back on that court and got two interceptions. She was sent off but when she came back it was with a controlled and very passionate drive. This player had the complete drive at that moment in time and she was going to get out there and do this well. In fact, it was the last thing she did … That does not happen by drilling. Another example is 100-metre sprinters who often run faster in a relay than they would ever run in just a flat race. That shows that element of people's desire and passion within them that will drive an exceptional performance at a particular time.

Lyn believes strongly that athletes have many learning experiences without coach interference. In many situations that Lyn sets up (e.g. a game or practice), the athletes set off to do things in their own way. She often waits on the sideline until she can determine that the athletes are stuck or an athlete asks for clarification. Their learning is enhanced because they are discovering and taking ownership of their understanding of the situation(s). Often when implementing activities or games, coaches tend to interfere, to jump in and tell the athletes how to solve the problem. In effect, athletes are giving the responsibility of understanding back to the coach and the coach is taking it away from the players. However, the coach's role should be to try to set conditions that will enhance the learning and accelerate it.

Conclusion

Lyn says that she continues to learn about her coaching and from the athletes:

> I think you learn all the time in different environments but you have to pay attention. I'd rather something emerges than is specifically created because people buy into it as something they own. I think the discourse crucial. If I expect people to be courteous to one another and share and perform to win, then how I spoke about that was really important. It wasn't the words, but the ideas behind the words. So by changing those you can set an environment that will indicate change in a lot of people's behaviour and expectation. I can remember teaching a seventh form [class] at school and they were talking to one another in very negative terms, as young people did at that time. We talked about it and suggested an experiment: to play a game of softball in the class and see whether they could actually not say anything negative. We agreed on a penalty if they did. They all bought into this and off they went. At the end of the session, they debriefed. They realised they couldn't get through the game. People would start to say something and then they'd stop midway and realise what they were about to say. They were all great about it, but what I was trying to do is just show them where they were at and what they were doing unconsciously. I didn't have anybody tell me to do that or teach me how or when to attempt it.

Lyn is an astute, insightful coach. Her ability to read people impressed me in watching her coach and interviewing her. She has a highly analytical mind, with a key ability to focus on the big picture.

Lyn also believes strongly in focusing on a quality team culture through the notion of community. This community is a group who come together to strive for a mutual direction, often an external goal. Through a coach's efforts to ensure this community works well together, it is possible to create a quality sport environment in which values and principles are adhered to and practised as individuals work together for a common purpose. To develop and maintain such a community, Lyn advocates the four principles of having direct communication, taking responsibility for your own and the group's performance, being honest and celebrating difference.

Lyn's use of athlete-centred coaching has been an asset to those athletes she has influenced. Her curiosity has inspired them to develop the same quest for knowledge. Through her, athletes have also been exposed to many valuable experiences that have enhanced both their performance and their holistic development.

If we would have new knowledge, we must get a whole world of new questions. – *Susanne K. Langer*

Schooling, instead of encouraging the
asking of questions, too often discourages it.
– *Madeleine L'Engle, US civil rights leader,*
clergyman

Freedom is the opportunity to make decisions. . .
– *Kenneth Hildebrand*

My grandfather once told me that there were two kinds of people: those who do the work and those who take the credit.
He told me to try to be in the first group. There is much less competition. – *Indira Gandhi*

Chapter Eleven

Rod Thorpe on Teaching
Games for Understanding

This chapter contains extracts from an interview with Rod Thorpe, from Loughborough University in England, which were included in *Developing Decision Makers* (Kidman, 2001). Also included are Rod's insights into the current trends and practices of the Teaching Games for Understanding (TGfU) movement in sport and physical education, which he developed as Game Sense in Australia and New Zealand. He gives his interpretation of an athlete-centred coaching approach and discusses how TGfU fits into this coaching philosophy.

Rod Thorpe and David Bunker (1982) were central to the development of TGfU in the early 1980s. In this approach a meaningful and appropriate games experience is a key to athlete learning. It requires the coach to move from one game to another using a progressive, purposeful activity that meets the needs of athletes' learning about the actual game they play. This model breaks away from the traditional approach of isolated skill practice, where athletes learn skills of the game separate from the actual game itself (Thorpe, 1990). By playing purposeful games, athletes enjoy training and their intrinsic motivation is increased which in turn enhances their desire to learn and encourages them to continue participating in sport.

It is interesting to note that many physical education teachers and coaches were taught to save the 'game' until the end of the session, at which stage individuals could apply the techniques that they had supposedly learned. Yet as physical education teachers and coaches, many of us used to complain that the students could never get the idea of the skill when they were actually playing a game. We were trained to use games not so much for learning but as a vehicle for teaching technique, while we tended to save the game for a 'treat' at the end of the lesson. TGfU offers a more exciting approach to motivate students and to enable them to learn and enjoy themselves.

As a key developer and practitioner of TGfU, Rod discusses the movement away from the traditional approach towards a TGfU approach, which enables students or athletes to learn about the game and practise the techniques within the context of a game rather than separate from it. Learning in context provides a better understanding of the game as well as many opportunities for decision making, a skill that is consistently considered desirable for athletes. Rod also discusses how athletes learn and why TGfU enhances learning opportunities. Reinforcing his argument, each of the coaches featured in this book believes in the value of using TGfU games to enhance athlete decision making in technical, tactical and attitudinal ways. At the end of the chapter, Rod elaborates on how skill is developed through TGfU before summarising his impressions of the current directions of the TGfU model.

The Development of Teaching Games for Understanding

In my earlier interview with Rod, I first asked why he originally had the idea of Teaching Games for Understanding, when it breaks away from a traditional skill learning model. He responds:

> That is quite an interesting question, there were many interlinked reasons that came out of our thoughts on skill learning—most pertinently, the then forgotten aspects of perception and decision making, motivation, social psychology, teaching methodologies, etc. I would also add that we were taught the value of small side games as students in the early '60s, even though we were taught to focus on the 'skill' part of the lesson.

> When we watched youngsters playing on their own, either in a recreation setting or, say, before a practice session or lesson, we often noted quite sophisticated movements and interactions. A few examples might help:

> - Youngsters put some coats down to make soccer goals for a game. There are seven of them but they decide to play three, including the oldest player, against four, including the two youngest.

> - There is a pick-up game (play rather than organised game) of three-v-three cricket in a rural area, mixed ages. The youngsters decide to make a rule that 'The big kids can't bowl fast'.

> - At the start of a basketball lesson, the coach has not arrived. The youngsters are playing two-v-two and using disguise, reverse dunks (or nearly). The coach walks [in] and coaches 'fundamentals', divorced from any game or individual need. The kids were challenging themselves and each other; the coach failed to do so.

> The common factor in our observations was that when children were getting on with it, uncluttered by teachers and coaches, they were often more productive in terms of learning in context, enhancing motivation through challenges, social interactions, etc. They were empowered by circumstance. When it comes to empowerment I would say we noticed that kids left alone often had it and were the better for it. If we accept that well-intentioned coaching is not always better than no coaching, we might examine our practice more carefully.

What is Rod's understanding of the empowerment approach as it is used to help athletes learn?

> Empowering literally means 'giving power to' and I think this is a good point to start. A coach can give power to an athlete to make decisions about all aspects of the learning and performance process. Of course the obvious [step] is to give the players the power to decide on which action to use to produce the most appropriate tactical outcome in an activity. Certainly a major push for this empowering approach at an elite level has come in activities where players have to take responsibility for decisions. I would contrast say rugby football, in which the coach is removed from the game,

with American football, in which coaches dominate decision making for most players. As players become more equally fit and technically efficient there is a split-second difference in decision making. This is often linked to a split-second assessment of the relative probability of success of a number of options, a vital part to the game, for example, 'Shall I pass left and short, go myself or send the long pass right?'

But this is only a small part of empowering. The athlete can also be given power to aid motivation, self-confidence, etc. For example, 'To determine goals, what should I be aiming at in my training? How much do I think I can do? How much can I improve?' Personal goal-setting can be applied to physical and mental training, to match performances and to things like social support of teammates.

The player can also be given much more power to determine the way he/she learns. For example, when learning a shot, a tennis player might determine which sense to use to monitor a shot. Some might use the feel of the shot, some the sound of the ball on the racket, and yet others the resultant flight of the ball.

Simply, what are sometimes called the 'traditional approaches' to coaching, in which the coach is the holder of power, the font of knowledge, the provider of information, the analyser or the source of feedback, are actually disempowering. Approaches that involve the performer as an active contributor, rather than a passive receiver, most notably questioning approaches, are empowering.

Why do many coaches use the traditional approach that tends to disempower?

I would think a number of things contribute:

- Coaches know, and/or are supposed to know, a lot about their area and feel it is important to pass this over to the player.
- Of course ego comes into this. I cannot deny that I get a buzz out of directly helping people; it takes time to develop an approach where you get athletes to learn. Of course, it's easy to do when teaching beginners so we begin our coaching careers telling people what to do and we fail to practise early in our coaching development other methods of coaching.
- Players, parents, other coaches expect the coach to be 'delivering'.
- Most worryingly for people like me, having trained lots of teachers and coaches, when we traditionally judged coaches we would concentrate on their performance; voice projection, presence, demonstrations, appearance, preparation, etc. We did not really look at the athlete—we often gave the coach a topic. We did not assess the 'learning environment' as a whole. We also assessed a lesson or session in isolation [see next point].
- Perhaps outweighing all the other points is that the prescriptive approach produces quick 'performance' changes, within the lesson. Remember that people judged the success of their coaching on the session: 'I think that session went well'. The coaches seemed to grasp that.

- The same people would be found the following session, or after the next game, to be complaining that the players had forgotten everything: 'Don't you remember what we did?' Of course they didn't [remember] because we taught for rapid performance change, not for deep-rooted learning.

Rod explains how this athlete-centred philosophy relates to the use of TGfU as follows:

There was no more obvious an example of disempowerment than in traditional games lessons in schools, or similar coaching lessons. Children were provided with a lesson of warm-up – skill – game dominated by 'technical instruction'. The teacher chose the skill (better called 'technique' as it rarely had any perceptual, decision-making or contextual elements) and presented it often with little reference to the game it was to be used in. Clear demonstrations were applauded, despite the fact that in many cases, a good percentage of the children could not really aspire to the 'perfect model' being presented and practice ensued. Conformity was expected. If practice of the technique was 'good' in the sense of behaviour, rather than performance or improvement, the children were rewarded with a game. What little teaching occurred in the game was normally in the form of directions from the teacher as to where to stand and what angle to run at, or more often what not to do.

Lessons of this type were punctuated with 'When can we have a game?' during the technique teaching, and looks of anguish when the only bit of freedom gained, in the game, was interrupted by the instructions from the teacher. Power lay completely with the teacher.

Teaching Games for Understanding was a reaction to this 'traditional instruction' in two ways:

- we could not understand how we could expect children to learn if they were not involved in the learning process and did not understand what they were trying to do; and moreover
- as sport psychologists, Dave Bunker and I could not continue to accept an approach in which children lost the motivation to play and improve.

We wanted an approach that we felt youngsters could contribute to, know what they were doing and where they were going. We found most children pre-12 years of age wanted to 'play', so we wanted to capture and keep this personal (intrinsic) motivation. We wanted to challenge and we wanted improvement and we realised we could not achieve any of these things if we continued to deliver a technical model, suitable for the average, using a 'prescriptive' style.

The value of questioning and problem-solving approaches in education had been well researched by the 1960s and 'educational gymnastics', an approach using problem solving, had been proposed. Games set problems; we don't even have to use words to set the problem.

Our answer was always to let children enter the game (after a warm-up). The game was suitable for their age and development and so in the model we used the term 'game form'. (Often our children would play several simpler games before they reached the mini-game typified by Aussie Sport and Kiwi Sport in their early forms.) We wanted to avoid the need for the teacher/coach to do too much 'management' which we often saw as opening up the prescriptional approach [see Playsport below].

So we set out a different format (model). We wanted to be sure the children understood the game they were playing: 'What am I trying to do?' So the games had to be simple and we included game appreciation, before we moved to tactical awareness. As children exploited the simple games, e.g. 'Coach, he/she holds the ball and we cannot get it', [their experience] might lead the children to introduce a three-second hold rule in netball.

The key element of the approach, however, is to design games that help children arrive at tactical understanding for themselves. Well-structured games give options, so that decisions have to be made. The teaching/ coaching of youngsters, as with all their learning, is to give them just the right amount of option. When we have made the decision, we have to act, but that action will be different according to physical ability (of course, ability influences the decision in the first place), hence teachers and coaches must be helping their players differentially.

When Rod introduced the TGfU approach to Australia, the name became Game Sense. What is the difference between Game Sense and Teaching Games for Understanding?

I am not sure, as some use the phrase interchangeably, [that] there is much difference, but I see Game Sense as incorporating more than the original Teaching Games for Understanding. It is important, however, to think through carefully what, as a coach, you mean by a phrase like this. Len Almond, a colleague at Loughborough, often used the phrase 'Game-Centred Games Lessons' to try to put the game back at the centre of the lesson. I saw this as useful, but it only described the structure of the lesson and it hid a philosophy. My central aim in the lesson was to ensure children 'understood' what they were doing and learned more about games. Let us look first at TGfU as this was in sense the starting point.

Teaching Games for Understanding was literally an approach in which we wanted children to understand:

• the game they were playing;

• what they were trying to do;

• why they might select a particular move/action;

• that you could play games with varying degrees of competitiveness;

• that there were no universal right and wrong answers. (The phrase of TGfU is 'it all depends': it depends on the opponent's move, it depends on your position on court, it depends on how much skill you have, it depends on the situation, etc.);

• why they might want to learn and practise skills; and subsequently

- that success was there for everyone, but depended on them not the teacher or coach who could only help.

TGfU was based on recognising underlying 'principles' of games, based on space and time. Tactical understanding was reduced to simple ideas that might cross games. A goalkeeper 'bisecting the angle' is only doing what a tennis player does when covering a shot from one wing of the court. It was a simple idea, but new to many teachers and coaches.

To expand on an innovative way of enabling teachers and coaches to learn about TGfU and use the model confidently, Rod and a research assistant designed Playsport. It may be this development that helps us understand the difference between Game Sense and TGfU:

It became obvious in the late eighties that, whilst many teachers saw the value of this model for teaching games, leaders, beginner coaches and many primary (non-specialist) teachers felt they did not know games well enough to teach in this way. Playsport was a series of mini games in a number of sports presented with instructional cards, which were designed to provide children, parents and teachers with progressive, easily used programmes. The cards had clear pictures of children playing the games, with a minimal [number] of rules, safety points and suggested progressions. They used equipment as appropriate to children.

The key element was [that] the games provided progressive challenges to understanding, decision making, skill demand, social interaction, etc. but the novice teacher, mum or dad could use them without knowing the intricacies of any of these factors—they were literally providing a play structure for the children. The 'game designers' had done the thinking as to the outcomes of this play.

The Youth Sports Trust (UK), with headquarters at Loughborough University, used these [Playsport games] as their basis for TOP play and TOP sport developing equipment bags and in-service training to match. They decided that marketing the 'starter' games in Playsport that were not really a recognised sport would be more meaningful [if they were presented] as 'TOP play', and as the games became 'recognisable', they would be called TOP sport and lead on to and beyond the mini-game.

The games can be operated with minimal knowledge of the sport as they are based on child-centred play. Children learn as they meet the challenges of the 'new' (but only slightly changed) next game. Games set problems, children solve them.

In a sense TGfU expects the teacher/coach to be able to frame the challenges and to react to the situation; Playsport (TOP play/TOP sport) does not. It should be said, however, that once teachers (dare I say particularly those teachers with no previous ideas of coaching) become comfortable in the 'play' situation, they start to ask the sort of questions that are obvious within the game.

And so to the southern hemisphere. Between 1994 and 1998 I developed a programme called Game Sense with teachers and coaches in Australia, and the Australian Coaching Council produced a video and instructional booklet. I should acknowledge that there were many teachers and coaches using similar approaches already, some as a result of TGfU. Whilst Game Sense is an Australian programme, it embraces elements of both TGfU and TOP sport.

Simply it *makes sense to play games* (TOP sport) because we learn as we play. (In my opinion the teacher/coach who presents children with a well-designed game, appropriate to age and ability, is doing far more good than one who struggles to try and teach a technique or rigid tactic.) This can be followed by the *making sense of games* phase, that is based on teaching games for understanding.

Once primary teachers and coaches have gained confidence from the well-designed cards and children are active in TOP sport, the skills of the teacher soon appear. Children are asked 'where they are aiming and why'. The first steps to Teaching Games for Understanding are not difficult if teachers and coaches understand they are not expected to know everything or to give detailed technical instruction. In fact, to enable athletes to learn, coaches should avoid any direct detailed instruction, but rather focus more on athletes solving problems through coach or teacher questioning. Indeed, I find primary teachers are very comfortable with this teaching style.

Interestingly, whilst the Australian video is called Game Sense, much of video is about empowerment; it leans heavily on questioning and player ownership. Some coaches even see the approach as important because of this change of style rather than the idea of understanding.

One of the strengths of the athlete-centred approach, as highlighted by coaches and players, is the strong team culture it can create. Rod elaborates on how the use of TGfU contributes to team culture:

Sports psychologists will tell you that two sources of motivation keep coming out at the top of why people play sport. One is achieving—doing something well (not surprising then that children who are not physically gifted drop away from activities which emphasise only the technical and physical). The other is 'affiliation'—being with others, interacting, friends, the social aspects. Clearly, sessions in which children, or elite sports performers, interact together are the most motivating, the very essence of teaching games for understanding.

Everything from rules to tactics to goal setting to team selection (and I do not mean picking sides in public) can involve interactions between players. They share success and they share failure, they learn how to get the best out of everybody, *but* we do it while children are young. The players introduce rules into games, or conditioned games (when older), and understand about the need for rules and officials. (Rules are things to help you play the game better, not things a referee uses to stop you doing things.) Perhaps most importantly, particularly at high levels, because players are given freedom to … decide on actions, their teammates are tolerant of inappropriate decisions, and learn how to remedy and counter the potential negative consequences. Nonconformity and individuality [are] accepted, as long as it fits within a grand plan, but the grand plan has to be mutually agreed.

Of course, there will be disagreements, but this is in itself a learning process. I often ask the teacher/coach first using small-sided games and a TGfU approach, 'If you see one game stop and children disagreeing what do you do?' For me, as long as you perceive no anger or distress in the situation, stand back for a few seconds and they will often solve it. Much of my philosophy is that players, particularly games players, learn much from 'play', not least how to work together. My concern is that with directive coaches and organised play, we lose some of the potential to learn about social interaction.

This learning idea spreads to leadership, captaincy, etc. Normally, someone has to make the final decision, e.g. 'Let's do this'. The tough call for the coach is to determine at what point the coach decides and at which point he/she leaves this to the players. We do have to be careful because players want to feel confident about what they are doing and so someone has to cement the ideas. There is some evidence that players like a more democratic coach in training, but prefer the coach to become a wee bit more autocratic toward competition time. The skill of coaching is getting this balance right. Confused players doing their own thing are not what an empowering process is all about.

As demonstrated by the coaches in this book, most athlete-centred coaches use TGfU games to practise and reinforce the established vision, values and goals of their team. Such purposeful games provide coaches with relevant opportunities for athletes to learn about the meanings of the vision and values by interacting with each other, as well as with scenarios to focus on particular situations that may arise in competition.

With reference to his experience and research, Rod relates how students and top-level athletes have responded to TGfU:

At school level, there is ample evidence that more of the children enjoy this form of lesson, and skill learning does not suffer. Children with low physical ability and/or disabilities can achieve because a specific physical movement is never an essential. Games are relative, i.e. we play against another person [or other people] for an outcome.

When speaking to coaches, I often use the phrase, 'You can play games well/badly'. What I mean is that I watch people with relatively poor techniques totally engrossed in [playing] a game of badminton. They have good tactical understanding, are totally absorbed, dash about the court and leave the session satisfied and want to come back next week. So? The toughest call for a coach is to decide 'not to do anything'. I know I could make them better players, but is it the right time to step in? Will I have enough time to ensure that my input will be positive? The coach who steps in and explains what a player is doing wrong, or shows a 'better' way is having a very negative effect if they do not have the time to spend or the player does not have the ability to incorporate a lasting improvement into their 'fun' game. This said, some would argue that the traditional lessons that do this are not well taught which results in poor responses to lessons by children, rather than the approach [as such] being incorrect.

It is important to remember that TGfU is a curriculum model that assumes some transfer between games and embraces a desire that children at least 'appreciate' what is involved in games. Many children enjoy the movement between games, particularly in the early years. The community coach who lets children play with the ideas of hitting to space and running in a rounders game, has only to introduce kicking instead of hitting to give a whole new game with common tactical principles. Little kids need change.

Top-level coaches who use the TGfU approach say to me that they feel players are better motivated and make better decisions (but they *would* say this to me). Players see that they can learn from other games and that it helps players to see beyond the 'prescribed' tactics of their own game. Because perception and decision making [are] a central focus, it is almost obvious that these qualities, often neglected in early coaching, are seen to improve.

The recognition that 'techniques are only means to an end' has also given some coaches more comfort when dealing with a nonconventional 'technical' player. Sometimes, particularly early on, we do things which some would see as 'sacrilege'. [For example,] we let rugby players run sideways, giving up the tackle line, so that they can assess their personal running potential against an opponent who has also been assessed. Of course, I might argue that the critical time for a rugby team is to defend the ruck or maul behind the tackle line that would result from an inappropriate lateral run. Mmmm.

The one certainty is that players at top level need continuous challenge. Training can get boring in a long season. The great players are students of their game and self-motivated. Of course, they will enjoy this sort of coaching and their tactical decision making will be enhanced.

Many coaches explain that these ideas of empowerment and TGfU are fantastic, but admit they have neither confidence nor ability to put these approaches into action. When asked what advice he would give to coaches who have never tried TGfU, so that they gain the confidence to begin to use such an approach, Rod replies:

Remember there is no 'right way' to coach, just as there is no single 'right way' to play. You will choose coaching methods to suit your persona. This said, just as a good player does not try only one method of beating an opponent, so a coach should develop a range of approaches. Consider adding this to your coaching portfolio and then decide if it works better for you. I am convinced that the traditional way has shortfalls, but I am quite willing to accept that many coaches will employ it at some points as part of a variety of approaches. Once you do this and see the 'power' of empowering, you may start to develop a philosophy which is much more about developing the player as a whole, and I do mean as a person as well as a sports performer.

Start small. You will have a well-tried coaching model in your head from your previous experience as a coach and very powerfully from the way you were coached. See if you cannot introduce elements into your sessions in which you give more freedom to players. We are all familiar with conditioned games. Choose one, but instead of diving in and telling the players how to exploit this, let them see what they can do. In a conditioned team game take out two key players from one side. Let both sides work out how to cope. It's only a five-v-three game, but let them work it out. Set a timed two-minute game, let them work out a scoring system that is fair; e.g. the three[-person] side gets five points for a goal or try, the five[-person] side gets one point. In a game of badminton or tennis, put 'no go' (for tennis ball or shuttle) zones on the court, let's see how they cope.

We have all done it, but what we usually do is select the activity that allows us, the coach, to 'tell' the players what we want them to do. The major difference is that we help them work out what they have to do to exploit the situation and this means 'questioning' either verbally or by setting a new condition in the game.

Play small-sided games, but see if you cannot select those [games] that allow you to observe decision making. Get used to trying to see what the player is basing the decision making on, watch the opponents first and then see if the response is correct, rather than only watching your player. We do it in when analysing matches; do we do it enough in practice?

In regard to the possible challenges or pitfalls to TGfU, Rod suggests the following issues:

Uncertainty. Coaching is a performance and, just as players can be confused by too much information or uncertainty, so can coaches. I have always said that I am perfectly happy if presenting an alternative has made coaches think, has produced *reflective coaches*. I have always been concerned that many coaches tend to settle into a comfort zone about the way they coached, even if they were diligent about the latest technical, tactical, conditioning or psychological developments.

It follows, however, that whilst experienced coaches have the confidence to try things, we must not [over]load the beginner coach, hence the reason for the TOP sport concept. Equally, whilst I believe that children might learn far more in a game than in some 'technical' lessons I have seen, I do not want teachers and coaches to see this as an excuse for 'giving them a game'.

Considerable time has to go into the games and practices designed to produce a particular outcome. At times the coach can seem to be somewhat redundant, as he/she watches and assesses, only to go away and spend hours thinking how best to get 'learning outcomes' from his or her players.

We all know that in games coaching, ... the coach who can assess what is needed ... is the most effective coach. This type of approach needs the coach to both do this and then to think how to achieve this whilst not taking responsibility away from the players.

I have recently watched coaches, and from different parts of the world, who have taken away the responsibility from the players by thinking that they still feel the need to give instruction after playing a game. The problem with this is that TGfU's intention is to use games as fantastic learning opportunities, whereby athletes become self-aware and the games provide a problem solving mechanism. These coaches and teachers, though well intentioned, spoil that learning opportunity by telling the athletes how they should play the game, or what tactic they should use. This way of teaching and coaching limits not only those learning opportunities, but intrinsic motivation as well, as the athletes stop to listen to the 'words of wisdom' reducing their own input and thus their ownership of learning. Ensuring athletes are provided with opportunities to solve problems themselves and understand why certain situations occur is the key to TGfU.

Someone said you have to be a good coach to coach this way. Of course you do and this is what we should be aspiring to. Coaching is a 'profession'—note the small 'p' (i.e. not always for money). We need to study our profession. And if this approach and the whole issue of empowerment has not convinced you of the need to look toward this type of coaching, the fact that the commercial world is now looking at this sort of approach to increase 'performance' in their workforce must say something.

How Skill Develops Using TGfU

Many coaches suggest that if athletes work too much in games, there is no opportunity for them to learn skill. It is difficult to convince these coaches that skill learning is part of the process of becoming self-aware and a game-like experience provides the stimulus to learn the skill. Rod expresses his opinion on this attitude, with reference to skill acquisition theory:

Of course, because people see the emphasis shifting to perception (reading the game) and decision making, based on players having knowledge and gaining responsibility for training and performance, people inevitably say to me, 'So you are not as interested in skill'. *Wrong*. If you don't have the skills to exploit the situations you are faced with, your performance has to be limited.

Rod does not believe that people must have the skills before they can play the game:

I think we have to develop games that ensure that skills occur and develop in context. I have, over time, entered debate with the 'fundamental skills lobby', people who believe we should give our children a good grounding in fundamental skills. As a physical education student in the early sixties, I was presented with 13 fundamental skills and I firmly believe we should encourage youngsters to master these. I do, however, believe that we master these skills by having lots of goes, so we have to provide our youngsters with lots of interesting ways to practise these [skills]. And games do this.

My approach to throwing for accuracy would be to let youngsters try to, for example, throw a ball into a bucket and at a circle on the wall (targets in the horizontal and the vertical planes—maybe some readers can see how these two targets prepare youngsters for later). I would watch the efficiency of the action and help the youngsters having 'particularly obvious' problems. The children are playing a game; I am observing and helping the skill.

It is why I am so convinced that the secret to good games skills is the development of progressive games for youngsters. Games use the skills as mastered to date, but allow refinement of that skill ready for the next game. I think those of us who developed a 'games first' approach always felt that if players understood what they were trying to do and 'wanted to learn' the skill to do it, we would have far more motivated people addressing the skill problem.

Once people are well motivated, do coaches then break out into the typical technical phase of the lesson, albeit perhaps following the game? For example, your session might be structured as: warm-up, game, skill interjection, game, skill interjection, and game. Rod responds to my question in this way:

Interesting how you use two words almost interchangeably—the typical *technical* lesson and *skill* interjection. Remember I see 'technique' as the physical movement and 'skill' as the movement in context. I am happy to say I might break out into a *skill interjection*. Rarely will I spend time on an isolated *prescribed technique*, as we used to, because I do not think it is the best way to become skilful.

Let us look at one or two ideas that are presented by people who have studied skill acquisition (learning). Many of us, teachers and coaches, realised many years ago that isolated drills transferred poorly to games. Recent skill acquisition findings would suggest that this is due to three major reasons.

1. Integration

The relationship between the environment and the physical movement is far more integrated than we previously thought. The idea that we see something, make a decision and then select a specific action is naïve.

Let us try and give a very simple illustration. How is [it] that someone can pass the ball in basketball when falling? They have to pick up signals from their surroundings but their eyes are much lower than usual. They will release the ball in half a second when they are much lower, so they have to compute this; the arms will have to move a little differently and they will be passing up more so need a little more power. They must make sure the body hits the floor safely, and so on and so on. Of course, perception and movement are integrated, so why are we surprised that a technique practised in isolation does not transfer to the game? The example does not do justice to the work of those scientists investigating skill acquisition, but perhaps does enough to convince the coach that we have to consider more carefully how we deal with 'technical' elements.

Of course, the speed with which we have to respond in games means that these links between perception and response have to be done in a split second—some would say automatically (autonomously). It is interesting to note the problems that exist when adults are suddenly asked to 'think' about the decisions they make. The thinking mind is far too slow, the moment has passed, it has to be more 'automatic' and so the importance of building this sort of approach from [when athletes are] very young is obvious.

2. Variable practice

The idea that as soon as a person has grasped the 'idea' of a skill, the practice should be varied has been in the literature for many years and yet we still see the tennis coaches feeding a constant feed for hours after hours, often with a ball machine. The literature would tell us that as soon as the basic idea of the shot is in place, then we should be building variable feeds, send one shorter, one longer, have targets near the net that require less hitting force, or more spin, etc. It seems so logical and the evidence is there, but why don't we do it?

Perhaps the answer lies in how we measure improvement. It gets right to the issue of why some coaches are reluctant to change. In a sense the skill-learning issues are not dissimilar to the empowering issues. Coaching is a long-term process but is often judged on short-term results. Let me give you one more example.

3. Memory

A researcher (Helen Wright), when doing her Masters degree at Loughborough, replicated a laboratory experiment in a basketball class. She had one group of boys learn a skill with the teacher giving information and feedback throughout the session. A parallel group, matched so she could compare, were given the same information and feedback for half the session time, but were left alone to practise on their own for the other half. Her results replicated most of what was found in the laboratory experiment. At the end of the lesson, the group with continuous teacher support was significantly better than the half-session teaching group but after a week this difference had disappeared and the group [who were] given some time to practise alone had retained more from the first lesson. The sports scientists would say that the parallel group had 'subjective reinforcement': they had to pay attention for themselves to feelings in the body, results of actions, etc. They had been actively involved in building up the memories, not relying on the teacher feedback.

If you are interested in memory, you will also be aware that some of the problem is in retrieving something from your memory: [e.g.] 'Oh I know that person—what is her name?' It is interesting to look at another very well-researched area hinted at above. Coaches may identify two aspects to work on following a match. Let us say [the aspects identified are] the short serve in doubles badminton and defence on the smash. Typically, the coach will work on one (short serve) as a block until he/she feels it is okay and then move onto the next (defence of the smash).

Research into massed/distributed, constant/random [i.e. skill acquisition theory] would suggest this [approach] is not appropriate for learning. The results are good in the session, but do not seem to last. One explanation is that if we spend some time on serve, then move to defence, then return to serve, back to defence, etc., every time we return to, say, the serve we have to try to pull it out of memory, the work on defence of the smash has pushed it out of our thoughts. Can you see the links to the Helen Wright example?

We can make very fast improvements in the performance of a skill in a single session, but this might be disadvantaging the long-term learning process. The parallel with direct teaching, in which some rapid short-lived improvements can be made, and questioning-type approaches, in which immediate improvement is less obvious, must be seen. And thereby lies the problem.

Community coaches say to me, 'But the players (and parents of young players) expect me to tell them their faults (negative) and to rectify them quickly in a single session.' Professional club coaches say to me, 'I agree with you but if I do not get a quick return on my efforts I will be out.'

We have to change the way we evaluate coaching—coaching is a long-term process concerned with the development of a player. I think many coaches are really instructors.

When asked to link all these thoughts about skill learning with ideas on coaching games and empowerment, Rod says:

I think two key messages come through this.

One is that players have to be involved in the learning process, sometimes consciously: [ask them,] 'What are you trying to do?' Sometimes [they should be involved] subconsciously, by providing game like situations that bring into play an integrated response to the situation.

The second [message] is that many of the games children develop when left to their own devices, in a play-like environment, provide better learning experiences than the situations we, as supposedly knowledgeable coaches, have evolved. In coach training we have concentrated on how we coach and neglected how our performers learn.

For skill learning, I become more and more convinced that the secret is to 'condition/modify' games to the extent that the 'movement' required occurs more often, but does so under varying conditions. This does not stop the coach clarifying when [he or she is] certain this will help: 'If you spread the fingers, you will have more control on the volleyball during the volley'. [However, this idea does suggest] that the sooner a practice can be put into more realistic game-like situations, the better.

The TGfU movement has been expanding greatly in recent years. There is now a taskforce to help increase the use of TGfU throughout the world. Two international conferences have been held to enhance professionals' understanding of TGfU and to present research on physical, cognitive and psychosocial processes of the model. Rod spoke at the second conference in Melbourne, Australia in 2003.

In my later interview with Rod, I ask if anything had influenced his thinking about TGfU or its variations since 2001 when I first interviewed him. He reflects:

> It was pleasing to see, at the Biennial Conference on Teaching Games for Understanding, University of Melbourne, December 2003, that so many people from so many countries were critically assessing the approach. There was some concern [from conference delegates] that the model was being adapted, but this should be happening. The real concern for me was that sometimes in a search for a more 'structured lesson' or 'physical education programme', many of the adaptations were at the expense of the individual and certainly at the expense of individual empowerment. I am convinced this is as a result of the culture in which the teaching occurs. I suspect in one case the 'national culture' demands structure, in another [it is demanded by] the need for 'objective' measurement within physical education; of course, there is a less institutionalised culture of coaching that has tended to be conservative.
>
> In the United Kingdom, two factors have tended to catalyse a movement toward empowering the individual athlete, and hence a renewed interest in TGfU/Game Sense. Firstly, there has been an arrival of a number of Australian and New Zealand coaches and coach educators who were convinced of the value of Game Sense (or similar) and quite comfortable in using it. Secondly, the development of the United Kingdom Coaching Certificate (UKCC), ongoing, has emphasised the generic *how* to coach, to balance the many years of coach 'training' of *what* to coach. This, set against the central focus on the *individual learner*, has prompted most national governing bodies to look again at approaches to hand and not surprising[ly] this includes TGfU and Game Sense.
>
> Teaching Games for Understanding/Game Sense is being embraced, adapted and developed. This is heartening to me and the many other people who contributed to the early models. But if the developments do not retain those elements that surround the concept of empowering the individual athlete, they miss the point.

References

Bunker, D., & Thorpe, R.D. (1982). A model for the teaching of games in secondary schools, *Bulletin of Physical Education*, *18*(1), 5–8.

Kidman, L. (2001). *Developing decision makers: An empowerment approach to coaching*. Christchurch: Innovative Print Communications.

Thorpe, R. (1990). New directions in games teaching. In N. Armstrong (Ed.), *New directions in physical education* (pp. 79–100). Champaign, IL: Human Kinetics.

Note

For those interested in the theoretical aspects of this work, research is ongoing in many countries, under the heading of TGfU and/or Game Sense. TGfU is essentially practical so coaches should contact their own sporting bodies, coaching associations and local universities and colleges to see if work is being done in this area.

For assistance in implementing this type of approach, coaches can access a range of resources including:

Australian Sports Commission (1997). *Game Sense: Developing thinking players: A presenter's guide and workbook.* Available from: www.ausport.gov.au

Butler, J., & Griffin, L. (2005) *Teaching games for understanding: Theory, research and practice*, Champaign, IL: Human Kinetics.

Griffith, L.L., Mitchell, S.A., & Oslin, J.L. (1997). *Teaching sport concepts and skills: A tactical games approach.* Champaign, IL: Human Kinetics.

Launder, A.G. (2001). *Play practice: The games approach to teaching and coaching sports,* Champaign, IL: Human Kinetics.

Information about TOP programmes can be gained from the Youth Sports Trust, Loughborough University, Loughborough, Leicestershire LE11 3TU, England. For research information, contact the Institute of Youth Sport at the same address.

It is amazing what can be accomplished when nobody cares about who gets the credit. – *Robert Yates*

Teamwork divides the task and doubles the success. – *Anonymous*

The way a team plays as a whole determines its success. You may have the greatest bunch of individual stars in the world, but if they don't play together, the club won't be worth a dime. – *Babe Ruth*

He whose ranks are united in purpose will be victorious. – *Sun Tzu*

Questions provide the key to
unlocking our unlimited potential.
– *Anthony Robbins*

Chapter Twelve

Asking Meaningful Questions

From all the coaches and athletes interviewed for this book and from David Hadfield in Chapter Two, a clear message about an athlete-centred approach to coaching emerges: to use it effectively, ask meaningful questions. When the coach asks questions, athletes must find answers, which in turn increases their knowledge and understanding of the purpose of particular skill performances and tactical plays in the context of competition. As John Dewey said, 'Thinking in itself is questioning'. Questioning stimulates athletes' thinking, providing them with a chance to be creative and make decisions. It is also an extremely powerful means to inspire in athletes an intrinsic motivation to learn.

An athlete-centred coaching approach is ineffectual without a high level of questioning and clarifying to generate answers from the athletes. It is known that athletes learn well and have higher retention rates if they are given the opportunity to work out for themselves what to do and how to do it. As part of becoming athlete-centred coaches, we need to learn to apply an effective questioning technique at training sessions, to enhance athlete learning.

As David Hadfield mentions in Chapter Two, implementing an empowerment approach and using questioning may be uncommon and, to some, feel unnatural. Athletes may initially be surprised that they can have input into solving problems and thus their immediate response may not be favourable. However, if questioning becomes part of a coach's repertoire and the coach focuses on questioning well, then athletes will enjoy solving problems and be successful.

To create situations where athletes learn best, by listening to their responses, then redirecting, prompting or probing for better or more complete answers, coaches must have an in-depth understanding of the material they are asking about and the context in which it will be applied. As Wayne Smith suggests:

> To truly empower athletes to take responsibility for their learning, use game specific activities, ensure that they have fun and use questioning for them to become self-aware … I believe at the elite level, the questioning approach really tests your knowledge and in particular your eyes and technical nous.

Ian Rutledge argues that solving problems in simulated situations enhances athletes' decision making and in-depth understanding. As coach in such situations, he says to his athletes:

> In this situation we need to achieve A, so what are the options available to you so you can do A? What are the options available if you don't do it?

When the coach poses questions and gives athletes the opportunity to solve a problem, the athletes will try hard to solve it. The solution they generate is theirs; thus they will take ownership of it and remember, understand and apply the content more effectively than if they were told what to do, when to do it and how to do it. Solving problems through coach questioning enables athletes to explore, discover, create and generally experiment with a variety of moving and tactical processes of a specific sport. Ruth Aitken enhances these decision making processes by:

> ... asking questions and posing problems rather than always telling them the answers ... I try and put groups together and give them tasks to do—for example, to come up with a play to counteract a particular opposition strategy ... I've always felt in sport that there's lots of different ways to skin a cat, so it's not just my way—it's, 'How else can we do it?'

Questions to Promote Low-order and High-order Thinking

The goals of effective questioning include actively involving athletes in the learning process, and enhancing their task mastery and conceptual understanding. Another goal is to promote both simple (low-order) and complex (high-order) thinking. These two forms of thinking require different types of questions.

When athletes need to remember specific ideas or concepts, *simple* or *low-order questions* are appropriate. These questions serve as reminder cues that might be important to a learning sequence. Low-order questions are often *what?* or *where?* questions asked during drills. Low-order questions are factual, generally with only one possible answer. Examples of low-order questions used in coaching are:

- 'What part of the hand should you contact the ball when you spike it?'
- 'Where should you aim when shooting in netball?'
- 'How many points do you receive for a goal in lacrosse?'
- 'Who is the captain of the New Zealand women's hockey team?'

Research indicates that coaches tend to use low-order questions and certainly in some instances low-order questions are appropriate. However, coaches should strive to ask more *high-order questions* to extend athletes' opportunities to self-evaluate.

High-order questions require abstract or higher-level thinking processes. These questions challenge athletes to apply, analyse, synthesise, evaluate and create knowledge. They are generally more appropriate for analysing tactics and complex skills. Although both children and elite athletes respond well to high-order questions, it is advantageous for coaches to create the questions according to the athletes' developmental needs. Designing high-order questions and questioning sequence is more appropriate when encouraging independent learning, where athletes are required to think in greater depth about the subject matter or context and can search for multiple answers. Examples of high-order questions in sport settings include:

- 'How can we get the ball down the court quickly?'
- 'In how many different ways can you balance on the balance beam?'

- 'How can you get around the defence?'
- 'Why should we push the defence to the sideline?'
- 'Why do we need to tuck when doing a somersault?'

Mike McHugh gives some examples of high-order questions he poses to the Wellington Saints:

> 'Is that the most effective to defend that screen? Is that good shot selection? What is the consequence of a bad shot? Why did we as a group of people make that play, when this might have been more effective?'

Why? and *how?* questions enhance athletes' ability to make decisions, one of the central goals of an athlete-centred approach emphasised in earlier chapters. It is important for coaches to allow athletes to think about questions and help and encourage them to answer. If athletes are having difficulty with the answer, a coach can redirect or rephrase a high-order question so they can think carefully about what has been asked. However, the coach should never give the answer itself, as it takes ownership of the problem-solving process away from the athletes. Mike McHugh affirms the need for coaches to be self-aware when they ask a question:

> They have to come up with the relevant answers. They have to answer it with some validity.

With high-order questions, there are no 'wrong' answers as the athletes generally interpret the questions at their own level of understanding. Coaches need to listen closely to the answers, interpret the significance and respond accordingly. Often athletes come up with answers that coaches may find useful to elaborate and apply within their game plan. By listening, in other words, coaches can learn much from their athletes.

Tactical questioning and technique questioning are two specific kinds of high-order questions that can be very helpful to the athlete-centred coach. Both strategies are detailed below, before consideration is given to a third strategy that forms a useful part of high-order questioning: movement response.

Tactical Questioning

Questions that call for decision making and problem solving with respect to the strategies of the competition are tactical questions. Prescriptive coaches often direct and decide on the competition plan. Yet unless athletes understand why the game plan exists and take ownership of it, coaches will find the athletes have difficulty accepting and understanding it. To increase tactical awareness and decision making, coaches should use many high-order questions that allow athletes to create and develop their ideas.

In an athlete-centred approach, coaches set up tactical situations as problem-solving exercises. They then ask *how?* and *why?* questions to solve tactical problems and enhance understanding. Examples of some useful questions might be 'Given a three-on-two situation, where is the space? Why?' or 'How would you finish the race in the last 100 metres?' It is important for the athletes to perform the actual movement so they solve problems, seek solutions through practice and try various alternatives, and thus build a better understanding of variable situations.

Technique Questioning

Formulating questions for athletes to become aware of their technique helps to provide them with purposeful feedback. Through this mechanism, coaches prompt athletes and compare their actions to an ideal model of performance. In Chapter Two, David Hadfield discusses this method as the 'query theory', which Kidman and Hadfield (2000, p. 14) summarise as follows:

> While words are different to bodily feelings and are associated with different parts of the brain, athletes must answer questions (such as 'what happened to your hips when you played that shot?') based on knowledge and understanding passed to their brain by their proprioceptive sensors. The basis of this approach is to increase kinaesthetic (body and sensory) awareness of appropriate skill execution and be able to make decisions about what strengths to keep and what weaknesses to fix (and how to fix it). In plain language, if athletes cannot feel it, they cannot change it.

To help the athletes gain kinaesthetic awareness, a coach uses demonstrations that provide them with mental images. The athletes then execute the skill based on their own knowledge and existing motor programme. In the process of skill execution, the coach observes and analyses the athletes and identifies strengths and weaknesses.

To aid the athletes in comparing their action with the ideal model, the coach asks *what?*, *where?*, *why?* and *how?* questions (e.g. 'What did your arms do when you released the ball?', 'Where was your head when the hockey stick contacted the ball?', 'Why is it important to have a follow through?', 'How did your legs move to complete the handspring?'). These types of questions should help athletes become aware of their own body movements in executing a skill. If athletes are still unaware of what their bodies are doing, the coach can use 'shaping' questions (e.g. 'What did the demonstration show you about using your legs?', 'How did you use your legs?').

Next the athletes execute the technique using their knowledge and kinaesthetic awareness. At this stage, the coach should allow the athletes to experience the technique several times before asking another question. The purpose of such sequences is to enable the athletes to become self-aware in using the technique and to take responsibility for making decisions. In this way, when they are performing the technique in a competition, the athletes can understand how to perform it and when it feels right.

Movement Responses

Although questioning has always been considered a mental strategy, athletes can learn much through problem solving and questioning using movement responses. A movement response requires an answer that involves a physical demonstration.

A typical example of a problem that requires movement response is 'Show us how to control the ball most effectively' or 'Show me how to grip the racquet'. Even though the coach does not express either of these statements as a question, the athletes must provide answers by showing the coach how they understand.

Posing movement questions is an effective tool to enhance physical skill learning. In providing movement responses, athletes can identify faults or determine correct skill technique. Consistent with the query theory, if athletes have input into correcting skill performance, along with appropriate self-awareness, they tend to retain the information they have discovered. Through this mechanism, some athletes may determine the correction they need for a technique that their coach has been trying to correct in them for years.

A Note on Rhetorical Questions

Coaches should avoid using *rhetorical questions*. A rhetorical question is one that coaches do not expect athletes to answer or that coaches answer themselves. An example is 'Can you please pick up that baton?' The response might be 'No, I can't ...' Other examples are when the coach asks, 'Will you please sit down?' but is actually giving a direction, or asks, 'What is the best way to pass to another player?' then gives the answer, encouraging the athletes to be passive.

Techniques for Effective Questioning

Questions are only as good as the answers they extract. What follows are some useful tips to enhance coaches' questioning skills.

Planning Questions

Formulating meaningful questions is a key element in establishing a great questioning environment. Planning the questions for the training session ahead is the most important step, especially if questioning is a very new part of the coaching repertoire. As noted in previous chapters Wayne Smith and Ian Rutledge encourage such planning. Wayne explains:

> On my practice plan, I have questions, general questions that I would be asking them. Like the decision, where I saw [someone] in an attacking situation that didn't pass the ball, 'What did you do, what did you see, why didn't you pass it?'—basically to get feedback and ensure they were developing self-awareness about skill execution and tactical understanding.

For his part, Ian is strongly committed to planning questions:

> ... If you have got purpose to a subject, you have to have a plan for questions. I think if you have no plan for questioning, you won't know what the problem is. You have a coaching plan, a training plan; you have to have a questioning plan. I think having an awareness of the coaching points [is important]. I still [see other coaches] who don't use training plans ... Even if you are

working with a mentor coach, you need to have training plans. I ask my students, 'Out of this drill, what are the coaching points that you are trying to achieve?' You need to plan that. Somebody had a simple drill set up the other day and asked the mentor coach to give them an example of each of the coaching points. He couldn't answer what they were ... you have to understand coaching points to ask the right questions.

To plan meaningful, clear and coherent questions, an athlete-centred coach will:

- consider the nature of the content to be mastered and the athletes' readiness to contribute;
- practise the questions for the next training session by writing them down;
- ensure there is a variety of high and low-order questions;
- ensure there is an answer to work towards (and know the answer), with the questions planned to lead systematically to the planned answer; and
- formulate the questions appropriate to the athletes' level of learning by reading the questions aloud (e.g. 'What flight angle will be most appropriate to get the ball through the goal post?' may not suit athletes under the age of six).

For example, a coach's goal may be for the athletes to learn the footwork involved in a bowl in tenpin bowling. The coach would like the athletes to find out what the steps might be. Before starting to question, the coach determines the steps up the bowling lane to where the ball is released. Then he or she begins to create the questions. The first question might be 'If you were to release the ball at the boundary line, which foot would have to be in the front?' Once the athletes have worked out the answer, the coach might ask, 'How many steps would it take to get to the line where you release the ball?' The next question might be 'So if it takes three steps to the release line, what should your foot position be at the start?' The athletes will give many different answers, but each of them will work out the answer in his or her own way. By the end of the set of questions, athletes will have solved the problem about their footwork, with no instruction from the coach.

In planning questions, it is also important to be flexible in both developing the questions and timing them. Among coaches who are new to questioning, it is common to ask the planned questions but not to move beyond those questions in the training session. However, the real art of questioning is to read the athletes, look at what is happening and ask relevant questions *when* the athletes are ready or need to solve a problem. For example, Wayne Smith plans general questions, then in training he formulates further meaningful questions based on the situation as he reads it.

After implementing the questioning strategy, coaches should evaluate the session to improve their questioning skills. To this end, they may write down questions used and determine their relevance, or get someone on the sideline to evaluate these questions.

Gain the Athletes' Attention

An important management strategy in questioning is to ensure that all athletes are quiet and listening to the questioning sequence. To this end, a coach may create rules to encourage attention. Useful examples of rules include 'When one person is talking, everyone else listens' or 'Raise your hand and wait to be called on'. Notice that to contribute to a supportive environment, both rules contain positive words, rather than negative words like 'Don't'.

Once the coach has the attention of all athletes, everyone can hear the questions, while the coach can make appropriate eye contact and look for nonverbal signs of misunderstanding or excitement among the athletes. At this stage, the coach can begin the planned segment using questioning strategies.

When Is It Appropriate to Ask Questions?

An issue that both Wayne Smith and Don Tricker raise is the need to choose the right moment for athletes to solve problems. The ability to pick this moment is considered part of the art of coaching. When Wayne first implemented his empowering approach, he noted that he often overquestioned in his enthusiasm to get athletes to take responsibility. Don suggests that understanding the individual athlete is one key to knowing when to question:

> Asking the right questions to the right athlete at the right time is often the most effective way of ensuring that a particular experience has been analysed and the key learnings identified. If any of these parts is missing then the communication will not be effective. Timing will always depend on the athlete and the nature of the experience. If the experience has been a pleasant one then questions may be asked immediately. If the experience has not been so pleasant then the first priority is the well-being of the athlete; questions that reflect on the experience can wait.

There is no formula for the right time to ask questions. The answer is 'It depends'. It depends on fatigue, it depends on 'teachable moments', it depends—as Don noted above—on individual differences such as intrinsic motivation and it depends on whether the athlete has managed to solve the problem by himself or herself. A coach should read or analyse each situation to determine if the athletes need to solve a problem at that time and in that situation. Often coaches jump in because they feel like they are not doing anything and need to advise. More often athletes can determine their own mistakes and fix them because of their own decision-making ability and self-awareness. When an athlete makes a mistake and obviously knows it, there is nothing so stressful as being reminded of it by some significant other.

Athletes are bright; coaches should allow them to determine their needs and have faith in their ability to solve problems. As Rene Deleplace says, 'There is no point in coaching unless the teaching you do helps the student to overtake you.'

Wait Time

One of the reasons for gaining and maintaining athletes' attention is to provide wait time for athletes to consider their responses to the question. Increasing wait time enables athletes to formulate better responses and encourages them to give longer answers because they have had the opportunity to think. When given this 'thinking time', athletes tend to volunteer more appropriate answers and are less likely to fail to respond. They are more able to respond to high-order questions because they tend to speculate more. With longer wait time, athletes tend to ask more questions in return. If they do not understand or they need to find out more information, athletes also feel they have been given an opportunity to clarify the question. With longer wait time, athletes exhibit more confidence in their comments and those athletes whom coaches rate as relatively slow learners offer more questions and more responses.

Ian Rutledge highlights the need to deal with those moments of 'uncomfortable' silence for coaches using wait time to enhance athletes' answers:

> … you have to feel comfortable during those uncomfortable times of silences. I reckon it is a true bit of advice because I think that when I ask questions, the thinking takes time and as a coach, you want thinking activity … As a naive coach, I used to feel uncomfortable by those silences and I would give the answers. Now, I just sit tight and allow players valuable thinking time and then get the players to answer.

Wait time is quite difficult for coaches when they are first learning how to question. Research on teaching suggests that teachers tend to answer their own questions when a wrong answer is given or tend to become impatient. As in teaching, an appropriate wait time in coaching is three to five seconds. Once they have mastered wait time, coaches will find that athletes benefit more from questioning than they do if the coach calls on them for an immediate response.

To increase wait time, an athlete-centred coach will:

- listen to athletes' responses without repeating what they have said (*coach echo*) and give them time to think in silence while they are formulating their thoughts;
- be careful not to call an athlete's name immediately after posing the question. Once the coach identifies an athlete to answer the question, the other athletes tend to relax and discontinue their thinking process;
- show he or she is listening by limiting comments and being aware of using 'uh-huh' and 'okay';
- avoid a 'Yes but …' reaction to an athlete's response, which signals that coach rejects the athlete's idea; and
- allow the athletes to provide the answers.

Reinforcement

As athletes offer solutions, either verbally or through a movement response, a coach should encourage their innovative ideas—no matter how silly or inadequate the coach may perceive those ideas to be. If they find no sincere support for answers (either verbal or nonverbal), the athletes will be less likely to respond next time they are questioned. If the response to an athlete's answer was 'What a stupid answer', how would the athlete feel? Would the athlete feel respected by the coach? Thus part of the process of questioning is to encourage athletes to continue to try for a solution, even though they may appear to be a long way from it.

All of the coaches in this book highlight the importance of establishing an environment in which athletes feel confident to volunteer responses. The difficulty here, when a coach is deciding how to handle an inadequate answer, is to determine whether the athlete is off task or deliberately trying to be silly. If the response is off task, the coach should refocus or ignore it, then reinforce the athlete's next attempt to respond. Sincere positive reinforcement will be more likely to motivate athletes to respond enthusiastically to later questions. It is also noted that different individuals respond to different types of reinforcement.

For effective reinforcement, an athlete-centred coach will:

- praise based on the athlete's answer—for example, 'That's an interesting answer, can you tell us why you said that?';
- praise with the focus on reinforcing the athlete's response;
- praise honestly and sincerely; and
- give nonverbal reinforcement such as eye contact, thumbs up, smiling, nodding, and clapping hands—all extremely useful as forms of praise.

Prompting

With prompting, a coach uses cues to 'remind' athletes of something that they have learned and help them to answer a question. Examples are 'What did you determine about using a fake on offence?' or 'How have you been putting the shuttlecock on the floor? Think about the racquet swing.'

It is important that in giving cues, a coach does not give athletes the whole answer. The purpose of prompting is to encourage athletes to provide a response. Prompting can help them gain the confidence to answer the question.

Probing

Probing is a questioning strategy in which a coach asks follow-up questions so that athletes can extend, amplify or refine their answers. Here the coach should avoid using 'uh-huh's or 'okay's as these comments show a lack of interest in athletes' responses.

The following is an example of an effective probing sequence.

Coach: 'How can we get the ball down the court?'

Athlete: 'Dribble it.'

Coach: 'Is there a way you can get it down faster?' *(probe)*

Athlete: 'You could run faster.'

Coach: 'That is a good answer. What other skill have we been learning to move the ball around?' *(probe)*

Athlete: 'Passing.'

Coach: 'Great. Now what is it about passing the ball that gets the ball down the court faster?' *(probe)*

Athlete: 'When you pass the ball to a person, the speed of the ball is faster than when you dribble.'

Coach: 'Now you are getting the idea. If the ball is faster when passing, what does that mean when you are being defended?' *(probe)*

Athlete: 'The defender has less time to recover when you pass the ball to someone else. When you dribble, the ball is moved more slowly and therefore the defender has more time to catch up.'

Probing and reinforcing promote learning through extending current thought processes and encouraging athletes' responses.

Equity of Directing and Distributing Questions

Coaches will notice that some athletes cannot wait to answer the questions while others prefer to remain anonymous in the background. The athletes who volunteer readily are probably the most confident in their skills and their cognitive abilities. Research in teaching suggests that the teacher tends to neglect the students in the back. This same tendency will be found in sport settings as well. A coach must make a conscious effort to include all members of the team or squad in problem solving.

A coach should allow equal time for all athletes to contribute to the discussion. Through skilfully directing and distributing discussion, he or she will provide a fair environment where athletes can contribute equally. Directing questions to athletes in a nonthreatening way can encourage those who still may prefer not to participate. If a reluctant participant responds to a question, the coach should praise this answer and use the content of the response in further discussion.

Guided Discovery of a New Skill

Many coaches believe that they must tell and show their athletes exactly how to perform a correct technique. In contrast, through Teaching Games for Understanding (TGfU; see Chapter Eleven) athletes learn technique through guided discovery (and through self-awareness). The coach gives guidance with a series of meaningful questions about the athletes' technique (while recognising that athletes are capable of participating in sport without being taught the perfect technique). Athletes then learn by discovering how to do the technique themselves, in a process similar to the query theory, but learning is a result of self-discovery rather than of watching a demonstration.

Techniques do not have to be taught explicitly as athletes at all levels can often figure out the approach needed. A good example is found by observing children in action in the playground, where they are highly capable of discovering how to perform the 'game' without being told by someone else.

To use guided discovery as a coaching tool, it is useful to plan the line of inquiry. The coach should first decide and plan the answer or ultimate technique, then arrange the questions for the athletes to discover the answer. Athletes then provide demonstrations of the techniques as they discover the solution.

This process may be illustrated through the following example, in which athletes discover how to find the open space after a dribble in soccer.

Coach: 'In a three-on-three situation, what is the best way to get the ball to your teammate? Let's try it.'

Athletes pass all kinds of different ways.

Coach: 'What happens if you pass the ball behind your teammate? Let's try it.'

Athletes pass to partners and aim everywhere. Some athletes have to turn around and run for the ball, some are going forward nicely.

Coach: 'Now, if you want to make sure that your teammate goes forward (towards the goal), where do you want the pass to go?'

Johnny: 'They should go behind the person.'

Coach: 'Great, let's see how that works, Johnny. All go out in your threes and try to pass behind the person'.

The athletes try this approach.

Coach: 'Did that work?'

Athletes: (In unison) 'No!'

Coach: 'Why didn't it work?'

Athletes: 'Because we had to keep coming backwards.'

Coach: 'So how shall we do it this time?'

Kirsten: 'We should pass it to the front of the player.'

Coach: 'Great, let's try what Kirsten said.'

From this step the coach might get the athletes to practise in a game, concentrating on passing forward or passing to the place where the athletes are headed. After the athletes have mastered the concept, the coach might call them in again and try the same sort of discovery for passing and running to a space. An example might be 'Now that we can pass it well, what do you think the player who just passed the ball should do?'

Notice that in the above example, the coach never provides an explanation or demonstration. Instead, the athletes figure out for themselves how to pass forward. With any method where athletes have to figure out how a technique is performed, they will not only retain and understand that technique more fully, but also get more practice opportunities and take control of their own technique experience. Athletes tend to remember more because they are doing it, rather than watching a coach explain and demonstrate.

Conclusion

Asking meaningful questions can give coaches a huge advantage in applying an athlete-centred approach. This chapter has highlighted some useful techniques to ensure their questions are meaningful. It is important for coaches to realise that it takes plenty of practice to use meaningful questions in a purposeful way. Moreover, coaches who use questioning well will enjoy it for the rewards it brings. While they need to be aware of the considerations that should shape the way they use meaningful questions, they can also be aware of how athletes will benefit from being able to work out problems, discover their own abilities and make informed decisions. The use of effective questioning will further enhance a coach's repertoire and promote the learning of his or her athletes.

References

Kidman, L., & Hadfield, D. (2000). Athlete empowerment. *New Zealand Coach, 8*(4), 14–15.

All the world is a laboratory to the inquiring mind.
– *Martin H. Fischer*

We learn more by looking for the answer to a question and not finding it than we do from learning the answer itself. – *Lloyd Alexander*

He who asks questions cannot avoid the answers.
– *Cameroonian Proverb*

Millions saw the apple fall, but Newton asked why. – *Bernard Baruch*

Chapter Thirteen

Children and Sport

Children Learn What They Live
Dorothy Law Nolte, PhD

If children live with criticism, they learn to condemn.
If children live with hostility, they learn to fight.
If children live with fear, they learn to be apprehensive.
If children live with pity, they learn to feel sorry for themselves.
If children live with ridicule, they learn to feel shy.
If children live with jealousy, they learn to feel envy.
If children live with shame, they learn to feel guilty.
If children live with encouragement, they learn confidence.
If children live with tolerance, they learn patience.
If children live with praise, they learn appreciation.
If children live with acceptance, they learn to love.
If children live with approval, they learn to like themselves.
If children live with recognition, they learn it is good to have a goal.
If children live with sharing, they learn generosity.
If children live with honesty, they learn truthfulness.
If children live with fairness, they learn justice.
If children live with kindness and consideration, they learn respect.
If children live with security, they learn to have faith in themselves and in those about them.
If children live with friendliness, they learn the world is a nice place in which to live.

This chapter on children in sport is included because coaches featured in this book continually highlight the need for developing athletes as people through all stages of sport. They suggest that coaches of junior sport are an extremely important influence on the development of our future athletes. Coaches interviewed also identify the need to develop decision makers at junior as well as other levels given that junior levels tend not to focus on learning. Many coaches at elite levels suggest that often they have to start from the beginning in teaching athletes to make informed decisions as they have never learned this skill in their earlier years.

An athlete-centred philosophy is an approach that junior coaches could use to encourage the development of well-rounded children; that is, children who are independent, value learning and enjoy participating in sport. As Dorothy Law Nolte (1972) richly illustrates in the poem that opens this chapter, children learn what they live. Coaches facilitate a significant part of this learning and have a big responsibility to develop an environment that enriches the lives of our young people.

Children are motivated and learn well when their coach uses an athlete-centred approach. As discussed in previous chapters, children learn by making their own decisions and through trial and error. Potentially, sport can offer them the opportunity to demonstrate flair and experience excitement. However, coaches (and other adults, such as parents) are notorious for taking decisions away from children by telling them what to do and when to do it, with an emphasis on robotic plays and perfecting technique (see Rod Thorpe's discussion of technique and games in Chapter Eleven).

There are a multitude of reasons why children participate in sport. Many children are prompted to start sport by suggestions or influence from their parents or other adults (Roberts, Treasure & Hall, 1994). While it is important for adults to support their children and encourage them to participate in sport, they should be careful to keep children's motives in the foreground. The adult-structured sport organisation and the pressure adults can put on children increase stress, which in turn can increase the risk that children will leave sport. Ultimately, recognising that children are the future in sport, adults must enable children to learn and experience success in their own terms, so they continue to enjoy and thrive in sport.

These issues are examined in more detail in this chapter. Discussed first are the benefits and disadvantages of competition for children. The chapter then moves on to the reasons why children participate in sport and why many drop out. Thereafter it addresses the kinds of pressure adults put on children in sport and the influence of comments that adults make in the 'heat of the moment' on the sideline during children's competition. The chapter concludes with a look at the importance of ensuring that children experience a balanced lifestyle, in which sport is only a part of their life.

Children and Competition

Traditionally, sport has been considered a means by which children can learn values and discipline, as well as develop morally and socially (e.g. by learning skills in teamwork and cooperation). However, there is a lack of research to show conclusively that participation in organised sport programmes leads to the development of appropriate values and attitudes, morals or other characteristics traditionally associated with sport involvement (Coakley, 1992). Indeed, contrary to these conventional associations, in many recorded instances sport has been shown to teach inappropriate values and attitudes (e.g. cheating and violence).

Thus sport involvement does not necessarily lead to positive socialisation. Rather, significant others, including coaches and other adults, contribute in positive and negative ways to the building of character and moral development. As well as influencing whether children participate in sport at all, adults have an enormous impact on the types of sports in which they become involved, and whether that sport experience is negative or positive. In children's sport, it appears that a number of social influences often produce a clash of values between adult expectations of success and children's expectations of fun (Roberts et al., 1994). Consequently, 'parents' value systems and the role they play in structuring children's attitudes to sport, where children's well-being can become secondary, is most disturbing' (Kidman, 1998, p. 1). Because the desire for adult approval is very strong before puberty, children's ability to perform at their own level and for fun can be inhibited. Therefore adults have a responsibility to consider which expectations are their own and which are their children's. This is a difficult task because it requires some degree of objectivity.

To the extent that parents value and give attention to sports, children learn to see sports as worthwhile activities. The problem is that children's participation in sport is determined by adults who have designed competitions that reflect adult expectations and are derived from adult structures. Adults, including coaches, believe that they know what is best for children. We tend to dismiss or ignore the reality that while adult-structured competition can enable children to have a wonderful experience, for many children their experience of it can be totally unsuccessful and sometimes dreadful. Adult-structured competition has an enormous effect on children's self-esteem and perceptions of their own ability.

General self-esteem, defined as one's evaluation of general self-worth, has been shown to play an important role in children's perception of and confidence in their ability to perform the task at hand, as well as influencing their social perception. Children low in self-esteem respond more positively to coaches who are trained to be reinforcing and supportive, and less positively to untrained coaches, than do children high in self-esteem (Smoll & Smith, 2002). Self-esteem is also related to how athletes perceive both positive and negative behaviours of the coach. Children with high levels of anxiety (which competition can create) are particularly sensitive when something threatens their self-esteem. For example, anxious children may perceive a coach as less reinforcing and encouraging and as more punitive than the coach actually is, because they are more likely to perceive behaviours as threatening. It is also possible that certain children are uncomfortable with high levels of reinforcement while, because of their life experiences, they expect and are relatively comfortable with negative interpersonal feedback. All life experiences, including sport, contribute to developing a balanced and healthy lifestyle and influence self-esteem.

The key ingredient to encouraging high self-esteem is to ensure children have personal success, as when they feel that they have accomplished something their confidence increases. All children need to have success so that they feel able to try new things and have fun with what they are doing. Inappropriate criticism can be a critical impediment to this learning. If they are constantly criticised for mistakes, children decide that learning is a dreaded thing. A child's low self-esteem comes from learning to expect failure when he or she does something.

Thus the 'win-at-all cost' attitude, which is largely associated with adult-structured competition and often comes from influential adults (such as parents and coaches), can significantly affect the way children perceive success. Winning promotes failure because 'winning' is often out of one's control and losing often equates to failure. Adult reinforcement is the main influence on the way children perceive failure. If adults make it clear that they expect their children to win, they insinuate that the children will fail unless they win. Constantly reinforcing this concept of winning perpetuates the adverse perception that if children do not win, they are not successful within their influential relationships. As a result, many children drop out of sport due to stress and their perception that they cannot be accepted.

As adults have such a major impact on young children, it is important for adults to use competition in ways that will teach sound values and attitudes. If competition meets children's needs for experience and life-long learning, it can be a positive tool. The following are some advantages to this kind of use of competition:

- Children can develop a positive self-image by participating in sport. If adults are encouraging and fair to all children and ensure that they are successful, children will value their involvement in sport and enhance their self-image.
- Children can learn the value of cooperation through sport. Indeed, learning to cooperate by being part of a team has been rationalised as a positive outcome of team sport participation for decades.
- Adults can reinforce the value of cooperation by ensuring that all children are treated fairly, by valuing the contributions of all team members, and by providing opportunities for all children to work together in practices and competitions.
- The powerful lessons that can be learned in such an environment may even be able to be transferred to other social situations such as family life and school.
- Children can develop social skills by participating in sport.
- One of the primary reasons that children participate is to meet new friends. Sport is simply one more avenue for children to develop friendships, and for many the friendships that are developed through sport become some of the strongest in their lives.
- If organised and conducted appropriately, sport participation can teach children fair play and sportsmanship.
- Unfortunately when winning is so important, children also learn how to cheat. Again, adults should teach fair play and respect by practising it themselves (Kidman & McKenzie, 1998, p. 11).

Competition is great if children see it to be successful. Success does not mean winning; instead it means enjoying the experience and learning. Remember that because young children do not really understand competition, they will listen and act the way parents and other adults do. For this reason, adults need to be particularly careful not to put too many pressures on children, or the result may be that the children do not enjoy their sport and ultimately drop out.

Why Do Children Participate?

According to research, the main reasons why children participate in sport are to have fun, be with friends and improve skills (Taggart & Sharp, 1997). These reasons are forms of intrinsic or internal motivation, where high self-concept and feeling good are related to being satisfied with participation. With internal motivation, children tend to want to participate and improve to satisfy themselves. On the other hand, if children relate achievement to external rewards, they generally want to participate in order to win or impress someone else.

As mentioned above, significant adults are a primary influence on the degree to which children enjoy their sporting experience. As having fun is one of children's main reasons for participating in sport, whether they experience enjoyment is a major consideration in a child's decision as to whether to continue participating. Behaviour of the individual parent, teacher, administrator or coach can affect children's enjoyment. More than that, it affects their psychosocial development (including attitudes, values and self-perception) beyond the influence of the school, curriculum, sport club or sport programme itself. Young athletes' perception of themselves as good, competent or otherwise in turn affects their reasons for participating.

Developing a Competitive Orientation

Sport psychologists have researched the influences on children's attitudes to participation in sport. Their focus is the concept of *competitive orientation* (Nicholls, 1989), which identifies some children as ego-oriented and others as mastery-oriented.

An *ego-oriented* child wants to look good for external reasons and compares himself or herself with others. Caring greatly about what others think, ego-oriented children are subject to pressures outside their control and the expectations of adults play a significant role. When under heavy pressure (as often applied by influential adults), they have a high ego orientation. Results of competition are important, as self-confidence is linked to performance. While ego-oriented children are winning they are confident, but if they fail they lose confidence and the desire to participate. For children with a high ego orientation, it is important to balance it with some degree of mastery focus.

A child who is *mastery-oriented* wants to become good at a sport for internal reasons. Such children want to determine how much they have improved. They will be satisfied with losing if they judge themselves to have performed well, or conversely dissatisfied with winning if they consider that they did not perform well.

Research is inconclusive about whether a child is born with a tendency to be ego- or mastery-oriented. It is believed that both tendencies can exist within each individual and that significant others can have a major influence in developing a particular orientation of a child (Murphy, 1999).

Social learning theory (Bandura, 1977) proposes that people learn new behaviours simply by observing and listening to others. Thus adults can influence children's cultural and social development. According to this theory, by observing parents and coaches on the sidelines, children learn to model their behaviours. These behaviours, in turn, can be perceived as appropriate or inappropriate according to cultural expectations and the existing values of parents and other adults.

These adult behaviours can also be categorised into mastery- and/or ego-oriented tendencies. If an adult is ego-oriented, children who have observed and listened to that adult will learn to be ego-oriented. Then if parents make negative comments (which have been deemed inappropriate in research findings), children often experience stress as they are publicly scrutinised and evaluated. With constant social evaluation, children have to be concerned with not only their ability to perform, but also how their parents behave during the competition. Consequently, if a child receives outcome-specific recognition, such as from a parent on the sideline (i.e. concerned with scoring, winning), then the child receives a clear message that the more important goals of achievement in sport are outcome-related. Conversely, if children receive recognition based on mastery (e.g. skill learning, performance) then they learn that the more important goals are mastery-oriented (Roberts & Treasure, 1995).

A child's need for adult and peer recognition highlights the influence of significant others on the environment and success in sport participation. The world of sport strongly reinforces an ego orientation because of the traditional expectations about 'winning'. Often the first question that parents ask children when they return home after a sporting event is, 'Did you win?', indicating that the adults see winning as the reward for sport and expect the children to fulfil the adult desire to win.

Research has also traced how children may develop towards a particular competitive orientation (Smoll & Smith, 2002). Before approximately nine years of age, few children distinguish between ability and effort. In other words, most children cannot determine whether someone beat them (outcome, comparison to others) because of his or her greater talent (ability) or because he or she tried harder (effort). They may begin to see that some have more ability than others, but they still believe that effort will overcome ability. As discussed above, young children are highly influenced by and dependent on adult feedback (approval or disapproval), such that competition is really an adult-structured phenomenon that adults perceive as important but children do not really understand.

As children enter the age group of 9–11 years, they begin to see the difference between ability and effort. Their judgement moves from an external source (adults, peers) to an internal source (self). By the age of 11, a perceived failure has a more significant impact on sporting self-confidence, because these children are likely to attribute it to a lack of ability. As this perceived lack of ability becomes significant to a child, this individual tends to leave sport because of the perception that he or she 'can't' do it well (Murphy, 1999). Based on this outcome of perceived lack of ability and the high drop-out rates that may result, it may be concluded that adult-structured competition and organised sport are not necessarily beneficial for children.

The Benefits of a Mastery Orientation

For children to have long-term success, it is important that they have a high mastery orientation, with adults encouraging and supporting mastery-type experiences for them in sport. A mastery climate encourages the child to apply effort, because it is associated with higher intrinsic motivation. Therefore significant others need to encourage the development of such motivation by emphasising process rather than outcome. In addition, sport psychology research has provided evidence that children tend to correlate fun and enjoyment with a mastery climate rather than with a climate focused on outcome (Cresswell, 1997).

A mastery orientation enables athletes to accept failure and to learn through trial and error. It focuses them on improving, rather than just on winning. To help develop this orientation, adults can encourage athletes to participate for their own goals and satisfaction (a goal in an athlete-centred approach), rather than for external reasons. Athletes need to learn how to judge their own progress, set their own goals and to take satisfaction from improving, even in defeat. The mastery approach enables athletes to think critically and independently, with both sport and life skills.

As the above discussion indicates, a mastery orientation is reflected clearly in the philosophy of an athlete-centred approach to coaching. Most coaches in this book actively promote the idea of mastery orientation when they are concerned with learning for the benefit of the athletes themselves.

Encouraging a Mastery Orientation

Given that mastery-oriented children are more likely to participate and continue in sport, it is important for adults to know how to encourage mastery in children. Success and winning are different. For success, striving to win is more important than actually winning. A child can execute the best performance of his or her life and still lose the competition. This child can still feel positive because, when success is determined by the individual child as it is among mastery-oriented children, success is equal to good performance and meeting self-determined goals. Every little success deserves to be rewarded through encouragement and support.

As Murphy (1999) suggests, in teaching young athletes mastery orientation, adults need to:

- Encourage realistic goal-setting,
- When finding a coach, look for,
    —Valuing qualities beyond winning (love of the game),
    —Knowledge of the sport,
    —Ability to encourage,
    —A love of teaching,
- Emphasise progress, not outcome,
- Emphasise participation for all,
- Reward skill development,
- Encourage self-awareness (problem solving).

All these qualities are closely linked to an athlete-centred philosophy.

Why Do Children Drop Out?

The discussion so far has indicated that children's sporting experiences can influence their individual development in both positive and negative directions. Research has suggested that a significant number of children drop out of sport because of their negative experiences of it. As adults, we are sometimes responsible for these negative experiences. Although we tend to know that children should be encouraged, our emotions, love of winning and pursuit of what we think is best for our children can override our intention to provide a positive environment.

Many studies have examined why children participate in sport, but few have focused on dropping out. Among the few studies conducted in this area, the reasons for dropping out tend to be that the children had other interests, the coach was too tough/mean, it was no longer fun or the children did not get enough chance to participate (Gould & Petlichkoff, 1988). Interestingly, children seldom say that their desire 'to win' (a characteristic goal of a tough/mean coach) is a reason for participating.

Although many coaches and other adults have tried to reduce the high drop-out rate in various sports, many still promote winning as all-important and put unnecessary pressure on children. These attitudes are encouraged by society more widely, which values winning and the competitive achievements of élite athletes. It is also obvious to all adults that society puts most of our sport-directed monies into 'élite' sport. It is what society values most. Yet this view overlooks the reality that there would be no élite sport unless children are developed and want to participate and stay in sport.

Contributing to such pressures is the value that professional sport attaches to certain kinds of performance. Professional sport emphasises winning, entertainment, money and, in certain sports, aggression. Despite children's limited skill, knowledge and understanding of tactics and strategies, many adults expect children to participate and act like professionals, when the children simply want to have fun and to be with their friends.

Certainly, there are many coaches who focus on attracting and keeping children involved by providing a positive, safe and supportive environment that caters for children's needs in sport. Not surprisingly, such a supportive environment is related to an empowering style of coaching. If adults can ensure that such positive environments can be provided for children, then fewer children will drop out. Unfortunately, these environments are not always established.

As indicated above, one of the main reasons that children drop out of sport is that for them it is no longer fun. In many instances, adults intend to encourage children to focus on having fun, being with friends and developing skills but, as the competition gets underway, some parents (a minority) become increasingly excited and concerned about the performance of their son or daughter, and the outcome of the competition. This emotion is also true of many coaches.

In clubs, the sport itself is geared towards competition, including for children. For example, there are sports where league standings are kept for under 10s and some sports even have national competitions for children under 10 years (despite the research suggesting that children under 11 do not really understand the notion of competition). This kind of environment is the perfect set-up for children to experience excessive stress and anxiety and maybe, as a result, drop out of the sport. If the emphasis is truly on having fun, being with friends and skill development, then why is there a need for league standings and competition points?

A focus on winning can have a secondary effect on coaching that also discourages children from continuing with sport. As reinforced by research findings, athletes do want to participate rather than sit on the sideline. It is important to find out the coach's philosophy and whether he or she intends to allow equal time for all. As part of an athlete-centred philosophy, all children should receive the opportunity to participate equally, which is the intention behind the various rotation systems of athlete-centred coaches in this book.

Parents have a range of expectations for their children in sport. Some wish their children to do well because they themselves missed out on opportunities in childhood, or live vicariously through their children, hoping to gain glory and satisfaction from their children's success (Brower, 1979). Worries about failure and living up to adult expectations and social evaluation add unneeded stress to children and can lead them to drop out. Adults who are participating in competitive sport tend to increase their children's anxiety and the chances of burnout because of the complex interplay of their values and the personal characteristics inherent in the child (Gould, 1993).

One of the mismatches in youth sport is that most children are actually mastery-oriented and parents reinforce winning, which falls into the realm of ego orientation (Cresswell, 1997). This conflict of interest increases the likelihood that children will drop out. Children still suggest that winning is important to them, but it is less important than having fun, being with friends and improving skills. Given that winning is generally out of the control of athletes (due to uncontrollable factors like opposition and referee calls), the most effective method of decreasing the drop-out rate appears to be focusing on the reasons that children play sport.

Adults on the Sideline

Children who perceive themselves as low in competence are particularly dependent on or are easily affected by external feedback (Horn & Hasbrook, 1987). Consequently, their experience of negative comments from their parents may be detrimental. On the other hand, if significant adults evaluate their performance attempts in terms of mastery and give them encouraging and contingent feedback, children are likely to perceive that they performed with some degree of success. They tend to develop a positive perception of their competence and a belief that they can control the outcome of future performances (Horn & Hasbrook, 1987).

The sideline behaviour of adults is most noticeable to young children. For example, a gentleman on the sideline at a soccer game of under-seven-year-olds yelled out to the children, 'Come on you guys, pull up your socks'. As a result, the game stopped and all of the players pulled up their socks! This true-life example shows how much such sideline comments and behaviours influence children who are participating. In other words:

> Children do hear and listen to what their parents and other adults are saying on the sideline. Most children don't say anything, but the negative or embarrassing feelings that they experience are real. When children are asked about what they want adults to say, they mostly suggest 'just cheering'! (Kidman & McKenzie, 1998, p. 20)

One of the common intentions of adults on the sideline is to ensure that their children do their best and do what they are supposed to do. They may shout out corrections or instructions, assuming they are helping. Unfortunately, their good intentions can backfire as these adults are being prescriptive in their behaviour, not empowering. As stated in previous chapters, for children to learn, they should make decisions in a variety of situations. When adults on the sideline relay instructions to children in competition, the children simply follow those instructions. The children lose the opportunity to practise decision making, and thus lose the opportunity for maximal learning (Hellison, 1985).

With the recognition that decision making is an important skill to develop, an athlete-centred approach gains more credence for its encouragement of decision making in athletes. If children are given opportunities to interpret information that is available to them while they are performing, and to decide for themselves the appropriate course of action, they will learn more and retain more information. They may not make the decision that an observing adult expects, but in making it the young athletes will have learned something about their performance as they are being encouraged to be self-aware. As Mark Norton highlights (Chapter Three), it is also amazing what children can teach adults when they are left to make unique decisions.

As some research has suggested, most comments from adults on the sideline are quite positive, but a significant proportion (about one-third) may be described as negative (Kidman, McKenzie & McKenzie, 1999). This proportion is far too high to create a positive sporting experience for children. Adults need to be made aware that negative comments from the sideline can put unnecessary pressure on the children who they are watching and supporting. It is important not to yell at them for making a mistake in front of their friends and other spectators, as it can decrease their self-confidence, increasing the likelihood of those children dropping out of the sport.

In a survey of hockey players under 12 years of age, Suzie Pearce (1996) examined the influences and comments of adults on the sideline. She found that although children generally like to have adults there for support, this need was not met: 50 per cent of parents came to watch their children play, but 95 per cent of the children reported that they would like their parents to come. Of those who did not want their parents to come, some said that they were embarrassed when their parents did come because of what their parents said on the sideline and because they did not want to fail in front of their parents. These results suggest that some adults who come to watch may put too much pressure on their children.

A good way to determine whether the sideline comments are helpful and supportive is to ask the children what they prefer to hear on the sideline, if anything. Some children do not hear what goes on. However, many children hear exactly what the expectations of adults are. It is important to listen to what children prefer to hear on the sideline and then try to put it into practice. Also, to support children, adults need to eliminate the question, 'Did you win?' when they come home from the game. This question sends a clear message that winning is what is important. Children often have goals they are working towards. Try asking them if and how they met their goals, or 'How was the game today?'. The types of questions that adults ask their children can convey a particular message.

In summary, adults (especially parents) need to reduce the level of negative and outcome-related comments in public (e.g. from the sideline) and in private (e.g. after the game). Instead, they need to encourage children's notion of success in sport (i.e. to have fun, meet new friends and improve skills) and enhance children's self-esteem by focusing on a process in sport rather than on its outcome.

Useful Guidelines for Adults on the Sidelines

- Yell encouraging comments and keep the voice tone positive.
- Let the coach do his/her job. Like the children, they are doing their best.
- Stay in the area designated for spectators.
- Understand that the referees/umpires are doing the best they can. Have faith in them and thank them for officiating at the end of the game or event.
- Offer to help the coach, referee or scorers.
- Show self-control. Remember, you are watching children participate in sport—it is not the Olympic Games.
- Cheer for the entire team and encourage all players.
- Provide support for your child by listening to them and trying to understand their feelings.
- Be a good role model. Avoid smoking and drinking at children's sporting events.
- Congratulate the opposing players/athletes at the end of the event (Kidman & McKenzie, 1998, p. 22)

Sport as Only One Part of a Child's Life

When adults get caught up in the emotions and challenges of sport, often—subconsciously—they encourage their children to neglect other important adventures in life. Children have homework, other interests, a family and friends. Sometimes sport can take over a young one's life because adults are 'overinvolved'. Adults, including parents and coaches, should reflect on their own priorities and encourage their child to achieve a balance by showing interest in other parts of their child's life. Children need to be allowed to balance their commitments, with sport as only a part of their young life.

As well as occupying a central position in the athletic setting, a coach can have an influence that extends into other areas of a child's life. Ultimately, a coach's effect on the athletes is determined by the meaning that athletes attach to his or her behaviours. In other words, the young athletes' processes of thinking and emotional well-being filter the obvious coaching behaviours, in their development of attitudes toward their coach and sporting experience. We would assume that athletes' expectations of how coaches behave would influence how they react to particular behaviours. For example, punitive behaviours may be expected and tolerated to a greater degree in a collision sport like football.

The adults who work with youth sport programmes would be wise to use what they know about children's informal sports to guide their attempts to organise those programmes to meet the needs of young people. If children enjoy what they experience in organised sport, they are more likely to be favourably influenced by the relationships they form through their participation.

Conclusion

Many highly competitive adults tend to 'exploit' children based on their own needs and values. It is not a question of blame: most adults are trying to do what is best for their children, but sometimes they get it wrong. The solution is to give priority to the development needs of children ahead of adult needs. Murphy (1999) suggests that in the context of competitive sports, coaches and other adults can achieve this focus by enabling their athletes to:

- learn emotional and psychological skills to help them become effective competitors and give them life-long skills;
- learn how to deal with loss, without transferring blame to children or reinforcing it on them;
- focus on achieving a mastery orientation in their approach to improving children's performance; and
- learn new skills, work on existing skills, set goals and try to achieve them, and work with others in forming a positive team culture.

All these skills are useful in everyday life as well as sport. As such, they allow all athletes to benefit from sport.

Teachers, coaches and parents have such a major impact on the quality of children's sporting experiences that we need to reflect on the opportunities we can provide for them. Our influence can help ensure a positive experience and a sound level of development. If children are happy and successful, under little or no pressure to win, they enjoy their experience in sport.

As Dorothy Law Nolte (1972) points out in her famous poem, children learn what they live. Therefore they should be taught and encouraged in a positive learning environment. Children and adults can share in the enjoyment of sport for a multitude of reasons. Enjoy your short time with your children. Help them to grow through sport. Help them to create fond sporting memories that they and you can enjoy for a long time.

References

Bandura, A. (1977). *Social learning theory*. Englewood Cliffs, NJ: Prentice-Hall.

Brower, J.J. (1979). The professionalization of organized youth sport: social psychological impacts and outcomes. *Annals of the American Academy of Political and Social Science, 445*, 39–46.

Coakley, J. (1992). Burnout among adolescent athletes: a personal failure or social problem? *Sociology of Sport Journal, 9*(3), 271–285.

Cresswell, S. (1997). *Intrinsic motivation in youth sport: The effect of goal orientations and motivational climate*. Unpublished dissertation. University of Otago, Dunedin.

Gould, D. (1993). Intensive sport participation and the prepubescent athletes: competitive stress and burnout. In B.R. Cahill & A.J. Pearl (eds), *Intensive participation in children's sport* (pp. 19–38). Champaign, IL: Human Kinetics.

Gould, D., & Petlichkoff, L. (1988). Psychological stress and the age-group wrestler. In E.W. Brown & C.F. Banta (eds), *Competitive sports for children and youth* (pp. 63–73). Champaign, IL: Human Kinetics.

Hellison, D. (1985). *Goals and strategies for teaching physical education.* Champaign, IL: Human Kinetics.

Horn, T., & Hasbrook, C.A. (1987). Psychological characteristics and the criteria children use for self-evaluation. *Journal of Sport Psychology, 9*, 208–221.

Kidman, L. (1998). Who reaps the benefits in coaching research? The case for an applied sociological approach. *Sociology of Sport On Line, 1*(2), article 1.

Kidman, L., & McKenzie, A. (1998). *Your kids, their game: A children's guide for parents and caregivers in sport.* Australian Sports Commission, Active Australia.

Kidman, L., McKenzie, A., & McKenzie, B. (1999). The nature and target of parents' comments during youth sport competitions. *Journal of Sport Behavior, 22*(1), 54–68.

Murphy, S. (1999). *The cheers and the tears: A healthy alternative to the dark side of youth sports today.* San Francisco, CA: Jossey-Bass.

Nicholls, J. (1989). *The competitive ethos and democratic education.* Cambridge, MA: Harvard University.

Nolte, D.L. (1972). *Children learn what they live.* Retrieved 8 October 2004, www.empowermentresources.com/info2/childrenlearn_long_version.html

Pearce, S.N. (1996). *Pre-adolescent hockey players' perceptions of parental behaviours.* Unpublished dissertation. University of Otago, Dunedin.

Roberts, G.C., Treasure, D.C., & Hall, H.K. (1994). Parental goal orientations and beliefs about the competitive-sport experience of their child. *Journal of Applied Social Psychology, 24*, 631–645.

Roberts, G.C., & Treasure, D.C. (1995). Achievement goals, motivational climate and achievement strategies and behaviors in sport. *International Journal of Sport Psychology, 26*, 64–80.

Smoll, F.L., & Smith, R.E. (2002) *Children and youth in sport: A biopsychosocial perspective.* Dubuque, IW: Kendall/Hunt.

Taggart, A., & Sharp, S. (1997). *Adolescents and sport: Determinants of current and future participation.* Perth: Sport and Physical Activity Research Centre, Edith Cowan University.

Those who educate children well are more to be honored than they who produce them; for these only gave them life, those the art of living well. – *Aristotle*

I believe that children are our future. Teach them well and let them lead the way. Show them all the beauty they possess inside. – *Whitney Houston*

Listen to the desires of your children. Encourage them and then give them the autonomy to make their own decision. – *Denis Waitley, US motivational speaker*

I have found the best way to give advice to your children is to find out what they want and then advise them to do it. – *Harry S. Truman*

Chapter Fourteen

So, What Now?

The coaches in *Athlete-centred Coaching* have highlighted their innovative coaching practices in which the athletes and the team environment are the keys to enhancing sport performance. Now that these coaches have 'convinced' you that this athlete-centred approach is successful and worth trying, it is important to know how you might begin. The coaches and other contributors to this book can also help here as they have suggested ways to trial the approach, illustrating its benefits and challenges based on their own successful experiences. So use their experiences to get out there and start.

This chapter begins by highlighting team culture, a key theme that has emerged from this book and an essential component of applying an athlete-centred approach successfully. Building on David Hadfield's ideas (Chapter Two), it then discusses initial implementation (giving it a go), before looking at how you might evaluate your athlete-centred approach and how you can continue to develop as a coach. It is important to note that the way you coach now is probably terrific and has great merit. What is being suggested here is a way to enhance your coaching and the performance of your athletes rather than 'the' correct way of coaching. As Rod Thorpe points out in Chapter Eleven, there is no single correct way to coach, but there are several *better* ways to coach:

> **Rod:** You will choose coaching methods to suit your persona. This said, just as a good player does not try only one method of beating an opponent, so a coach should develop a range of approaches. Consider adding this to your coaching portfolio and then decide if it works better for you. I am convinced that the traditional way has shortfalls, but I am quite willing to accept that many coaches will employ it at some points as part of a variety of approaches. Once you do this and see the power of 'empowering', you may start to develop a philosophy which is much more about developing the player as a whole, and I do mean as a person as well as a sports performer.

Team Culture

Before discussing the ways to put an athlete-centred approach into action, I believe that it is important to reiterate that, as each coach has pointed out in this book, without any focus on team culture, the athletes have little chance for real success. Team culture is basically the environment that the athletes, coach and manager create. It defines the purpose of the team, establishing a mutual direction so that everyone is on the same wavelength. Team culture is based on standards and values that direct how things are done. The way a team behaves on and off the field or court is a reflection on the team culture (Hadfield, 2002).

Don Tricker (Chapter Four) highlights the importance of each individual. It follows that coaches need to understand each individual and draw all the individuals in the team together to establish a quality team environment:

> **Don:** … the common denominator in sport is that it is played by individuals, each with different needs and expectations. Therefore, when building teams, it all comes down to ensuring that individual expectations are satisfied when developing the core components of the team culture. The components include ownership of a shared vision or common purpose, clearly defined values, standards and role definitions.

While recognising individual differences, we usually have the added challenge of finding a way to encourage these individuals to form a team. Bringing a group of athletes together does not automatically create a harmonious team (Kidman & Hanrahan, 2004). In a quality team culture, the athletes work together in pursuit of the group's goals or objectives. Creating this team culture is a process; it does not just happen. Coaches must focus on it and prepare the athletes for it.

Most of the coaches in this book advocate that every person on the team needs individual roles and responsibilities, as a way of helping the team to run smoothly. If a quality team culture is to be created, athletes need to feel that they have ownership of the team. If they feel they have nothing to contribute to the team, then they will not feel they are a part of the team, which in turn will detract from team culture. Additionally, each member of the team should be acquainted with the roles and responsibilities of other members and appreciate their importance.

One of the roles that each athlete should have is that of a leader. Shared leadership has been a theme with every coach. As Mike McHugh (Chapter Seven) says:

> **Mike:** … one of the things I try and do is teach them all to be leaders … even the ones who are quiet and shy, after a while, they will feel confident enough to say, 'Oh I think it is this', or 'This is how we do this'. So it is a bit of a trick to allow that to happen. Obviously, they don't assert themselves right away. But I want everyone to be leaders. I don't subscribe to the team captain theory at all. I subscribe to the collective responsibility concept. That's taking ownership; it's about everyone being leaders, [and] at the same time, everyone being helpers as well. I want leaders and I want them all to be leaders in their own way … I think, if you are going to play sport at a high level, you have to be an assertive person. Assertiveness is one of our guidelines and, while being assertive, you are being a leader.

Mark Norton (Chapter Three) puts his beliefs about shared leadership into practice in this way:

> **Mark:** Within the overall squad, we created smaller groups, which were responsible for different aspects that we were trying to do. I empowered each student to have some leadership or have some responsibility. Without responsibility, you can't learn how to use it, learn how to develop.

In team sports, role rotation during training has been cited as a key way to develop empathy towards teammates and understanding of their individual responsibilities to the team. Playing other positions in this way can help athletes understand the demands on their teammates. Alternatively, athletes may be given the task of performing team drills with one position removed, which highlights the importance of that position (Kidman & Hanrahan, 2004).

One very important aspect of a quality team culture, as presented in Chapter One, is trust. Individuals who trust each other are more likely to be open with their feelings, ideas and information, which will enhance communication. The day-to-day behaviour of athletes has a powerful impact on the establishment of trust. Trust can be also enhanced by giving athletes a sense of ownership of the team by allowing and encouraging them to become involved in decisions that affect the team and them personally, such as decisions about team direction, training times, drills or tactics. Another way of strengthening a sense of ownership is to encourage the athletes to choose how they will be distinct from other teams (Kidman & Hanrahan, 2004).

Using team-building activities is a practice mentioned by a couple of coaches in this book. The lesson from their comments is that it is important to carefully think through the purpose and nature of those activities. It is easy to organise a ropes course, run by someone else, or to go through an obstacle course at the local army base. However, any effective team-building activity will also have a clear purpose. Sometimes the purpose is to get to know each other better; sometimes it is to perform an activity in which each team member has a responsibility. Fundamentally, each team should evaluate their vision statement and gear any team-building activity towards teaching or promoting that vision.

In *Championship Team Building* (2002), Jeff Janssen suggests seven components of team building for coaches to focus on in developing and maintaining a quality team environment:

1. Common goal—successful teams have a vision or common focus. This common goal or vision gives a team its mission or purpose.
2. Commitment—successful teams are committed to the vision or common focus. The athletes have a sense of responsibility to contribute to this vision and demonstrate effort and intensity.
3. Complementary Roles—successful teams take pride in performing their various roles. Athletes realise that every role (large or small) is important to the vision of the team.
4. Clear Communication—successful teams have communication processes set up and communicate effectively on and off the field or court.
5. Constructive Conflict—all teams experience conflict, it is the resolution of this conflict that ensure that it does not interfere with the team's vision.
6. Cohesion—all athletes on any team like and respect each other.
7. Credible Coaching—the coach plays a major role in facilitating athlete development and maintaining quality team culture, through monitoring and practising the values established by the team.

A Process of Developing a Team Culture

A step-by-step method of creating a quality team culture is presented here as a useful guide for coaches interested in putting an athlete-centred approach into practice. It focuses on establishing the team's overall mission, in which the athletes are involved in making decisions about and developing the vision and values and the coach's role is to facilitate the process. Once created, the values and strategies that are established must be taught, nurtured and practised for the team culture to work. Many companies and teams have been caught out because they hang up the poster or sign announcing their vision and key values and then forget about it.

The following steps, then, represent one approach to creating a quality team culture, which was successful with Mark Norton's volleyball team. (For the full story of the process, see Chapter Three.) It is important to note that many other different strategies could be used for the same purpose; this is just one way that worked:

Step 1: Establish the goals and dream goals for the season. As Mike Chu (c. 2004) says, 'A team without a vision or team goals is like a team without a rudder.' It is useful to establish these goals by asking athletes meaningful questions. Mark's approach was to ask, 'If you were at the end-of-season dinner and had to make a speech and talk to everyone about the sort of team that we are, what would be the things that you would liked to be able to say?' An example of such a dream goal might be to win the local championships or place in top 10 at Nationals.

Step 2: Establish the strategy to meet the goals. Once goals are established, ask, 'How do we do these things?' This step is the start to developing the actual values. But first, it is important to have an idea of what the team needs to do to be able to meet the vision. For example, as a way to achieve the dream goal of winning a local championship, the team might choose to be the most exciting team to watch.

Step 3: Formulate the values. Values are non-negotiable rules with which the team will live. Some examples are respect, unity and honesty. In this step, Mark gave a list of values to the athletes, and then had them pick six and define each one. The meaning of the values must be interpreted in the same way by everyone. A good place to start the process of choosing values is with the 30 values listed by Jeff Janssen (2002).

Step 4: Develop strategies to meet the values. The purpose of these strategies is to set up some action so that the team can live by the values. An example might be, 'Take care of things outside the sport so we can enjoy our sport more'.

Step 5: Create a single mission statement. This statement serves as a reminder to the athletes of their campaign—it is what they decide as a team to follow, For example, 'Brothers in Arms' which might refer to the unity and respect for each other, the commitment to the team.

Step 6: Find a symbol to represent the whole mission. An example from the volleyball team was a gluestick, which symbolised 'Binding together to be better' (their mission statement). The New Zealand women's hockey team carried around laminated cards emblazoned with the team values.

Step 7: Practise and reinforce the values.

After formulating the vision, values and strategies, some teams confirm their commitment to the team's mission through some formal method of agreement, such as a poster, a card, a song or even a certain handshake. The form of agreement can also continue to remind athletes of their commitment and strengthen the team bond.

There are many other examples of ways to set up the vision and values for a team. The Internet is one useful source (see, for example, Mike Chu at www.nzrugby.com. Whatever process you choose to follow, it is important to revisit and practise the vision and values regularly once they are established, rather than leaving them to hide in the cupboard. As Mark Norton has shown, the process of establishing the team mission and then monitoring it is a key to developing a quality team culture and creating that team spirit (wairua) in your team.

Putting Athlete-centred Coaching into Practice

In looking at how to get started with an athlete-centred approach, we will pick up on crucial tips from the various coaches in this book. Every one of them has suggested that it is important to at least 'give an athlete-centred approach a go'. You will probably not feel accomplished the first time you try it but, as you develop it, an athlete-centred approach becomes a powerful way to enable athletes to learn, to be motivated to put in huge effort, and to enjoy their sporting experience. As a result, their performance will naturally improve.

If you have never tried this approach, you need to implement it in small steps. Rod Thorpe sums up this strategy well:

> **Rod:** Start small. You will have a well-tried coaching model in your head from your previous experience as a coach and very powerfully from the way you were coached. See if you cannot introduce elements into your sessions in which you give more freedom to players … We have all done it, but what we usually do is select the activity that allows us, the coach, to 'tell' the players what we want them to do. The major difference is that we help them work out what they have to do to exploit the situation and this means 'questioning' either verbally or by setting a new condition in the game.

One of the real hurdles to overcome is a lack of confidence to try an athlete-centred approach. It is important to accept that you may not be successful the first time; remember that a big step towards success in your use of the approach is just getting in and learning it, applying it and seeing how the athletes respond. Mark Norton says that, although he had been using an athlete-centred approach in some form for a while, he needed more confidence to extend his coaching to incorporate other parts of the athlete-centred approach:

Mark: ...it's more involved, there is more to it. It's the approach I wanted to do but I didn't know enough about it. So, now that I have learned these things, it is the way I want to coach, so I'll continue to do it. No doubt, I won't get it perfect, there are still lots of things that [have been] pointed out to me that I had to do...There are always going to be things that you don't get, and you don't get it all together perfect every time. It's like anything. So, if you let those things worry you, then you will never do anything. You have to be confident with what you do know and what you are going to do.

Ian Rutledge (Chapter Six) highlights where he obtained his confidence to use an athlete-centred approach:

Ian: I always ask myself this question, 'Where do I get the tenacity to be brave?' ... If you are going to do the job and be successful, you have to do it your way. If you are going to fail, you might as well fail doing it your way ... If you are going to be successful, you do it your way and you take great confidence out of each time you step up to the challenge. My attitude is always live by the sword, die by the sword and that is why if I am going to go down, I am going to go down my way, then I can take confidence out of that ... I suppose it was the fact that my mum told me she had confidence and believed in what I was doing as a kid, that is probably where I get the confidence... you take confidence out of knowing that you can work with other people. Then you still have to have the conviction to do it yourself. When you think about the philosophy of coaching, it's uncharted territory and I don't think you can show fear of looking back. If you've got people following you, it's like a new frontier ... the philosophy of New Zealand hockey, winning the gold medal would be lovely for us. It might never be done, but we are going for it.

Don Tricker says he personally obtained the confidence to try this approach because:

Don: I just believed that it was what the athletes wanted. I just believed that it is right for us in terms of our stage of development. I believe it was the right way to go in terms of coaching and hadn't been convinced otherwise through my previous experience. It was these experiences that conditioned me to realise that this is the way forward.

Where does Mike McHugh gain the confidence to tackle an athlete-centred approach?

Mike: The fundamentals of success are communication, trust, collective responsibility, caring, and pride. I think you have to instil these principles and then demonstrate belief in the players. You've got to let them know that you believe in them, you care about them and you trust them. Once they are convinced of that, once they are confident that you have belief, trust and care, they will respond in the same way. Sometimes that is ... not an easy lesson.

The athlete-centred approach does not succeed simply because the coach applies it. It is important for you as coach to continually develop and practise your empowering strategies (just as in any skill learning). In addition, your athletes (if they have never been coached in this way) must buy in to the approach before it can be successful. Gaining the support of some athletes may take time, along with effort in facilitating and nurturing. Wayne Smith (Chapter Nine) reinforces this idea with reference to his own development of the approach with the Canterbury Crusaders:

> **Wayne:** It is going to take a while … and that's what people don't understand. If the quality outcome you are after is satisfaction, then we got that straight away. My first year with the Crusaders [of building the team culture, without actually winning the Super 12s] was exciting. Since then, we have won the tournament twice, but to me it's not the winning that counts—it's doing your best to win. Having fun and learning together is a rewarding experience. We've had hard times, but generally the smile on their faces is the biggest indicator to success. Seeing a group of talented individuals selflessly giving to each other and enjoying the experience makes coaching worthwhile.

Because the entire team may not catch on to the athlete-centred approach at the same time, the coach must cater for individual needs and nurture each athlete. In a sense, the coach has to continue to 'sell' the approach and enable athletes to understand the benefits they may gain through it. Don Tricker and Ian Rutledge tell of their experiences in winning athletes over:

> **Don:** When building the culture of the 2000 World Champion team I was probably a little bit [coach-centred]. This was because of the athletes' maturity level with an athlete-centred approach in developing team culture. In 2000 I met with the athlete leadership team and explained what I was looking for in terms of culture. The athlete leadership team then facilitated a meeting with the rest of the athletes. The outcome of the meeting was a perception that the athletes built the culture of the team, when in reality they delivered pretty much what I sent them away to do. In 2004, the process was very different, with the athletes taking complete ownership of developing the culture of the 2004 team. The captain of the side facilitated a meeting with the athletes; the outcome was the core components of the culture.

> **Ian:** I take great satisfaction out of … the pride in knowing that you have the ability to get people to do a certain thing … Then they take that pride into doing it as well. As long as they can see the benefit, I think our athletes will buy into being empowered. If they don't understand the benefits, they don't know why they are doing it; they will do it, but they do it because the coach wants them to do it. If you explain the purpose behind asking questions, what you are trying to achieve from using such an approach and how it is going to make them a better team, by [encouraging] the individual to achieve a goal, then that is when the athlete buys into it. Until you actually get to that stage, they don't really buy into the approach … or dedicate themselves to the task. But when they understand that this way will make us a better

team, allow us to win and allow [the athlete] to achieve [her] dreams, that is when she buys in … she has to see how this is going to make her achieve her dream and justify the sacrifices she has made.

One of the most challenging yet rewarding aspects of this coaching approach lies in drawing on the art of coaching. This art includes the ability to read and understand your athletes, then help them by using great communication and coaching strategies that are suitable for the athlete in that particular situation. Ruth Aitken, Leigh Gibbs and Mark Norton elaborate on what it means for a coach to successfully apply the art of coaching through an athlete-centred approach:

Ruth: Some athletes like it more than others; some just want you to, 'Let's cut through this and tell me what you really want me to do'. I think there is a fine line. I think it can cause a bit of frustration with some players that if we want them to do a lot of self-evaluation, they would still like to be told what we think, and so there is still that balance and I'm not sure if I get it right all the time or at all.

Leigh: Knowing the right time to stop and question or when to let the activity run without interruption. Then with skill development, how many times or repetitions are really going to cause a change, for that group or for that competition that we are leading into? How many will we have to do? Is it enough to just get through it a couple of times and hopefully they have got it?

Mark: Sometimes a lot of what happens in the gym, it's hard to pick up on because I know that a lot of the time, when they are playing the game, I am commenting and giving lots of feedback, talking about decisions they are making on the court and I am often focusing on the people who are immediately in the drills or in the game … I found a number of times a couple of things that are happening out the back were highlighted. Perhaps a rude gesture or a comment that somebody else made that was perhaps not living up to the values and needs to be addressed. That's quite good because [it is] highlight[ed] for me and then we address it at the end or there at the time.

Determining when to jump in and when to leave the athletes to make their own decisions is another important facet to the art of coaching. Judging the situation correctly takes time while the coach tries it out in different contexts, and it is not uncommon to make mistakes along the way. We learn best through trial and error.

As Wayne Smith points out, one of the most 'different' aspects of the athlete-centred approach is that the coach stands back and observes for longer, enabling the athletes to make decisions. If we, as coaches, jump in and try to take over, athletes learn very little. So, when observing and analysing your athletes, you might try counting for 5 to 10 seconds, or allowing several trials of the game, before providing feedback. Then when providing feedback, jump in with a meaningful, open-ended question that enables athletes to think and become self-aware (see Chapter Two).

Clearly, then, when the coach interjects, it is important to ask the right question. As most contributors to this book point out, it can be tempting to tell people what you know. That is certainly a temptation for a lot of coaches who have never tried an athlete-centred approach. On many occasions, even when posing a question, they also answer it for the athletes. With reference to the ideas from this book, what outcomes are likely from this kind of coaching approach? How do athletes feel when their knowledge is undermined? Questioning is not easy but it is thoroughly worthwhile when athletes make informed decisions because of what they learn. Therefore, planning and practising are critical. In discussing their own processes of learning how to question in previous chapters, the athlete-centred coaches offer ideas that will be helpful to someone new to the approach.

As coaches, we continually look for better ways to enhance the performance of our athletes. Our search is for a process of learning and practising that will give that edge to us and our teams. So allow your athletes to interact and question. It will enhance your coaching approach even further, once they understand it, value it and become more self-aware and better decision makers.

In summary, the following are some key points for putting an athlete-centred approach into practice:

- Go for it. An athlete-centred approach is fantastic, enhancing learning and the sport environment.
- Take small steps. You cannot be proficient immediately; it takes practice.
- Tell your athletes about the approach so they can begin to understand why you are using it.
- Add the approach to your current practice as another part of your coaching repertoire.
- Cater for athletes. Remember patience is a virtue.
- Observe your athletes for a period before interrupting. Often athletes are already self-aware and can fix errors on their own.
- Ask meaningful questions. Remember that learning this technique takes time, so practise it.
- Evaluate:
  —how your approach is working;
  —how athletes are responding to it; and
  —your questioning repertoire.
- Be careful not to overquestion and not to answer your own questions.
- Most of all, enjoy using the athlete-centred approach—your athletes sure will.

Self-reflection: A Key to Developing and Improving Your Coaching

An important part of learning any approach is to reflect on your own coaching. Self-reflection is a particularly significant part of an athlete-centred approach, in which a core component is that coaches themselves take ownership of their own learning and decision making. Each coach should take responsibility for evaluating the way he or she coaches, the way the athletes respond and the general team environment.

Just as they expect athletes to practise to improve their performance (physical, mental and social), coaches need to practise their coaching performance. Extending this principle, we would expect that if coaches do not evaluate what they do, it is difficult for them to achieve a high standard of performance. A successful athlete-centred coach should practise and understand the theoretical elements of sport and coaching as well as technical fundamentals of instruction. After gaining feedback and advice about his coaching (from me during my research observations), Mark Norton reports he enjoyed the experience and found it helped with his self-analysis:

> **Mark:** Getting advice was great. It fast-tracked the learning process. It helped having someone chipping in the odd suggestion. Even just a question like 'Why are you running this drill?' made me think about the benefits of the drill and that there may be a better way of doing it. It also meant there was another set of ideas looking for team dynamics and cohesiveness. So I think that it is certainly beneficial to have someone who is experienced and someone who knows what they are doing to give you suggestions along the way.

Wayne Smith also suggests that self-analysis is a way to continue improving and learning about coaching at both elite and junior levels:

> **Wayne:** When I first committed to using empowerment in my coaching, there was no one else really using it, so I needed to look at other sports to keep learning. I still like to see what other coaches do and whether I am on the right track or not. I know the way I want to go … to continue empowering my players and to get better at questioning (rather than instruction). I also want to be my own person and develop my own style. I work hard not at copying, but at understanding and adapting what I learn.
>
> I have to work on my ability to discriminate between the need to ask questions about the skill and the need to ask about the tactics, i.e. understand whether it's a skill issue that let the player down or a game understanding one. Did he fail to pass because he couldn't technically execute it quickly enough, or did he pass because he didn't see what was [going] on? You can get the answer quickly … by asking, 'What did you do?', 'What did you see?' and 'What did you want to do?' You can soon find out whether he wanted to pass and couldn't, or whether he ran with it because he didn't see that the pass was on.
>
> The skill is in understanding how to use the questions and doing it quickly and selectively so that you're observing more than talking. Let the players have a go, then if you see the activity being done correctly you don't need to step in. My biggest fault is overquestioning.

As part of their self-reflection, Ruth Aitken and Leigh Gibbs ask players to evaluate how things are going with the team, including their coaching:

Ruth: ... after our tours and camps, we have a detailed debrief from each of the players. They're actually very good now, their evaluations are very useful. We ask for opinions on the trainings, team talks and other aspects of the team environment and performance. We also get feedback during a series or camp from our Senior Player Group, who in turn report back from the player-only meetings that they hold. So nothing much is held back.

Ian Rutledge describes his self-reflective process, which he sees as an essential part of his coaching:

Ian: What I do after each training session is to go through a self-reflective process where you ask a whole series of questions, such as 'Could I have done it better? What areas didn't I cover, was I you happy with it? Did the finish reflect the planning?' From there, it gives me the direction for the next game or training. You need to be reflective in your learning. There is never a point when I don't go home and say, 'Oh I could do better'. I walked out of this meeting with you thinking that there is a process that I could have done better.

Don Tricker constantly analyses other coaches, which helps his self-reflective process:

Don: I can't watch sport now without trying to break it down into understanding what happened and more importantly why it happened. Why were poor decisions being made, those sorts of thing ... This is in every sport. I go to watch rugby, I go to watch netball, I am not looking in terms of the result, in terms of who won or lost, I am looking at how it happened. I am looking at particular players and attempt[ing] to understand why they chose to execute a particular play that is clearly not part of the role or skill set.

Self-reflection empowers coaches to accept the challenge to become the best coaches they can be. Videotaping, a useful tool for self-reflection in teacher education, has gained great status in coach education as a means to self-train, as Wayne Smith describes:

Wayne: Sometimes it is because of frustration or time pressures, or things not going right ... we film our trainings to look at the drills we are doing and make sure they are valid, see whether the players are doing them really well and to check our way of communicating. Quite often I go home and think, 'Gee that wasn't the right way to handle that player tonight'. I've had to learn strategies to cope with people making mistakes. I have very competitive instincts and like to see everything done well. It has been an ongoing learning experience allowing the players to make errors along the way, which is now an important part of our team environment.

Many coaches already use videotapes of their trainings as an insightful means of observing their own coaching. Trying it for the first time can be daunting as many people, when confronting themselves on videotape, are surprised at their physical image. This confrontation is a barrier that you overcome by getting accustomed to and accepting mannerisms that only you notice. Thereafter you can objectively and realistically look at your coaching, how your athletes are empowered, and what impact your philosophy and methods are having.

Figure 14.1 illustrates a model of how self-reflection works, whether or not you are using a videotape of your coaching to assist you in the process.

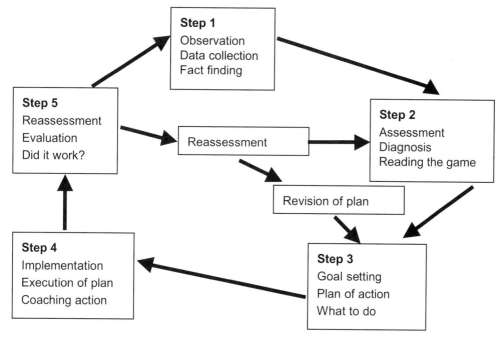

Figure 14.1: The Coaching Process—A Five-step Model for Self-reflection.
Source: Fairs, J.R. (1987). The coaching process: essence of coaching. *Sports Coach*, *11*(1), 19. Copyright 1987 by Australian Coaching Council. Reprinted with permission.

The five-step model shown in Figure 14.1 is designed for coaches to self-reflect by analysing, evaluating and modifying their coaching skills. In reflecting on what they do, coaches observe certain elements of the training session in a process of:

- collecting pertinent information;
- analysing the information;
- using the information to formulate goals and directions;
- designing a plan of action;
- implementing the plan of action;
- reassessing the outcome of the plan; and
- continually repeating the cycle.

The cycle continues for every aspect of coaching that a coach may wish to improve.

As highlighted consistently in this book, to enhance an athlete-centred approach coaches frequently use questioning and problem solving as tools to develop their athletes.

Coaches should also ask themselves reflective questions as an important element of their ongoing self-analysis. Reflective questions provide guidelines and information about your coaching. They can also be designed to suit your own development needs. You may find it useful to ask sport-specific personnel or another respected person to help develop reflective questions about a particular strategy that you wish to analyse or change. This person would also be a good source for advice about your coaching (provided he or she has nothing to do with your coaching career, as that person's objectivity may be lost, while you may find your coaching becomes unrealistic and unnatural).

Sample Questions: A Starting Point for Self-analysis

Below are some examples of very general reflective questions about coaching. Although not specific to individual needs, they may be a starting point for your self-analysis (using your videotape to answer each question):

1. What did you learn about your coaching? and about your management?
2. What did you learn about the athletes?
3. What did athletes learn about themselves?
4. What effects did your coaching have on the athletes? Discuss benefits and barriers.
5. How can the athletes rectify any barriers discussed? How can you rectify any barriers discussed?
6. How do you think the session could be improved?
7. Do you think you can solve any identified coaching difficulties by yourself?
8. How do you plan to follow up in the next sessions?
9. How was this session relevant or transferable to other aspects of the athletes' lives?
10. What did you learn about yourself?
11. Describe in detail one significant event that happened during your lesson. It may be significant because it was something that excited you, bothered you, made you rethink your intentions/beliefs, or made you realise that your intentions/beliefs were sound.

Sample Questions: A Starting Point for Reflecting on Your Athlete-centred Approach

The next set of general reflective questions may help to get you started in looking at how you focus on being athlete-centred (again, referring to the videotape from the training session!):

1. How was the session designed to empower athletes? Analyse your planned questions.
2. Did athletes have input to training? How or why not?

3. Reflect on your session by answering these questions:

    (a) What did you like best about the session?

    (b) What did you like least about the session?

    (c) How would you improve the session plan?

    (d) What did the athlete(s) learn?

4. Analyse your line of questioning. Did it encourage athletes' learning? Were the questions clear? Were you flexible in your ability to ask purposeful questions?

5. Explain the general motivational climate of the session.

6. How well did you plan for different ability levels?

7. How well did you cater to athlete-centred learning? Explain.

8. How did athletes respond to being empowered? Give examples.

9. Explain how this training session nurtured the holistic needs of the athletes.

10. Are athletes' needs identified and how do you encourage independent development?

Sample Questions: A Starting Point for Reflecting on Your Use of Teaching Games for Understanding

As Chapter Eleven discusses, many athlete-centred coaches make use of Teaching Games for Understanding (TGfU). The following reflective questions may help you to analyse how you use TGfU in your training session:

1. Discuss how this session was designed to cater for TGfU.

2. Analyse the games you provided. How can they be improved?

3. Analyse the purposefulness of the games.

4. How did athletes respond to the TGfU session?

5. Did the athletes learn anything beneficial to their development? Why or why not?

6. Explain the social benefits and/or challenges of applying TGfU in this session.

7. Analyse the enjoyment and motivation of the athletes participating in this session.

8. Were you happy with the amount of time that the athletes were able to practise for the session? Why or why not?

9. Analyse the questions you asked. Were they predominantly high-order or low-order questions?

10. How do you think the training session could be improved?

Sample Questions: A Starting Point for Reflecting on Your Questioning

Chapter Twelve focuses on asking meaningful questions. Here are some questions for you that will help you reflect on your questioning of your athletes (using your video!):

1. How clear and coherent were the questions that you asked your athletes?

2. When asking questions, did you have the attention of all the athletes?

3. Analyse the responses to the questions. Who answered them? Did they give the answers that you expected? How well did you probe?

4. How well did you listen and accept athlete responses?

5. Did learning occur? Explain your answer.

6. List the questions that you asked during the session. How many were high-order questions and how many were low-order questions? Was the ratio effective? Why or why not?

7. Discuss any thinking that occurred (or did not occur) after you asked high-order questions.

8. Were the questions meaningful to the purpose of the training session? Explain.

9. Were you flexible in accepting and exploring athletes' responses?

10. How well did you encourage your athletes to reflect and process what they learned? Explain.

To enhance your use of videotapes to analyse coaching, show the videotape to a colleague, coach, teacher or any respected person and ask for feedback. It is an advantage if this person comes from a similar philosophical belief so that he or she can help to analyse how you are using a particular empowering approach. The feedback enhances your learning, verifying what areas you need to develop, and is ultimately beneficial to the athletes. Your colleagues will also gain a lot from observing and analysing you; in this way, the learning process spreads throughout the coaching world.

Finally, coaches should obtain positive feedback both from other people and from themselves. Identify your positive strategies and pat yourself on the back as much as you try to improve yourself.

Continuing Coach Development

As presented above, self-reflective analysis is a means of learning about and improving an athlete-centred approach in coaching. An advantage of using videotaping as a tool in this process is that it is easy to apply. It does take time to sit down and analyse these videotapes, but once coaches become accustomed to using videotapes, they can participate in a self-directed training approach when it suits to their own needs and time.

An Example of Self-reflective Analysis

The following outline of a self-reflective analysis process can aid in reviewing your coaching and targeting parts of your coaching you might want to improve.

Step 1: Videotape a training session and conduct a self-reflective analysis of your coaching. Identify one or two parts of your coaching you want to change or improve. Give the videotape to a critical friend and gather feedback about your coaching. Tell the friend your philosophy and what you are intending to focus on. It is important that this critical friend acts as a sounding board rather than an adviser. You need to feel empowered with the process, meaning that it is you who decides what to change, for your reasons.

Step 2: Develop a plan of action for changing or improving the parts you have identified. Ask yourself, 'How can I design a method to change/improve this part of my coaching?' You can get relevant reflective questions from a critical friend, another respected individual, or written resources (like this book or others that are in the library).

Step 3: You will need several training sessions to work on improving each of the parts you identified. Use the first few training sessions to practise these parts. After practising, videotape another training session. Ensure you have prepared some reflective questions to help in the self-reflective analysis of this videotape.

Step 4: Repeat the above process to focus on other parts of your coaching or to revisit parts you may have identified in the first process. Remember you can only work on one or two matters at a time, and it takes a long time master or get where you want it to be with some strategies (Kidman & Hanrahan, 2004).

Self-reflective analysis is one method that will help you to continue developing as a coach. Another way to continue developing as a coach is to do research. Research does not mean having to understand academic language and gobbledegook. What it does mean is read books, search the Internet, network with coaches, observe other coaches who use an athlete-centred approach and attend conferences. Asking athletes can also help in your research.

Gathering Information and Continuing to Learn

In some countries and some sport cultures, people do not communicate with the 'enemy' for fear of giving away secrets about team strategies. This attitude seems absurd, given that one of the main reasons we coach (at least from an athlete-centred perspective) is to develop athletes. To develop philosophical beliefs, we need to talk with other people, including coaches, parents, administrators, athletes and educators.

By talking with other people who have insights from their own experience of what has and has not worked, we may gather ideas that may help individuals and teams. Perhaps you have a specific problem in designing a game that enhances an old drill that was used in a sport, so ask another coach for advice. You are not admitting defeat; you are demonstrating a desire to search for knowledge or new methods and to help athletes learn. It cannot hurt to ask. The worst that can happen is for someone to say, 'No'. All coaches in this book are always looking for advice to improve their coaching. A commonality of an athlete-centred approach seems to be that such coaches admit to still needing to learn, so they continually search for better ways. Other coaches, parents and administrators have some great ideas. Ask anyone; everyone has an opinion, especially in sport.

Most athletes may have experienced several different coaches. Ask them for their opinion—and in the process apply a key element of an athlete-centred approach. Ruth Aitken and Leigh Gibbs have found that gaining a written evaluation from their players is extremely useful to their coaching development. The player evaluations pointed out positives and negatives of the season, information the coaches can use to better their coaching for the next season. Through an athlete-centred approach, coaches are constantly asking for player feedback, reading them and interpreting their ideas and values. Through an athlete-centred approach, you can make a natural evaluation from the players when they answer questions and you read them, which is useful to everything that occurs in the sporting environment.

Educators (teachers, university lecturers, coach educators) can offer great advice and information. Although some coaches may see educators as too academic or out of their league, there are many educators who understand coaching as they have been there. Educators are able to benefit from keeping up to date with current research and many put these new strategies into practice. This perspective is where empowerment came from: coaches who have achieved great success, but realised that through an empowerment approach they can enable greater success and fulfilment among their athletes. Coaches should be empowered to enhance their coaching by having the 'nous' to search for better approaches.

Some speak of a gap between educators and coaches but, in reality, many of us are trying to get rid of this perceived gap. Educators and coaches learn from each other; educators and coaches learn from athletes (and students). The athletes are the ones to benefit from this sharing of ideas. Through this sharing, coaches can provide terrific learning experiences that enhance athletes' lifestyles, in which sport is a means to an end, rather than the end. No one has all the answers, but through conversations and observations we can learn from each other. Among the coaches interviewed for this book, a common characteristic is their belief that they are still learning. Their ego does not get in the way; rather, the athletes are truly more important than the sport.

Conclusion

It has been an intention of this book to inform and teach coaches about an athlete-centred approach, including how athletes learn and enjoy their sport. Another goal has been to empower coaches themselves to increase their knowledge, practise more, reflect and analyse, and continue to improve in their own time and using their own methods. Coaches should provide athletes with choice and control; this book provides coaches with choice and control. Take bits from it that you think will work, and skip the bits that you have trouble with. The previous chapters have illustrated some successes, but this book does not have all the answers. It simply shares ideas so that coaches can take the ones that suit their philosophy and purpose and apply them to their sport.

In this chapter, you have been encouraged to obtain feedback. You should also provide feedback to other coaches. Based on your thinking and understanding and all the research that you have completed by reading through this book, you can offer valuable information to aid other coaches in their development. Coaches should serve as critical friends who can provide sound advice and at the same time identify the positive aspects of others' coaching.

Those who endeavour to be a thinking, proactive coach, and who take advantages of opportunities to improve their athletes' performance, enjoyment and lifestyle, will be the most successful coaches. These coaches will make a difference to sport and athlete development. An athlete-centred coaching approach encourages a holistic learning environment in which athletes can learn about life and about sport.

References

Chu, M. (c. 2004). *High performance with Mike Chu*. Retrieved on 11 October 2004 from www.nzrugbynet. com/NZRFU/Coaching+Info/gameplanRUGBY/gameplan+Rugby

Fairs, J.R. (1987). The coaching process: essence of coaching. *Sports Coach*, *11*(1), 19.

Hadfield, D.C. (2002). Developing team leaders in rugby. *Rugby Football Union Technical Journal*. Retrieved on 7 October 2002 from www.rfu.com/pdfs/technical-journal/Developing_leaders_captains.pdf

Janssen, J. (2002). *Championship team building*. Cary, NC: Winning the Mental Game.

Kidman, L. (2001). *Developing decision makers: An empowerment approach to coaching*. Christchurch: Innovative Print Communications.

Kidman, L. & Hanrahan, S. (2004). *The coaching process: A practical guide to improving your effectiveness* (2nd ed.). Palmerston North: Dunmore.

The spirit, the will to win, and the will to excel are the things that endure. These qualities are so much more important than the events that occur. – *Vince Lombardi (1913–1970) US football coach*

Cowardice asks the question, is it safe? Expediency asks the question, is it politic? Vanity asks the question, is it popular? But conscience asks the question, Is it right? And there comes a time when one must take a position that is neither safe, nor politic, nor popular, but he must take it because his conscience tells him it is right … – *Martin Luther*

Good character is more to be praised than outstanding talent. Most talents are, to some extent, a gift. Good character, by contrast, is not given to us. We have to build it piece by piece-by thought, choice, courage and determination. – *John Luther*

Treat people as if they were what they ought to be and you help them to become what they are capable of being. – *Johann Wolfgang Von Goethe*

If a team is to reach its potential, each player must be willing to subordinate his personal goals to the good of the team. – *Bud Wilkinson (1916–) US football coach*

About the Author

Lynn Kidman is a coach educator at the Christchurch College of Education in Christchurch, New Zealand. Lynn has authored another book, *Developing Decision Makers: An empowerment approach to coaching* and co-authored a first and second edition of *The Coaching Process: A practical guide to improving your effectiveness.* Lynn has coached many teams, mostly secondary school age, in the sports of basketball, swimming, softball, and volleyball. Currently, she is taking on a player manager role, where she can help promote the team vision, enable athletes to learn best and become great human beings.

About the Contributing Authors

Dave Hadfield is one of New Zealand's best known and most experienced sport psychologists and coach educators. Previously a University lecturer in coaching, sport psychology and leadership, Dave has since spent the last 5 years working both for Wellington and Hurricanes Rugby, and since ending his contract with them, he has formed his own company, MindPlus. He currently works extensively in NZ sport (primarily for NZ Rugby), working both with elite players and coaches throughout the country. He has worked with 3 Super 12 teams in the last 4 years. Dave also holds elite level III coaching qualifications from New Zealand Cricket and the Australian Cricket Board and was a Central Districts senior selector last season, having previously been Coaching Director for C.D. in the early 1990s. He developed the Query Theory approach to coaching a number of years ago and describes his coaching philosophy as "A caring guide to self-discovery and improvement". He is now introducing his coaching and self-improvement approach to the business world.

Rod Thorpe trained as a Physical education teacher in the early 60s, joining Loughborough University (then Loughborough College of Education) in 1968. Through the late 60s and 70s Rod at Loughborough evolved his own approach to teaching and coaching and then with colleagues at Loughborough and many teachers and coaches refined the thinking. In 1982 he and David Bunker produced a model that became known as Teaching Games for Understanding. Whilst much of the work in the 80s was developing games teaching in Physical Education, Rod was also developing ideas to enable less experienced non specialists offer valuable games experiences (that evolved into TOP play and TOP sport in the UK) and introducing ideas to coaches, even those working with elite players (not least Games Sense in Australia and New Zealand). Rod retired from Loughborough in 2003 after spending 6 years developing a major sports development concept with new sports facilities to the value of £40m. Rod has been inducted into the UK Coaching Hall of Fame, was awarded the prestigious Munrow Award for Services to University and College Sport and the Biennial IOC award for services to sport.